JAMES HALL

Spokesman of the New West

JAMES HALL

Spokesman of the New West

By Randolph C. Randall

Ohio State University Press

To Ellen Randall

 PREFACE

JAMES HALL's life began when Washington was President
and extended until three years after the death of Lincoln.
Born into an old family of Maryland planters and Philadelphia intellectuals, Hall in his twenty-third year forsook the
security of the settled East and rode over the mountains to
become a lawyer in Pittsburgh. Four years later, he took
a keelboat for Shawneetown, Illinois, and definitely cast his
lot with the new West. During the thirteen years of his
residence in backwoods Illinois villages, he wrote most of
the works upon which his literary reputation rests. After
this rigorous apprenticeship in frontier life, he settled in
Cincinnati in 1833 and lived there until his death thirty-five
years later.

Similar as the outline of his life is to that of many other
bright and personable young men who went west during
those stirring times, Hall's career has an important distinc-
tiveness. Brought up as a cultivated young gentleman and
tempered by war, he embodied an unusual combination of
courage and discrimination. He appears to have been quite
without what we ordinarily think of as fear, and could face
violence with complete coolness. At the same time he had
the sensitivity to recognize the subtle poetry of Hawthorne's
short stories when other Americans overlooked them. He
was endowed with a special kind of loyalty, which impelled
him to embrace difficult causes. He realized from the first
the immense significance of the western migration and spir-
itedly defended the West against its detractors, interpreted
it to itself and the rest of the world, aroused the cultural
consciousness of the western people, and recorded western
life in history and in fiction.

In assessing his achievements at his death in 1868, the
Nation observed, "Nobody who would understand how the

people of the great Valley became what they are should neglect Judge Hall." He established the first magazine in Illinois, conducted the first successful magazine in the Middle West, edited two newspapers, and brought together in *The Western Souvenir* the first collection of western short stories. Early in the 1830's, he was, through these journals, the West's most eloquent and powerful advocate of public education. The foremost author of the midwestern frontier, he appears to have been the first to portray in fiction the uncouth western frontiersman proliferated later in narratives like those of Mike Fink, Davy Crockett, and Paul Bunyan, and he delineated the western boaster later portrayed by Mark Twain. His writings influenced, besides a number of lesser figures, Robert Montgomery Bird and William Gilmore Simms, and they affected the work of Herman Melville. Although Irving was the predominant author of short tales of the period, Hall was a leading writer of short stories between 1824 and 1832, when Irving published no short narratives and before Poe and Hawthorne had demonstrated their best artistry in brief fiction.

No just record of Hall's achievement in American literature can be written without attention to the peculiarities of his environment, and I have been more than ordinarily concerned with the social trends of his time and the circumstances in which he wrote.

The changes during the half-century of his life in the West must have seemed as wonderful to Hall and his contemporaries as those of the last fifty years do to us. In fiction, the sketch was evolving into the modern short story, and the trend toward regionalism, in which he was a noteworthy pioneer, got under way. In politics, he saw the rise of Jacksonianism, the upsurge of religious intolerance, the rise of the antislavery movement, and its convulsive culmination in war. The landscape, perhaps, changed most. Forests were transformed into farms. Villages and towns like Cincinnati, St. Louis, and Chicago grew into vibrant cities known for their luxuries and for the social ills that afflict a concentrated population. The wonder of the frontier westerner may have been excited even more by the effects of the industrial revolution upon transportation and communication. Canals were dug; the keelboat was outmoded by the steamboat, and the steamboat by the railroad. When the telegraph proved successful, its creation was thought of as the work of God.

Yet the immediate circumstances in which Hall wrote in Illinois were not entirely propitious. The life of a pioneer author was, in its own way, as barren as that of a backwoods farmer or hunter. As a professional man, Hall had to earn a living in a society blessed with only a few crude institutions. Although his business journeys on horseback over the prairies could be delightful in certain seasons, they were sometimes fraught with pain and danger. The frontier villages in which he lived had aspects of ugliness and dullness that would in comparison make a Gopher Prairie of the 1920's seem like a paradise of convenience and pleasant streets.

Although he was strong enough to fashion a makeshift cultural climate of his own, his life was often intellectually lonely. He lacked especially the professional advice and encouragement that writers hunger for and that he might have found in some older communities. He was without convenient reference books, and his knowledge of the main streams of contemporary art and thought depended chiefly upon publications that had survived the perils of more than a thousand miles of freightage by boat and wagon. Most of his fellow westerners were necessarily engaged in the stern business of clearing land, building homes, and producing food. In the absence of public schools, many were illiterate. Religiosity was widely diffused. At a time when authorship was meagerly rewarded anywhere in America, he encountered his share of indifference to his publications and at times experienced the open hostility of many of his western contemporaries. In short, the West that Hall and his fellow frontiersmen knew is generally foreign to our generation.

In preparing this narrative of his life, I have attempted to identify his writings, to search out the available manuscripts pertaining to him, and to use not only the magazines and newspapers that he edited but also the other principal journals published in the towns where he lived. As a result, it has been possible to correct errors and misunderstandings in previous accounts, to present knowledge from hundreds of manuscripts not used before in studies of Hall, and to add nearly three hundred items to the list of his known writings. From these records he emerges as the leading figure in the cultural history of the Middle Western frontier.

R.C.R.

Fenn College
July, 1963

  ACKNOWLEDGMENTS

THE PREPARATION of this book has extended over a period of many years, and in the search for information and in the writing I have had the help of many kind persons. I am particularly grateful to Frank W. Scott, who, in the beginning of my study, welcomed my investigations and sent me a copy of a part of Hall's journal; to Charles B. Anderson, of Mamaroneck, New York, who facilitated my pursuit of Hall's paths in southern Illinois; to Eugene Carroll, of Chicago, who cordially allowed me to use the Eddy papers; and to Donald R. Tuttle, of Washington, D.C., and William T. Christian, of Indio, California, each of whom transcribed certain manuscripts for me. The particular assistance of others is indicated in the notes or the bibliography.

For many courtesies, I wish to thank Julian P. Boyd, of Princeton University; Mrs. Alene Lowe White and Miss Mary Ruth Russell, of the Western Reserve Historical Society Library; Miss Elizabeth Beam and Emil J. Stefancic, of the Fenn College Library; Miss Margaret Cross Norton, of the Archives Division of the Illinois State Library; Miss Eleanor S. Wilby, formerly curator of the library of the Historical and Philosophical Society of Ohio; and Miss Donna L. Root, Mrs. Arline Welch Colgrove, and especially Miss Louise Boutelle, for many years a devoted collector of historical works, of the Cleveland Public Library.

Hall's descendants have generously granted me the use of their family records. To Miss Margaret Yost Kent and Francis Hall Kent, of Philadelphia, and to Nicholas Van Antwerp, of Cincinnati, I am indebted for permission to use their manuscripts; to Mrs. Juliet R. Frazier, Miss Charlotte Wright, and Mrs. Elmer J. Rodenberg for providing me with photographs of portraits of several members of the Hall family; and to Miss Alice Hall for taking me to visit the old Hall farm at Loveland, Ohio. Miss Mary Posey Foote, Hall's granddaughter, carefully related to me her amazingly particular recollections, and with her sister, Miss Louisa Bowler Foote, allowed me to use the family documents in their possession.

Many who have read the manuscript in its various stages have offered recommendations resulting in its improvement. For reading an early draft, for painstaking comments, and for encouragement at critical times, I am deeply grateful to Herbert Brown, of Bowdoin College. R. Carlyle Buley, of Indiana University, heartened me with cordiality to my work. I am thankful also for the suggestions of other kind readers, all now or formerly of Columbia University: Susanne Howe Nobbe, David Donald, James L. Clifford, Mark Van Doren, and especially Lewis Leary, for his friendly advice and encouragement during the later stages of my study, and Ralph Leslie Rusk, under whose guidance this book was far advanced and to whose scholarly example I owe much.

Over a period of more than a decade I have had the privilege of frequent consultation with my colleague William Cherubini, who, with unflagging attention and generosity, always gave me the advice that I sought.

One other debt, for discerning judgment and consummate patience, is recorded in the dedication.

CONTENTS

ILLUSTRATIONS

JAMES HALL

Spokesman of the New West

I

Young James Hall

JAMES HALL was born in Philadelphia on July 29, 1793,[1] in circumstances distressing to his well-rooted and comfortable upper-class family. The year was notable for the city's most severe plague of yellow fever. Before James was born, the season had been unnaturally and ominously sultry. Three weeks after his birth, the nature of the epidemic was recognized. As the death list grew and terror mounted, three of Philadelphia's four newspapers suspended publication, and a third of the residents fled from the city. James's parents, John and Sarah Hall, probably joined the flight as soon after James's birth as Mrs.

Hall was able, for the baptism of James was delayed until January 19,[2] when all danger from the epidemic had passed. Plagues of yellow fever broke out again in the summers of 1797, 1798, and 1799. In 1798, when James was five, two-thirds of the inhabitants deserted the city, and hundreds of them pitched tents in the fields along the Schuylkill between Spruce and Chestnut streets.

The Halls were well-to-do, with firm roots in the country, and their probable retreat during pestilence, as it was from time to time in financial misfortune, was Mount Welcome, a plantation sixty-four miles from Philadelphia on the eastern shore of Maryland, where James's father had been reared and where the Halls had owned land since the establishment of their family in America about the time of Cromwell's death. Certainly during his childhood James spent much time on the plantation. A brick house about a mile east of the Susquehanna River on the north side of the Baltimore-Philadelphia road is still pointed out to the visitor as part of the original Mount Welcome residence. From the homestead on the high ground the Halls of several generations could look out over their great farms and into the hills beyond the broad, shallow Susquehanna. James, evidently describing Mount Welcome as it was in his childhood, wrote of a mansion that was once "thought to be a noble specimen of architectural skill and magnificence." According to his account, "it was surrounded by a very large plantation, appropriated chiefly to the culture of tobacco and corn, and studded in every direction with little cabins inhabited by negroes. A fine garden, an extensive orchard, and a meadow, in which a number of high-bred horses sported their graceful limbs, showed the proprietor to be a gentleman of easy fortune."[3]

James has also told how, as a child, he gazed with admiration at family portraits hanging in the hall at Mount Welcome. He might have seen, among the likenesses of some of the great landed proprietors there, the portrait of Richard Hall, the family's first American ancestor, a Quaker who entered land rights in Maryland in 1663.[4] It was he who had acquired much of the land on which the family fortune

depended; at the time of his death he was the owner of
2,400 acres and lived at Hall's Hills, a thousand-acre estate
in Calvert County, on Maryland's Western Shore. As a
child James might also have seen a painting of Richard's
son Elisha, who had inherited three-fourths of Hall's Hills
and, like his father, had represented his county in the pro-
vincial legislature. The portrait of his son Elihu (1692-
1753), a handsome man with a sensitive, cultivated face,
may still be seen.[5] The last of the family known to have
been a Quaker, Elihu married Elizabeth Chew and established his branch of the family in Cecil County, on the
Eastern Shore of Maryland, where the Halls had owned six
hundred or more acres since the time of Richard Hall.

James tells us that he took special interest in the portraits
of Elihu's son, also named Elihu (1723-1790), and of his
wife, Catherine Orrick Hall.[6] These were James's grandparents. As James gazed "with admiration" at their portraits, it seemed to him that some of the glamor of the
Revolution still hung over the mansion. Elihu and his only
two sons old enough to fight had served in the Revolutionary army. The younger of the two boys was James's own
father, John, who had enlisted in 1777, at seventeen.[7] James
as a child was no doubt told how, when the British army
threatened to occupy Philadelphia in August, 1776, his
grandparents, though they then had twelve children of
their own, had welcomed to the manor the wife and children
of their kinsman Dr. Benjamin Rush and had sheltered
them there for two years. Dr. Rush's son John was born
there,[8] and a daughter born to the Halls in 1778 was named
Julia Rush Hall.[9]

At the close of the war, on February 20, 1783, James's
father, John Hall, had married Sarah Ewing. During the
first year of their marriage, they lived in Philadelphia, where
their first child, John Elihu, was born on December 21 and
baptized a month later.[10] The next year they took up their
residence in Maryland on the ancestral lands at Mount
Welcome, a part of which had been given to John Hall at
the time of his marriage. But Sarah Hall had come from
a family of intellectuals and was used to cultivated society

5

in Philadelphia; to her the following six years that she and her husband spent at Mount Welcome seemed like a dreary exile. "She was naturally gay," James wrote later, "and she loved books, society, and her friends too dearly, to be satisfied with a country life, in a secluded neighborhood."[11]

Probably to some extent through her urging, the Halls moved back to Philadelphia in 1790, where they were to live the three years before James's birth and the eight years immediately afterward. About the time of their return to the city, Thomas Mifflin was beginning his nine-year administration as governor of Pennsylvania. John Hall soon afterward entered politics, and for a time enjoyed the favor of influential men. By 1794, he had won the confidence of Governor Mifflin, who appointed him agent of information with the duty of determining for the governor exactly what progress had been made in the execution of contracts for the improvement of roads and rivers.[12] In February, 1795, Mifflin showed his satisfaction with Hall's work by renewing the appointment at the handsome salary of five hundred pounds a year.[13] With such political figures as Jacob Hiltzheimer; Daniel Brodhead, surveyor general of Pennsylvania; and Joseph Hopkinson, later United States senator, Hall was a guest at the lavish dinners with which Governor Mifflin entertained his friends in his home at the falls of the Schuylkill.[14] On August 1, he became a member of Mifflin's official family by accepting the position of secretary of the land office.[15] His salary of five hundred pounds a year—two-thirds that of a Justice of the United States Supreme Court and double that of the Attorney-General of the United States — insured the family's prosperity during James's childhood.

In later life James himself wrote as one familiar with the household of his Philadelphia grandparents. His mother, born October 30, 1761, was the daughter of John and Hannah Sergeant Ewing. At Princeton, where he was graduated in 1755, John Ewing is said to have been the favorite student of Aaron Burr, the president of the college.[16] From 1759 until his death in 1802, Ewing was the pastor of the First Presbyterian Church in Philadelphia. He was acquainted with several languages and was a scholar of some originality in philosophy. When he was visiting in Britain, from 1773 to 1775, the University of Edinburgh honored him with the degree of Doctor of Divinity. At a dinner in London he met Dr. Samuel Johnson and replied so graciously to one of his anti-American remarks that the gruff lexicographer was disarmed and sat talking with Ewing until midnight.[17] In America, Ewing was appointed provost of the University of the State of Pennsylvania when it was chartered in 1779. Upon the amalgamation of that institution with the College of Philadelphia in 1791, he became the first provost of the University of Pennsylvania, which was created by the merger; and he served in that office, as well as in the pastorate, until his death.

James's grandmother Hannah Sergeant (1739-1806), whom Ewing married in 1758, also belonged to an intellectual family. Her father was Jonathan Sergeant, treasurer of Princeton; her foster mother's father was Jonathan Dickinson, founder and first president of Princeton; and her half brother was Jonathan Dickinson Sergeant (1746-1793), attorney general of Pennsylvania and an active and radical republican.[18]

The education of the twelve children of John and Hannah Ewing was an important concern to Dr. Ewing even while he was in England. From London he wrote to his wife, "Let the children be kept constantly at School. . . . As we shall be able to give them little or no Fortunes they should have as good Learning as we can give them."[19] The result of his determination was that each of James Hall's four Ewing uncles was graduated from the University of Pennsylvania and, exactly three years afterward, proceeded to the Master's degree.[20] Even though girls in that age were not generally encouraged to obtain an education, Sarah Ewing, James's mother, found in her childhood home exceptional opportunities for learning. "Her father was a man of social habits," James later recalled, "fond of the society of his own family, and endowed with rare talents for conversation. Few men ever possessed in so high a degree, the art of communicating to others, the acquisitions of his [sic] own

7

mind. He had the faculty of rendering science familiar and agreeable, and of bringing the most difficult attainments within the comprehension of the common intellect. . . . His religion," James remembered, "was of a cheerful character, which, while it enabled him to maintain the dignity and sanctity of his office, threw no gloom upon surrounding objects. His fireside, while it was the scene of hospitality and cheerfulness, was always enlivened with literary and scientific discussion. . . ."[21]

In describing the education of his mother in Dr. Ewing's household, James observed, "If she had not the regular means of instruction, nor opportunities for study, she was surrounded by the light of knowledge. . . ." Undoubtedly she had an uncommon hunger for learning. He listened with admiration to his mother's "animated description of the eagerness with which she gleaned instruction, while a mere child, from discourses which were intended for the ears of others. She obtained," he said, "a critical acquaintance with the principles of grammar, and an extensive knowledge of the ancient classics, by hearing her brothers recite their Latin and Greek lessons to their father, and by listening to the conversations of the learned men, who frequented his house. . . . Her reading . . . [before her marriage] was rather choice than extensive; and was confined chiefly to history and belles lettres. For the latter," James believed, "she always had a decided and refined taste; and as it was not thought necessary, then, for females to read at all, and no course was marked out for her, she perused with avidity, all the most elegant productions of the press which fell in her way. Even this much was often done by stealth, in those leisure moments which the industrious economy of her mother allowed her to call her own."[22]

II

The Philadelphia of the 1790's was a city whose importance must have been discernible, even to a child. In the year of James's birth, the settled portions of the United States lay almost entirely east of the Alleghenies, and far-away Pittsburgh was then, and for two or three decades afterward, regarded as "one of the outposts of civilized America."[23] With 45,000 inhabitants, Philadelphia was the most populous city of the republic. It was the principal port of immigration, was foremost in business and culture, and was the nation's capital until 1801, when James was eight. Franklin had died there in 1790, and Washington lived there as President.

During James's childhood, his family lived amid scenes fresh with the glory of the stirring events of the nation's founding. From 1796 or 1797 until about 1800, his home was at 301 High Street (now Market). Down the street, No. 190 was occupied by President Washington until March, 1797, and afterward by President John Adams and his family.[24] Apparently in 1800, when James was seven, John Hall moved his family to 159 Chestnut Street, opposite the Supreme Court building on Independence Square. Near the Halls, at No. 173, lived Phineas Bond, his Britannic Majesty's Consul General; and No. 181 was the home of Jared Ingersoll, counsellor-at-law and attorney general of Pennsylvania. In 1797 or 1798, the land office was in Carpenters' Hall, the meeting place of the Continental Congress, where John Hall might well have taken James to visit. From the Hall residence in High Street it was little more than a block to Independence Square, where the Hall children may have played on the lawns. In 1800, when the Halls lived across the street from the Square and while the federal government remained at Philadelphia, James, young as he was, must have become familiar with the faces and figures of some of the great men of that brilliant decade in American government. It may well be imagined that patriotic parents like John and Sarah Hall would call their children to the window to see such eminent men as President Adams, Vice-President Jefferson, or Alexander Hamilton walking or alighting from their carriages to enter the government buildings. Such impressions, which could so easily have been stored during a childhood lived within the very shadow of his country's government, would have played a part in nourishing the intense patriotism of James's later life.

9

Sometimes, too, in the city's streets he caught glimpses of frontiersmen. "I shall never forget," he recalled, "the intense interest which I felt, while a boy, in gazing at the brawny limbs and sun-burnt features of a Kentuckian, as he passed through the streets of Philadelphia. The rough, hardy air of the stranger, the jaded paces of his nag, the blanket, the bear-skin, and saddle-bags—nay, the very oil-cloth on his hat, and the dirk that peeped from among his vestments, are still in my eye; they bespoke him to be of distant regions, to have been reared among dangers, and to be familiar with fatigues. He strode among us," James declared, "with the step of an Achilles, glancing with a good-natured superciliousness at the fragile butterflies of fashion that glittered in the sun-beams around him. I thought I could see in that man, one of the progenitors of an unconquerable race; . . . he had the will to dare, the power to execute; there was something in his look which bespoke a disdain of controul, and an absence of constraint in all his movements, indicating an habitual independence of thought and action."[25]

James had no formal schooling until he was nearly twelve; before that time he was taught chiefly by his mother. Although she must have been very busy—she had seven children by 1799,[26] when James was six—he was fortunate to have her for his teacher. With rare energy and persistence she became one of the best educated women of her time. During the forty years between her marriage and her death, James wrote afterwards, she usually studied until midnight, and often until two or three o'clock.[27]

She reared James with cheerful friendliness, and he learned easily. In relating an experience of his first days in school, he said that he had never been whipped by his parents. In fact, they seem to have spoiled him somewhat by allowing him to learn their high opinion of him. "For some reason," he recounted, "I was not sent to any school, until my twelfth year, but having an ardent thirst for knowledge, and ample means for the gratification of this appetite, the love of reading became in early infancy a powerful passion; and," he continued, "although I acquired but little of the technical learning, usually taught in schools, every day added to my attainments in literature. Books were my favorite, and almost my only companions, and these were never willingly forsaken, except when opportunities occurred of listening to the conversation of my seniors. Hidden in a corner, I have sat for hours absorbed in the perusal of a favorite author; but often, while apparently thus abstracted," he remarked, "I have been a silent and curious auditor of dialogues, which were intended for other ears. . . . By my mother I was pronounced to be a great beauty; by my father, a wonderful genius; and both, however they might differ upon other subjects, agreed, that I should certainly cut a figure in the world."[28]

Among the books he read were tales of terror. "I look back upon my infancy with pain," he wrote; "the tales which astonished and alarmed my imagination are still vividly impressed upon my memory; hours and nights of fear and anguish are freshly remembered as the events of yesterday; and I cannot think of a chambermaid, or a nurse, without some gloomy associations of spectres, raw heads, and bloody bones."[29]

Fortunately, his mother knew how to guide him to better books. Sarah Hall's method, as he later remembered, was not to drive her child to study but to lead him into reflection upon the reading he had undertaken of his own accord. It was not enough for her to let books fall into her children's hands. She strove "to allure their minds to study" and "to instil into them such principles, as would induce them, of themselves to make the proper selection" of books. She casually began her conversations by asking the child what he was reading, what it was about, whether he would read some of it to her. If she considered the book worthless or harmful, she pointed out its faults; and "such were her powers of ridicule," James recalled, "that she readily put the young reader out of conceit of his author, while he remained in perfect good humour with her, and with himself." If she considered the book worth while, she commented upon the subject and the style. She asked the meaning of parts read to her, required the child to identify persons and places,

11

asked why the author employed a particular phrase, and inquired whether the expression were elegant or the thought morally sound. These discourses were familiar and cheerful, but they "had the appearance of being entirely accidental."[30]

James was trained in writing perhaps as much by the literary atmosphere in which he lived as by direct instruction. Both his mother and his oldest brother, John Elihu, wrote with careful attention to form and were contributors to the *Port Folio* throughout its long life of a quarter of a century. This magazine, established in Philadelphia in 1801 by the exacting stylist Joseph Dennie, soon became pre-eminent in the United States. Dennie, who made the magazine largely a community enterprise, achieved success by means of his great charm, by his leadership of a social-literary circle in Philadelphia, and through his own column addressed to the contributors, in which he flattered, condemned, counseled, or prodded his authors. James's brother John Elihu, one of Dennie's admirers, observed that such a spirit of literature prevailed among Dennie's associates "and the young men generally" at the height of the magazine's popularity that his editorial table "abounded with contributions" for the *Port Folio*.[31] Small wonder that some loyal Philadelphians began to speak of their city as the Athens of America.

Among the magazine's contributors during the first two years or longer were James's twin uncles, John and Samuel Ewing; his mother; his brother John Elihu; Samuel Ewing's friend John Quincy Adams; and John Elihu's beloved friend Charles Brockden Brown.[32] Dennie himself, according to Samuel L. Knapp, was an intimate in the Hall household. Sarah Hall's disposition, Knapp said, "was cheerful and she looked on the bright side of every thing. At her hospitable mansion, the feverish scholar [Dennie] found more charms to cure his misanthropy than could be found elsewhere. . . . When the evil spirit came over him . . . he went, to use his own words, to the house of Mrs. Hall, to drive off all his blue devils. Her conversation abounded in classical recollections, in playful remarks, and in delicate satire, and like the harp of David, gave new soul and life to the gloomy editor."[33] James himself later wrote that his mother was a member "of the literary circle with which he [Dennie] associated," and he recalled Dennie's "wit, his gentlemanly character, and companionable qualities" as if he had known him.[34] At any rate, it is not difficult to imagine the excitement with which an intelligent boy would turn the freshly printed pages of a journal in which each Saturday he might find the productions of his mother, his brother, or his uncle.

Whatever political influence the *Port Folio* had upon the young James was in the direction of Federalism. The magazine's first number appeared on the first Saturday of the nineteenth century, but its editor looked backward rather than forward to the new age symbolized by the election, in the House of Representatives six weeks later, of Thomas Jefferson to the Presidency. Even John Elihu Hall, a militant Federalist with an almost fervent admiration for Dennie, observed that he had "a degree of bigotry and prejudice on certain topics which was strangely contrasted with the virtues of his heart and the gentleness of his deportment."[35] Democracy, to Dennie, was vicious and intolerable. As a Federalist, he favored rule by men of wealth and position.[36] He was an Anglophile who attacked democracy so virulently that he was once tried for seditious libel. In the *Port Folio* he printed sordid slanders of President Jefferson. It is likely, also, that the political views of Dennie and his circle were sometimes reflected in their literary tastes.[37] When Thomas Moore visited Philadelphia in June, 1804, Dennie and his Federalist friends—apparently regarding the poet as a symbol of political conservatism—feted him lavishly during ten long-remembered "days of ease and nights of hilarity."[38]

The election of Jefferson soon brought changes in James's life. In the election of 1799, his father had supported his friend James Ross, a Federalist of Pittsburgh, for the governorship of Pennsylvania.[39] But the Republicans won; and, on December 17, John Hall resigned as secretary of the land office. On December 9, however, President Adams had already provided for Hall by appointing him United States Marshal for the District of Pennsylvania.[40] It was probably unfortunate for Hall that, as marshal, he had had a small part in the trial of the leaders of the Fries Rebellion, an uprising of eastern Pennsylvania farmers in opposition to the Federalists' property tax. The Federalist prosecution of Fries recoiled, and was a factor in the Republican victory of 1800. John Hall had probably been stamped in the minds of politicians as the enforcement officer of a hated Federalist law. He served as marshal a year and three months, but, in spite of his pleas and in spite of the intervention of such powerful friends as Joseph Anderson, Richard Peters, and William Rawle, he was forced out of office in April, 1801.[41]

In the same year, the Halls moved to Lamberton, New Jersey, thirty miles north of Philadelphia. They lived in the village four years.[42] About the time of their removal to Lamberton, James's brothers John Elihu and Harrison withdrew from the University of Pennsylvania.[43] John Elihu entered the class of 1803 at Princeton, eleven miles from Lamberton, but left the college near the end of his senior year.[44] To Sarah Hall the Lamberton residence meant a degree of isolation. Although her family duties were increased by the birth of two more sons, she was able to write at least two pieces for the *Port Folio*.[45]

Apparently during the Lamberton period, in James's "twelfth year"—so runs his account in "The Academy," written twenty-two years later—his father entered him in an unidentified school known "time out of mind" as "The Academy" and situated "in the outskirts of a populous town in Pennsylvania."[46]

On his first visit to the Academy, James was accompanied by his father. The boy was eager with anticipation. He had built grand dreams of schools, and expected kindness from his teachers and friendship and devotion to learning from his future fellows. He was disappointed from the beginning. He and his father were met by a "small dapper man," to whom James, sensing in him pettiness, jealousy, and a taste for revenge, took an instant dislike. The students were equally disconcerting. While the teacher talked with James's father, the pupils whispered, made faces at James, and played tricks upon one another. But when the master turned his attention to the boys, they instantly appeared

14

to be busy. So great was James's disillusionment at these evidences of hypocrisy and at the obvious coercion on the part of the teacher that his family had some difficulty in persuading him to return the next morning to begin his studies.

There were three teachers. One, James declared, whipped the very young through the spelling book. The second "scourged into larger lads a competent knowledge of arithmetic, English grammar, and geography," and a third taught Homer and Horace by whipping off the pieces of skin inadvertently left by the other two.

James ran into a crisis when he had been at the school only a few days. He was not only rebuked for having handed his teacher an exercise containing an interlined word but was threatened also with a beating. "I was astounded by hearing him vociferate, 'How do you dare, Sir, to hand me such a paper?' I was silent with astonishment. 'Why don't you speak, Sirrah! are you dumb?' 'No, Sir, I am not dumb.' 'Don't repeat my words, you rascal!—don't be insolent, or I'll flog you within an inch of your life!' 'I am not insolent' said I, 'nor will I suffer myself to be flogged.' 'What's that you say, you villain?—you scoundrel, do you dispute my authority? I'll teach you, who I am!' and, rushing toward me with his scourge uplifted, his eyes glaring, and his visage bloated with fury, he seemed ready to immolate me, when I replied 'Stop, Sir! remember that I have never yet been struck even by my parents; and never will I submit to a blow from any other hand but theirs. It is an insult which I will not bear, and never will forgive!' The tyrant recoiled. The firm remonstrance appalled his coward spirit—I escaped the rod; but became the object of his lasting hatred."

In this story of his formal schooling, written primarily as an argument against whipping schoolchildren, he very likely remembered best those details which made him out the hero. The result is that he portrays himself as something of a prig —unless, of course, the relation is mainly true. Strange as it may seem to us, it probably was. One finds it difficult to account for the kind of fierce, fearless pride built into upper-class young men of the day—pride that flared at the least

15

suspicion of insult and endured the epoch's resolution-gauging methods of warfare and its nerve-testing duels—except by the conjecture that it was taught at home from earliest childhood.

At any rate, James found that the boys on the playground, where the weak cringed to the strong, were as tyrannical as the teachers. The polite James, who had played with the nice boys and girls of some of the best families of Philadelphia—such as the Hopkinsons and Davidsons, and apparently the Gratzes, the Whartons, and the Biddles—found on the playground of the Academy neither amiability, forbearance, nor justice.[47] "From such companions," he wrote, "I fled with horror."

The result of his experiences at the Academy was that he acquired an aversion for schoolmasters, copy-books, and everything else pertaining to schoolrooms. He learned to dislike Greek and Latin and to avoid any serious study of "squares and angles." Instead, he turned to romance, to tales of chivalry, to poetry, and substituted imagination for science. Apparently, he soon left the Academy. His writings reveal, however, that either at home or at school he attained some knowledge of Latin, became fairly well grounded in history, and probably learned to read and speak French.

III

James's schooling was probably shortened as much by changes in the family fortunes as by his "disgust" for schoolmasters. In 1805, the last year of the residence at Lamberton, his father, James wrote later, was "suddenly reduced from affluence to poverty."[48] Neither the nature nor the cause of the misfortune is known, but in that year the Federal government entered suit against him to recover public funds which he had retained to reimburse himself—at the time he left the Marshal's office—for his expenses in the trial of John Fries and in the upkeep of prize vessels lying in the port of Philadelphia.[49] John Hall's loss of fortune, therefore, may have been the result of a settlement of his accounts with the government. At the same time, he was

16

so "dreadfully afflicted with the gout, which at last destroyed his health," that he was able to do little effective work. "His family," James wrote later, "from that time were left to struggle with adversity."[50] When these blows struck him, John Hall was forty-five and had nine children, six of them between the ages of one and fourteen. Blessed with a wife who had "a flow of spirits which forsook her not even under the severest trials," he met his misfortunes, or submitted to them, by retreating to his paternal estate on the Susquehanna in Maryland. There the family lived on Octorara Creek, about a mile south of Mount Welcome.[51] Sarah Hall described the region near her home in a poem inspired by the singing of birds during some unusually warm weather of February, 1806:

> Hills rise on hills —
> An amphitheatre, whose lofty top,
> The spreading oak or stately poplar crowns —
> Whose ever-varying sides present such scenes
> Smooth or precipitous — harmonious still —
> Mild or sublime, — as wake the poet's lay. . . .[52]

To James, the beauty of the neighborhood was unforgettable, and his life there was one of the happy periods of his boyhood.[53]

In 1811, James's parents brought the family back to Philadelphia, where John and Sarah Hall were to live the rest of their lives.[54] A little later, John Hall had sufficiently recovered from his illness to be able to travel in western Pennsylvania as an agent for Eastern landowners.[55] The indefatigable Sarah was soon engaged in writing a book about the Bible, to consist of a series of imaginary conversations between a mother and her children. Although she was well fitted for the task by her experience in educating her own children, she undertook the study of Hebrew "to enable herself to make the necessary critical researches."[56]

James must have been about sixteen or seventeen when

17

his father, "intending to educate him for the mercantile profession . . . placed him at an early age in a counting
house." But "the business was not congenial to his tastes."[57]
A poem probably written by James and printed in the *Port
Folio* reveals the poetic aspirations of one ensnared in the
routine of commerce:

> In a cold empty warehouse I peevishly write
> With no spark to warm, but the Muse's dim light;
> Dim light! ay to me — for those coquetish lasses
> Shed all their bright radiance on pitiful asses,
> While I am left pining alone in the dark,
> And praying, in vain, for one — only one spark. . . .

But the Muse answered the prayer with scorn:

> "Thou merchant! begone, learn to herd with thy race! . . .
> Remain where thou art with thy gold-seeking clan!"[58]

By 1811, James had left "the cold empty warehouse" and
in that year began the study of law in the office of his uncle,
Samuel Ewing.[59] Ewing had many qualities to interest his
eighteen-year-old nephew. He was a lawyer, a poet, an
editor, a wit, a patron of the arts, and a man about town.
He had been graduated from the University of Pennsylvania
and had gone on to the Master's degree. When Dennie established the *Port Folio*, Ewing, with such young men as
the outgoing President's sons Thomas Boylston Adams and
John Quincy Adams, was one of Dennie's inner circle; and
for a long time he contributed a column of poetry, entitled
"Reflections in Solitude."[60] It is said that, as a young man,
Ewing loved the beautiful Jewess Rebecca Gratz and she
returned his love, but the difference in their religions prevented their marriage.[61] In 1809, he established the *Select
Reviews and Spirit of the Foreign Magazines* and, as both
owner and editor, conducted the magazine profitably for

three years. At the end of 1812, he sold the periodical to Moses Thomas; and he may have been in part responsible for Thomas's choice of Ewing's and John Elihu's friend Washington Irving for the editorship of the journal, published, after Ewing sold it, as the *Analectic Magazine*.[62] James could have met Irving at his uncle's law office. The likelihood of their acquaintance is enhanced by the fact that Irving, although he rarely printed verse in the *Analectic*, published one poem written by James and one signed with John Elihu's pen name.[63]

During the years of his law studies with his uncle Samuel, James was gay, energetic, high-spirited, and—if we may judge from a later portrait—handsome.[64] Some friends of the Hall family, such as Rebecca Gratz, may have mistaken his good humor for irresponsibility. She wrote that two or three of Sarah Hall's sons were considered geniuses, but James was "the one perhaps from whom least was expected."[65] As a member of the Washington Association, he moved in the society of gentlemen's sons. He had known Thomas Biddle, brother of Nicholas Biddle the financier, since boyhood.[66] In a diary Thomas Franklin Pleasants (1790-1817), Master of Arts from the University of Pennsylvania, mentioned James as if he were a friend and indicated that Thomas Isaac Wharton (1791-1856)—a contributor to the *Port Folio* and the *Analectic*, and, in 1815, Irving's successor to the editorship of the *Analectic* — was also James's friend. Others referred to in the Pleasants diary and probably members of James's circle by 1813 were Edward Ingersoll, Condy Raguet, and Rebecca Gratz's brothers Joseph and Benjamin.[67]

In the midst of these genial years of James's youth, Congress, on June 19, 1812, declared war against England. The Federalists at once raised a bitter antiwar clamor. Toward the struggle which developed, James appears to have been at first indifferent. His brother, however, played a leading part.

After leaving Princeton in 1802 or 1803, John Elihu had studied law in Philadelphia, first with his uncle John Ewing, and then with Joseph Hopkinson.[68] In 1805, he opened an

19

office and began to practice in Baltimore. There he seemed destined for eminence. In 1808, he began his editorship of the *American Law Journal* and by his editorial duties was soon led into correspondence with outstanding jurists. In Baltimore in 1809, he published his first book, *The Practice and Jurisdiction of the Court of Admiralty.* Meanwhile, he continued faithfully to send Dennie verse and prose for the *Port Folio.* He also entered politics, and in 1812 was allied with Alexander Contee Hanson and Jacob Wagner, publishers of the Baltimore *Federal Republican.* On the day after the declaration of war, they printed an incendiary antiwar editorial. Late in July, a mob beat and brutally tortured Hanson and eight of his friends, including John Elihu, and left them for dead in a mangled heap. John Elihu managed to crawl away from the pile of dead and broken bodies and succeeded in reaching Philadelphia by August 14, afflicted with a "particular sort of pain" in his head that was to remain with him for at least eight years, and probably until his death.[69] In his home city he asked an aroused public to wait for a truthful account of the riots; and two weeks later he was able to bring out his version, "The Narrative of John E. Hall," in a Philadelphia newspaper.[70] Not long afterward, at the request of Federalists in Philadelphia, he edited an antiwar pamphlet containing his narrative and the accounts of several other defenders of Hanson's house.[71] Using the riots as a political windfall, the Federalists won the elections of 1812 in Philadelphia and parts of Maryland. Reinvigorated, they went on protesting against the war.

James was then nineteen; these were his dancing days. Although he must have been sobered by the spectacle of John Elihu arriving in the city, battered and broken, and although he must have been moved by the other grave events leading to and following the declaration of war, there is little sign of his concern in the three poems that are all he is known to have written during 1812. He was having fun especially with "Othello," a poem sketching farcically the career of Shakespeare's Moor:

For his trouble he gave her a bushel of sighs,
 And swore that she lov'd a bold knight;
He declared that he valued her more than his eyes
So he made her dad drunk, bore her off by surprise
 And married her that very night.[72]

In May, 1812, "Miss W," chronologically the first of an impressive number of girls to whom James wrote verses, was the subject of his dreams. He had, perhaps, spent the previous evening dancing, or at least talking, with her:

So I last night when sunk to rest,
 In fancy still remained with you;
I heard your voice — your hand I prest,
 And sigh to find my dream untrue.[73]

After the declaration of war, James answered a "Miss M" with languid levity:

Ah! with joy would I fly to proud victory's field —
 But *freemen* alone may enlist in her train;
And I am a slave forced by Cupid to yield
 Long since, lovely girl, to your magical chain![74]

The military events of 1812, however, were of a kind to beget gravity.

II
The First Campaign, 1814

JAMES's frivolity was the effervescence of health and youth. He was fearless, intensely patriotic, and ready to rally to a cause when the need was plain. Certainly he was not dominated by the Federalist zeal of his brother; when at last the war began to threaten Philadelphia, James became a soldier.

The war, during its first six months, had brought a series of almost uninterrupted disasters to the American armies. From the Canadian frontier, reports of defeat arrived with dismal monotony. On August 16, General Hull surrendered at Detroit, leaving the British masters of a large American area in the Northwest. On October 13, General Van Rensselaer was forced to surrender a thousand men. Late in the same month, General Dearborn failed. On November 28, the army of General Smyth, whose military methods have been characterized as grotesque, dissolved in wild confusion, the soldiers firing their muskets in every direction, but most frequently toward Smyth's own tent.[1]

The coming of spring brought sudden danger from the south. In early March, 1813, a unit of the British fleet blockaded Delaware Bay and began to raid the farms and towns on its banks. After the bombardment of Lewes, Delaware,[2] militia companies sprang up in Philadelphia. The Washington Association, a patriotic society of young men, called a meeting at Washington Hall in Goforth Alley and, on March 22, formed the Washington Guards.[3] This fashionable corps of 116 volunteers was "composed from the most respectable young men of the city."[4] Forgetting the Federalist antiwar views of his brother, John Elihu, and even the "magical chain of Miss M," Hall busied himself in organizing the Guards, and his name is said to have stood first on the recruiting list.[5]

The Guards held their drills at six o'clock in the morning in the State House Yard. On April 5, they paraded in uniform, marching to the Centre Square for exercise in firing. On April 13, they joined their regiment at the State House Yard and began their thirty-mile march down the Delaware to Camp DuPont, at Stanton,[6] where they spent the next three months guarding against landing parties from the British fleet. On July 28, when danger was over, the Guards returned to Philadelphia. Three days later the troops were mustered out and honored with a feast.[7]

II

Not long after the end of his summer duty with the militia, Hall enlisted again and spent the winter at Fort Mifflin on Mud Island in the Delaware, seven miles below Philadelphia. The commandant was Captain Thomas Biddle, a younger brother of Nicholas Biddle, the financier. Acquainted since boyhood, Hall and Biddle entered now upon a friendship to be ended only by death. Two years older than Hall, Biddle had spent the previous summer fighting with the army on the Canadian frontier. At his own request, Biddle was ordered to select from the recruits at Fort Mifflin one subaltern and ninety men, to organize them into a company of artillery, and to lead the detachment to the northern border for the summer campaign.[8]

Hall was chosen as Biddle's subaltern and was commissioned as a third lieutenant in the Second Artillery on March 30, 1814.[9] Two weeks later, on May 1, he was promoted to a second lieutenant.[10] Near that date, the company left for Buffalo.

The company traveled from Fort Mifflin to Trenton by water, marched from Trenton to Brunswick, and then boarded shallops for Albany. During the voyage, Biddle was confined to his bed by an ague contracted during the previous summer's campaign. At Albany he was too weak to travel and was left behind to follow in a stagecoach as soon as he was able. The company went ahead under Hall's command.[11]

Hall suddenly found himself in charge of not only a company and its equipment but also the wives and children of some of the men, for it was still an age when the campaigning soldier might be accompanied by his family. But in spite of these stern and varied responsibilities, Hall enjoyed the journey. He was twenty, but nobody, he said, would have taken him for more than eighteen. He was resplendent in a new uniform with "the glittering epaulet, the gilded sword-knot, and the scarlet sash." The road from Albany to Buffalo, he wrote later in a thinly disguised description of his company's march, led through three hundred miles of forest broken only by an occasional village, lake, or farm.[12] It was late May, and the "romantic lakes, the fertile valleys, and the boundless forests" were at their loveliest. The company of recruits, no matter how jaded, was carefully arranged before being exhibited to a secluded hamlet. At the leader's command, Hall remembered, "the drum strikes up a lively march—the little fifer sends forth his shrillest notes," the stragglers are called in, and the company "moves forward with a firm and rapid step." Not the least of the company's attractions was its wagon train. "In the rear," Hall writes, "comes the baggage-wagon loaded, followed, and preceded, by men, women, and children—the sick, the weary, and the lame. But even these are not without their pride. The poor soldier with his knapsack at his back—his child on one arm, and his wife leaning upon the other, feels himself as much

'his country's stay
In the day and hour of danger,'

as the stoutest comrade in the ranks"

When evening came, Hall marked off the ground for his camp, surrounded it with sentinels, and supervised the pitching of the tents "in a regular line, with technical accuracy." He sent parties for water, wood, and straw. Then fires were kindled in the rear of the camp, and cheerfulness reigned throughout.

Biddle overtook the company at Utica but was again taken ill and left there, and Hall led the troops until they were within a few miles of Buffalo. There his anticipated pleasure of leading the fine body into headquarters was prevented by Biddle's rejoining the company.[13]

At the camp near Buffalo, the company was united with the army of General Jacob Brown. Brown, decidedly a man of action, was preparing for an invasion of Canada. His subaltern, Brigadier General Winfield Scott, was drilling officers of all ranks with the aid of a single copy of a French military manual. Brown's force at its maximum contained about 3,500 men, exclusive of some six hundred Indians.[14] His artillery consisted of four companies of approximately one hundred men each, and each company had three brass field pieces. By early July, Brown was ready to strike.

The scene of his ensuing campaign was the western or Canadian shore of the Niagara River. Before daylight on July 3, Brown's army crossed into Canada at Black Rock, at the head of the river. A battalion of infantry and Biddle's company of artillery were immediately detached from the main force to take nearby Fort Erie. Biddle's company formed battery in the open plain in front of the fort, but the 170 British officers and men surrendered without firing a shot. Ordered to take possession of the stronghold, Biddle's company occupied it during the night.[15]

Having secured Fort Erie, General Brown's army hastened down along the Niagara toward Chippewa, about twelve miles below Fort Erie. The artillery arrived there at eleven o'clock in the night of July 4, two or three hours after the main body. The next morning, the British attacked.

Hall and his company, held in reserve during the early part of the Battle of Chippewa, had an excellent view of the field. Hall himself afterwards described it memorably: "The battle took place on the margin of the Niagara river, on an extensive plain, which had once been covered with fine farms, but now, forsaken by its inhabitants, and desolated by war, it exhibited only a barren waste. The river at that place begins to acquire some of that terrific velocity, with which it rushes over the awful precipice three miles below . . . the noise of the cataract is heard, and the column of foam distinctly seen from the battle ground. On the other side the field is bounded by a thick forest, but the plain itself presented a level smooth surface, unbroken by ravines, and without a tree or bush to intercept the view, or an obstacle to impede the movements of the hostile bodies, or to afford to either party an advantage. From this plain the American camp was separated by a small creek. In the full glare of the summer sun, on the morning of the fifth of July, the British troops were seen advancing toward our camp, across the destined field of strife, their waving plumes, their scarlet uniforms, and gilded ornaments, exhibiting a gay and gorgeous appearance—their martial music, their firm and rapid step, indicating elastic hopes and high courage. The Americans, inferior in number, were hastily put in motion to meet the advancing foe; they crossed a small rude bridge, the only outlet from the camp[,] under a heavy fire of the enemy's artillery; and moved steadily to the spot selected for the engagement. The scene at this moment was beautiful and imposing. The British line, glowing with golden and crimson hues, was stretched across the plain, flanked by pieces of brass ordnance, whose rapid discharge spread death over the field, and filled the air with thunder; while the clouds of smoke enveloping each extremity of the line, left the centre only exposed to the eye, and extending off to the river on the one hand, and the forest on the other, filled the whole back ground of the landscape. The Americans were advancing in column. They were new recruits, now led for the first time into action, and except a few of the officers, none of all that heroic band had ever before seen the banner of a foe. But they moved steadily to their ground, unbroken by the galling fire: and platoon after platoon wheeled into line with the same graceful accuracy of movement which marks the evolutions of the holiday parade, until the whole column was deployed into one extended front; the officers carefully dressing the line with technical skill, and the whole brigade evincing by its deep silence, and the faithful precision of its movements, the subordination of strict discipline, and the steady coolness of determined courage. Now the musketry of the enemy began to rattle, pouring bullets thick as hail upon our ranks. Still not a trigger was drawn, not a voice was heard on our side, save the quick peremptory tones of command. General Scott rode along the line, cheering and restraining his troops:— then passing from flank to flank to see that all was as he wished, he wheeled his steed into the rear of his troops and gave the command to 'fire!' A voice was immediately heard in the British ranks—supposed to be that of their commander—exclaiming, 'charge the d——d Yankees! charge the d——d Buffalo militia! charge! charge!' The American general ordered his men to 'support arms!' The British rushed forward with bayonets charged; but they were struck with amazement when they beheld those whom their commander had tauntingly called *militia*, standing motionless as statues: their muskets erect, their arms folded across their breasts, gazing calmly at the hostile ranks advancing furiously with levelled bayonets! It was a refinement of

27

discipline rarely exhibited, and here altogether unexpected. The Americans stood until the enemy approached within a few paces:—until the foemen could see the fire flashing from each other's eyes—and each could read the expression of his adversary's face; then, deliberately, as the word was given, the Americans levelled their pieces, and fired,—and the whole line of the enemy seemed annihilated! Many were killed, many wounded, and some, rushing madly forward with a powerful momentum, fell over their prostrate companions, or were thrown down by the weight of succeeding combatants. In one instant the ground lately occupied by that gallant line, was covered with flying Britons; in another, a second line had advanced to sustain the contest, while the broken fragments of the first were rallied behind it. The 'Buffalo militia' were now the assailants, advancing with charged bayonets. Then it was that the young American chiefs, who led that gallant host, displayed the skill of veterans, . . . Five-and-thirty minutes decided the contest, and the retiring foe was pursued, and driven to his fortress. . . ."[16]

"About the time the enemy commenced their charge and at the moment they broke," wrote Major Hindman in his official report, "Captain Ritchie's Company of artillery, and one piece (a 12 Pounder) of Captain Biddle's Company of artillery under Lieut. Hall, participated in the action. . . . The whole artillery then on the field pursued, under the fire of the Enemy's batteries, with rapidity and saw them precipitate themselves within their works."[17] It was Hall's first experience under fire.

Brown's army forced General Riall to blow up his fort at Chippewa and retreat down the Niagara to Kingston. Brown followed him there so aggressively that Riall moved on downstream all the way to Fort George, where Brown soon cornered him in the angle formed by Lake Ontario and the mouth of the Niagara. When Brown's pursuing army reached Queenston Heights, the crimson line of retreating British troops was still visible in the distance below. From the Heights the view of Lake Ontario, of Forts George and Niagara, and of the boundless forest of the American shore made Hall catch his breath. Here, under a clear sky, was "a brilliant landscape, glowing with the luxuriance of summer" and providing one of those rare hours in perhaps every man's life "when a coincidence of happy circumstances" creates unforgettable beauty.[18]

Brown's army descended to the village of Queenston, remained there two days, and then proceeded to Fort George. Camping before the fort and just beyond the range of cannon fire from its ramparts, Brown prepared to attack.

But, it is said, he then received word that General Drummond was advancing to the aid of Fort George with five thousand men recently freed from the war with France.[19] Brown retreated to Chippewa on July 24 and camped on the battle field. Riall promptly followed and, on the morning of July 25, camped a few miles downstream at Lundy's Lane. There, at five o'clock in the evening of the same day, Scott's brigade began an attack upon a superior British force. The resulting engagement was the Battle of Bridgewater, or Lundy's Lane.

Scott's troops fought tenaciously until nine o'clock, when in the darkness the rest of Brown's army, including Biddle's artillery, came on the run to his aid. At that hour, about 1,900 men with seven field pieces faced about 2,600 British with the same number of cannon. Biddle's battery was stationed within sight and hearing of the Falls and at the junction of Lundy's Lane and the main road along the Niagara to Queenston.[20] Hall again commanded one of the twelve-pounders. The battle was murderous. The muzzles of the American cannon were advanced within a few yards of those of the British. The Indians, both by their war cries and their stealth, doubtless added terror to the darkness. The companies of artillery were posted in different parts of the field. "Unable to follow the frequent and rapid movements of the line," Hall wrote, "and often unable to distinguish friend from foe, they were . . . sometimes exposed to capture. Hindman dashed from one company to another, his horse reeking with blood. Towson's veteran company, so often distinguished, was now dreadfully mangled. The gallant Ritchie fell, literally covered with wounds. Biddle's company suffered considerable loss, and he was wounded in the neck, by a musket ball."

After midnight when the fighting was over, General Brown had lost 853 men, nearly half his force, and the British an equal number. Three American generals were wounded. Biddle, though wounded twice, had refused to leave the battle. To please him, his "subordinate," very likely Hall, lashed a British gun, "a beautiful six-pounder," behind his own caisson and wheeled it off as a trophy, which, Hall noted, was "the only piece of field artillery captured from the enemy during the war."[21]

The next day, July 26, the American troops retired twelve miles up the river to Fort Erie, situated on a bluff looking out over Lake Erie, and camped there in the evening. They spent the next few weeks feverishly strengthening the fort. Biddle's battery was placed in front. On August 2, the British laid siege.

III

During the three-months' siege of Fort Erie, General Brown singled out Hall for the performance of confidential missions.[22] At least once he sent Hall under a flag of truce with dispatches to the commander of the British forces. In Hall's two accounts of a part of the errand the dates of the journey conflict, but it probably occurred between August 5 and September 16. It may be that the real object of the mission was not merely to deliver dispatches to the British general but to secure information about the enemy.

A part of the enemy, it has been explained,[23] were supposed to be encamped on the Canadian side of Grand Island, lying in the Niagara River. But the troops had been moved during the night and, upon landing, Hall found himself in their rear. He was taken prisoner and held, he said, "while these exalted personages [Generals Brown and Drummond] were settling a controverted point of etiquette" regarding his status.[24] General Drummond freed Hall, but, to guard against his returning to Brown with information of any value, decreed that he could rejoin his forces only by a circuitous three-hundred-mile route leading along the Canadian shore of Lake Ontario to Fort Prescott on the St. Lawrence. Hall was paroled, was allowed to keep his sword and epaulettes, and was placed in the care of a veteran British officer, "a companion rather than a guard," who was to guide him to Fort Prescott. This officer was a man of middle age, a genial and worldly veteran of many foreign campaigns. On the first day's journey, Hall related, the two officers rode their horses from the head of Lake Ontario to Dundas and there stopped for the night. Encamped in that village was an army of Indians allied with the British. During the night the chief of the tribe strode into Hall's room and warned Hall to stay away from the open window lest he be killed by the savages raging in the yard outside. At dawn the two officers set out without breakfast on a path "along a broken ridge skirted with precipices." As they rode through the "thick and lofty forest," Hall's companion tried to divert their minds from hunger by whistling and by pointing out the scene of a bear fight, a murder, or an Indian ambuscade.

Late in the day, they stopped at the farm house of Major Thomas Merritt, the fifty-five-year-old sheriff of the Niagara District and commander of a troop of Niagara cavalry. His house was a mile or two upstream on Twelve Mile Creek, fourteen miles north of the juncture of the Niagara River and Lake Ontario.[25] Hall later remembered Mrs. Merritt as a "cheerful and complaisant" lady. The Merritts had a son, William, who had been captured at the Battle of Lundy's Lane,[26] but they had at home a daughter, Maria, who was about eighteen and "whose glowing cheek, and sparkling eye," Hall thought, "might have warmed the dreary bosom of an anchorite. This lovely girl, bred in the wilds of Canada, was intelligent, well educated, and easy in her deportment."[27] He and his companion stayed for a meal and possibly spent the night at Major Merritt's. The charming Maria presided at the table, and Hall came near being "desperately smitten." In his journal there is a playful four-line poem entitled "On Miss Maria Merritt" and dated "12 Mile Creek, Upper Canada, September, 1814," a copy of which he possibly gave to Maria at parting or left in his room:

> Let toasted beauties boast their charms
>   Their taste or wit, or sense, or spirit; —
> They cannot lure me to their arms,
>   For I admire *modest merit.*

The officers rode on their way, and the romance was over. There is no record that Hall ever saw the girl again. She married two years later;[28] and within a few years, Hall had written verses to pretty girls in more than half of the states of the Union. Of the journey itself, little more is known except that Hall, traveling, it is said, sometimes on foot and at night, managed to rejoin his corps by September 16.[29]

He took part in most of the three-month battle of the siege of Fort Erie. It is possible, though not likely, that he was present on August 14, when the British attacked after midnight but were finally driven off at five in the morning after losing a third of the 2,150 men in the attacking force.

He later described his own and the garrison's plight during the latter part of the siege:

> For more than six weeks there was scarcely an hour in the day or night, in which bombs and shrapnell [*sic*] shells were not bursting in the air, and cannon balls sweeping through the area of the fort — not a day or night, in which a number were not killed. Nor was any spot secure. . . . The troops were all in tents; the one occupied by captain Biddle and his lieutenant [Hall], was destroyed by piecemeal during the siege, being torn in nearly twenty places, at different times, by fragments of shells, and other missiles. One of these, a fragment of more than a pound weight, pierced entirely through the mattrass [*sic*] on which those gentlemen were sitting. Biddle himself was struck down on one occasion by a small fragment of a shell, which fell perpendicularly on his shoulder, pierced through the strap of the epaulet, and penetrated to the bone; on another, a soldier who stood at the opening of the tent, had his head completely crushed while the

brains were thrown upon a dish, which the captain's servant was about to place on the table. Unfortunately for the garrison, the season was remarkably rainy. The fort was situated on a level plain . . . ; the heavy rains pouring continually upon it, and the treading of so many men, reduced the whole ground to one great mud puddle. The service itself was severe. The artillery especially were ordered to sleep in their clothes and accoutrements, and to man the guns at every alarm. These occurred, not only every day and night, but often, every hour. The real alarms were numerous; the false alarms, occasioned by the mistake or inadvertence of centinels, or the accidental firing of guns in the woods, were still more frequent. In every such instance the artillery paraded at the guns — remained perhaps long enough to be thoroughly drenched with the rain, then returned to their tents, to sleep for an hour in their wet clothes, and be again called on for duty. . . . Sickness began to prevail to an alarming degree; and even those who remained on duty, were enfeebled and worn down by fatigue and exposure. Add to this the continual exposure of ghastly corpses, the dreadful groans and excruciating pains of the sick, the wounded, and the dying — the sick destitute of every comfort, and the dying of every consolation — and it will be seen that this little army endured a complication of dangers and sufferings, which can scarcely be realized by any who have not had the same experience. . . .[30]

Weak as the garrison was, on September 17, the day after Hall is said to have written a letter from the fort, General Brown slipped out during a heavy rain with about two thousand men, attacked the British camp, blew up its powder magazine, and destroyed a third of the British force. Four days after Brown's smashing sortie, the British gave up the siege and withdrew.

But Brown was eager for more fighting. About three days after his sortie, he received word that General Izard was bringing a large army to aid him. Izard planned to voyage up Lake Ontario to the mouth of Eighteen Mile Creek, near the head of the lake. From that place his course would be directed by information that he might receive from Brown. It is probable that Hall was "the young artillery officer," described in his story "The Bearer of Despatches,"[31] whom Brown selected to deliver the message to Izard. The route lay through territory thick with enemy spies. According to Hall's account, the messenger crossed the arm of the lake to Buffalo, got a horse from the quartermaster there, wrapped himself in a great cloak to hide his uniform and insignia, and rode down the Niagara's eastern bank on a road that led near Fort Niagara, then in the possession of the enemy. He passed Schlosser before sunset and then fell in with a suspicious looking "boor," who was a little drunk or else acted as if he were. At dark, the two men passed through a village of the Tuscarora Indians at Lewiston and, about midnight, arrived at a village inn situated in or near enemy territory. There the messenger spent the remainder of the night. Sleeping little, he twice frightened away men who, he thought, were trying to break into his room. Before daylight, as he was leaving, the landlord tried to stop him by seizing his horse's reins but the messenger broke away and rode on into the darkness. Not finding Izard's army at Eighteen Mile Creek, Brown's courier rode on some sixty miles to Genesee, where Izard had landed on the twenty-second. He finally found Izard at Batavia and delivered the message there on September 27.[32]

General Izard's army at last joined Brown's on October 13, but, except for a brief artillery duel at Chippewa, the campaign was over. On November 5, Fort Erie was abandoned and blown up. Brown moved his troops to the American side and went into winter quarters. The daring and resolution of his campaign made a deep impression at home. "So famous did Brown's little army become," Henry Adams observed, "that the details of its force and organization retained an interest equalled only by that which attached to the frigates and sloops of war."[33]

Hall himself was cited to the War Department for his part at Chippewa; General Brown spoke well of him; General Scott said he had behaved "like a soldier"; and General Ripley praised him and recommended, though belatedly, that he be brevetted for his conduct at Lundy's Lane.[34] More valuable than the honors were his new friends and his new views of life and of his country. He had seen human nature stripped to its elements. He had tested his own endurance and had learned that he "could eat salt junk, drink dirty water, or nestle composedly in a thick settlement of bedbugs."[35] He had made friends among his fellow officers, several of whom later spoke not only of his strict attention to duty but also of his "pleasing man[ners] & address," of his "having a great share of what is commonly called *good nature*," and of his "m[ore] than common gayety & sociality of heart."[36] Perhaps of even greater significance for his later career was a new understanding of the size of his country and of the nature of its hinterland.

At Fort Erie, probably about the middle of October, he became ill and was sent to the base at Williamsville, near the ruins of Buffalo. The Harvard-trained surgeon's mate at the hospital, James Bates, diagnosed the complaint as "a disease of the Liver."[37] The hospital contained nearly two thousand patients, "principally under tents."[38] The post was almost as wretched as Fort Erie—"a licentious camp," Hall wrote, one of those "which, though containing the bravest of men, were surrounded by the worst of women."[39]

Supported by the consent of Biddle, who was still at Fort Erie, and by Dr. Bates's prescription of "a change of place and objects," Hall applied for leave to go on recruiting service in Philadelphia, stating that his illness precluded all hope of performing any kind of duty on the frontier that winter. On November 3, the leave was granted.[40]

According to his story "Empty Pockets," he was soon in New York. "Fresh from the scenes of tumult and danger," he wrote, "with a heart sickened among the gloomy scenes of the hospital . . . I gazed with delight upon my countrymen . . . and contrasting this placid and cheerful display of national happiness, with the vice[,] dejection, and disease which I had left behind, my heart was filled with delight."[41] He took a room at the City Hotel and went to see a production of *Romeo and Juliet*. The next morning he boarded a steamboat for Brunswick. As the boat slipped down the harbor, he found that, during the previous night, his head had been so full of the sorrows of Romeo and Juliet

35

that he had lost his purse. But he was relieved of his difficulty when a stranger on the boat offered him his pocket-book and asked him to take what he needed.

Probably by mid-November, he arrived at his home at 108 South Fourth Street, Philadelphia.

III

Service Afloat and Ashore, 1814-16

On November 30, 1814, Hall was assigned to Captain James Nelson Barker's company at Fort Mifflin, just outside the city.[1] His new commanding officer, like Hall a native Philadelphian, was a successful playwright who was later to become alderman of his native city and Comptroller of the Treasury of the United States. He had spent two previous winters as an artilleryman on the Canadian frontier, but, having been shot through both thighs in a duel there, was no longer fit for active duty.[2] Both these veteran artillerymen were high-spirited enough to take to military life, and both were literary. They appear to have remained friends for several years.[3]

During the winter, Hall no doubt enjoyed some distinction as a minor hero of the northern campaign. He could wear the dashing blue uniform trimmed with yellow.[4] The tight-fitting swallow-tail coat was set off with epaulettes, and a sash was tied around the waist. The bell-shaped hat was heightened by a cockade or pompon. Tufted sideburns to the lower edge of the ear were in fashion among military men, and Hall doubtless yielded to the mode. We may be sure he dressed fastidiously for the dinner of the Third Company of Washington Guards at the Washington Hall Hotel on January 20, where he proposed a toast to "The Volunteer Companies of Philadelphia—the pride ornament and protection of their native city."[5]

But the war was already over. News of the signing of the peace treaty arrived in Philadelphia at noon on Sunday, February 12.[6] A week or two later, Hall was on furlough in Baltimore, probably as the guest of his brother John Elihu.[7] There James amused himself by inditing "The Soldier's Invitation," a not very weighty set of verses printed in the Baltimore *Telegraph* the same month and notable chiefly because it left little doubt that he had already embraced soldiering as a profession.[8]

While Hall was still on furlough in Baltimore, President Madison asked Congress for a declaration of war against Algeria. Congress complied just a week later. Although this contest with the Mediterranean nation was clearly a task for the navy, Hall was determined to have a part in it; and he went at once to Washington and offered the Navy Department his services as a midshipman.[9] His proposal was rejected, and he poured out his disappointment melodramatically:

> I'll not repine if niggard fate
>   Less kind — more cold — each moment grows
> And with a vengeful, pois'nous hate
>   A baleful vapour round me throws;
>
> She cannot turn my friends away
>   She cannot make my heart despair. . . .[10]

But Hall's "niggard fate" suddenly beamed upon him;
the Navy Department was persuaded to send with the naval
expedition a small detachment of artillerymen with "some
mortars to be used in the bombardment of Algiers."[11] Hall
was one of the five army officers selected; and, on May 10,
he was ordered to report at New York to Commodore
Stephen Decatur, commander of one of the two squadrons
being fitted to sail against the Algerines.[12] He said farewell
to his family and friends, and arrived in New York probably
between May 15 and May 20, where he found Decatur's
squadron in the bustle of last-minute preparations for sail-
ing. On presenting his orders, he was told by the young
commodore that the principal part of the artillery stores
was in Boston with Commodore William Bainbridge's
squadron. Since Hall had been placed in charge of the army
ordnance, Decatur gave him an order to report there.[13] Hall
was probably still in New York when Decatur's squadron
sailed on May 20. He must have felt a chilling disappointment as he turned from the wharf, for Decatur, who had
stunned the Mediterranean pirates with the swiftness of his
attacks eleven years before, was the very symbol of military
valor. At the dock Hall may have met Washington Irving,
one of John Elihu's acquaintances. Irving and Decatur had
become warm friends, and the commodore had invited the
New Yorker to go with him and share the danger and the
glory. Irving had accepted, and on May 18—about the
day Hall was conferring with Decatur—had stored his bag-
gage on the flagship. But at the last minute he changed his
mind; he was to sail for Liverpool instead.[14]

Hall could only go on to Boston, where he reported to
Bainbridge within three days after Decatur had sailed. In
comparison with the exciting hum of the fleet in New York,
the preparations of Bainbridge's squadron must have seemed
a slow-motion pantomime. Bainbridge was cordial enough
to Hall, but punctilious. He explained that he outranked
Decatur and could hardly be expected to consider his orders.
He was, however, kind enough to say to the eager soldier
that "his services would be useful and he would accept them
with pleasure" if the Navy Department would give him an

order. All this Hall reported to Secretary of the Navy Crowninshield.[15] It was more than two weeks before the requisite order was in Bainbridge's hands, but that was more than soon enough: none of the squadron's vessels sailed before July 5, and Hall's ship was delayed until August.

For more than ten dragged out weeks, Hall tried to amuse himself. Suspicious of New Englanders, he made no lasting friends in Boston.[16] From a poem in his journal, it appears that in June he journeyed to New York to visit Daniel Sackett, who had been an infantry lieutenant in the northern theater of the war and whom Hall described as "the dearest of friends."[17] Apparently the two had studied together long before:

> With minds independent and free
> Unshackled by any controul
> Together we plough'd learning's sea
> Together we feasted the soul.

Hall spent glorious days with Sackett and his friends. Among them, it seems, were the lovely creatures described in the poem beginning "If I were Persia's king, my dear." But bewitching as they were, Hall's fondness was restrained by the memory of a Philadelphia girl named Ann with whom he had exchanged vows.

Hall was back in Boston in July. When most of Bainbridge's squadron sailed on July 5, Hall's vessel, the "Enterprise," still required a month's preparation. With his fellow officers, Hall passed some of the weary time in the careful choice of meats, wines, and liquors for the voyage. At last, at two o'clock Sunday afternoon, August 6, the "Enterprise" weighed anchor and sailed down the bay.[18] The rest of Bainbridge's squadron had already left; the "Enterprise" was to cross alone.

II

The "Enterprise" was a brig of fourteen guns commanded by Lawrence Kearny, a twenty-six-year-old lieutenant. She was a "wet" vessel: except in fine weather, on deck one was constantly drenched with spray; and the water was always ankle deep. During the first fifteen days of the voyage, the weather was rough. Although Hall's curiosity was too strong to allow a mere drenching to keep him entirely from the deck, he spent most of the time in his stateroom. He kept a journal of the voyage out and recorded the ship's position, the temperature of the water, and various events of the journey. Entries in the journal show that he was reading the Bible, Shakespeare, and Goldsmith, and that he was finding William Falconer's *The Shipwreck* and parts of Byron's *Childe Harold's Pilgrimage* pertinent to his voyage.

Because Hall was a soldier, the naval officers aboard looked forward to his seasickness with special mirth; but he surprised even himself. The first rough weather bothered him little; subsequently, at the beginning of a storm, he went below and slept; and even when the brig rolled and pitched in the Gulf Stream, he was able to conceal his giddiness. His good spirits forced his companions to acknowledge that, if he was no sailor, he was at least "an old man o'-war's-man."

The storm struck at three o'clock in the afternoon of the fourth day. For three hours the wind blew with such a fury that Hall frankly acknowledged his inability to describe it; few, he thought, would have believed him if he had. Two days later both Kearny and the master of a British ship hailed by the "Enterprise" agreed that they had never seen a harder gale. But afterwards there were days and nights of ease. Hall amused himself by watching the flying fish and the porpoises. Sometimes he and Kearny sat on the sunny deck talking and smoking their cigars. Once, at midnight, they found the moonlight so fair that they lounged on deck talking until nearly dawn, when they had a cold supper in Kearny's cabin before retiring.

In Boston, Hall and the officers of the "Enterprise" had gone to great trouble and expense to lay in provisions of the best quality. "Knowing by repute the kind of people" they had to deal with, they had selected every article themselves.

41

But at sea, Hall recorded, they found all their care of no avail:

> By the mystical operations of these Eastern magi our fine old madiera [*sic*] was changed to Sherry, Jamaica Spirits to New England Rum, and Holland Gin to American whiskey; . . . and our corned beef and pickled port [pork] became *salt junk*. . . . After venting our indignation we began . . . to *guess* that we had come off pretty well, as any honest man may congratulate himself on doing who leaves *Boston* with the loss of nothing more than his money;—if he preserves his watch, his toothpick and his tobacco-box he does well and deserves credit for his vigilance; but if he retains his honesty he does better, and may stand an honourable exception to the rule that evil communication corrupts good manners.

This hoodwinking was no doubt a factor in Hall's long-lasting wariness of New Englanders. But, for the voyage, the loss of the delicacies mattered little. Anyone who had endured the siege of Fort Erie could accustom himself to the food of a war vessel.

On Sunday, August 27, the brig reached São Miguel, an island of the Azores, where she was becalmed. As she drifted in near shore, Hall climbed to the main top and sat for a long time gazing at the neat white houses and even at the islanders dressed in their Sunday clothes. On September 1, the brig spoke a British vessel whose captain shouted indistinctly either that "Buonaparte was dead," or "gone to H-ll" or "to St. Helena." The next day, when the ship was more than a hundred miles from land, a dove settled on her rigging. "We looked upon it," Hall records, "as a bad omen —it looked too much like peace." Three days later, when there was little or no wind, suddenly out of nowhere came a squall that carried away the brig's main- and fore-topmasts and with them a sailor, who was drowned in spite of all the crew's efforts. The "Enterprise" passed on down the Spanish coast within view of Cadiz. As she rounded Cape Trafalgar and sailed over "the scene of Lord Nelson's glory and his death," Hall heard the fateful battle explained by a sailor who had been with Nelson's fleet. The next morning

42

Hall saw ahead "the narrow defile" of the Strait of Gibraltar and, far beyond it, the sun rising out of the Mediterranean and "gilding at once the rocky shores of Europe and Africa." As the "Enterprise" glided through the passage, he contrasted the crags on either side with Byron's description of them.[19] The same morning, after a voyage of thirty-three days, the brig anchored at Gibraltar.

The first news Hall heard was that the swift Decatur had already swooped upon his enemies, conquered them, and forced them to sign agreements before Bainbridge's squadron even arrived in the Mediterranean.[20] Hall expressed his disappointment in a solemn display of heroics:

Our long and disagreable [*sic*] voyage was now over, and the brilliant hopes we had indulged almost within our reach. We looked forward with delight. A few days would bring us to the scene of action, and of glory, where we expected to reap the laurels of victory. But how soon were these pleasing anticipations changed to the most bitter disappointment! The first news we heard was that which must ever be the most disagreable to a soldier, the news of peace. . . . I used frequently during the voyage to think, "is it possible that so much good fortune is intended for me—no—something will interrupt—something will frustrate it," and the event proved my thoughts prophetic, and confirmed me a predestinarian.

While new topmasts were being installed in the "Enterprise," Hall and a Mr. DeBree explored the caves and fortifications of Gibraltar. They climbed to the pinnacle and, standing on the leveled surface only twenty feet wide, found that they could see not only across the Strait but as far as Cape Molerino, thirty leagues away. "The pages of history," Hall wrote in a Byronic vein, "opened itself to my view, and the tales of chivalry rushed across my recollection. I saw at once the countries of the haughty Spaniard and the daring Moor of ancient days."

About September 11, the "Enterprise" sailed to join the rest of Bainbridge's squadron at Malaga, where she lay at anchor several days. Hall was impressed by the city's labyrinth of irregular streets, not as wide as many modern side-

43

walks. Sauntering on the promenade in the evenings, he saw "the lean monks, the fat friar, the tawny mountaineer, and half a dozen other classes of degenerate Spaniards." But he acknowledged the beauty of Malaga's ladies, whose striking dress and manners gave them "a momentary charm over the more modest and retiring graces we had been used to at home." Under the serene skies of Malaga, Hall sighed,

> Oh, happy if the stream of life,
> As smooth as now forever flowed.

The journal breaks off with the entry for September 16, while he was still at Malaga. One wishes he had continued it. His observation was acute; and although he is self-conscious and literary in the early pages, he soon relaxes into a simpler prose, not without charm.

Bainbridge's squadron, including the "Enterprise," was back at Gibraltar on September 26, and sailed for home on October 6. On the return voyage, Decatur's vessel overtook the "Enterprise"—which the Commodore had commanded when he performed his spectacular feats against the Tripolitans eleven years before—and escorted her the rest of the journey.[21] Hall had to be content with so slight a share in Decatur's victory. The "Enterprise" anchored at Newport, Rhode Island, during the night of November 8.[22]

III

Three weeks after his return, Hall reported for duty and was assigned to Captain Howell's artillery company at Newport, where he was stationed during the next nine months.[23] Soon after his arrival, he began to press for promotion. To General Brown he wrote that everyone except himself, from the commanding officer to the sergeant, had been promoted, brevetted, or honorably mentioned: "Had I but one companion in this disgraceful exception," he lamented,

> I could have borne it with more patience—but when one officer alone in a whole Battalion is neglected, it is reasonable to

presume that he is the only one who has not done his duty. . . . and I feel myself already as much disgraced as if my unworthyness has [*sic*] been publickly announced.[24]

Early in January, John Elihu took up his brother's cause in letters written, "entirely without the knowledge" of James, to General Ripley and the Secretary of War.[25] In the June number of the *Port Folio*, he published one of James's anonymous poems with an introduction reciting the injustices he was suffering:

His merits have been great, but he has neither been feasted or flattered; his shoulders are racked by rheumatism, contracted when his "lodging was on the cold ground," instead of being graced with the badge of promotion.[26]

Perhaps as a result of John Elihu's prodding, General Ripley recommended that James be brevetted for gallantry at Lundy's Lane.[27]

At the turn of the year, the War Department disheartened Hall by transferring him to the Ordnance Department. He wanted the fame that could come only with a display of heroism in battle, and his protest to the War Department was as quick and heartfelt as would have been that of a Decatur doomed to a counting house.[28] Hall also enlisted the aid of powerful officers. Lieutenant Colonel Abram Eustis of the Light Artillery at Newport wrote that he would like to have Hall on his staff.[29] General Ripley himself vouched that "Lieut. Hall is one of the most deserving officers of his grade in the army" and concluded by asking as "a personal favor" that he be allowed to remain an artilleryman.[30] The salvo from these howitzers did not succeed in removing Hall from the Ordnance, but may have been influential in his promotion to a first lieutenancy in May.[31]

One would expect that the ten poems that Hall wrote in Newport and copied in his journal would reflect envy, burning ambition, or racking rheumatism. On the contrary, nearly all are frivolous addresses to girls. He also records that he went to church every Sunday; but, for his taste, the

45

minister dwelt far too much upon "the pains of death and the joys of immortality."[32]

IV

During the summer or early autumn of 1816, Hall made an important decision. Offered his choice of posts,[33] he elected the arsenal in remote Pittsburgh. Here, under the direction of his father's friend James Ross, he could resume the law studies interrupted by the war. Hall no doubt already had acquired some knowledge of Pittsburgh from a fellow artillery officer of the Niagara campaign, Presley J. Neville, a younger brother of Morgan Neville.[34] Now, also, his adventurous spirit was roused by the westward migration of his older brother Sergeant, a wandering printer who, in October, was to try to establish a newspaper at Vincennes, on the extreme edge of Indiana Territory.[35] A still more compelling factor in Hall's decision, it seems, was his romantic notion of the frontier. He still cherished his boyhood memory of the bronzed Kentuckian, with saddlebags, bearskin, and dirk, riding his horse through the streets of Philadelphia, "glancing with a good-natured superciliousness at the fragile butterflies of fashion that glittered in the sunbeams around him," and like an Achilles, evincing "the will to dare, the power to execute," and "a disdain of controul."

Hall left Newport about September 12, under orders to proceed to Charleston, South Carolina.[36] Apparently, he discharged his duties there with reasonable diligence, for by mid-October he had arrived in Pittsburgh.

IV

Court-Martial

PITTSBURGH, between 1816 and 1820, the period of James Hall's residence there, was a city of about seven thousand people. Its buildings were clustered on the low, flat, triangular piece of ground between the Monongahela and Allegheny rivers, which join at the tip of the triangle to become the Ohio. The hills that rise in the rear to form the base of the triangle and those that, on the far shores, tower over the city were heavily forested then and furnished a setting of unusual magnificence. Yet, by 1820, Pittsburgh had already become a busy manufacturing city. "The clang of hammers arose from its numerous manufactories—the rattling of carriages and the hum of men were heard from its streets." Even then the town was enveloped in an "eternal veil of smoke" from the factories burning the coal dug nearby; soot and cinders filled the atmosphere, and everything in Pittsburgh wore "a sombre hue."[1]

Before the completion of the National Road to Wheeling, Pittsburgh's situation on the three rivers made it the chief station beyond the mountains for the stream of traffic moving to the farther West. Each year, several thousand loads of merchandise were painfully hauled in Conestoga wagons over the mountains and shipped from Pittsburgh down the Ohio to Western merchants. The city was a bottleneck. There were periods, sometimes of several months, when the Ohio was too low even for keelboats to navigate, and tremendous stores of goods piled up on the docks awaiting shipment to the West.[2] The city became choked with settlers bound for the new lands, whose destitution—and often disease—made it necessary for the citizens to provide aid through organized benevolence.[3]

Two miles above Pittsburgh, the new and splendidly equipped United States Arsenal stood on an oblong tract of thirty acres adjoining the Allegheny. A great tower 120 feet high dominated the lower buildings, which were arranged in a square.[4] Among them were the officers' quarters, a barracks, various shops, and a brick office building. The arsenal was both a supply depot and a factory producing military supplies. Some of the mechanics employed there lived with their families in the barracks. A part of the labor was performed by deserters, in whose capture the commanding officer was zealous.

The commandant was Major Abraham R. Woolley,[5] who had supervised most, perhaps all, of the arsenal's construction. Soon after Hall reported to Woolley, about the middle of October, 1816,[6] Woolley gave him command of the detachment, including soldiers and workmen, and entire control of the laboratory and workshops. The quartermaster's department and the erection of new buildings remained in Woolley's charge. In December, Lieutenant Charles Ward arrived and was placed under Hall's direction.

48

The events growing out of Hall's relations with Woolley not only colored Hall's life during his three and a half years' residence in Pittsburgh, but left their impression on him for many years afterward. At first, the two officers appear to have been friendly. Hall—according to his own later account—freely communicated to the older officer his plans for a career and his desire to participate in the future of the West; but this early friendliness quickly chilled. Within a few weeks after his arrival, Hall complained of Woolley's interference with his command. Woolley replied curtly with a threat to order him back to Washington. The dispute was patched up when Hall wrote a respectful, if not humble, note stating that he would be glad to remain if he could do so without violating his self-respect.[7] But soon Hall was objecting again to Woolley's practice of issuing orders, and even passes, over his head.

Eight weeks after Woolley had given Hall command of the detachment, their relations were further strained by a letter of Woolley's minutely specifying Hall's duties. Woolley was clearly determined to circumscribe Hall's command:

> You will keep constantly in mind that I am your commanding officer, that, being stationed at this Depot & in command here, I have the supervision and control of all its operations. . . . The subordinate officers should act under the orders . . . of the senior officer, should advise him of all the operations daily, & keep him constantly advised—Nothing should transpire without his knowledge, & nothing should be done without his previous instructions or sanction.[8]

Hall disclosed his pique in his reply of the next day to Woolley:

> I have received your letter divesting me of the command & responsibility which I have held. The instructions will of course be implicitly obeyed & I can assure you, that I am happy to be releved [sic] from a charge, which was equally arduous and unprofitable.[9]

Just a week later, their antipathy was fanned into hostility by an unfortunate incident. Both Hall and Woolley afterward related biased accounts of it, out of which it is possible to construct a reasonably impartial narrative.[10]

It was Christmas time. Major Woolley asked Hall to give the arsenal's employees a vacation beginning the day before Christmas and ending the morning after New Year's Day. Hall complied by granting leaves to all the detachment except thirteen men reserved for the guard. On Tuesday, the day before Christmas, Henry Beech—a pensioned old soldier, an invalid, and a trouble-maker possibly hoping for a reward—came into Woolley's office with information that a deserter, William Williams, was living only two miles away in the home of his employer, Henry Ray, a coal digger. Woolley brought the informer to Hall, who ordered a sergeant to arrest Williams quietly sometime during the holidays. As was customary, Hall also wrote to Peace Officer Hubly in Pittsburgh and offered him a reward for the deserter's arrest.

On Wednesday, Christmas Day, Hall was absent. Beech again came to Woolley and said that the deserter was still at Ray's house. Woolley took Beech to Hall's subordinate, Lieutenant Ward, and asked him to attend to the matter. Ward sent two men with Beech, but the party met with such resistance from Williams's coal-digging friends that the soldiers were driven back. Beech himself was severely wounded.

At the arsenal the next morning, Hall learned of Woolley's interference and of the defeat of the expedition. He informed Woolley of his regret that soldiers had been sent on the errand and reminded him that he had given orders for the arrest to both the sergeant and the peace officer.

Woolley then sent Hall to take the post surgeon, Dr. Hanson Catlett, to dress Beech's wounds and, on the same journey, to reconnoiter the house where the deserter was staying. Dr. Catlett and Hall were friends, and on that same day, Hall called upon Catlett at his office in Pittsburgh. Hall, and probably Catlett as well, had little enthusiasm for the errand. The two rode out—not toward the arsenal's neighborhood, where Beech and the deserter were supposed to be — but up the Monongahela. When questioned later about Hall's attitude toward the mission, Dr. Catlett seems to have been cleverly evasive in replying that he gave to it "every anxiety that the circumstances called for."[11]

The next morning, Beech hobbled into Woolley's office and disclosed that he had not seen Dr. Catlett. When asked for an explanation, Hall told Woolley that he and the doctor had explored a good deal of country but had not been able to find either Beech or the house containing the deserter. Then, Woolley later related, "I spoke [to Hall] authoritatively, & said, here is Beech [;] he can show you the house of Ray, I leave my saddle horse for you to ride, I am going to town on business—."[12] When he returned in the evening, he asked Hall for a report on the assignment. Hall's written reply blandly ignored Woolley's order to go with Beech to Ray's house, and merely repeated that Sergeant Fitzpatrick and Peace Officer Hubly had orders to take Williams. He concluded, "I believe these measures to be all that my duty required me to take, unless otherwise ordered—."[13]

Thoroughly roused, Woolley immediately gave Hall an unmistakable written order: "You will tomorrow morning take effectual measures to apprehend William Williams a deserter. You will proceed yourself, Sir, on this service, taking such men of the Detachment under your immediate command, as you may think proper—You are to leave no stone unturned, until you arrest this deserter—."[14]

According to Hall, Woolley added to the written order an oral explanation:

> He wished me to attack the house of Mr Ray, to break it open, to take the man dead or alive—and as he expressed it "to shew the citizens by G——d that he was commanding officer here!"[15]

Hall protested—somewhat legalistically, perhaps—that such measures were unlawful, because he had no right to force the house of a citizen; impracticable, because all of his men except the guard were on pass; unnecessary, because Williams could be arrested at any time by Peace Officer Hubly; and inexpedient, because of the unnecessary risk to the lives of his men. But Woolley was obdurate.

The next morning, Saturday, December 28, Hall rose at daybreak only to find that Woolley had infringed so far upon military practice as to give passes to all personnel of the guard except those actually standing post.[16] Left without a single man, Hall went to town and searched until noon for Hubly, who then promised to have Williams in custody by seven o'clock. Hall then searched the grogshops and other haunts of the soldiers and succeeded in finding Sergeant Fitzpatrick and four others whom he directed to meet him at Gibson's hotel at seven o'clock. At that hour, Hall saw Hubly at the jail; he had not made the arrest, but promised to deliver Williams early in the morning. Hall then met his soldiers at Gibson's. He ordered Sergeant Fitzpatrick to get Beech to guide the party to Ray's house. Because the soldiers were in civilian clothes and not entirely sober, Hall ordered them to go to the neighborhood of Ray's house and remain there until Hall joined them. He ordered them to guard against Williams's escape, but not to take arms and not to fight, and to attempt the arrest only if there were an easy opportunity. About ten o'clock, Hall rode out to join his party; "but," he later explained, "being unacquainted with the country[,] was unsuccessful." Having heard that there were ten or fifteen armed men in Ray's house, he rode back to the arsenal for reinforcements in the hope that some of his men on leave had returned. There, however, Lieutenant Ward told him that no men were available. Tired and disgusted, he threw himself on his bed and went to sleep, leaving his men in the field under a subaltern.

An hour or two later, he was startled out of his slumber by Sergeant Fitzpatrick, who told him that there had been fighting between his soldiers and the coal diggers—apparently started by Beech's taunts—and that one soldier, Daniel Decker, had been killed. Already the news had spread like wildfire, and several soldiers had come running back to the arsenal "calling for vengeance." Hall collected eight or nine men, went to a house near the scene of the fight, and there found Decker, "the bravest man in the Detachment," dying with a bayonet wound in the breast. Hall sent for a doctor, meanwhile dressing Decker's wound himself. The messenger returned without a doctor. Hall rode into town and, near daylight, brought back Dr. Catlett. When it was light, Hall went to Ray's house, persuaded Williams to submit to arrest, and took him to the arsenal.

Hall then wrote a note to Woolley:

> I have the honour to report to you, that, agreeably to your order, directing "effectual" measures to be taken, for the apprehension of William Williams & prescribing what those measures should be, I proceeded on that duty with a party— Williams is taken and is in confinement here, Decker is mortally wounded with a bayonet in the breast—I feel very happy, that the measures which led to the death of this man, are not my own, & that I did every thing in my power to prevent such a catastrophe. Dr. Catlett is at the house where Decker was left, I wish Lt. Ward to go out there to assist him. I propose going to bed.[17]

But Hall was to get no sleep that day. Here was a matter of public moment, a killing for which Hall had recklessly blamed Woolley. Woolley, determined to exculpate himself, kept Hall in his room all that Sunday writing reports to justify his own conduct. Hall, only twenty-three, rash and high-strung, weary from more than twenty-four hours' duty endured with only an hour's sleep, and distressed by the dying agony of his bravest soldier, was matched against the older officer—strong-willed, calculating, and experienced.

Woolley first sent for Hall and asked him to explain in writing the sentence stating that the measures leading to Decker's death were not his own. Hall's cautious reply reviews the steps he had taken to arrest Williams in the usual way, and attempts to justify Hall's contention that Woolley, by his interference, had botched Hall's plans for an orderly arrest. He left out of the account, however, the evident fact that, in his expedition with Dr. Catlett on Thursday and again on the day before the fiasco, he had made no determined attempt to find the deserter.

Woolley soon discovered the omission and strode to Hall's room in wrath. Confronting him with the letter, he charged,

"This report by God is false." Hall replied hotly, but caught himself just in time: "Whoever says so tells a ——," leaving the sentence unfinished. Hall's relation states that Woolley then walked up and down menacingly, swearing furiously.[18]

Woolley next wrote to Hall demanding a full written account of his proceedings in the arrest of Williams. In this report it came out that Hall had not accompanied the party that fought at Ray's house. At two-thirty in the afternoon, Woolley submitted to Hall all of his letters and ordered him to comment upon them and return them. In a weary but respectful answer, Hall hinted that Woolley could waive his rank so that Hall could challenge him to a duel: "There is," he wrote, "also distance between our respective rank[s], which make it impossible, we can meet each other, in a case of this kind upon terms of equality——."[19]

Woolley's reply lends a momentary element of comedy to the struggle. Major Woolley, Ward reported to Hall, was willing to waive his rank, but he could not, of course, waive his status as a married man; if Hall would get married, Woolley would fight him; if Hall would not meet the marital requirement, the major could offer an unmarried younger brother as an opponent.[20]

Having Hall on record in four separate reports, Woolley the next day ordered Ward to arrest him, take his sword, and confine him to the arsenal grounds. The man with whom Hall had trifled now had him in his grip.

There is no doubt that Hall was partly to blame for the bungling that ended in Decker's death. He was insubordinate. In the beginning, he probably felt that tracking down a common deserter was beneath a commander of a detachment and a hero of Bridgewater and Fort Erie. Fourteen years later, he explained, "I refused to obey an order which I though illegal. . . ."[21] But his failure on two occasions to find Ray's house was probably simple shirking, and he was ignobly in bed when his men needed him. But Woolley cannot be excused. His zealous pursuit of deserters was petty. Resentful and litigious, he seems to have been incapable of building loyalty in his subordinates. Worse yet, after having given his drastic order for the deserter's arrest, he invited bloodshed by depriving Hall of the men needed for a show of strength.

II

Hall's friends soon came to his aid. One was Dr. Catlett, a Kentuckian with eight or nine years' service in the army. In 1806, he had been the second for Charles Dickinson, who had been killed in his duel with Andrew Jackson.[22] Catlett visited Hall the day after his arrest and tried in talks with both Hall and Woolley to smooth over the quarrel. A few days later came another friend, William B. Foster, a well-to-do commission merchant known to history as the father of the song writer, Stephen Collins Foster. As Woolley's agent and a former army officer associated with Woolley in early plans for the arsenal,[23] Foster was in a position to request of him both a list of the charges against Hall and permission for him to visit at the home of Dunning McNair, four miles away, and at Foster's own home in the nearby village of Lawrenceville. Woolley evaded the request for charges but granted the other request, and within a few days Hall was a guest of the Fosters at their white house on Bullitt's Hill, commanding a view far up and down the Allegheny.[24] No doubt the visit with the Foster family soothed Hall's over-wrought nerves. Even thirty years later, when his fortunes were ascending and those of the Fosters declining, he appears to have remembered their kindness with a business reference for their son, Stephen, then just beginning his career.[25]

During the first week in January, in letters to Daniel Parker, adjutant and inspector general, and to Colonel Decius Wadsworth, head of the ordnance department, Hall urged that he be furnished with a copy of the charges, for which he had applied in vain to Woolley, and that he be allowed to reside in Pittsburgh.[26] To Wadsworth he wrote of Woolley's surveillance, "I have been galled, & goaded, untill I can bear galling & goading no longer," and adds that he was suffering "under insult, injury, & oppression." Wadsworth granted the requested permission to live in town, and Hall took quarters there in early February,

1817;[27] but nearly four months elapsed before he received a copy of the charges. Woolley evidently preferred to wait for the civil trial for the killing of Decker, at which he might obtain evidence to strengthen his case against Hall. After the failure of several letters asking for the charges, on March 27, Hall wrote again to Wadsworth, declaring that he was the victim of oppression and demanding a court-martial.

Two poems that Hall wrote in January and early February show no loss of faith in the rightness of his conduct. Indeed, from the first and third quatrains of "Stanzas," one might believe he was chained in a dungeon because of his heroic beliefs:

> The captive whom oppression binds,
>> May carrol gaily as a lark;
> His thoughts are free as passing winds,
>> Altho' his cell is lone and dark.

> .   .   .   .

> But trembling is the coward heart,
>> Of him whose arm has wrought the chain;
> No soothing balm his thoughts impart,
>> For they are full of guilt and pain![28]

In a gloomy essay, he went so far as to say that adversity is generally the result of virtue, and prosperity the fruit of vice. But "by adversity," he continued virtuously, "the passions, though at first roused, are ultimately corrected, and they subside into dignity and firmness."[29]

There is little evidence, however, that the passions of either Hall or Woolley were subsiding. Stephen Barlow, a friend of Woolley and a nephew of the poet and diplomat Joel Barlow,[30] reported to the major a conversation of March 1, at the dinner table at Gibson's Hotel, where Hall appears to have been a boarder. Here, Barlow declared, Hall had called Woolley a swindler and a coward, and had said that he would feel justified in assassinating him. Although Hall later in court severely damaged Barlow's credibility, it seems true that Hall was insulting Woolley, perhaps from uncontrollable anger, perhaps with the cold intention of provoking a duel.

Nor was their malevolence allayed by the events of the civil trial for the killing of Decker. In these proceedings before the court of Oyer and Terminer between April 10 and 13, [31] Hall was an important witness; and Woolley employed his friend Henry Baldwin, counsel for the prosecution, to record Hall's testimony. In some way Hall learned that Woolley, Baldwin, and Barlow were acting together against him.[32] Just an hour after the case was given to the jury, Hall, with some friends, entered Kerr's Hotel, where Barlow was sitting. Hall called for brandy and water, said that he wanted to drown his sorrows, and declared that he had been so persecuted by Woolley and Baldwin that he did not know which end he was standing on.[33] Barlow asserted his own and Baldwin's innocence of any such conspiracy. A violent quarrel ensued, and Hall used words "tantamount to calling Mr. Barlow, either a damned rascal, or a damned liar," and said that "he had already pronounced Major Woolley a rascal & a coward, & that no gentleman would associate with him. . . ." [34] As Woolley's guest at dinner the next day, Barlow dutifully reported Hall's remarks. Woolley then had enough evidence; Hall received a copy of the charges eleven days later.

Exasperated by the delays in military justice that had kept him in arrest five months, Hall in early May appealed to Richard Rush—Acting Secretary of State, and probably a friend of Hall's family—with a request that he intercede with President Monroe to obtain an early trial.[35] So effective was his plea, through Rush or others, that in July the War Department took Hall out of Woolley's jurisdiction, permitted him furloughs to visit his friends, and assumed a kind of guardianship over him.[36] With this new freedom, he went to Washington, where both the Secretary of War and General Parker offered him his sword; but Hall insisted upon the right to prove his innocence in court.[37]

Hall had been under arrest nine months when the court-martial convened in Pittsburgh on September 11. It was in session two weeks. Hall's friend and former superior Major Thomas Biddle was president; two officers of the Artillery and two of the Ordnance completed the court. The formality of the proceedings was manifested by the president's challenge of the right of one justice to sit as a member of the tribunal because he had come without his chapeau bras, the ceremonial three-cornered hat.

Major Woolley was prosecutor, and Hall conducted his own defense. Among the witnesses were such citizens of Pittsburgh as William Wilkins, later United States senator and minister to Russia; Henry Baldwin, then a congressman and later a justice of the United States Supreme Court; Dr. Hanson Catlett; Mr. Wallace, a merchant; Charles Shaler, later a judge; William B. Foster; and John Irwin Scull, editor of the Pittsburgh *Gazette*. Woolley's three charges— unofficer-like conduct, disobedience of orders and neglect of duty, and conduct unbecoming an officer and a gentleman —were supported by fifteen specifications, of which the principal ones accused Hall of responsibility for Decker's death, of either a false report to Woolley or a false oath in the civil trial, of public insults of Woolley, and of false assertions that he had challenged Woolley and that Woolley had refused to meet him.

On the second Sunday, after seven days of testimony, Hall submitted his defense, still extant in his own handwriting.[38] One of Hall's contemporaries, an attorney and judge, described the defense as "masterly, exhibiting not only forcible argument, but . . . rich style and exuberance of expression. . . ."[39] Judged as the work of an unfinished law student of twenty-four, the plea still seems, in many respects, brilliant. Lucid and graceful, sparkling now and then with sallies of humor at the Major's expense, it generally demonstrates Hall's facility with language. And it goes far toward establishing, if not his innocence, at least a justification for some of his errors, even though he overdramatized his wrongs and made unsupported jibes at Woolley's character.

The court, however, was not convinced, and, on September 24 and 25, declared Hall guilty of all three charges. But his judges did acquit him of the two specifications most threatening to his honor: he was innocent of the charge of perjury and of being the cause of Decker's death. Moreover, with a stinging rebuke of Woolley for the long delay of both the trial and the presentation of charges, Hall's judges showed their understanding that, especially in times of peace, game-cocks like Hall needed careful handling: "Such relaxations," the court believed, "tend to foster & encourage the malevolent passions and turbulent tempers." Hall was sentenced to be cashiered.

Soon after the court's adjournment, he was ordered to Washington. There, he said, he found "men in high stations who could feel for the wrongs of a subaltern."[40] Perhaps he referred to his great-uncle, John Sergeant, then a congressman, or to John Quincy Adams, Secretary of State and friend of another uncle, Samuel Ewing. Hall asserts that he used influence only to gain a respectable introduction to President Monroe, and that, although some unsolicited representations were made in his behalf, the President "never was asked to travel out of the record of the court." President Monroe approved the court's sentence. He believed that Hall's conduct merited the censure; but, "because of his fair character & . . . his brave and meritorious conduct during the late war," he remitted the punishment, restored him to his rank, and apologized for the delay in holding the trial.[41] Hall then asked for a furlough of six months, probably on the ground that the long arrest had injured his health. The leave was granted on December 9.[42]

With Woolley's prosecution turned into something of a triumph for the accused by President Monroe's reversal and by the gift of a six-months vacation, Hall was back in Pittsburgh by February 3, 1818.[43] There, he tells us, Woolley's conduct toward him was the subject of ridicule. Hall resolved to forget the preceding year's events, which were "like the recollection of a sickening dream."[44] But the enmity between the two officers still smoldered and, a year and a half later, it was to flame forth briefly once again.

At the expiration of his furlough on June 10, 1818, Hall resigned his commission and abandoned the profession that he had followed for five years.[45]

V

Pittsburgh Lawyer, 1816-20

IT WAS PROBABLY soon after his arrival in Pittsburgh in October, 1816, that Hall began his legal studies under the direction of James Ross.[1] A resident of Pittsburgh since 1795, Ross had been one of the early protégés of Judge Hugh Henry Brackenridge, author of the satirical novel *Modern Chivalry*. Ross had twice been United States senator and three times the Federalist candidate for governor. He was easily the outstanding lawyer of western Pennsylvania.[2] Hall's father, the former marshal of Pennsylvania, had been a friend of Ross; and Hall's own acquaintance with him might have extended back to his boyhood, for it is possible that Ross had visited in the Hall home in Philadelphia. If so, Hall would have been attracted even then by Ross's gracious manners as well as by his professional reputation. The Hall family and Ross must have remembered vividly, if not painfully, that Hall's father had supported Ross in the gubernatorial campaign of 1799 at the cost of his marshalship.

Hall's time- and energy-consuming dispute with Woolley late in 1816 and early in 1817 left him little time for study. But for a year beginning in the spring of 1817, he was comparatively free. His defense of himself in military court served as a very practical thesis. Altogether his studies with Samuel Ewing and James Ross, though much interrupted, occupied about three years. He was admitted to the bar on April 9, 1818, upon the motion of his friend William Wilkins.[3] Sometime within the next two months, he opened his office on the south side of Fourth Street, between Market and Wood streets, and "nearly opposite to Patterson and Lambdin's book-store."[4]

The surviving records of the Pittsburgh court are too fragmentary to divulge the nature and extent of Hall's practice, but in the city's newspapers his advertising pertaining to legal transactions probably exceeded that of any other attorney. Within a month after opening his office, he was Isaac Craig's agent for the sale of Monture's or Nevill's Island, a thousand-acre estate lying in the Ohio five miles below Pittsburgh; and he was the agent of Charles von Bonnhurst, son of a Prussian nobleman, for the sale of other large tracts of land.[5]

Hall early attracted young legal friends. One was Henry Eddy, a bookish youth with an interest in printing and with some local reputation as an orator in the Pittsburgh Quintilian Society. Eddy studied under Hall apparently as early as 1817 or 1818. Probably about the beginning of 1820, Hall took as a partner Edward J. Roberts, son of the scholarly Judge Samuel Roberts.[6]

Neither Hall's law practice nor the bitterness of his quarrel with Woolley prevented the quick resumption of his essential light-heartedness. He tells us he "mingled in the gayest circle" of Pittsburgh society and partook "of the hospitality of the wealthiest and most honorable" of his fellow citizens. As always, he appears to have been acutely aware of "the sweetness and affability of the young ladies," among whom there was in Pittsburgh "a sufficiency of beauty and grace to decorate a ball room to great advantage. Indeed," he added, "I have seldom seen finer displays of female loveliness than I have witnessed here." Soon after his arrival in town, he testified in frivolous verse to the witchery of the Misses Kerr, Lea, and Beelen, and gaily declared that while he was trying to decide which of them was his favorite, he fell "deeply" in love with all three. In a poem entitled "Sleighing," he described his winter excursions with some of Pittsburgh's young men and women across the snow to a village inn, where they danced to a violin and drank until they were "boozy" before returning merrily home in their sleighs. Apparently he continued his revelries during the August preceding the court-martial when he was at Bedford Springs, a watering place fashionable among Easterners and Southerners. Never before, he wrote, had he seen such elegantly attractive girls.[7]

In Pittsburgh after the court-martial, Hall became a member of the city's Thespian Society, which produced plays "about once in three weeks" for the double purpose of "gratifying the public taste by a moral and rational amusement" and of adding to the funds of the Male Charitable Sunday School. In his letter of December 7, 1818, to his mother, Hall said that the group consisted of about thirty persons, mostly junior members of the bar and, he assured her, "all gentlemen." Among them were "some beardless youths who personated the females." To escape the censures of the church they sometimes called themselves the Dramatic Benevolent Society and as a result found among their audience some of Pittsburgh's most religious ladies. In the city's small theater, "occasionally occupied by strollers," the Thespians played to full houses; and the boxes were crowded "with beauty and fashion." Seats could be had in the boxes for a dollar, and admission to the pit was fifty cents. The doors opened at five o'clock, and the curtain rose at six-thirty.[8]

In his letter Hall told his mother that he participated in

63

the plays partly to gain popularity but much more to acquire a knack as a speaker. In view of his later success as an orator and lecturer, it is surprising to learn that he then thought himself timid. After a few more performances, he told her, "it will be strange if I cannot muster strength to face a jury—and yet few persons would believe how hard it is to me." "I used to fancy myself as something of a hero —but . . . I would rather face a dozen canon [*sic*] than the same number of stupid blockhead jurors. . . ." His appearances in court during the eight months since his admission to the bar, he said, had "all proved abortive, and while the old lawyers pat me on the back, and tell me that I am destined to shine as an orator, I no sooner rise than I am seized with a feeling which I can compare to nothing but sea sickness. When I made 'my first appearance on these boards,' in Vortex, while the audience was convulsed with laughter at my comic phiz, and the humor with which they were pleased to say I represented the little Nabob, I was in agony—the objects before me were dancing about—the audience sometimes under my feet, sometimes over my head, and I was totally incapable of distinguishing the face of a single person in the pit or boxes."

Apparently his stagefright did not entirely incapacitate him, for he quoted a critic who had said his acting received "great and merited applause from a liberal and enlightened audience." To overcome further uneasiness, Hall was determined to take a part in every play; and in spite of his nervousness, his fellow actors complimented him with the award of leading roles in later productions. When he wrote to his mother, he had already appeared as Captain Beauguard in the younger George Colman's *The Review*, Captain Faulkner in Thomas Morton's *The Way to Get Married*, and Dick in *The Apprentice* besides his performance as Vortex in Morton's *A Cure for the Heartache*. For later productions, he was cast as Plastic in Morton's *Town and Country*, Jeremy Didlow in *Raising the Wind*, and Iago in *Othello*.

Hall diverted himself also with the militia. During the

four years of his stay in the city, he was captain of the Pittsburgh Fencibles in friendly rivalry with Morgan Neville, who led the Pittsburgh Blues. Proudly parading with their plumes tossing, Hall's Fencibles added pomp to such an event as a public hanging, the visit of a famous person, or the funeral of a notable citizen. In a typical celebration of Independence Day, the company paraded on Grant's Hill, marched through the city, and took a boat—on which a band was playing—to the mouth of Saw Mill Run. There they banqueted, drank toasts, and celebrated with what is described in the newspapers of the period as "temperance and harmony."[9]

Hall became also a director and, later, secretary of the Sabbath School Association, which, with the Philosophical Society and the Library Society, made up most of the organized cultural life of the city.[10]

On February 2, 1817, a few days after he moved into town, he became a Mason in Ohio Lodge 113 and thenceforward took a serious part in the activities of the order. Secretary of his lodge during 1818, master of ceremonies in 1819, and junior warden in 1820,[11] he was further complimented by being asked to deliver the St. John's Day anniversary oration at a joint meeting of two Pittsburgh lodges on June 24, 1818. The address was so well received that his own lodge asked permission to print it, and it became Hall's first separate publication—a spirited defense of his order and an exposition of his own orthodoxy. "I can only say as an individual Mason," he told his audience, "that I should have spurned with indignation the honourable task which I now with so much pride perform, had its performance been incompatible with an independent candour; and that I should have shrunk with burning shame from *that* threshold, and from the insulted presence of this respectable assemblage, if I came as the advocate of principles in any manner varying from those, which are promulgated from the sacred desk, before which with reverence I stand. . . . I am no free thinker—I advocate no false philosophy, no licentious doctrine; my position is simply this: that in a temporal institution, formed for the dissemination of knowledge, and the exercise of benevolence, if we agree in that one great fundamental principle, which, by holding out the hope of reward, and the fear of punishment, renders our obligations to each other binding, and teaches us to consider ourselves responsible at a future day for our conduct to each other, and to society, we have no right *as members of that institution* to enquire further."[12]

II

Throughout the four years of his residence in the city, Hall wrote for the *Pittsburgh Gazette,* the oldest newspaper west of the mountains. In 1816, the editor was John Irwin Scull, a Federalist like his father, the founder and first editor.[13] Three years older than Hall, the younger Scull had studied at the Pittsburgh Academy and had been graduated from Princeton. Upon his graduation, he had, like Hall, read law under James Ross and, in 1813, been admitted to the bar.[14] He had taken over the editorship of the *Gazette* only a few weeks before Hall's arrival in the city.

Hall had been with Scull at Kerr's hotel the night of his violent quarrel with Stephen Barlow, and he had been greatly helped by Scull's strong support as a witness at the court martial. Scull's *Gazette* was silent upon Hall's conviction but triumphantly announced the news of his restoration to the lieutenancy as "gratifying to an extensive acquaintance by whom he is highly appreciated."[15]

Hall's first contribution to the *Gazette* was "Eugenius," a feeble sketch over-burdened with the moral that virtuous people should be cheerful. The story is noteworthy only because it is Hall's first known attempt at prose fiction and because it bears his new pen name, "Orlando," which, with its variant "O," was to mark much of his writing of the next twelve years. The tale was followed by several poems— of which the most interesting was possibly the widely copied burlesque "Othello"—and by a prose defense of Major André's captors, whose integrity had been attacked in the Pennsylvania legislature. After the court-martial,

when Hall went to Washington, he left with Scull an enlarged version of the journal of the voyage to the Mediterranean. With a burst of rhetoric, Scull proudly introduced
it in the *Gazette* and printed it serially during October and
November, 1817. A writer in the *Pittsburgh Commonwealth,*
however, scoffed at Hall's account as unseamanlike. He was
answered in the *Gazette* by "Old Bung" (possibly Scull),
who based his claim to nautical authority upon a voyage to
Kentucky in a keelboat and an excursion up the Allegheny
in a canoe.[16]

III

During the remainder of his stay in Pittsburgh, Hall was
more and more influenced by the partisan Westernism and
glamorous history of Morgan Neville. Neville became Scull's
partner on May 1, 1817, and took over the editorship of the
Gazette, a position he was to hold until the autumn of
1821.[17] During the three years that Hall continued to write
for the paper, he profited from association with this frontier-
bred editor, who was, in Pittsburgh at least, conspicuous
both for his literary tastes and for his colorful history.

Hall was no doubt already acquainted with Neville's
younger brother Presley J. Neville, a fellow lieutenant in
the artillery during the Niagara campaign.[18] At any rate,
Hall and Morgan Neville soon became intimate friends,
living and working as neighbors. Both Hall's and the
Gazette's office were on Fourth Street "nearly opposite to
Patterson and Lambdin's Bookstore," and Neville's home
was close by on the same side of the street. When Neville's
father died, Hall wrote a eulogy of him for the *Gazette;* and
when his remains were brought back to Pittsburgh for
burial, he "wept at his grave."[19] Hall was ten years younger
than Neville, who was thirty-five in 1818. Both were high-
spirited. They shared interests in law, Masonry, the militia,
and literature; and both were warm champions of the West.
Later, Neville was to aid Hall in his attempt to found a
nativist Western literature and in that endeavor was to
write one memorable and influential narrative, "The Last

of the Boatmen."[20] There can be little doubt of the significance of Neville's influence upon Hall's development.

Hall must have found Neville's conversation absorbing, for Neville's life, to one who views the frontier romantically, had been unusually rich in stirring events and in association with men of historic significance. He came from a family that had once been wealthy and powerful in Pennsylvania. Both of his grandfathers, John Neville and Daniel Morgan, had been generals in the Revolutionary army.[21] Neville's father, Colonel Presley Neville, educated at Newark Academy and the University of Pennsylvania, had been for three years the aide-de-camp of General Lafayette, with whom he carried on a lifetime correspondence. The family was conspicuously Federalist. During the Whiskey Rebellion of 1794, when Morgan was eleven, his Grandfather Neville's home overlooking Chartier's Creek had been burned to the ground by the insurgents.

Neville, who had been educated at Pittsburgh Academy, was considered by Henry Marie Brackenridge "the first of the first" of his schoolfellows there. During his boyhood, Neville had associated with frontiersmen of many sorts. New vistas of learning and the outside world were revealed to him by the Chevalier du Bac, a French exile who, having bought a few hazelnuts and some maple sugar, was successfully operating a candy shop in Pittsburgh. Du Bac was an intimate in the Neville home. Neville later described him as "one of the worthiest of men, and an admirable philosopher." To him, Neville was indebted for a knowledge of "some of the richest treasures of French literature" and for a series of visits by the exiled Duke of Orleans—later Louis Philippe, King of France—and his brothers, the Duc de Montpensier and the Comte de Beaujolais. During these visits, which occurred when Neville was fourteen, he and the future king amused themselves by sitting at the fireside reading favorite passages from French literature to each other.[22]

In his young manhood Neville had "spent some happy hours" at the Ohio River island home of Harman Blennerhassett, "when it was the favourite residence of taste and hospitality." When Neville was twenty-three, he and William Wilkins had been seconds in a fatal duel, after which Wilkins took refuge for a year in Kentucky.[23] Whether or not Neville also left town is unknown, but the same year he came under the sway of Aaron Burr. The suave former Vice-President had induced a number of Pittsburgh's citizens to join him in an expedition whose purpose is still a mystery, but it has been thought his aim was to conquer Mexico, to detach the western states from the Union, or perhaps only to take up a land claim he had purchased in western Louisiana. Conspicuous among his associates was Blennerhassett. Neville, apparently an innocent recruit, commanded one of the boats intended to carry Burr's supplies down the Ohio. In this escapade, he was one of the fourteen men who were arrested by the militia at Blennerhassett's Island and who, upon their release, escorted Mrs. Blennerhassett and her children down the Ohio to join the Burr expedition. In the late summer of 1807, Neville was summoned to Richmond to testify for the government in the trial of Burr and Blennerhassett for treason against the United States. There he was again in Blennerhassett's company and apparently Burr's as well.[24] After his return to Pittsburgh, Neville settled down, was admitted to the bar the next year, and, in 1809, married Nancy Barker. In the autumn of Hall's arrival in Pittsburgh, he was elected cashier of the Farmers and Mechanics Bank. But he was still the stormy petrel. In 1818, the bank was sacked by robbers and soon afterwards was forced to close.[25]

Under Neville the semi-weekly *Gazette* became an outstanding newspaper. He bought new type and widened the pages from four to five columns. The other two newspapers published in Pittsburgh—the *Mercury,* edited by Philip Snowden; and the *Commonwealth* (later the *Statesman*), edited by Ephraim Pentland and subsidized with federal legal advertising—were published weekly and were too dull to furnish serious competition. The *Gazette,* with its fresh news stories and literary columns, was respected—and frequently quoted—in the East. John Elihu Hall, in a note for the *Port Folio,* warmly applauded the staff of the invigorated *Gazette:*

> Our old correspondent "O" or "Orlando," sometimes forsakes our pages for the columns of the Pittsburgh *Gazette;* but as we are unwilling to let these ultra-mountain wags have all the fun to themselves, we have copied several of the latest communications of this sprightly writer. We cannot permit this opportunity to pass without testifying the great satisfaction which we derive from the manner in which this gazette is conducted. Mr. Neville holds the pen of a scholar, and he is actuated by the independent candour of a gentleman. His political paragraphs are pleasantly diversified by the frolic of the wit and the song of the muse.[26]

The "frolic of the wit and the song of the muse" were furnished almost entirely by Hall. Neville was a clever writer and, on occasion, charming; but he was heavily burdened with politics, with vexatious family responsibilities, and with the disaster caused by the robbery of the bank. Three weeks after he became editor, the first number of Hall's essay series, "The Wanderer, by Edward Ennui," was printed in the *Gazette.* Appearing weekly from May 22 to June 19 and irregularly during the remainder of the year, the fourteen "Wanderer" essays contained probably the best writing of Hall's Pittsburgh period.

Hall's taste for the essay form and for the periods of Addison and Steele can surprise no one. The publication of more than eighty editions of the *Spectator* in less than a century indicates that the journal enjoyed a popularity exceeded by no work of its size except possibly the Bible, and the essay periodical, it has been said, "determined, to a great degree, the literary history of the eighteenth century." During the hundred-year period beginning with the appearance of the *Tatler,* more than four hundred essay series in the *Spectator* tradition were printed in British periodicals.[27] In America, the Addisonian essay was probably not much less admired. During the brief period between 1785 and 1800, perhaps a hundred series of light essays appeared in the newspapers of New England alone.[28] By

70

1810, many of the better known American authors—Timothy Dwight and John Trumbull, Benjamin Franklin, Royall Tyler, Joseph Dennie, James Kirke Paulding, and Washington Irving—had tried their hands at the essay of manners.

The essay tradition on which Hall had been richly nourished was probably nowhere more vigorous than in the Philadelphia of his boyhood. In the fashionable drawing rooms of the city and perhaps sometimes in the streets, where Hall himself noted "the fragile butterflies of fashion," the leisurely, fastidious life of Will Honeycomb and Sir Roger de Coverley might not have seemed entirely foreign. There Joseph Dennie, the persistent foe of democracy, dressed as elegantly as Goldsmith, graced the parlors of the literati, and swayed the discourse of the Tuesday Club at the printing house of Asbury Dickins.[29] The Federalists found in Dennie's journal what their British counterparts had found in their own periodical essays—a reinforcement of their conservatism, an emphasis upon leisure-class concerns, and a kind of retreat from the stirring changes of the age.[30] The pages of the *Port Folio* were turgid with essay series. Among the authors of letters to Dennie (addressed as Mr. Samuel Saunter) and contributors to his various columns "The American Lounger," "Colon and Spondee," "An Author's Evenings," and "Reflections in Solitude" were Charles Brockden Brown, Royall Tyler, Dennie, Hall's mother, his brother John Elihu Hall, and his uncle Samuel Ewing.[31]

Hall was familiar not only with the Philadelphia Addisonians but probably also with a number of English and other American imitators, and certainly, as the quotations in his writings reveal, with the *Spectator* itself. His title "The Wanderer," he owes to others: at least four essay series entitled "The Wanderer" had been printed in Britain between 1783 and 1810,[32] and there was "The Rural Wanderer" in the *Port Folio*. Strictly in the convention, he began his first essay in the *Gazette* with a description of himself as an idle lounger, exceeded in his ennui not even by Ichabod Idler. In the third number he went so far as to include a letter playfully attributed to Sophia Sparkle, a character of Irving and Paulding's *Salmagundi*

71

series (1807). Probably in imitation of Dennie's "The Lay Preacher" series, he began number six with the arid Biblical text "Like unto a householder which went out early in the morning."

But imitative as the "Wanderers" were, they were significant in Hall's development and noteworthy for their divergences from the tradition. In number two Hall apparently recognized the incongruity of an Edward Ennui and a Sophia Sparkle transplanted into the rough frontier Pittsburgh of 1818, and confessed that, since Addison's time, "foppery has gone very much out of fashion"; ladies "have discarded their patches" and "have withal become so learned" that the Will Honeycombs would "encounter fearful odds in attacking them." Frequently in the later numbers, he drops the lounger pose. He was working toward the short story in numbers eight, fourteen, and fifteen.[33] Some of the essays were also significant expressions of his early interest in recording unusual phases of frontier life. In the fifth number, for example, he described the resort of Bedford Springs, and, in the twelfth, the impressions of his visit to the communist colony led by George Rapp at Harmony, twenty-five miles north of Pittsburgh. In the eighth number he related an episode in his captivity during the War of 1812. With a boldness which was later to become characteristic, he proposed in the eleventh essay what he was to make a reality twelve years later—a Western periodical, "which will yield us enjoyment at home and respectability abroad."

Although two of the essays, it is true, were remarkable only as tours de force in the art of saying nothing gracefully,[34] others attain an urbanity worthy of the tradition. But, on the whole, we must accept Hall's own estimate of the "Wanderer" essays—implicit in his neglect of them— as bagatelles in which he quickly lost interest. They lack the lightness of touch and the buoyant humor of the Salmagundi, and they do not reach the classical purity of Irving's prose. Buried as they were in a frontier newspaper, they have had, at most, a modest effect upon American culture. He reprinted none of them and used only the relation of his military experience in number eight as the nucleus for a later story.

Of the twenty-seven *Gazette* poems that may now be identified as Hall's, twenty-three appeared during Neville's editorship. Most of them are either humorous or farcical—more "frolic of the wit." These coltish antics in verse, widely copied in frontier newspapers,[35] reflect the scarcity of money, urge ladies to make haste in love, extol the pleasures of tobacco and wine, or make fun of political opponents. Of the twelve *Gazette* poems with a serious intent, most are delicately amatory, such as "The Rose":

> Lady, the rose
> Pluck'd by thy hand is doubly blest:
> For though it knows,
> No more its native bed of rest,
> By beauty's hand that flow'r was prest.
>
> Thus should you steal,
> Some light heart from its home away
> It soon would feel,
> That beauty's eye could shed a ray,
> To keep the wand'rer from decay.[36]

Probably the most nearly successful is "Night Thoughts":

> Star of the night!—whose friendly brilliance oft,
>   Didst guide my weary wand'ring steps aright,
> When from my downy couch and pillow soft
>   I flew, the child of sorrow and of night!
> How have I lov'd thee! not inconstant thou,
>   Like earthly things, still glittering to deceive,
> Whose gleams alternate light and cloud the brow,
>   And, when they gladden, give us cause to grieve!
>
> Oh could my heart be taught by thee to fly,
>   From worldly pleasure and from worldly care,

73

Fix'd on a steady light my eager eye,
 Would dwell untir'd and with rapture glow.
Delusive hope no more—nor trait'rous love,
 With thoughts unholy should disturb my heart,
My first, my only wish, to find above,
 An ark of refuge, and a couch of rest![37]

Hall's verse of the Pittsburgh period, and even later, owes much to the metrical forms of Thomas Moore's *Irish Melodies* (1807) and *National Airs* (1815). In some poems Hall reflects Moore's tender sentiments; in others, he merely adapts the verse forms to rollicking treatments of timely or Western themes.[38]

His political writings for the *Gazette* began to appear in the autumn of 1819, when he entered the lists for Neville. Neville was trying to improve his circumstances, severely straitened as a result of the panic and the robbery of the bank, by running for the sheriff's office. During the campaign, he was driven to abandon his pride so far as to inform the electorate that "he did humbly hope that the circumstance of the crippled widow and five unprotected children of a revolutionary officer being thrown upon him for support, would plead for him with every man of feeling. . . ." At the height of the contest, Hall aided Neville with a poem which, printed in the *Gazette*, neatly disposed of two of Neville's opponents whose letters had appeared in the *Statesman*.[39] Neville was elected. Afterwards, Hall wrote for the *Gazette* two letters and another poem in support of Neville's program for the West, which included the building of a good highway between Philadelphia and Pittsburgh, the clearing of the Ohio's channel, and the encouragement of domestic manufacturing. In the first letter, addressed to Snowden of the *Mercury*, Hall set forth and supported Neville's agenda for the West; but he could not resist including a jeer at the intelligence of the *Gazette's* two rival editors, Snowden and Pentland. Hall's second letter consisted almost entirely of abuse of Pentland. But a serious quarrel between Hall and the two editors was somehow averted, for the controversy was concluded with an exchange of good natured poems—the first by Hall in the *Gazette,* and the other, presumably by Snowden, in the *Mercury* a week later.[40]

IV

In Philadelphia at the close of 1815, while Hall was still stationed at Newport, John Elihu Hall had become editor and Harrison Hall the publisher of America's leading magazine, the *Port Folio.* This periodical, founded in 1801, had probably enjoyed and deserved its greatest popularity during its first five years under Dennie's editorship. After Dennie's death, in 1812, it had continued in its long and respectable career under the direction of Nicholas Biddle and, later, Dr. Charles Caldwell. John Elihu Hall, who had written faithfully for all three of these editors, remembered Dennie reverently as "the Columbus of polite literature in this hemisphere."[41] Taking over the editorship with the January, 1816, number, he soon evinced an intention to restore to the *Port Folio* that Federalist dignity which had distinguished it during Dennie's time. John Elihu was widely known in his party as the hero who, during the riots in Baltimore, had suffered in the defense of Federalist principles. He seems to have expected the Federalists to support him as they had supported Dennie. The Federalist party, however, was dying. Joseph Hopkinson, Federalist member of Congress and an old friend of John Elihu, answered his request for aid by frankly warning him that the magazine probably could not be restored to its original vigor.[42]

John Elihu, having been editor of the *American Law Journal* (probably the first American magazine of its kind and "certainly one of the most notable"),[43] professor of rhetoric and belles lettres at the University of Maryland in 1814 and 1815, and a member of the American Philosophical Society since January, 1814,[44] was acquainted with many potential writers for his magazine. But during the twelve trying years of his editorship, he was to rely upon contributions not only from his mother and James but even from the youngest brother, Thomas Mifflin Hall.[45]

In the March, 1816, number, probably the first prepared under his sole direction,[46] John Elihu had revived two of the best known columns of Dennie's editorship—"The Lay Preacher," for which he found an unprinted lay sermon of Dennie's; and "The American Lounger," for which Sarah Hall contributed a letter, as she had done in the old days for Dennie. John Elihu's aim, apparently, was to recapture some of the playfulness that would be remembered by Philadelphians who had feted Tom Moore eleven years earlier.

It was for their humor, lightness of touch, and adventurous spirit that John Elihu valued James's writings from the first. In April, 1816, while James was in Newport, John Elihu printed the "Description of St. Michael's Cave, in the Rock of Gibraltar," the first of a series of three short selections from the journal of James's voyage to the Mediterranean and, so far as is known, his first published prose. Also, nine of James's poems appeared in the June, September, and October, 1816, numbers of the *Port Folio*. Some of them, already described,[47] had a somewhat serious tone appropriate to war time. "The Power of Madeira" and "To a Young Lady Who Mended the Author's Stockings," perhaps the most successful of the group, were in his most frivolous manner.

From the December, 1816, issue to the end of the second number of 1820, roughly the period of James's Pittsburgh residence, the *Port Folio* contained twenty-nine poems and four prose pieces that can be identified as Hall's.[48] Ten of the poems and the biographical sketch of Presley Neville had first appeared in the *Pittsburgh Gazette*. Of the remaining *Port Folio* poems of the period, "The Hermit Mouse," translated from La Fontaine, and "The Dream" were probably the best. "The Smile," however, was an interesting imitation of Byron's "The Tear," and "Song" was modelled after Scott's "Soldier Rest." Of the prose contributions, "The Adventures of a One Dollar Note,"[49] adhering to a form frequently employed in eighteenth-century British fiction, was apparently patterned particularly after Addison's "The Adventures of a Shilling," the two hundred and forty-ninth number of the *Tatler* (1710). The substance of Hall's narrative, however, is thoroughly American and noteworthy for its glimpses, even though tantalizingly brief, of the younger circle in fashionable Philadelphia society. The somewhat unconventional views of Hall's essay on adversity[50] were evidently inspired by his differences with Woolley. "The follies that produce adversity," Hall observed, "generally 'lean to virtue's side;' while the arts which lead to prosperity, are too often closely allied with vice. Fools and knaves thrive where better men must beg." Ten of his poems printed during 1818 and 1819 were included in a little volume, *The Poetry of the Port Folio*, which was edited by John Elihu and published, in 1818, by Harrison Hall.

V

Still another of Hall's publications had its unhappy origin in his quarrel with Major Woolley, a quarrel that continued throughout Hall's stay in Pittsburgh. Soon after Hall had returned to the city in the winter of 1817-1818, having been restored to his rank by President Monroe, it became evident that Woolley shared none of the President's opinions of Hall's "fair character." In early May, 1818, Hall wrote to Woolley, reminding him that he had been ordered to resume his sword and asking that it be returned by an officer, according to military custom.[51] Woolley did not reply; Hall appealed to General Parker. After waiting two months for an answer, Hall wrote to him again and observed that in Woolley's hands the sword was being polluted. Woolley replied to his superiors in Washington that Hall could have the sword if he would call for it, but in the same letter he expressed his determination to arrest him again whenever he reported for duty.[52] After four more months of protest and delay by Woolley, Parker and Wadsworth finally compelled Woolley to yield. Woolley ordered Lieutenant Ward —then stationed 513 miles down the Ohio at Newport, Kentucky—to journey to Pittsburgh, call for the sword at the arsenal, and deliver it, in his apparently contemptuous phraseology, to "the said James." On September 14, 1818,

Ward brought the sword to Hall in his office and gave him a copy of Woolley's order.

There the quarrel might have ended had not Woolley, in the meantime, slandered Hall. In an attempt to force Woolley either to fight or to retreat, Hall sent a friend to him with a blunt letter, dated August 30, 1819: "Sir, I have understood you have lately stated to officers of the army that I was reinstated upon the express condition that I would immediately resign my commission. You will be good enough to state to me whether you did, or did not, make this assertion. My friend, who will deliver this, is authorised to give you the name of my author [informant] if necessary, and to accept such explanation as he may think proper."[53] Woolley acknowledged that he had made the statement, said that he believed it was correct, and refused to retract it. Again Hall sent the emissary to Woolley with a letter from General Parker affirming that, not only was there no condition to the President's restoration of Hall to his rank, but the words of the President were very complimentary.[54] Woolley informed the envoy that he could enter into no dispute with Hall, avowed that what he had said was spoken in private, and again stubbornly refused to retract.

There is no record of a duel. Hall determined to publish an account of all his dealings with Woolley. On the last day of 1819, Eichbaum and Johnston, printers of the *Gazette,* published *The Trial and Defence of First Lieutenant James Hall,* consisting of the proceedings of the court-martial, a preface relating incidents that had occurred since the court martial, and an appendix devoted to documents pertinent to the dispute.[55] The pamphlet, no doubt, was gratifying to Hall, who had the satisfaction of describing Woolley in print as "a poor, pitiful reptile." But Woolley's litigiousness and his inability to get along with his officers have been better established by other records. In 1819, he prosecuted Hall's friend, Dr. Hanson Catlett and Lieutenant W. B. Davidson in courts-martial. No doubt there were other victims of his legalism and vindictiveness in the subsequent ten years in which Woolley rose to the lieutenant colonelcy and the command of a regiment of infantry. Not until 1829, when he prosecuted Captain John Gantt, was he finally brought to book. The justices of that court staged a rebellion which Hall, if he learned of it, undoubtedly relished. They pronounced Woolley's charges "malicious, oppressive, vexatious, and frivolous," and ordered the arrest of Woolley on charges of oppressive conduct, maladministration, and striking a soldier. He was tried and found guilty; the verdict was sustained, and he was dismissed from the army.[56]

VI

In the spring of 1820, Hall determined, apparently suddenly, to leave Pittsburgh for the newer frontier of Illinois. "Having no dependence but my own exertions," he explained, "—with great ardor and hopefulness of spirit, and energy of purpose, I resolved to go to a new country to practice my profession where I could rise with the growth of the population—but [I was] allured in fact by a romantic disposition, a thirst for adventure, and a desire to see the rough scenes of the frontier."[57] Other important factors in his resolution, however, were probably a commercial panic and a fever generated by the increased tempo of westward migration. The panic occurred in 1819, and the hard times lasted until 1824.[58] Pittsburgh was severely affected. It was reported at a town meeting that only a third as many hands were employed in the city in 1819 as there had been in 1815. The value of the products of the city's largest industry, the manufacture of steam engines, fell to one-seventh of the 1815 value. In the autumn of 1819, Neville spent a day on Neville's Island and saw only one boat pass on the Ohio instead of the fifty boats of normal times.[59] The poverty of immigrants stranded in Pittsburgh stirred public pity. Sometimes whole boatloads arrived sick and destitute. Neville solicited funds for the relief of the poor; and it was probably Hall who, a little earlier, had written for the *Gazette* a plea for the establishment of a city poorhouse.[60]

Hall described the flood of immigrants that he saw as he was returning on horseback from a visit to Philadelphia. "I found these roads," he observed, "crowded with emigrants of every description, but the majority were of the poorest class. Here I would meet a few lusty fellows, trudging it merrily along; and there a family, more embarrassed, and less cheerful: now a gang of forty or fifty souls, men, women, and children; and now a solitary pedestrian, with his oaken staff, his bottle, and his knapsack; and, once a day, a stage-load of tired travellers, dragged heavily toward the west." Later, as he watched the emigrants leaving Pittsburgh— some taking furniture, farming implements, and servants; some bearing only a handful of goods; some, single men, leaving all their cares behind them—he was reminded of the invitation of a camp meeting song:

Come hungry, come thirsty, come ragged, come bare
Come filthy, come lousy, come just as you are.[61]

Not all were poor or unlettered. Many of Hall's own class, cultivated men of action, were launching new careers in the West. Dr. Charles Caldwell, formerly editor of the *Port Folio* and teacher at the University of Pennsylvania, passed through Pittsburgh that autumn on his way to Lexington, Kentucky, to open a medical school at Transylvania University, 250 miles west of Pittsburgh. Richard Flower, in a letter in the *Gazette,* described the success of a colony of middle-class Englishmen at Albion, Illinois. The frontier had made enormous leaps. Pittsburgh was now only a forwarding station for the real frontier, as was dramatically demonstrated, late in the autumn of 1819, by a great banquet held in the town to celebrate the completion of a new bridge over the Allegheny. For the feast, a table "several hundred feet long" was laid on the bridge. One can imagine Hall, who was present, listening to James Ross, the orator of the day, as he spoke of the bridge as a symbol of Pittsburgh's absorption into the stable Eastern community. The assimilation had been rapid. Ross himself could remember, he said, when the country beyond the bridge was "the haunt of savages, where no white man dared to place his foot." No doubt the address helped Hall to realize that opportunity lay farther west.[62]

In the spring of 1820, having promised Neville that he would write an account of his adventures,[63] Hall boarded a keelboat bound for Shawneetown, Illinois, a thousand miles down the Ohio.

VI

All the Way to Shawneetown, 1820

HALL's keelboat left Pittsburgh probably early in the morning of April 17, 1820.[1] Before 1820, steamboats appear to have visited Pittsburgh only rarely.[2] Keelboats were able to navigate low water, and passage on them was cheaper. "The keel," Hall wrote, "is a long, sharp vessel, drawing but little water; when loaded, the hull is nearly all immersed, but there is a deck or roof, about six feet high, covered on all sides so as to exclude the weather, and leaving only a passage of about a foot wide, which is called the running board, along the gun-wale, and a small space at the stem and stern. The deck, or roof, affords an admirable lounge in pleasant weather, but at other times the passenger is limited to very narrow bounds below; the oars, which are placed at the bow, are from eight to twelve in number, and are used only in descending the river. By means of these the boat is propelled at the rate of two or three miles an hour faster than the current, which has an average velocity of about three miles. The oars are applied during the day, and at night the boat is suffered to float, with a man at the helm, and one at the bow to look out. . . . A hundred miles in twenty-four hours is accomplished with ease."

Hall's particular boat was one of about forty-five tons, loaded with merchandise, and manned by eight or ten oarsmen. There were, at first, only two other passengers, both ladies—neither "young nor lovely"—who occupied the cabin in the stern. Hall's "stateroom" was in the forward part of the vessel among the boxes and barrels, some of which were arranged to support a mattress on which he slept. He took along his own food, and used the top of a box for a table.

The journey was leisurely, occupying nearly three weeks; in high water it might have been accomplished in half the time. On April 19, when the boat stuck on a sand bar, he took his gun and went hunting. The squirrels—against which he waged war in "Virginia, Ohio, or Kentucky, as was most convenient"—and the milk and bread, which he obtained at farmhouses, added to his diet. "By walking at a brisk pace along the shore," he explained, "I could keep in advance of the boat when the men were not rowing, and could pop over the squirrels, talk to the men, take a peep at the women, and kiss the children, while jogging on my way." On board, the journey was enlivened by "Pappy," a robust boatman of about fifty, who was popular because he told "merry and marvellous tales," played his violin, and hailed with some pleasantry every boat encountered. "He was a man of endless humour—a fellow of infinite fancy." Sometimes when the boat tied up for the night, he was chief musician for dances on shore.[3]

Not searching the shores with an eye to commercial advantage, but primarily impelled by a romantic spirit,

Hall recorded some of the scenes and events even as the boat floated along. The "gracefully rounded hills" had not yet been "shorn of their forests,"[4] and the season was appropriate to his mood. Just below Marietta, the fruit trees were blooming; at Cincinnati, the dogwood, red-bud, and tulip trees were in flower, and the locust bent "with the exuberance of its odorous blossoms." Below Louisville, the air was filled with the scent of wild grape bloom. After considering the beauties of the other rivers he had seen—the Niagara, the St. Lawrence, the Hudson, and the Susquehanna—he concluded that the Ohio had "a wild solemn, silent sweetness, peculiar to itself. On each side rise the romantic hills, piled on each other to a tremendous height; and between them, are deep, abrupt, silent glens, which at a distance seem inaccessible to the human foot; while the whole is covered with timber of a gigantic size, and a luxuriant foliage of the deepest hues. Throughout this scene there is a pleasing solitariness, that speaks peace to the mind, and invites the fancy to soar abroad, among the tranquil haunts of meditation. Sometimes the splashing of the oar is heard, and the boatman's song awakens the surrounding echoes; but the most usual music is that of the native songsters, whose melody steals pleasingly on the ear, with every modulation, at all hours, and in every change of situation."[5]

At Parkersburg, where—apparently on April 19—the boat was tied up for the night, the crew found a whipping post in the town, confiscated the undemocratic relic, and threw it into the river. Exhilarated by their adventure, they sat on the bank in the moonlight and sang their river songs. Hall wrote them down, delighted to find poetry dressed "in the robes of Nature" and, "like a good republican, dispensing her smiles as well upon the lowly as upon the great." He liked one song especially:

> "It's oh! as I was wal-king out,
>   One morning in July,
>   I met a maid, who ax'd my trade—
>   Says I, I'll tell you presently,
>   Miss, I'll tell you presently.

And it's oh! she was so neat a maid,
    That her stockings and her shoes
She *toted* in her lilly white hands,
    For to keep them from the dews," &c, &c.

Later, even while he was copying the verses, the boatmen were singing in the night and timing the strokes of their oars to the rhythm:

"Some rows up, but we rows down,
All the way to Shawnee town,
    Pull away—pull away!"[6]

Hall also drew clear-cut word pictures of emigrants traveling on the river, which was burdened with craft of almost every description. The passengers were as varied as their conveyances. On April 19, near Marietta, he saw several New England families traveling on two large rafts lashed together. "Each raft was eighty or ninety feet long, with a small house erected on it; and on each was a stack of hay, round which several horses and cows were feeding, while the paraphernalia of a farm-yard, the plows, waggons, pigs, children, and poultry, carelessly distributed, gave to the whole more the appearance of a permanent residence, than of a caravan of adventurers seeking a home. A respectable looking old lady, with *spectacles on nose,* was seated on a chair at the door of one of the cabins, employed in knitting; another female was at the wash-tub; the men were chewing their tobacco, with as much complacency as if they had been in the 'land of steady habits,' and the various family avocations seemed to go on like clock-work." Near Guyundat, Hall was attracted by a rude skiff. Rowing out to investigate, he found a man and woman, both gray-haired, "tugging deliberately at the oars." "This primitive couple," he said, "looked as if they might have been *pulling together* down the stream of life for half a century, without having grown tired of each other's company; for while their oars preserved a regular cadence, they were chatting sociably

85

together, and they smiled as they invited me into their skiff. . . . Neither of them could have seen much fewer than sixty years, and both were withered, wrinkled, and apparently decrepit; but they were sprightly and social, and spoke of clearing *new lands* in the wilderness, with a confidence which evinced nothing of the feebleness or indecision of old age." They passed their whisky bottle to Hall, and all three drank to their better acquaintance in the woods. He left them with the feeling that this courageous old Kentuckian was "worth a hundred dead Greeks or living Scotch reviewers."

Near Maysville, a European came on board as a passenger and at a landing bought a fishing line from a Negro who had lost both feet. In the transaction he cheated the Negro. The incident roused Hall's wrath against European authors of travel books defaming the United States. He observed that anyone who would cheat a Negro would steal without shame and that anyone who would wrong a cripple would commit murder. Such travelers, he remarked, caused the injured person to treat all their countrymen badly.[7]

On about April 24, the boat stopped at Cincinnati and remained there several hours. But Hall made only a scanty record of his first view of this city, which then, with a population of more than nine thousand, was the metropolis of the Middle West.[8] He spent most of his hours there in visiting "a lovely female," a companion of his *"dancing days."* He could not, he explained, make descriptive notes when he had a chance to talk over old courtships or dance once more his old cotillions. He did record, however, his general impression of a port crowded with boats, wharves covered with merchandise, and streets thronged with people, many of them with "genteel forms and busy faces." "The indications of wealth, of business, and refinement," he noted, "were too striking to pass unobserved, by one who reflected how recently the forest frowned on this spot." But in the afternoon, as his boat left the wharf and glided downstream, he was struck with the quickness with which the busy little city passed out of sight and hearing. Soon nothing could be seen but the woods, and nothing could be heard but the squirrel, the woodpecker, and the mocking bird.

Below Cincinnati, high winds frequently forced the crew to shelter the boat for hours together under the bushes on the shore, and rain frequently drove the passengers from the deck. At Louisville, on April 28, he ate an excellent dinner at Allen's Hotel, took a hack to Shippingport, where he examined some fine steamships, and boarded his keelboat, which was then piloted down the Falls of the Ohio. Below the mouth of the Green River, passed on May 3, he observed a flatter country of frequent bayoux and cane brakes. He saw extensive groves of large and extremely tall cottonwoods, gigantic sycamores, pecan and catalpa trees growing in the lush bottoms, and mistletoe in the highest limbs of the great trees. In this jungle, grape vines were sometimes a foot in diameter, and in the brakes the evergreen cane was from ten to twenty feet tall. There were also large flocks of parakeets "sporting their bright green plumage in the sunshine." On May 4, when violent winds forced the crew to seek shelter at the mouth of a small creek in Indiana, he pushed a little way into a cane brake and saw several deer and a flock of wild turkeys.[9]

On May 6, the boat reached Shawneetown, where Hall left it. The town was to be his home during the next seven years.

VII

Frontier Editor, 1820-22

In 1820, most of the 53,787 white residents of Illinois were settled in the southern third of the state, principally along the Wabash, the Ohio, and the Mississippi, which, bordering that region, formed a giant V.[1] Inland from the rivers, the settlements were rare. The state's central and northern portions were still inhabited by Indians: the Kickapoo in the central areas, the Sauk and Foxes northwest of the Illinois River, and the Potawatomi and Winnebago east of them. Chiefs Black Hawk and Keokuk still dwelt in their native Sauk Village near Rock Island. The white settlers were just beginning to work inland. A few had voyaged up the Mississippi, turned into the Illinois, and made homes on the land to the east. Here were the prairies—great, flat, grass-covered tracts having a deep, fertile soil and needing no clearing—but their lack of wood for fuel and fencing delayed their settlement. The land southward, within the lower part of the V, was chiefly forested. A few settlers had been attracted there because an easy living could be had by hunting. There were bear in the woods, and deer and wild turkey abounded.

On the emigrants' main highway, nine miles below the Wabash and one hundred and twenty miles above the Mississippi, Shawneetown was the front door to Illinois. Its population in 1820 may not have exceeded six hundred; yet, in all the four hundred miles of the Ohio below Louisville, it was easily the most important of the two or three towns that peeped out of the forest at the river traveler. With the possible exception of Kaskaskia, it was also the chief town in Illinois. It had one of the state's three land offices; it was the port used by the greatest number of emigrants moving overland to both the eastern and western settlements of Illinois or even to Missouri; and it also had an industry, the manufacture of salt.[2] The Indians long before had discovered the saline springs seven miles inland and had built a village on the site of Shawneetown. In 1820, their white successors shipped salt to places hundreds of miles away.

As seen from the river, Shawneetown probably seemed to be little more than a line of log cabins. After Hall had walked up the sloping bank that Saturday in May, he found a primitive settlement. Most of the eighty or a hundred buildings were ranged on a single street parallel to the river. Nearly all of them, including the Bank of Illinois at least as late as 1817, were built of logs, although several frame houses and perhaps one or two of brick sheltered the town's wealthiest people. There were taverns, the postoffice, a printing shop, the land office, and stores with both a retail and wholesale trade.

Surely the town could have been better located. Every spring the river grew turbulent, lapped at the very doors of the houses, and usually crept over the low ground in the rear before subsiding. The dank backlands were overgrown with great cypresses, cottonwoods, and pecans. Some travelers believed this low land made the town unhealthful. Hall disagreed, but he gave full credit to the agility and muscularity of the mosquitoes that flourished there and advised care in tucking in the mosquito net at night.[3]

Any officer of the peace in Shawneetown would have faced heavy odds. Like other river towns, it was subject to frequent invasion by the crews of flatboats and keels. Sometimes the boatmen, often drunk and quarrelsome, were so numerous that the order-loving citizens were powerless. Frequently described by their contemporaries as "half horse and half alligator," the rivermen fought in the frontier manner, "trying to put out each other's eyes with their fingers and thumbs, and sometimes biting off each other's noses or ears."[4] When John Audubon tied up his boat at Shawneetown on the night of November 7, 1820, one of his crew had part of his nose bitten off in a fight,[5] and in the same place and manner a neighbor of John Woods had suffered a similar loss. The increasing use of the steamboat, which required a smaller and more responsible crew, was, however, gradually lessening the number of foreign rowdies. Shawneetown still had plenty of its own. In 1821, Hall complained that citizens as well as strangers were shooting at marks within the town limits, so that it was dangerous to walk the streets. He objected also to "several contemptible riots and affrays," and to Negroes, free as well as bond, who stalked about the town with guns and pistols and collected at grogshops on Sundays. In 1822, the town's trustees found it necessary to prohibit horse racing except on the race track in the upper part of the town. In the same burst of progress, they made laws requiring sidewalks. Although Shawneetown was the county seat, it was long without a courthouse. Visiting the town on a Sunday late in 1819, John Woods remarked that there was no church and that the Sabbath "was not much observed. . . . There was much drinking and fighting, nor was work wholly laid aside."[6]

90

Yet brutal events were probably remembered more for their luridness than for their frequency. Even rioters must rest. "No place in the western country," Hall writes, "has been more vilified than Shawnee Town."[7] At least some of the residents were gentlefolk. On a visit to the town in 1817, Morris Birkbeck, founder of the English settlement at Wanborough, found "a greater number than we expected of agreeable individuals."[8] The Methodists sometimes held meetings at one another's homes. There were small libraries, too; Mrs. Sarah Weed owned nine volumes from the same set of the *Spectator* that was once owned by Benjamin Franklin and which were given to her by Franklin's grandson.[9] Henry Eddy owned *The Federalist,* a beautiful edition of Cowper's poems, and two encyclopedias, one Rees's, in forty volumes, and the other Nicholson's.[10] At the store of Samuel and Joseph Hayes, according to the *Illinois Gazette* of September 30, 1820, one could buy not only books like Cramer's *Navigator,* addressed primarily to the traveler, but also textbooks in spelling, arithmetic, reading, and chemistry. And for the more advanced reader, there were Henry Marie Brackenridge's *View of Louisiana,* William Grimshaw's *History of the United States,* William Paley's *Principles of Morals and Political Philosophy,* Robert Adam's *The Religious World Displayed* (in three volumes), and Abraham Booth's *The Reign of Grace.* Medical and theological dictionaries, family Bibles, and John Walker's *Dictionary of the English Language* were for sale. Only two works of fiction were listed, both English; one, advertised as "Sequel to Cœlebs," was probably Harriet Corp's *Cœlebs Deceived* (1817); the other was *Ivanhoe,* which had required only ten months to find its way from Britain to the lonely frontier village.

And there was beauty. There were days—perhaps, even weeks—in the 1820's, when the town was undisturbed by any sounds ruder than "the boat song which broke the sweet silence of the wilderness at sunrise, and the blast of the horn which came winding on the evening breeze, as the boat glided into sight from behind the island of willows." Hall

91

thought that Shawneetown "occupied a beautiful situation," and, twenty-five years later, he still remembered the songs and horn blasts of the boatmen.[11]

To his new life on the frontier, Hall brought an unusual combination of talents and accomplishments. He could write; he knew something about managing a newspaper; he was a practicing lawyer; and he had, he believed, "a somewhat richer store than ordinary of history, poetry, and romance."[12] Soldiering had taught him how to deal with danger and how to endure hard living. He had vigorous health, high spirits, and a special loyalty to his neighbors.

He was not slow to begin. He soon bought or leased a house next to Captain Hobson's Steamboat Hotel. Within sixteen days after his arrival, he had bought a half interest in the town's newspaper, the *Illinois Gazette,* and had become its editor. Two months later, on July 22, he advertised that he would practice law in the Illinois counties along the Ohio and Wabash.[13]

II

The newspaper, first known as the *Illinois Emigrant,* had been founded only two years earlier by Peter Kimmel and his nineteen-year-old son, Allen.[14] Before the year had ended, another youth, Henry Eddy, had bought a half interest. The next year the name had been changed to the *Illinois Gazette.* Now its owners were Eddy and Allen Kimmel. It was the latter's share that Hall bought.

Hall's partner, Henry Eddy (1798-1849), was something of a prodigy. He had entered the war when still a boy and is said to have been wounded at the Battle of Black Rock.[15] After the war, he settled in Pittsburgh, was for a time a teacher, became a printer, and took up the study of law.[16] Apparently he left a favorable impression on his other acquaintances there. Morgan Neville, who had not known Eddy intimately, observed in the *Pittsburgh Gazette* of September 11, 1820—two years after Eddy had left for the West—that his friends still spoke highly of his intellect. In Illinois he was to win the friendship of politicians and the respect of lawyers. Many years later, Usher F. Linder, after watching him plead in the Supreme Court of Illinois, noted his magnificent appearance, his close knowledge of the law, and his ability to recite from memory whole pages of Shakespeare and Milton.[17] However, he had an avowed distaste for rough-and-tumble politics, and his political career was limited to brief service as prosecutor and later as judge.[18]

Like other frontier newspapers, the *Illinois Gazette* was a single, folded sheet. Each of its four pages had four columns and was about twelve inches wide and twenty long—four inches longer than most of our tabloids but not quite as wide. There were two other papers in the state: the *Spectator,* published at Edwardsville by Hooper Warren; and the *Illinois Intelligencer,* published at Vandalia by William H. Brown.[19] These papers were made up almost entirely of advertisements and items of foreign intelligence from Eastern papers and contained little local news. During political campaigns, however, their columns bristled with scurrilous partisan attacks on each other. It was in the midst of such a contest that Hall took the editorship of the *Gazette.*

He at once stated that he was "decidedly friendly" to President Monroe, who had received him with understanding in his trouble three years before.[20] But for the time being he shrewdly avoided becoming embroiled in the state campaigns. Illinois's political groups had no basis in national parties, but originated in feuds of territorial days and "were founded on the principle of personal affection to one set of men, and personal hatred for another. . . ."[21] United States Senator Ninian Edwards and his son-in-law, Daniel Pope Cook, were the leaders of one party. Governor Shadrach Bond, Elias Kent Kane, and John McLean were important in the other. But there was so much intrigue, even within the parties, that the membership fluctuated greatly from campaign to campaign. With these squabbles, Hall said he would have nothing to do "simply because we know nothing about them."[22] Kane and Cook were candidates for Congress. Henry Eddy, then twenty-two, offered himself for the legislature; John McLean was one of his opponents.

Agitation for a convention to amend the state constitution in order to permit slavery had a part in the canvass of 1820, and the slavery issue was a dominant one during the next four years. In his campaign for the legislature, Eddy frankly

93

favored changes that would permit the operation of the saline springs with slaves.[23] Then and later, the Edwards party tried to convince the public that the Bond party in general and McLean in particular were the sponsors of the convention movement. McLean vehemently denied this charge in the *Gazette* of July 29, 1820. The Edwardsville *Spectator,* probably referring to Eddy's proslavery declaration, charged that the *Gazette,* in supporting McLean, advocated slavery. In the issue of July 22, Hall denied the *Spectator's* accusation and explicitly disavowed the proslavery views of his partner; furthermore, on August 5, he printed Morris Birkbeck's letter ending with the appeal to "send no advocate for slavery to represent us either in our State Legislature or in Congress." Upon this conclusion Hall commented, "From this state it [slavery] is excluded; it cannot now be introduced; and were an attempt to be made for that purpose we should be among the first to oppose so material a change in our Constitution." Hall's real view is obscure, but he seems to have expected that a convention would allow the limited use of slaves. Less than four years later, according to the *Gazette* of April 24, 1824, he was to come out clearly for a convention; he was never to become a militant public opponent of slavery.

In the election in August, Cook received a majority of the votes for congressman. McLean, with 288 votes, and Eddy, with 218, both won seats in the state legislature. As editor, Hall had carried out his promise of neutrality, and had impartially printed the letters of Edwards and Cook as well as those of McLean and Kane.

Possibly Hall hoped he might always avoid being drawn into the state's political vortex. Politics had brought loss of office and perhaps loss of fortune to his father, and had made his brother a partial invalid. But for James Hall, neutrality was usually difficult. The first sign of his political alignment in Illinois came a month after the election, when, in the *Gazette* of September 9, he and John McLean announced that they had formed a law partnership. In the same number, Hall advertised that he had moved his office to McLean's, and that his own house was for rent. There-

94

after both probably lived in the house containing their office.

John McLean (1791-1830) was a Kentuckian who had fought under General Jackson in a campaign against the Indians. He had become a lawyer in Shawneetown in 1816. Now, at twenty-nine, he had already completed his term in Washington as the first congressman from Illinois. Only the general agreement of his contemporaries stifles our doubt as we read their descriptions of the powers of his mind and body. Governor John Reynolds, who knew him well, wrote, "Probably of all the pioneers in Illinois, nature did the most for John McLean of Shawneetown. His gigantic mind, his form of noble and manly symmetry, and his lofty and dignified bearing, all demonstrated him to be 'the noblest work of God'. . . . His eloquence flowed in torrents, deep, strong, and irresistible."[24] Reynolds's sonorous and oratorical judgments usually needed discounting; but his opinion of McLean was substantiated by Governor Thomas Ford, who had a far more incisive mind. Ford also saw much of McLean and found him "naturally a great and magnanimous man, and a leader of men," and "possessed of a fertility of genius and overpowering eloquence." [25] Other credible commentators described him as "tall, strong, and stately" and "well nigh resistless with a jury." In town he was dignified, but at his farm, a mile and a half west of Shawneetown, he liked to wrestle, run races, jump, and hunt foxes. "People almost worshiped him." [26] Hall had aligned himself with one of the most powerful men in Illinois politics.

Near the time the legislature convened, the *Gazette* suspended publication and did not print an issue for at least eight weeks, and possibly twelve.[27] The lapse has been cited to illustrate the difficulty that frontier editors had in getting paper; but since the period of suspension was roughly that of the duration of the legislative session, it seems reasonable to believe that Hall wished to see the government in operation and to meet the men who formed it. The assembly convened on December 4 in the new state house at Vandalia. McLean was elected speaker of the House of Representatives. Evidence that Hall's friends—or possibly McLean alone—had busied themselves in his behalf came six weeks later, on January 16, 1821, when Hall was nominated for the office of attorney general. But he received only six of the possible forty-three votes distributed among a half dozen candidates.[28] On February 12, Governor Bond commissioned him aide-de-camp to the major general of the Second Division of the Illinois militia, and Hall became one of the state's four colonels. To this partially honorary position, certainly not a lucrative one, Bond two days later added the more substantial office of circuit attorney of the Fourth Judicial Circuit, in which Shawneetown lay.[29] For one who had been in the state only nine months, Hall had made an impressive beginning. He was to hold various public offices in Illinois during the next ten years.

III

The *Illinois Gazette* was probably composed and printed in a log cabin. It was issued on Saturday and carried to subscribers in Shawneetown by the printer's devil, who was sometimes also the compositor.[30] It was a little paper and its business affairs were small. Local advertising, at a dollar and a half a square for the first three insertions and fifty cents thereafter, may have yielded as little as eight hundred or as much as seventeen hundred dollars a year, and federal government printing one or two hundred more.[31] Subscriptions, at three dollars a year, were sometimes obtained by politicians who desired the *Gazette's* good will.[32] The price, however, was beyond the reach of many a poor frontiersman. Eddy once had 250 subscribers, but collections from most of them were slow. Printer William Orr observed, "The great majority of subscribers do not even *dream* of paying —their idea of *'taking the paper'* is merely *paying the postage.*"[33] But Orr was trying to depreciate the newspaper that he was thinking of buying. On the frontier, pushing debtors too hard was frowned upon.[34] Even so, Eddy once wrote for Peter Kimmel a list of subscribers delinquent two or three years and asked him to sue certain ones if they would not settle otherwise.[35] Money was scarce; Eddy was offered corn for a subscription; and he and Kimmel once had their paper bill credited in Pittsburgh for fifty-seven dollars in payment for nine and a half dozens of deer skins.[36] But if the *Gazette's* income was small, so were the expenses. Hall probably paid about eight hundred dollars for the half-interest in the press and materials;[37] rent was only forty dollars a year; and the annual cost of paper seems not to have exceeded two hundred dollars.[38] One could live cheaply: early in the business depression of 1819-1822, beef could be had in Shawneetown at three cents a pound;[39] venison and other game were cheaper. Yet the *Gazette* was sometimes forced to suspend publication. During the two and a half years that Hall was editor, the paper missed issues which, altogether, represent a period of at least twenty-seven weeks. Hall's expressed reasons for suspensions should not be taken too seriously, for he sometimes offered two or more. Once he pleaded sickness of workmen and shortage of paper when he was really absent to attend court.[40] The following explanation, a typical one, emphasizes his difficulties in getting printing materials from Pittsburgh. "In the first place," he wrote, "the profits of our establishment do not enable us to pay our papermaker in *advance,* and he cannot indulge us with a year's supply on such a credit as would give us time to make collections to pay him. In the second place, owing to the uncertainty of navigation, and the carelessness or misfortunes of the boatmen, we are often disappointed, as now, in the due receipt of what had been long before shipped and paid for."[41] One shipment of paper ordered in November had not been delivered in March. At least five numbers were printed on a half sheet.

Yet one cannot say that the financial difficulties of the *Gazette* were due entirely to the indifference, dishonesty, or poverty of the frontiersman. Hall regarded his editorship as the profession of a gentleman and, figuratively at least, had no intention of exchanging the ten-dollar beaver hat that he had bought in Pittsburgh for a coonskin cap to wear in the woods.[42] When the printer was ill, Hall did not set the type or man the press to get the paper out on time.[43] The *Gazette* employed two workmen, at least one of them by the year; these and the two owners were a burden upon a paper that might have been produced entirely by one person.

IV

The chief subject of Hall's spirited editorials in the *Illinois Gazette* was the development of the West. Western poverty, general during the 1820's, was caused in part by the tendency of the pioneers' money to go to the manufacturing East and remain there. Morgan Neville and Hall, observing the disheartening stagnation of Pittsburgh's industry and of traffic on the Ohio River in 1819, aided each other in reaching the conclusion that the remedy lay in the development of Western manufacturing. After reading some of the earliest editorials that Hall wrote in Shawneetown, Neville expressed his gratification at having a brother editor who was "an able advocate in the *great cause.*" As early as the second number of the *Illinois Gazette,* that of June 3, Hall's bias against the East and in favor of the West was evident. In later editorials he encouraged immigration and urged better mail service. He advocated the culture of flax and hemp and sought generally to improve Western farming.[44]

He also nurtured with great care the tender shoots of Western culture. The *Gazette* of August 26, 1820, contained a friendly notice of the monthly *Western Review,* edited by William Gibbes Hunt, at Lexington, Kentucky. A year later, on July 28, 1821, Hall welcomed the second of Hunt's magazines that fluttered and failed, the *Masonic Miscellany and Ladies Literary Magazine.*[45] He gave space to accounts of the meetings of the Albion Reading and Literary Society at the English settlement at Albion, and he reviewed the "Anniversary Discourse on the State and Prospects of the Western Museum Society," by Benjamin Drake, of Cincinnati.[46] He began to notice resentfully those British travelers who defamed the West. Probably most readers will believe that loyalty to the West, rather than sober critical standards, led him to defend Angus Umphraville's unworthy *Missourian Lays and Other Western Ditties.*[47]

More courage was required for Hall's severe castigation of the merchants of Shawneetown, some of whom were his

98

advertisers, for their refusal to accept Illinois State Bank paper at par. He praised those who exchanged goods for farm produce. Nor was it an entirely comfortable task for him to rebuke Shawneetown's trustees for neglecting to keep the town clean, mow the weeds, and dig a town well. Alluding to his duty as prosecuting attorney, he warned the village's six justices of the peace that he would not tolerate the riotous behavior that had disgraced the town. "For ourselves," he declared, "we owe certain duties to society, and we mean to fulfill them." He deplored the necessity of holding court in the back room of Peeples and Kirkpatrick's store and advocated the erection of a court house. The town's lawyers, he wrote, should form a society.[48]

Hall almost certainly was the author of "Obediah Mifflin," a grandiloquent essay in the editorial column of the *Gazette* for June 2, 1821. Mifflin was a free Negro who made a living in Shawneetown as a barber-surgeon. During the sessions of the legislature, he went to Vandalia and was there accused of theft. In spite of his pleadings that he had free papers, he received a beating "perpetrated by clergymen." After his return to Shawneetown, he was frequently whipped, so that he had to return to Kentucky, "where a free man is always sure of protection, if he has his free papers in his pocket." Although Mifflin served chiefly as the butt of the author's humor in the essay, there was some satire directed against those who, while professing zeal for the exclusion of slavery, treated Negroes with a brutality like that of the worst slaveholders. But the basic purpose of the editorial, which was not obvious, probably was to argue that Southerners knew better than Northerners how to deal with Negroes.

Just eight weeks later, in the *Gazette* for July 28, Hall was asking if the increase in the free Negro population of Illinois ought not to be discouraged. "We need not refer," he wrote, "to the disturbances which, not long since, took place in this town among the blacks, for they at all times and in all places, [are] worthless vagabonds." To circumvent the Federal Constitution, Hall proposed that Illinois adopt such severe conditions for the settlement of free Negroes as "to amount to exclusion." "We can see no inhumanity," he concluded, "much as has been said and written on this subject, in excluding a set of beings who will not work, and who cannot aid in supporting the public burthens."

Probably because Eddy had frankly favored modification of the state constitution to permit slavery, Hall felt compelled to reiterate his antislavery views expressed on July 22. In the extant copies of the *Gazette,* he discussed slavery in three editorials. In two of them which have already been cited he stated flatly his opposition to its introduction into Illinois. In the third, which appeared April 6, 1822, near the end of his editorship, he expressed doubt that the people of Illinois would "consent to a proposition so pointedly opposed to their former sentiments [expressed in the state constitution]."

Except in his attitude toward Negroes, Hall was usually progressive. His condemnation of imprisonment for debt and of capital punishment for minor offenses contained a challenge: "Let us reflect on the law which condemns to incarceration the honest man who is 'found guilty of being poor,' and boast the superiority of our legislation if we dare."[49]

Throughout his editorship, Hall printed letters from the public with apparent impartiality. The authors of these communications, most of which were signed with pseudonyms, debated many of the state's important questions. It is known that, under the cover of a fictitious signature, he himself wrote some of the letters. But meanwhile he zealously maintained the same privilege for the public. When proponents of slavery sent letters to be printed, he wrote: "Let those who advocate the measure exhibit their manifesto, 'that the people may the better judge.' Our *Gazette* is at the service of all who choose to make it the medium of *temperate* discussion, on this or any other subject. . . ." When a subscriber advised the *Gazette* to take a certain stand, he demonstrated that freedom of discussion was more to him than a vague doctrine. "We would not wantonly offend one honest man"; he declared, "but if the full and

candid expression of opinions, in which we and our subscribers may happen to differ, should cause their defection,
we shall obey their order to strike their names from the roll
with more cheerfulness than we felt in placing them there.
. . . Let those who dislike any of our positions oppose
and refute them, if they can,—they shall have fair play in
our columns."[50] Yet in the frontier newspapers of Illinois,
the practice of anonymous political bickering hindered good
government; for the masked controversialists tortured one
another sickeningly with irrelevant personal abuse to the
neglect of sound civic programs.

V

In spite of Hall's public and private legal duties and his
work as general editor, he still wrote enough essays, stories,
and poems to give the *Gazette* a decidedly literary character.
During the summer and autumn of 1820, he printed a series
of travel essays. In a note introducing the first of these,
which appeared without a title on July 15, he sought to
conceal his authorship: "A young gentleman of our acquaintance, who recently passed down the Ohio, has been
good enough, to leave with us some extracts from his journal,
and some copies of letters to his friends, with permission to
lay them before our readers. . . . We are always happy to
make room for any thing about the Western Country, and
if the following letter has no other merit, the writer has at
least treated of us in a very good humoured style." In the
essay, Hall described and approved back-country people
and their manners. During the next six weeks, he appears
to have reworked his material into a series. The issue of
September 2 contained "Letters from the West, No. 1"; the
remaining six appeared regularly thereafter through October
14. They were addressed to "N"—doubtless Morgan Neville
—who, at Hall's departure from Pittsburgh, had urged him
to write an account of his adventures. The letters, however,
were not personal; the salutation was only a friendly sign of
the fulfillment of the pledge to Neville. The second letter,
containing a discussion of the Cumberland Road and the
improvement of the Western rivers, clearly echoed Neville's

101

reasoning on these matters. In most of the other "Letters from the West" that survive in the fragmentary files of the *Gazette,* Hall described the country and the people that he had observed on his keelboat journey down the Ohio. Since, during the next few years, he added fifteen letters to this nucleus of seven, a more complete discussion of them belongs to a later chapter.

More than a year later, during the Christmas season, one essay and one story appeared, both by Hall, but signed "By a Village Beau."

In the essay, "Cool Reflections," printed December 22, 1821, he posed as a bachelor playfully extolling the advantages of married life:

> In this inclement season, when Nature, like a lovely nun, has veiled herself in snowy vestments, and no longer spreads her roses, and her lillies [*sic*], and her thousand soft enchantments to the delighted eye of man, it may not be unprofitable to indulge those meditations which the passing hour inspires. "The father of the tempest" has come forth in all his majesty, and the little creatures of this world fly before him, or sink benumbed at his approach. The songster has left the grove, the beast retired to his cover, and even the poet finds the current of his genius frozen. To the poor this is the season of extreme poverty, and the wretched feel that the hand of God is upon them. But of all the animated world the solitary Bachelor has most reason to dread the approach of winter —cold and comfortless is his habitation—the raging blast whistles mournfully to his ears, for, like Park in the wilderness, he has "no mother to bring him milk, no wife to grind his corn." He was idle in the harvest, and has gathered no grain; he strolled in the vineyard until the grapes grew sour.[51]

Hall's quotations in the essay reveal his careful reading of the *Spectator* and Thomson's *The Seasons,* but the more immediate inspiration of his subject matter and especially of his prose style, with its frequent echoes of the Bible, may well have been Numbers I and XXIX of Joseph Dennie's *The Lay Preacher;* in fact, John Elihu Hall reprinted James's essay in the *Port Folio* as No. 520 of "The American Lounger" series founded by Dennie.

Fortunately for his purposes, Hall seems to have been losing his taste for this kind of incongruous elegance. Somewhat like Hazlitt and Lamb at this time,[52] he was apparently beginning to feel that the essay form that for a century had been dominated by the writings of Addison and Steele was no longer appropriate to the temper of the times—especially on the frontier. Although he was to use the sobriquet of "A Village Beau" in four more instances, he did so only as a writer of narratives, one of which had a Western theme. "Cool Reflections" was his last essay strictly in the Addisonian tradition.

Appearing successively in the *Gazette* of December 29, 1821, and January 5, 1822, were Hall's "Christmas Gambols" and "Fiddlers' Green," actually one story in two parts and reprinted in the *Port Folio* a year later as "The Bachelors' Elysium."[53] This humorous tale combined the real and the fanciful. The narrative opens in a parlor, presumably in Shawneetown, where a company of young ladies and gentlemen bearing such *Spectator*-like names as Absalom Squaretoes, Miss Fanny Flirt, Miss Tabitha Scruple, and Mr. Smoothtongue were gathered for a Christmas frolic. They at once fell into a discussion of the comparative advantages of marriage and single life. However, one of the company, Mr. Drywit, fell asleep and dreamed that he had died and been whisked away to the Bachelors' and Maids' Elysium, where those who could not prove themselves blameless for their earthly celibacy were given partners and compelled to spend eternity in dancing. In his dream Mr. Drywit, amazed by his new surroundings, strolled about the Elysium watching the newcomers arrive. Soon he observed a backwoodsman gliding into the Elysium. "He was a tall, gaunt, hard-featured personage, whose beard had evidently not known the discipline of a razor for a month before his decease. His feet were encased in moccasins, and his limbs in rude vestments of buck skin; a powder-horn and pouch were suspended from his shoulders, and a huge knife rested in his girdle."

A dandy, who had recently arrived at the Elysium, made fun of the backwoodsman's dress. For these insults the irritated hunter threatened "to flirt him sky high." The dandy, "assuming an air of vast importance, declared, that if a gentleman had used such language to him, he would know what to do."

" 'I tell you what, stranger,' the woodsman retorted, 'you musn't [*sic*] intimate any thing of that sort to me—I don't want to strike such a mean white man as you, but if you come over them words agin, drot my skin if I don't try you a cool dig or two, any how.' "

Called before the Elysian judge, the hunter explained that he had indulged in only one courtship in all his life, that the object of his brief attentions had been a backwoodsman's daughter, but that he had not liked the "signs" and had given up in disgust. The judge asked him to stand aside and await the decision.

Eventually "a languishing beauty," one who embodied "all that was soft and sweet," approached the judge's stand. "Gently raising her downcast eyes, [she] ogled the judge with a most bewitchingly pensive smile, which seemed to say, 'Oh! take me to your arms, my love.' "

After hearing her case, the judge turned to the backwoodsman, directed him to take the lovely girl as his partner, and the uncouth hunter capered away with her into their eternal cotillion.

Though "The Bachelors' Elysium" is told with a suave good humor and, for the time, with an extraordinary sense of structure, it is more remarkable as being a very early American piece of prose fiction—if not, indeed, the earliest —in which an uncouth frontiersman is the leading character.[54] Cooper's first Leather Stocking novel, *The Pioneers,* was published two years later. James Kirke Paulding's play *The Lion of the West* and his novel *Westward Ho!* appeared nine and ten years respectively after the first printing of "The Bachelors' Elysium."[55] In writing his story, Hall, like some other authors of the period who developed the character of the backwoodsman in fiction, was concerned with the behavior of his "natural man," not in his sylvan environment, but in a society with a highly developed etiquette regarding such social functions as dancing, dueling, courtship, and marriage. The result is a gentle satire upon the preciosities of fashion, not unlike that produced by Goldsmith's Lien Chi Altangi in his comments upon London society in the 1760's. The same conflict of etiquettes is effectively used in both *The Pioneers* and *Westward Ho!*[56] Hall's demonstration of the superiority of the backwoodsman in a contest with a fop was frequently a theme of later story tellers, notably of Mark Twain in "The Dandy Frightens the Squatter" (1852).

"The Bachelors' Elysium" did not appear in the *Port Folio* until November, 1823, and the chance that Cooper had read it soon after it appeared in the *Illinois Gazette* in late December, 1821, and early January, 1822, or was influenced by it in his creation of Natty Bumppo in *The Pioneers,* is slight. Yet Hall's story may have been reprinted in Eastern newspapers, and Hall's mother, for whom Cooper had esteem, may have encouraged Cooper to read the newspaper work of her son. In her letter to James of May 28, 1823, Sarah Hall discussed Cooper's *The Spy* (1821) and *The Pioneers* (February, 1823) and revealed that she was on close enough terms with Cooper to have received a copy of *The Pioneers* from him—"one of a few printed in a superior style, with his name on the title page"—and to be aware that artists "both at New York and Philadelphia" were at work on illustrations for forthcoming editions of *The Spy* and *The Pioneers.*[57]

Seventeen of Hall's poems, most of them parodies, are scattered among surviving copies of the *Gazette.* One, signed Valerius, in the paper of September 30, 1820, is apparently his. Unswervingly anapestic, it is not without some feeling for the Western scene:

By thy dark woody shore, gentle Wabash! I strayed
    As the owlet's hoarse whoop marked the close of the day;
Through the wide spreading valley the distant wolf bayed,
    As he prowl'd by the stream that bore Mary[58] away.

The 1822 "New Year's Address," probably printed originally as a broadside for the carrier of the *Gazette* to distribute to his patrons on New Year's Day, is worthy of remark because it tells us something of the contents of the paper, its distribution on Saturday morning by John,[59] the printer's devil, and its value to the backwoodsmen.[60]

VI

By the spring of 1822, Hall was ready for state politics. His newspaper partner, Henry Eddy, perhaps already friendly with the Edwards-Cook faction, was a candidate for the legislature. Hall's law partner, John McLean, was campaigning for the seat of the incumbent congressman, Daniel Pope Cook. Hall announced in the *Gazette* of March 30, his own candidacy for the legislature but, concluding that attending to his private practice, running a newspaper, and enforcing the law in six counties was enough for one man to do, withdrew on June 1. He was then free to aid McLean, who faced a hard battle against Cook. Cook was a frail young man of twenty-seven, weighing about a hundred and twenty pounds, and his features were delicate; but he was erect and quick, and to his schooling in the political battles of the frontier he had added some acquaintance with life in Washington and London.[61] In 1817, he had been attached to the staff of the United States Minister to Great Britain, John Quincy Adams. The next year he had become the first attorney general of Illinois. Since 1819, he had been the state's only congressman. In 1821, he had married Julia Edwards, whose father was a senator from Illinois and chief of his party in state politics.

Hall's carefully prepared case against Cook was divided into four letters addressed "To Mr. Cook" and signed "Brutus." The last three of these survive in the *Gazette* of June 29 and July 6. Hall's purpose was to strip off Cook's philanthropic disguise as a friend of the poor settler and reveal him as he was, a land speculator allied in marriage with another great landowner-politician.[62] The keystone of Hall's argument was that Cook had used his seat in Congress to enrich himself, particularly by voting against the reduction of the price of public land from two dollars to a dollar and a quarter per acre. "Why did you do this, Mr. Cook?" he asked. "You tell us that the poor man would be injured by the reduction. Was this a sufficient reason—was it *true?* The indigent and honest citizens who constitute a large majority of your constituents, can answer the question. . . . They will tell you, sir, that none were injured . . . but extensive speculators, who had made large purchases of land at the old price, and whose interest it was to prevent the value of land from being depreciated. You are one of those wholesale dealers in land; and some of those with whom you are most nearly connected in office, interest, and affection, are large land holders." The land-hungry Edwards-Cook combination was, Hall hinted, dangerous to democratic government in Illinois. "It is also said," he continued, "that there is a large amount of *available funds* in the *Edwardsville family,* laid by for the express purpose of purchasing the land which is to form the inheritance of a future generation of patriots, to be born and bred in that nursery of political eminence. . . ."

In the *Gazette* of July 6, Hall concluded his accusations. He also announced that the illness of one of his workmen, the occasional illness of both of them, and the beginning of the sickly season led him "to anticipate a temporary suspension." About this time, he left for Kentucky. Soon afterward, Cook came to Shawneetown. Eddy was at home; and apparently with his aid and in the *Gazette* office, Cook wrote his "Reply to Brutus," dated July 23. It was printed on the *Gazette* press as a handbill. Cook and Eddy then rode away together.

In the "Reply to Brutus," Cook made some show of answering Brutus's arguments point by point; but probably there was no defense that would have been acceptable to the majority of the electorate. Cook tried to escape from his predicament by maligning his accuser. Brutus, he charged, was worse than a murderer to attack a public official behind a false name. Brutus had descended to vituperation by calling Cook "a shallow-pated fool—a designing knave—a demagogue, and a hypocrite."[63] He had stolen a letter from the postoffice, Cook insinuated, and as prosecutor was in the habit of taking bribes. He had, moreover, been dismissed from a public office. "Does not Brutus know," Cook hinted broadly, "that other publick officers are sometimes suspected of acting corruptly in office for the sake of gain?—Has *he* never heard the uncharitable charge made, that, by corruption even in the officers of justice, criminals have improperly escaped punishment? But Brutus has been too long mixing with the world, witnessing its *ups* and its DOWNS, not to know that men are sometimes even *dismissed* the confidence of the people without just cause, and it would seem charitable, therefore, for *him,* at least to attack others with caution, and to be sure that he utters nothing but the truth."

Three days later, on Friday evening, Hall returned from Kentucky and read Cook's handbill. He was furious, but he still regarded his newspaper as a public forum. He reprinted Cook's "Reply to Brutus" in the next day's *Gazette,* though there was not time for him to include a letter of rejoinder. A week later, in the *Gazette* of August 3, he concluded the controversy with "To the People of Illinois," signed with his own name. *"I am Brutus,"* he declared. But he defended his former pseudonymity. He printed new documents to substantiate the charge that in the land question Cook had voted for his own gain. Much of the rest of Hall's rejoinder was not to his credit. He ignored Cook's hints of bribery but struck madly at his feelings by sneering, in a reference to his slight body, that he was "one of the last men who would ever be asked or expected" to fight a duel. He even swaggered: "He came to Shawneetown when he knew Brutus was absent from home, and vapoured about the streets with the courage of a magnanimous mouse, bragging about what he *intended to do*—while he knew well that he would have trembled to have looked Brutus in the face."

Cook was elected on August 5 with 55 per cent of the votes. In the southern counties, where McLean was best known and where the *Gazette's* influence was probably strongest, McLean had a strong majority, receiving in Gallatin County four times as many votes as Cook. But the state's center of population was shifting rapidly northward

108

as the new settlers came in, and Cook won there as well as in his home counties in the "American Bottom," opposite St. Louis. Although Cook was not finally driven from office until 1826, Hall had set in motion the arguments that seem eventually to have destroyed his power.[64] The Edwards men, on the other hand, for years taunted Hall with the nickname of Brutus.[65]

During the eleven years following the election, Eddy's favorable references to Hall and Hall's notes to Eddy show that their friendship endured in spite of political differences.[66] But Hall had decided, apparently before the campaign began, to quit the *Gazette*; he had printed in the issue of May 25 a notice stating that a half-interest was for sale. On or before November 9, Eddy bought Hall's share for eight hundred dollars.[67] Hall may never have known that— just a week earlier, on November 2—Ninian Edwards had lent Eddy 350 dollars, a loan that was not repaid until seven years later.[68] Edwards, it seems, was perturbed by Hall's gift for stating political issues unforgettably, and felt that the Edwardsville political family would be safer if the *Gazette* as well as the *Spectator* were entirely in friendly hands. The *Gazette* for November 16, 1822, marked the close of Hall's spirited and often distinguished editorship. He had given Illinois a newspaper such as it had never had before.

VIII

Circuit-Riding Prosecutor, 1821-24

As STATE'S ATTORNEY for the Fourth Judicial Circuit, Hall was law-enforcement officer for the six southernmost counties of Illinois. Later subdivided, these counties, in 1821, constituted an almost unbroken wilderness of three thousand square miles, and the prosecutor who attended all the courts in his district was required twice each year to travel two hundred miles on horseback. There were two terms of court every year, one beginning in April or May, the other in September or October. The first court was convened on the first Monday of the month in Franklin County at Moses Garrett's—

probably a log house in a clearing—on the Kaskaskia Road about forty-five miles west of Shawneetown.[1] Although the records of this court have been destroyed, its business each term was probably finished in a day or two. The judge and lawyers next rode southwest twenty-seven miles to Jonesboro, where the court was called to order the Monday following. By Thursday, the cases there usually had been disposed of. The next Monday, court convened twenty-five miles southeast in America, a village on the Ohio; and the Thursday following, in Vienna, an inland hamlet twenty-three miles northeast of America. On the next Monday, the bench and bar were on the river again at the village of Golconda, forty miles east of Vienna. A week later, they concluded the circuit forty miles northeast of Golconda in Shawneetown, where the litigation might require three weeks.[2]

Many years later, Hall was still fondly recollecting those fall and spring excursions into the backwoods. "The country," he wrote in his description of the circuit, "was thinly inhabited; between the settlements were vast districts of wilderness, over which the traveler might ride whole days without meeting with a human habitation. The panther and the wolf still lurked in the forests, the marshes and pools were alive with water-fowl, and the broad plains, covered with unbroken carpets of verdure and wild-flowers, were tenanted by myriads of prairie fowl."

"The lawyers not only rode large circuits, embracing nine or ten counties each, but those circuits were so arranged to follow each other in succession, that the bar could pass from one to another through several of them, and an industrious practitioner passed half of his time on horseback. The counties were extensive, and the county seats being widely separated, the journeys were long and toilsome. There were no hotels, few roads, and fewer bridges. The traveler often passed from county to county by mere bridle-paths, leading from one settlement to another, crossed streams where 'ford there was none,' and when the channels were filled by heavy rains, found both difficulty and danger in getting over. Sometimes the close of the day found him far from the shelter of a human habitation, and then, like the hunter, he must light his fire, and encamp under a spreading tree, the want of an *inn* obliging him to camp *out*. The more usual resting-place was the log-house of a farmer, where a cordial welcome and a board spread bountifully with the products of the field and the forest awaited him.

"The seats of justice were small villages, mostly mere hamlets, composed of a few log-houses, into which the judge and bar were crowded, with the grand and petit jurors, litigants, witnesses, and in short, the whole body of the county—for in new counties every body goes to court. Here was no respect to persons; they ate together, slept together, congregated together in the crowded court house, and assembled together around the stump to hear the bursts of patriotic eloquence from the candidates for office."[3]

There can be little exaggeration in Hall's description. Until 1821, not even a seat of justice had been designated for Franklin County. The minutes of the court of Johnson County indicate no courthouse there until 1823.[4] Gallatin County's court was held in Peeples and Kirkpatrick's store until 1823, and in other buildings such as the house or tavern of Moses M. Rawlings until after 1825. The log jails were inadequate. The woods and the transient nature of most of the people made the arrest of criminals difficult and their escape easy. Court procedure also lacked some formalities. The summoning of grand jurors from among the bystanders, noted in the Union County minutes of 1825, was probably frequent. Sections of the courts' minutes surviving in the handwriting of Hall and others indicate that the circuit lawyers were sometimes the only available clerks of the courts.[5]

The rigor of travel, especially in the rough terrain of the Fourth Circuit, in part explains the youthfulness of most of its lawyers. Of eight whose birth years are known, the average age in 1821 was twenty-four; of these, McLean at thirty and Hall at twenty-eight were among the oldest. Most of them were unmarried. These young men, who rode their horses along the forest trails between the courts and lodged together in the villages or the woods, did more than try cases for fees. They met the leading citizens, attended lodge meetings, formed political alliances, and bound settlement to settlement and circuit to circuit. They were the bone and sinew of state government, and Hall's associates in the Fourth Circuit, then and later, held prominent state or federal offices. The careers of a few of the lawyers were typical. Sidney Breese (1800-1878), a graduate of Union College and, in 1821, the postmaster in Kaskaskia, later became United States district attorney and United States senator. Eddy, a member of the state legislature in 1821, later became circuit attorney and circuit judge. McLean, three times elected to the Illinois House of Representatives and three times elected speaker of that body, was twice United States senator. Samuel McRoberts (1799-1843), who was graduated from Transylvania University in 1819, became circuit judge, state senator, United States district attorney, and United States senator.

The fragmentary records of the six counties in Hall's circuit portray a violent community. Between 1821 and 1825, the preponderance of the indictments, especially in the five river counties, were for assault and battery, affrays, and riots. There seems also to have been a high proportion of murders. Horsethievery and hogstealing, though sometimes considered common on the frontier, are not often mentioned in the court records of this period. But Hall had to contend with the age-old offenses of larceny, adultery, fighting, sodomy, perjury, counterfeiting, fornication, forgery, rape, and trespass.[6]

II

Many criminals found an easy refuge in the Western wilderness. The names of a few brought fear to lonely outlying cabins from the Alleghenies to the Mississippi. The region along the Ohio below Shawneetown, the north shore of which lay in Hall's circuit, had been the haunt of perhaps more than its share of these desperate men. One of their dens was Cave-in-Rock, twenty miles below Shawneetown. Twenty-four years before Hall became prosecutor, Samuel Mason, a notorious land and water pirate, had used the

113

cave as a base from which he and his men descended upon passing flatboats, stole the money and cargoes, and sometimes murdered the crews. But the outlaws who for nearly a decade chilled the blood of the frontiersmen of Kentucky, Tennessee, and Illinois and who have become the subjects of history, song, and story were Micajah and Wiley Harpe. Two years after Mason's use of the cave, these men, who appear to have killed principally to satisfy a lust for brutality, hid with their women and children at Cave-in-Rock, where, it is said, they committed one of their especially revolting murders.[7] Both the Harpes, as well as Mason, had been captured and beheaded by 1804, but the *Illinois Gazette* of July 16, 1825, reported that there were still people living in the county who could relate the deeds of the Harpes minutely and who could point out, ten miles below Shawneetown, the spot on Potts's farm where they had murdered two men named Stighall and Freehart.

During Hall's term as prosecutor (1821-1824), there grew up in the region another outlaw, Roswell Sturdivant. Sturdivant was, Hall writes, "a man of talent and address. He was possessed of much mechanical genius, was an expert artist, and was skilled in some of the sciences. As an engraver he was said to have few superiors; and he excelled in some other branches of art."[8] As early as 1819, on his way to Vandalia, John McLean, having had a brush with a gang of swindlers and counterfeiters, had gathered a party and caught some of them. One carried a letter revealing that Merrick Sturdivant, brother of Roswell, was the leader of a band at Manville Ferry on the Kaskaskia River.[9] By 1822, Roswell Sturdivant was turning his skill as an artist to counterfeiting and had established himself in a house on the cliff by the river ten miles above Golconda. Hall records that "all his immediate neighbours were his confederates or persons whose friendship he had conciliated. He could, at any time, by the blowing of a horn, summon from fifty to a hundred armed men to his defence; while the few quiet farmers around . . . really not at all implicated in his crimes, rejoiced in the impunity with which he practised his schemes." His confederates were scattered over the

114

whole Western country; they regularly received supplies of Sturdivant's notes, and for each one hundred dollars of them paid sixteen dollars in good money.[10] The man had a sense of humor. He sent the cashier of the bank at Shawneetown some samples of counterfeit notes drawn on it, asked him to warn the public that such bogus money was in circulation in Pope County, and signed the letter with his own name. The *Gazette* of December 29, 1821, solemnly reported the warning, apparently unaware that it was the communication of the criminal himself.

In the *Gazette* of April 20, 1822, Hall announced, in his capacity as prosecutor, that counterfeit notes were in circulation in Shawneetown. Within a few weeks, one of Sturdivant's confederates was captured there. Hall and four other citizens determined to capture Sturdivant himself.[11] On June 29, armed with a warrant, the five men rode to Golconda, where they spent the night and added a constable and about three others to their party. The next morning they proceeded to Sturdivant's house. Hall and one other person "entered the house by strategem, unsuspected, and," according to the *Gazette* account, probably written by Hall, "the remainder immediately pressing forward, the gang within, consisting of six or seven persons, was completely surprised. They were evidently at work when the house was first entered, but broke off, and were busied in attempting to conceal their implements when they were discovered." The raiders saw the work benches, tools, and the "large flat stone" upon which the counterfeiters "were grinding or mixing ink when surprised." The invaders, however, were compelled to give up their search for evidence when they learned that an alarm had been given to Sturdivant's confederates in the neighborhood. "The apprehending party, being only eight or ten strong, therefore withdrew with Roswell Sturdivant and his brother, Merrick Sturdivant, who alone were named in the warrant." Nine of Sturdivant's men promptly took up the pursuit and were soon joined by twelve more. After a race of twenty miles, the posse reached a settler's house ten miles from Shawneetown before the pursuers overtook them. Here the arresting party "were

115

surrounded by these villains the whole night, and threatened with an attack; which, however, was fortunately not made—the resolute deportment of the party in the house being such as to intimidate their pursuers." On Sunday morning the prisoners were taken to Shawneetown and put under close guard.

But Roswell Sturdivant was too wily, and Hall could not convict him. Almost a year later, the *Gazette* of May 17, 1823, relates that a party from Golconda, after a bloody battle, again captured Sturdivant. In the Golconda courthouse there is an indictment in Hall's handwriting, dated September term, 1823, in which Sturdivant is charged with making counterfeit paper.[12] It appears, however, that Hall was unable to bring the slippery counterfeiter to trial, and that in the end the problem had to be solved extralegally by a community outraged by his felonies. "The enraged people, who rose almost in mass," formed a "regulating party," and probably beat him severely. Certainly they drove him from the community.[13]

The *Gazette* describes four murder trials that Hall prosecuted in Shawneetown. The issue of May 19, 1821, describes the trial of John Choiser for the killing of John Young. Henry Eddy and John McLean secured Choiser's acquittal. On October 11, 1823, the *Gazette* recounts two trials for murder. In one, Jordan Lacy was found guilty of manslaughter and sentenced to pay a fine of five hundred dollars and to be imprisoned for a year. During the same term of court, Hall prosecuted John Darr. According to his indictment, Darr, "not having the fear of God before his eyes, but being moved and seduced by the instigation of the Devil, on the 7 day of September, 1823, with force and arms, feloniously, willfully and of malice aforethought,"[14] with a knife did stab William Thomason in the right side to a depth of eight inches. But Hall ought to have done the jailer's work as well as the prosecutor's; for although Darr was found guilty and sentenced to be hanged, both he and Lacy escaped from the jail. The *Gazette* of May 8 and May 22, 1824, records the trial of Martin B. Frazer for the murder of Thomas B. Dryden, who worked for Frazer and whom Frazer killed to get his wife. All the frontier legal skill of McLean and Eddy, Frazer's attorneys, could not save him. He was sentenced to be hanged on Monday, May 10, between the hours of ten and three. Some of the great throng that witnessed the hanging may have remembered the ever disturbing remark that Frazer had made after he was arrested. When the searching party arrived, Frazer had run. Caught and brought back, he was asked why he had killed Dryden, and, if he wanted his wife, why he had not taken her and let him live. His reply was "that he did not know—the like might have happened to any one of you." Surely there was foundation for Hall's belief that his profession "above all others, opens to its members familiar views . . . of much of all that passes in the business and bosoms of men."[15]

Western Man of Affairs: Judge Hall

HALL had not been in Shawneetown long before he met Mary Posey, whose home was forty miles east in Henderson, Kentucky. She was twenty-one in 1820, have been born January 22, 1799, in Virginia.[1] She had both a grandmother and a grandfather who were cousins of George Washington. Another grandfather, Thomas Posey, was a lieutenant colonel in the Revolutionary army and later United States senator from Louisiana Territory and governor of Indiana Territory. He died at Shawneetown in 1818, while performing his duties as Indian agent. Miss Posey's father, John Posey, had been a captain in the war against the Indians in 1793 and had emigrated to Kentucky when Mary was a child of three or four. About 1804, he settled on a plantation called Walnut Spring, near Henderson.[2]

In the 1820's, there was a little colony of the Poseys in Shawneetown. Among them was Mary Posey's aunt, Eliza, the wife of Joseph M. Street, who had built one of the first log cabins in the village. There was also an uncle, Dr. Alexander Posey, who, it is said, had studied medicine in Philadelphia and had taken a degree there.[3] As a doctor practicing among superstitious frontiersmen, however, he had one asset that was more precious than academic degrees: he was a seventh son, and therefore had magic healing power. Hall later was to use his presumed gift as the basis of an amusing story.[4]

The only known portrait of Mary Posey, a large one in oils said to have been painted under Hall's direction eight or ten years after they met, and possibly not from life, shows a person of dignity and poise, with a face whose prettiness was not enhanced, at least according to modern taste, by the hairdress then fashionable.[5] Of more importance is Hall's description of her as "very lovely," "delicate and fair," with soft blue eyes, "pretty arched brows," and "a fine white forehead."[6] Certainly she appears to have been attractive, pleasant, and possessed of strong character. She was uncommonly devoted to her family. Once when her parents fell ill and Mary was with them at Walnut Spring, "for more than a week," Hall said, she "watched over them without once retiring to her bed. . . ." "Her father . . . had been given over by his doctor, and was only saved by Mary's fortitude and unremitting attention, by which she carried him through the crisis of his disorder before the arrival of Dr Posey whom she had sent for to Shawnee." "Her good sense, firmness, and remarkable sweetness of temper make her one of the best of nurses, and in the common diseases of the country her skill in medicine is about equal to that of our country physicians."[7] Her only known letter reveals her intelligence, her superior education, and her humanity. From Hall's correspondence with his brother John Elihu, he appears to have valued her judgment and customarily to have asked her opinion of his writing.[8] She and Hall were married at Walnut Spring on

February 2, 1823, and after a honeymoon of two weeks began housekeeping in Shawneetown.[9]

During the first two months of their marriage, Hall kept a household expense account.[10] Some of the purchases of the first day were

5½ lb loaf sugar	specie	$2.—
½ lb Tea . . .	do	1.50
1 Bush. meal . . .	S. P. [specie]	1.—
43½ lb salted pork		
191½ ——— do	S. P.	19.12½
8 Fowls . . .	S. P.	2.—
2 Loads wood	S. P.	4.—
1½ Bush. potatoes		
4 Bush. Turnips	S. P.	5.50
½ Bush. salt . . .	sp	1.25
2 Gallons molasses	S. P.	4.—

This list of expenditures suggests a robust appetite. To the 225 pounds of pork that the Halls bought on February 18, they added 410 pounds three weeks later; they bought flour by the barrel; and their bushel of meal appears to have lasted only nineteen days. Probably there were guests; probably also Mary brought to her new home some of the family slaves to serve as indentured servants. The account book throws no light on Hall's income, but his salary as prosecutor was 250 dollars a year.[11] He also received fees, usually five dollars, for each case brought to trial.[12] His private practice, which extended beyond his own circuit, was probably more remunerative; for, according to his own account, he was "a laborious practitioner" and "obtained also a large practice on the civil side of the court."[13]

Mary Hall's first baby was a girl, Sarah Frances, born November 27, 1823.[14] But the child lived only nine days and was buried in the cemetery on the hill a mile or two west of town. Her next child, Sarah Ewing Hall, was born October 2, 1824, at Captain Posey's seat, Walnut Spring. Hall was with Mary then, and six days later joyfully wrote to his mother that all was well. No other document portrays so vividly his boyish playfulness and his affection for his family:[15]

MY DEAR MOTHER,

Although I cannot promise you a weekly bulletin of Miss Sarah's health, I know that for a little at least you will expect it. This is her sixth day, and still keeps in fine health, and Mary is sitting up and has even been at her needle today. She is by no means well yet, but the weather is so very fine that she is tempted to be up a good deal, and is I think in no danger from exposure. It is [sic] has been as mild and as attractive as spring during the whole week, and she had her doors and windows open from the first. As for little Miss—— she has won "golden opinions" by her modest unassuming deportment. She has petted a little when hungry, as who would not—but has never once violated good manners by crying. She lies upon the bed by herself and sleeps for hours, and when she wakes I go and tell her stories and sing to her, and she falls asleep again—for all rocking, dandling, and walking about with her is forbidden by Mary who says it will spoil her, and that she must learn to sleep without it. I tell her the indians do so, and that it is using my daughter like a little Pottawatamy —and her grandmother says that she has a *right* to rock her and kiss as much as she pleases—and so between us little Miss gets a good deal of nursing against orders. But indeed she does not require it. She lies awake for half an hour at a time, and kicks, and laughs, and grunts, but never cries. I have got a great name in the nursery—there has been no medicine to administer, but I make all the drinks, hold the baby's feet to the fire, can handle her without any fear of breaking her in half, and last night took her to my bed and put her to sleep in my bosom, which I hold to be a feat of no small merit. The important question, who is she like? has been discussed over and over, but we cannot find out that she is like anybody—I believe however, from a very diligent perusal of her features, that her head, eyebrows, and eyes, will resemble mine, her mouth chin, and nose are the ditto of her mothers, and if so, she will have a lovely nose chin and mouth—but what a soft pair of blue eyes—what pretty arched brows,—what a fine white forehead she has lost by not taking them from the same side of the house.

I have amused myself in my leisure moments in writing the annexed piece. next week I shall send John [Elihu] something more. Mary says that she will write to Alexander as

121

soon as she is well enough, as he is the only one of her Phil[a] brothers who has written to her and she is fully sensible of the honour. I believe we shall call our daughter Sarah Ewing *anyhow,* unless you can shew good cause to the contrary, and I can assure you though she is "half horse and half alligator" she merits no worse a name. Mary says its a shame to be making fun of her baby so—and therefore I stop here. Capt and Mrs P. desire their compts to be presented you and my father & Mary sends her love to you all.

Probably for a few months, Hall's older brother Sergeant was a member of the Hall household in Shawneetown.[16] In the winter of 1816, this evanescent figure had failed in his attempt to establish a newspaper in Vincennes, but had managed to get into a newspaper controversy there in the spring of 1817.[17] On May 17 of that year, he printed at St. Louis the first number of the *Western Emigrant,* the third newspaper in Missouri, but less than two years later it had passed into other hands.[18] In 1821, he appeared in Shawneetown and advertised himself as an attorney available for consultation at the *Gazette* printing office. He was still in town in June, 1823.[19] Sergeant had an able pen, but he seems to have been lacking in tenacity. On September 13, 1827, John Elihu wrote to James that both Sergeant and Thomas Mifflin Hall, a brother five years younger than James, were out of employment. Sergeant had come home *"for another start."* "What with the laziness of one [Thomas Mifflin] & the want of steadiness in the other [Sergeant]," John Elihu wrote, "they give us a good deal of trouble." No record has been found of Sergeant's life after the date of John Elihu's letter.

II

Hall had been a resident of Shawneetown only two months when he was asked to read the Declaration of Independence at the Fourth of July banquet attended by the town's leading citizens. The reading was a rite, and to perform it was an honor. Forty gentlemen sat down to dinner, and twenty-six toasts were drunk. At subsequent Independence Day celebrations, Hall either read the Declaration or presided at the dinners, and no doubt shared fully in "that enthusiasm which the genial influence of good wine, and the inspirations of the occasion, were calculated to arouse." Sometimes at these celebrations, the men sang. Usually they fired the artillery of the state militia. Although ladies were once invited to Mr. Weed's tavern ballroom for a party following the dinner, the dinners themselves were gentlemen's affairs. The "gentlemen" were the merchants, the bankers, the professional men, and the officers of the state militia, as distinguished from those who worked with their hands or, in some instances, earned their living from trade. In 1825, the farmers and merchants had an Independence Day dinner of their own at the upper end of town.[20]

Hall during this period also played a leading role in the military organization of the state. On February 12, 1821, he began four years of service in the state militia, first as aide-de-camp to the major general of the Second Division, and later—with the rank of colonel—as brigade inspector. In 1823, he was appointed quartermaster general and held the office until 1825.[21] Doubtless, with his strong taste for ritual and ceremony, Hall enjoyed parading at town festivals and governors' reviews; however, in the 1820's, the frontiersman, spurred by an uneasy consciousness of the Indian tribes living in the northern half of the state, went through his military duties with some attempt at seriousness. Hall's resignation from the militia on January 4, 1825, was probably due principally to his acceptance at that time of other responsibilities in the state government.

His interest in Freemasonry, which he reverenced especially for its religious teachings, lasted longer. During 1821 and 1822, he was master of the Shawneetown chapter, Lawrence Lodge No. 34; and in 1823, he was the St. John's Day orator. In the winter of 1822, at Vandalia, he was a leader in the formation of the Grand Lodge of Illinois, serving on a committee to draft the constitution. He was elected Deputy Grand Master of the Grand Lodge in 1824, Grand Master in 1825 and 1826, and, in 1827, Grand Orator.[22]

Public records, of course, can disclose only a portion of

those daily acts by which a man is known to his friends. Hall was the kind of person who would hasten with his fellow townsmen to the river bank to gaze at some unusual vessel that was passing or tying up at the town; and he was eager to meet interesting travelers or settlers. He was a hunter. There can be little doubt that, in the *Port Folio* for June, 1824, it was Hall's own letter from Illinois that mentioned one of the backwoods diversions. "I have just returned from a wolf hunt," the writer said. "We found a wolf's den, and caught six young ones, two of which I am raising. The Indians frequently employ wolves in hunting, instead of dogs. You may smile at our amusements, but we have nothing better, and habit renders them pleasant."[23]

Like many other frontiersmen, Hall found both a social and a religious satisfaction in attending camp meetings. Near Shawneetown a grove was prepared especially for the services. Joseph M. Street, Hall's brother-in-law, wrote in a letter of 1827 that Hall "always" kept a cabin in the camp and took his family to stay throughout the meetings.[24] Street also recorded some of the grosser aspects of the gatherings, such as the "drunken, blackguard fellows" whose affray in the nearby woods ended in brutal stabbings that broke up the particular meeting that he was reporting. Hall, in his story "The Backwoodsman," vividly described a camp meeting, omitting the uglier side of the institution and dwelling on the sweet, majestic beauty of the services and the scene. On a knoll in the forest, he related, the small trees and underbrush were removed so that the great trees formed a canopy fifty feet above the ground. "The camp," he continued, "was laid off in a large square, three sides of which were occupied by huts, and the fourth by the *stand* or pulpit. The whole of the enclosed area was filled with seats roughly hewed out of logs. . . . The persons resident in the immediate neighbourhood had each erected his own hut, with the intention of accommodating, besides his own family, a number of guests; large quantities of game had been taken, beef, pigs, and poultry had been killed, and the good wives had been engaged for several days in cooking meat, and preparing bread and pastry."[25] In their own huts,

Hall explained, the families began worship at daybreak. They then congregated under the trees and sang without books, sometimes adapting popular ballads to religious themes. Then there was preaching, followed by breakfast. For several days or weeks, the services went on throughout the day and into the night.

In the *Gazette,* Hall had bluntly criticized Shawneetown's ugliness and dirtiness, for which he had blamed the trustees. Less than a year later, on November 4, 1822, he was himself elected town trustee. Hall and his fellow officers—John Seebolt; Michael Jones; Joseph Hayes, the merchant; and John Marshall, the banker—met in Hall's office several evenings in November, 1822, and passed laws to civilize some of the wilder residents and visitors. They provided penalties for obscene language and drunkenness and forbade shooting at marks in or near the town, as well as the racing of horses in the streets.[26]

Living in a comparatively inarticulate community, Hall performed wedding ceremonies, and was likely to be asked to make remarks upon the deaths of citizens.[27] His leadership was nowhere more evident than in the records of General Lafayette's visit to Shawneetown. Early in the first week of May, 1825, the townspeople were excited by the news that the general would visit them the next Saturday.[28] At a hastily called public meeting at Moses Rawlings's tavern on Wednesday evening, the citizens adopted Hall's motion for the appointment of a committee to plan the reception. On Saturday afternoon, May 7, about four o'clock, Lafayette's steamboat, the "Mechanic," was sighted coming upstream. As the boat edged toward the landing, the militia on shore fired a salute of twenty-four guns. The people of the town and countryside formed two lines from the water's edge to the entrance of Rawlings's Hotel. Calico was laid upon the ground over which the general was to walk. As he was escorted up the bank, the people reverently uncovered and "observed the most perfect silence" until he reached the tavern, where the ladies of the town were assembled. There Hall delivered the address of welcome. In listening to oratory on this famous tour, Lafayette earned as great a name for kindly patience as he had achieved for valor in the Revolution. Hall's speech required only ten minutes for delivery and was fairly simple; but parts were ornate, and, brief as it was, it seems now to have kept the sixty-eight-year-old guest standing a little too long. Nevertheless, Hall, who was the son of a Revolutionary soldier, in some passages spoke with an affecting appreciation of the symbolism of the occasion: "The little community which has the honor, today, of paying a small tribute to republican virtue, was not in existence at the period when that virtue was displayed in behalf of our country. . . . There is no sensible object here to recall your deeds to memory— but they dwell in our bosoms—they are imprinted upon monuments more durable than brass. We enjoy the fruits of your courage, the lessons of your example. We are the descendants of those who fought by your side—we have imbibed their love of freedom—we inherit their affection for *La Fayette.*"

In the hotel Lafayette and his party, including his son George Washington Lafayette, Governor Carroll of Tennessee, and Governor Coles of Illinois, sat down to "a handsome collation" with the ladies and gentlemen of Shawneetown. Toasts were drunk. One was to the immortal memory of Washington (drunk standing and in silence), and another was to the 19th of October, 1781 ("may that day never be forgotten by those who honour Washington and love La Fayette"). In the evening the general was conducted, again between the two lines of citizens, back to the "Mechanic," and a farewell salute was fired as the boat steamed away.

In the election of August, 1824, the voters of Illinois were called upon to decide whether they would admit slavery to the state. Those favoring slavery proposed a convention that would be authorized to amend the state constitution. A letter—probably written by Hall—in the *Port Folio* for June, 1824, described the battle's intensity:

With us, the convention is the most interesting subject. It is a dish which is daily, nay hourly served up. It furnishes all our food for conversation, for reading and newspaper scribbling. Party feeling is carried farther here than it ever was in Massachusetts. It destroys, in a great degree, all social intercourse between persons of different parties. . . . [29]

Hall seems to have taken a considerable part in the struggle. The account of a public meeting at Golconda in the *Gazette* of April 24, 1824, showed him on the side of slavery. There he proposed a resolution containing the clause, "That we use our best endeavors to procure a convention." It seems unlikely that he wanted to change the constitution for any other purpose than the legalization of slavery in Illinois. His stand is not surprising; though he had not, like the overwhelming majority of his neighbors in southern Illinois, been reared in a slave state, he had obtained, during some of the impressionable years of his boyhood, an acquaintance with and presumably a tolerance for slavery on the family plantation in Maryland. Fortunately for the Union, the proposal for a convention was defeated.

On September 25, 1824, a month after the Illinois elections, Hall wrote to his mother from Shawneetown. His letter was principally devoted to his family and friends, and to literature, but he commented upon the Illinois elections, the Presidential candidates, and the offices at the disposal of the Illinois legislature. Although Andrew Jackson was becoming increasingly popular, especially among Westerners —many of whom regarded him as a symbol of equality and as a person of their own fiber—Hall must have assumed that his mother would know that he would not favor him, for he did not mention him in his letter. On the other hand, he could not bring himself to vote for a friend of the family, John Quincy Adams. "[William H.] Crawford is certainly one of the most honest men in the nation. . . . I should like to see Crawford elected—but as a Western man shall vote for Clay."

Hall reported that former Governor Ninian Edwards had recently stopped in Shawneetown on his way to Mexico and "for the first and only time done me the honour of a call.

. . ." Hall's dislike of Edwards was no secret, but apparently the former governor had thought he might propitiate him, perhaps through pleasing Mary. "As he would not presume to talk of politics, or his little son Cook, or his great grand Master Adams, to me, who he knew despised him and them, he told us of the Washington ladies, the parties, Mrs. Adams' Ball, & Prince Hohenloe." Whatever Mary may have thought of this discourse on Washington society, Edwards's efforts were lost on Hall: "Edwards has always been an abandoned, unprincipled man—" he told his mother, "proverbial for his bold, artful, and successful villainies—and sustained by a well organized party. And bye the bye I think his friend & patron John Q. Adams, who makes such a man his friend and tool no better than he is."

Mary, who was going to have a baby, was then in Henderson with her parents. Within the next two days, Hall expected to complete his work in court at Shawneetown and join Mary in Henderson, where he would remain several weeks. He had been informed that his brother Harrison might visit him and Mary during the autumn. "Should Harrison come, he had better stop at Henderson which is directly in his route, where he will be sure to find Mary and perhaps myself. Should he come here first and find me gone —he must follow me to Vandalia, it is but 110 miles—and he will there see all Illinois assembled to witness the great contest for the loaves and fishes." "Should he not arrive within a month, I shall not see him—unless he extends his ride to Vandalia, which I hope he will do. I shall go there about the middle of Novr and be detained, I know not how long—perhaps all winter. Mary will be delighted to see him or any of my relations. . . . "

The result of the Illinois elections of members of the legislature, he said, had made the two parties nearly equal, "so that my chance for a Judgeship is about as good as ever—but I do not of late years indulge very sanguine hopes about any thing. . . ." "That pityful little tool Cook is again elected [to Congress] in preference to one of the most substantial men in our state [Shadrach Bond, the first governor of Illinois]." "I shall meet much opposition—I am the only man in the State who has written with much effect against Cook, and his party will oppose me to a man. They have been heard to acknowledge that I am the best writer in the state—and they fear to give me influence by elevating me to high office."

When the legislature met on November 15, Hall was managing or helping to manage McLean's candidacy for the United States Senate.[30] In the balloting, the only other candidate to receive a substantial number of votes was Ninian Edwards. McLean was elected on November 23, and left immediately for Washington. Five weeks later, on December 30, the lawmakers elected Hall judge of the Fourth Circuit, consisting of the counties of Gallatin, Franklin, Hamilton, Jefferson, Clay, and Wayne.[31] He was to serve only two years, but during the rest of his life he was known throughout the West as Judge Hall.

III

Back in Philadelphia, John Elihu and Harrison Hall's *Port Folio* had, in 1819 and 1820, been ploughing through rough seas. "Indeed," John Elihu wrote on March 20, 1819, "if my pride & my zeal were not largely embarked on this bottom I should suffer it to become stranded, for I am very certain that if there were not some extraneous means resorted to I could not have bubbled along."[32] He supplemented his income by practicing law, editing a law journal, and compiling books for the use of lawyers. In 1820, the *Port Folio* appeared irregularly, although it managed to complete both its volumes for that year. But before the end of 1821, it rallied and absorbed the *New York Monthly Magazine*. Then it went on to several years of health, and was respected in some localities as the *Atlantic Monthly* is today. But John Elihu was not well. He still felt the pain in his head resulting from the beating by the mob in Baltimore, and, about 1819, he had begun to suffer from apoplexy. He did a prodigious amount of work, but without the literary support of his mother and James he probably would have surrendered.

Sarah Hall, by a strength of will demonstrated in her

midnight studies, had emerged as a writer of solid reputation. Her *Conversations on the Bible*, first published in 1818, went through one English and four American editions. She gave John Elihu more than encouragement: her essays and reviews helped fill the magazine's pages.

Yet it was James's contributions that gave timeliness to the *Port Folio* and helped feed the general American hunger for information about the West. The seven *Gazette* "Letters from the West" appeared in the *Port Folio* between September, 1821, and August, 1822. A year passed before there were any new "Letters," and then seven more were printed between August, 1823, and March, 1825. In this later series, Hall continued the description of places and events that he had observed in his voyage from Pittsburgh to Shawneetown. Other "Letters" were devoted to accounts of little-known figures of the westward migration who had captured his imagination or his fancy. At the end of his relation of an incident in the career of Daniel Boone, Hall wrote, "If many of the heroes of Greece and Rome derived immortal fame from a single act of heroism, how much more does Boon [*sic*] deserve it whose whole life presents a series of adventures of the same character as those I have related." [33]

The *Port Folio* for October, 1824, included Hall's "Major General Thomas Posey," a biographical sketch of Mary Hall's notable grandfather, probably written in the autumn of 1824, while Hall was at Walnut Spring with Mary during her confinement. In this article, Hall made use of General Posey's documents preserved by his family.

Two other backwoodsmen who were to draw Hall's interest again and again were of a far different character. These were Micajah and Wiley Harpe, who spread death and terror throughout the Western wilderness in the 1790's. Hall could have learned about them from Mary Hall's father or from General Posey's widow, who, in 1827, was living in Shawneetown.[34] Near the close of the century, both had resided near scenes of the Harpes' violence. In any case, Hall briefly described the lurid career of the brothers in the *Port Folio* for April, 1824. In some settled sections to the east his account was read with incredulity. John P. Foote, in his *Cincinnati Literary Gazette* of May 28, 1825, frankly avowed his unwillingness to believe that such bloody murderers ever roamed the West. With all the alacrity of one defending his own reputation, Hall took up the challenge. For the August *Port Folio*, he contributed a longer account of the Harpes, which he supported with documents and punctuated with gibes at Foote and his little journal.[35]

In 1825, Hall sent John Elihu two narratives. The structure of both reveals a story-writer in the apprentice stage. The first, "Fashionable Watering Places," is a humorous relation of a man and woman who, during a vacation at Saratoga Springs, married because each was taken in by the false report that the other was wealthy. The introduction is nearly as long as the main body of the narrative, but this fault is in part offset by the clever ending. The second tale, "The Bearer of Despatches," already mentioned, is apparently a factual relation of the mission of one of General Brown's confidential messengers—probably Hall himself—in the War of 1812. The story's conclusion is weak, possibly because the mission itself ended lamely.

Of Hall's fourteen poems printed in the *Port Folio* after 1820, only six or seven had not appeared first in the *Gazette*. A few exhibit some craftsmanship but have only a fragile substance. "To Fanny," in the December, 1822, number, illustrates their album-verse prettiness:

> FANNY, while a lock of thine,
> O'er that snowy brow shall twine,
> Cupid, reckless of the snare,
> Soft shall sleep a captive there.
>
> Laughing eyes and cheeks of rose,
> Charm the urchin to repose;
> Sleeps he there, and ne'er will wake
> Till a frown his dream shall break!

All the pride and labor of John Elihu Hall and his mother could not keep the *Port Folio* going forever. In 1825, Sarah

Hall's brother, Samuel Ewing, died. Her husband, John Hall, died in September of the next year.[36] Soon afterward, it was clear that John Elihu's health would not permit him to continue the editorship, and the issue for December, 1827, was the last. The *Port Folio* had rounded out a lifetime of twenty-seven years; no other American magazine had lived so long.[37]

X

Spokesman of the New West, 1826-33

THE ILLINOIS elections of 1826 brought important changes to James Hall and his family. In that year his friend Thomas Sloo, Jr., opposed Ninian Edwards for the governorship. Edwards won, but by a margin of only 375 votes; and his chief aide, Daniel Pope Cook, again a candidate for Congress, was defeated.[1] Although the defeat broke the power of the Edwards-Cook combination, the Edwards party, during the next legislative session, succeeded in pushing through the legislature a bill replacing the circuit judges with the justices of the Supreme Court. Hall, in Vandalia at the time, was one of the supplanted judges. He immediately wrote and published a protest subscribed to by his fellow judges.[2] He also directed the circulation of petitions calling for the repeal of the new law. These measures failed. On January 15, in a letter to Sloo, who was at home nursing his own political wounds, Hall expressed his disappointment and his indecision: "Whether to go to the North, or the West or quit the State and its cursed politics, I am uncertain. It is a hard thing to be so poor that we must bend to circumstances."[3] But Hall's bitterness was premature. On February 10, 1827, the same legislature elected him state treasurer.[4] Apparently by March 3, he had established himself and his family in Vandalia, the state capital.[5] This town, which was to be his home during the next six years, was an important factor in his development, just as it was, shortly afterward, a significant element in the growth of Abraham Lincoln.[6]

At a meeting in the state house one evening in December, 1828, less than two years after he had moved to Vandalia, Hall reviewed the village's history. "It is but eight years," he told his audience, "[since] the axe was first laid to the tree, on the spot where we are now assembled. All around was one vast wilderness. The gentle stream that murmured past our town, had never been traced through its meanders, by any but the hunter. A rich growth of majestic oaks, covered the site . . . and tangled thickets, almost impervious to the human foot, surrounded it. . . . The gentlemen who attended the first session of the Legislature, which sat at this place, sought their way through the neighboring prairies, as the mariner steers over the trackless ocean, by their knowledge of the cardinal points. Our Judges, Legislators, and lawyers, came pouring in from opposite directions, as the wandering tribes assemble to the council; and many were the tales of adventure and mishap, related at their meeting. Some were lost in the prairie, some slept in the woods, some were almost chilled to death in plunging through the creeks and rivers."[7]

At least until 1832, and probably much later, Vandalia was still surrounded by forest. During the winter hunting season, peaceful bands of the Kickapoo and Potawatomi tribes

camped in the neighborhood of the village.[8] At Shawneetown, James and Mary Hall had been used to the bustle of
a river port, the brisk business of wholesale houses, carousing
boatmen, the boat horn, and the steamboat whistle. But in
Vandalia from early spring until late autumn, there was
little to disturb the silence of the enveloping woods except
the occasional howling of wolves or panthers. In 1828, the
town had perhaps four hundred inhabitants. The two-story
brick statehouse was the central building. By 1830, Matthew
Duncan had built a brick tavern that would accommodate
a hundred guests. Thomas Redmond's hostelry, the Sign of
the Green Tree, faced the public square; and John Charter
kept a house of entertainment at the sign of the eagle.[9] In
1832, Hall estimated that the population of Vandalia had
grown to eight hundred; and he reported that the town had
four retail stores, a church, three schools, and a combination
gristmill and sawmill run by water-power. Three doctors,
four lawyers, and one Presbyterian preacher lived there, and
a Methodist circuit rider came once a fortnight.[10]

Although the surveyors of the Cumberland Road reached
Vandalia in 1828, and were toasted at a public dinner, the
Illinois section of this national highway during Hall's residence in the town was nothing more than a cleared path
through the forest.[11] While Hall lived in Vandalia, two
important roads connected the hamlet with the outside
world. One, originating in Tennessee, entered Illinois from
Kentucky and, after passing through Vandalia, led off into
the wilderness of northwestern Illinois.[12] The other led west
from Vandalia to St. Louis, sixty-five miles away; over this
road manufactured goods were brought to Vandalia by
wagon. In winter, these thoroughfares brought throngs of
visitors to the village: legislators; justices of the Illinois
Supreme Court; politicians; delegates to religious, cultural,
and fraternal associations; and private citizens out for a holiday. The crowds milled about on the square and in the
lanes, slept in crowded rooms, went to meetings, heard lectures, and, once during every legislative session, attended a
grand ball.

In autumn, especially after 1827, large numbers of emigrants, chiefly from Kentucky and Tennessee, passed through Vandalia. On November 8, 1828, the town newspaper, the *Illinois Intelligencer,* recorded the daily passing of large parties of settlers bound for the northwestern part of the state. The next year, on October 31, it noted hundreds of wagons rolling through town to the north in a single week. One autumn, Hall observed the variegated emigrants strung along the road "in such numbers, that there seemed to be no end to the cavalcade." [13]

Beef and pork were plentiful in Vandalia at three cents a pound. Hunters sold venison hams in the village at twenty-five cents a pair and turkeys at 12½ cents apiece.[14] Hall tended his own large garden and kept a record of the flowers and vegetables that flourished in the virgin soil.[15]

During most of the years that he lived in Vandalia, he was prosperous and happy. His salary as state treasurer was eight hundred dollars a year—sufficient to place him among the well-to-do of the town; in addition, his prestige as state treasurer and his residence at the seat of the circuit court, the federal court, and the state Supreme Court gave him an unusual opportunity to try cases before these tribunals.[16] If Hall had wished, he could—with clear conscience—have relaxed into enjoyment of his family and his social position; but he had a concern for the destiny of the West. Even while he was becoming more actively involved in the shaping of this destiny, he found time to record frontier life as it was.

II

In September, 1827, a few months after the establishment of the *Western Monthly Review* at Cincinnati, Hall's poem, "The Indian Maid's Death Song," appeared in the magazine.[17] Two months later, two more of his writings were published in the *Review*: "To a Coquette," a poem; and "The Academy," an essay.[18]

In "To a Coquette," a parody of Edmund Waller's "Go, Lovely Rose," a rejected lover theatrically expresses his pique:

Go, fickle girl,—
Take to those syren arms of thine
Some wealthy churl;
Let him with thorns thy heart entwine,
Then think of those, you've plac'd in mine!

"The Indian Maid's Death Song" is the first of six poems in which Hall employs Indian themes. In all of these compositions, written over a period of five years, the savages are treated in a highly romantic fashion. Since the Indian wars were so recent that the frontiersman still regarded the Indian with hatred, Hall, in order to make his idealizations more plausible, usually related his characters to some distant tribe or to one without any indentifiable locality.[19] In "The Indian Maid's Death Song," Winona, a Dakotan betrothed to an absent hunter, is threatened with a forced marriage to another tribesman. She chooses suicide instead. As she stands ready to cast herself from a cliff, she sings of the fidelity of her absent lover:

His heart is so true, that in death he shall not
Forget the sad scene of this blood sprinkled spot;
But swift, as the feet of the light-bounding doe,
He'll fly through the current of darkness below,
To join his Winona in regions of truth,
Where love blooms eternal with beauty and youth.

"The Academy," which sheds much light upon Hall's own schooling, is significant chiefly as an early plea for the abandonment of corporal punishment in schools and antedates by several years Thoreau's rebellion against the whipping of school children. After relating his own narrow escape from a flogging at the hands of a tyrannical schoolmaster, Hall condemns the practice. "Few men of real learning," he declares, "will condescend to assume the laborious, thankless, and unprofitable task of teaching. When they do it, they confer an honour and a benefit on society, for which they should be

137

liberally paid in money and in gratitude, in esteem and reverence. But they should not whip our children." The editor of the *Western Monthly Review*, Timothy Flint, gave Hall's article the leading position in the November number, but Hall's proposal was so advanced that Flint took the precaution to state in a preface that he "did not wish to be understood to assent to all the remarks in the following spirited essay." Indeed, Hall himself let the article appear under his pen name.

Hall and Flint met sometime before the summer of 1828, and at this period they were friendly; but Hall appears to have contributed nothing for the remaining nineteen numbers of Flint's pioneer magazine.[20]

Probably while he was still living in Shawneetown, Hall had written three essays intended for publication in his *Port Folio* series of "Letters from the West." One of these deals with the superstitions of backwoodsmen, another describes Shawneetown, and the third controverts defamations of America written by English travelers.[21] He collected and rearranged the "Letters from the West" already printed in the *Port Folio*, added the three essays just described, and sought to have the whole published as a book.[22] Apparently Washington Irving, who was then living in England, had some influence in Hall's decision to seek a British publisher. John Elihu had written to Irving in London for advice about marketing such books there. On June 30, 1822, Irving replied that in England "a lively interest exists, on the subject of America and American literature."[23] Hall himself related the adventures of his manuscript. "In 1820 when descending the river Ohio," he recalled many years later, "and afterwards during the early part of my residence in Illinois, I wrote a series of 'Letters from the West'. . . . A friend who was going to England offered to place them in the hands of a London publisher. My friend died abroad, and I heard nothing of my 'copy' for nearly a year, when a very handsome volume appeared,—accompanied however by a blunder so whimsical and so sad—that I have scarcely yet got over the mortification it occasioned me. I had written a series of letters under the assumed character of a youth, traveling for amusement and giving the rein to a lively fancy, and indulging a vein of levity, and rather extravagant fun. The whole affair was anonymous, and was intended to be kept so. My title page, as prepared for the London edition read 'Letters from the West. By a Young Gentleman of Illinois.' Of course there was none of the pruning which would have taken place, in a work to be acknowledged as ones [sic] own. Imagine my dismay when the work appeared with the title 'Letters from the West. By the Hon. Judge Hall.' How this came about, I have never found out. I became a judge about the time I sent off the Mmss. and either some inconsiderate friend, who thought my new title would sound very grand, or the London publisher, who had found it out and thought it might help to sell the book, made this foolish change. The English reviews took up the book and made all sorts of fun of it. They acknowledged a certain sort of ability about it, and confessed that the author wrote very good English—but sneered at the levities and asked the English public what they would think of a learned judge who should lay aside the wig and robe of office, and roam about the land in quest of 'black eyes' and 'rosy cheeks,' dancing at the cabins of the peasantry, and 'kissing the pretty girls.' The *venerable* Illinois judge they pronounced to be a 'sly rogue,' and wondered if the learned gentleman was as funny on the bench &c &c. I never allowed the book to be republished—and was near never writing another." [24]

In arranging for the publication of the work by Henry Colburn, Hall's agent more than made amends for any indiscretion in proclaiming Hall's name and office on the title page. Colburn, who specialized in fashionable novels, was at that time the most enterprising publisher in London.[25] In printing *Letters from the West* late in 1828, he used excellent taste and materials, and produced a beautiful volume.[26]

The character of the *Letters* was such that the British reviewers were inclined to devote but little attention to the purely literary merits of the work. The reviewer in Colburn's own *New Monthly Magazine* described the *Letters* as "elegant and amusing," but observed that Hall's style "to our sober English tastes, is by far too flowery and ornate." Influenced perhaps by the circumstances of publication—the book's publisher, Colburn, was also the owner of the magazine and his employer—he was patronizingly generous: "Judge Hall's nationality, though often ridiculous, is never offensive; for it is accompanied by much truth, an hilarity of spirits, a vivacious manhood, and it is without personal rancour." He was, however, unable to forbear remarking that Hall's excellent descriptions recorded the Western pioneers' "descent . . . from civilization to semi-barbarism." [27]

The Tory *Quarterly Review* was less gentle. In *Letters from the West*, Hall had aggressively expounded his belief in democratic principles. He had exulted in the settlement of the West by freeholders. He had avowed that "in all ages, and throughout almost the whole of the habitable globe, . . . *the few* have cruelly oppressed the *many*—when we know that a people have but to *will* their freedom to obtain it, and that their happiness, and moral improvement, depend entirely upon their own desire for knowledge, and practice of virtue—we readily perceive how effectually ignorance may be deceived by art, how chains may be rivetted, and darkness perpetuated, by delusion and prejudice." Moreover, he had gone out of his way to upbraid the *Quarterly*,[28] rebuking it by name for its unfairness to the West. Accepting the challenge, the *Quarterly* for April, 1829, included a full-dress review of the *Letters*. The critic John Barrow, breathing forth fourteen pages of antirepublican prejudice, charged that Hall was enthusiastic about the West only because he was a "land-jobber." He called the *Letters* "a silly book" and Hall "a judicial blockhead." "God knows," he declared, "this country has little cause to be satisfied with the conduct of America; she has taken every occasion to injure our commerce . . . without benefiting her own; and her unjust and ungenerous attempt to wound us at a time when maintaining a struggle for existence, is too recent not to be remembered."[29]

Most American magazines were indifferent to *Letters from the West*. The *North American Review* ignored it. In several newspapers, however, the book was praised, notably by Robert Walsh in the *National Gazette*.[30]

In *Letters from the West*, as Hall states in the Preface, "neither a history nor a book of travels is attempted, but a mere collection of sketches, with but little choice of subjects, and still less attention to the order in which they are arranged." The twenty-two letters of the volume are, however, loosely unified by the narrative of Hall's keelboat journey from Pittsburgh to Shawneetown in 1820. A letter describing Pittsburgh, the starting point, is followed by one about Wheeling, which, as the western terminal of the Cumberland Road, inspired a history of the highways over the mountains and a discourse on the necessity for thoroughfares between the East and the West. The passing of Blennerhassett's Island evoked a communication on Aaron Burr's conspiracy, and Neville, Ohio, called forth a biographical sketch of General Presley Neville, one of the founders of the town. The departure from Cincinnati was the occasion for a section on General Arthur St. Clair's unfortunate campaign against the Indians. After the arrival at Shawneetown —which he described, as might be expected, considering his intimate acquaintance, with vividness and humor—he branched out into more general Western subjects: accounts of the adventures of Daniel Boone, the outrageous careers of the outlaws Wiley and Micajah Harpe, and the miraculous escapades of the Missouri River trapper Hugh Glass. Interspersed among the discussions of these topics, and sometimes a part of them, are frontier anecdotes and discourses on the character and manners of the frontiersmen, all generously punctuated by assaults upon the misrepresentations of the West by British travel writers.

Hall's principal aim was to write an entertaining book about the West. The letters have a pervasive gaiety, and the variation of description with anecdote, biography, and history sustains interest. The style, though sometimes self-consciously literary, is usually graceful and always lucid.

As an important record of a distinctive phase of American history, *Letters from the West* will continue to attract the reader seeking the early travelers' own accounts of the frontier. Few if any Western travel writers except Hall had the sensitivity to record the songs of the rough boatmen. Hall

141

heard them with the feeling that poetry "has again appeared in her native integrity":

> Oh, its meeting is a pleasure,
>   Parting is a grief;
> But an *on*constant *lovyer*
>   Is worse nor a thief!
>
> A thief and a robber
>   Your purse he will haave;
> But an *on*constant *lovyer*
>   He will bring you to the grave![31]

His descriptions of scenery, like those of people, show a predilection for the romantic, but he could be almost ludicrously explicit. Usually his mood was tender, as in the description of the view below Muskingum Island: "The river, making a long stretch to the west, affords an uninterrupted view for several miles. On one side are seen several log-houses, surrounded by newly cleared fields, exhibiting the first stage of the improvement; a little further on, a neat brick-house, with a numerous collection of fruit trees, just putting forth their blossoms, indicate[s] a more advanced state of civilization, and mark[s] the residence of a wealthier or more industrious citizen. Beyond these are lofty hills, whose long shadows fall upon the water, and all around is the gloom of the forest." [32]

On the other hand, he sometimes falls into the pedestrian manner of a bank appraiser: "There are now five salt works in operation [near Shawneetown] in the hands of different individuals, at the whole of which an aggregate of immense amount in bushels of salt are [*sic*] manufactured annually, which sells at from thirty-seven and a half to fifty cents a bushel, at the works, or in Shawneetown. It is sold by weight, the bushel being estimated at sixty pounds; about one hundred and twenty gallons of water yield sixty pounds of salt. The large tract of land reserved is devoted solely to the purpose of making salt, no part of it being leased for tillage; the object of this regulation is to preserve a supply of timber for fuel." [33]

Probably most enduring are his likenesses of persons bound for the West. Among the most memorable of them are two descriptions, already quoted in an earlier chapter: of the New England family, with all their livestock and farming implements, floating placidly downstream on two flatboats lashed together; and of the elderly couple (as resolute as Wordsworth's leech-gatherer) gaily rowing their skiff down the river to begin a new life in the wilderness.[34] Even more symbolical of the Western migration is the account, based on an earlier journey, of another migrating New England family struggling up to the highest point of the Alleghenies. The father, Hall recalled, "was guiding a pair of small, lean, active horses, harnessed to a light waggon, which contained the bedding and provisions of the party, and a few articles of household furniture; two well-grown, barefoot boys, in home-spun shirts and trowsers, held the tail of the waggon, laudably endeavouring to prevent an *upset,* by throwing their weight occasionally to that side which seemed to require ballast, while the father exerted his arms, voice, and whip, in urging forward his ponies. In the rear toiled the partner of his pilgrimage, conducting, like John Rodgers' wife, 'nine small children and one at the breast,' and exhibiting, in her own person and those of her offspring, ample proof, that whatever might be the character of the land to which they were hastening, that which they had left behind was not deficient in health or fruitfulness. Nor must I omit to mention a chubby boy of six years old, who by sundry falls and immersions, had acquired the hue of the soil from head to foot, and though now trudging knee-deep in the mire, was craunching an apple with the most entire composure. They had reached the summit of the mountain just as I overtook them, and as they halted to rest, I checked my horse to observe them. As they stretched their eyes forward over the interminable prospect, they were wrapped in silent wonder. . . . They looked back with a kind of shuddering triumph at what they had accomplished; they looked forward with a trembling hope at what was to come." [35]

143

Less sensitively written, but more widely appreciated by later writers, is the account in Letter XIX of the adventures of Hugh Glass. Glass, an old man, was a hunter attached to the expedition of Major Andrew Henry. While hunting ahead of Henry's party in the Grand River region, now northwestern South Dakota, Glass was attacked by a white bear and was so severely lacerated that, when his companions found him, they thought he would surely die. Major Henry, by offering "an extravagant reward," induced two of his party to remain with Glass until he should die or recover sufficient strength to endure removal. After five days, however, his two guards decided Glass could not live and abandoned him, taking his rifle and all his equipment, "leaving him no means of making fire or procuring wood." They then rejoined Major Henry's party and reported that Glass had died and that they had buried him. But Glass lived. He managed to drag himself to a spring, where he lay for ten days, subsisting on berries hanging within his reach. He then began crawling painfully toward Fort Kiowa, a trading post 350 miles distant. He was twice attacked by Indians, and twice escaped. After months of solitary travel, he reached Fort Atkinson in June, 1824, and told his story to the gaping garrison.

Someone who had heard Glass's narrative at the garrison retold it shortly afterward to Hall, then living at Shawneetown. Hall wrote down the story in detail and sent it to the *Port Folio*, where it appeared in March, 1825, nine months after Glass had told it to the troops at Fort Atkinson. The first printed account of Glass's adventures, Hall's *Port Folio* version gave the Glass legend its heroic aspect and made Glass, as one writer has said, "a symbol of the unique qualities of physical stamina and will that a frontiersman must have to survive in the extraordinary conditions of the far western wilderness." [36] Since 1824, the exploits of Glass have been the subject "of a continuous stream of oral legend and literary treatment." Washington Irving heard it in his tour of the prairies in 1832.[37] In the 1840's, trappers along the Santa Fé Trail related it to the English traveler George F. Ruxton.[38] The legend has had in literature a career no

144

less remarkable than in oral tradition. Eight early written versions have been collected. In modern times, it has been the subject of John G. Neihardt's narrative poem *The Song of Hugh Glass* (1915), Verne Bright's poem *Mountain Man* (1948), and Fredrick F. Manfred's novel *Lord Grizzly* (1954).

The fact remains, however, that *Letters from the West* never aroused enough enthusiasm to demand an American edition. The book does not even pretend to be more than a series of letters—a miscellany of anecdote, data, description, biography, and "tall story." Ornateness, sermonizing, and a tendency toward Anglophobia and Tory-baiting can all be fairly charged against *Letters from the West*. Probably under the influence of James K. Paulding's *Letters from the South* (1817), Hall overdoes digression. On the other hand, in regarding the *Letters* as evidence of the success or failure of the American democratic experiment, both British and American critics overlooked the book's chief merit: Hall, one of the few American writers aware of the epic nature of the westward migration, had succeeded in capturing some of the poetry of that movement and in portraying the Ohio Valley wilderness before the great tide of emigrants had changed the whole face of the country. He was both an accurate and a sensitive observer. His portraits of common travelers along the migration's greatest river highway show his human sympathy. He catches the gaiety of westward movers, old and young, when adventure and the hopefulness of spring lifted up their hearts. River mist and the smell of the woods are in some of its pages. Only twenty years after he had written his descriptions, the pristine grandeur of the Ohio's forested hills was gone. As the early settlement of the Middle West recedes further and further from our view, the book will grow in value, both as a storehouse for the social historian and as the delight of Americans interested in the West as the early beholders saw it.

III

Hall's use of literary annuals or giftbooks as an outlet

for his writing was due largely to the pioneering giftbook publications of his brothers John Elihu and Harrison. Prepared especially for the Christmas trade, the giftbooks contained short sentimental pieces in verse and prose. They usually were expensively bound and bore such titles as *The Forget Me Not* and *Friendship's Offering*. As early as 1818, John Elihu had edited and Harrison had published, in giftbook style, *The Poetry of the Port Folio*. In 1824, John Elihu planned a second volume. Published in 1826 as *The Philadelphia Souvenir* and regarded by one scholar as, in a sense, the first of the sort projected in America, this giftbook was intended to be reminiscent of intellectual Philadelphia in Dennie's day.[39] It contained chiefly selections from the writings of Dennie, Samuel Ewing, and other members of Dennie's circle. Two of James Hall's frivolous poems were included: "To My Glass" and "There's Nothing True but Heaven."

John Elihu's next giftbook, *Winter Evenings* (1829), contained Hall's story "The Soldier's Bride."[40] In the original draft of "The Soldier's Bride," John Elihu—formerly a professor of rhetoric and belles lettres at the University of Maryland—found much to censure: "If you send anything for the Christmas book, it must come as soon as possible, as the work is now in the press—& moreover it must positively be revised with care. You do not prune enough—you have too many adjectives ushering in the substantives which are generally able to stand by themselves. I have riddled your 'Soldier's Bride' without mercy—& after all—why— you ought to have sent something better. The story is defective. Your lover could draw the portrait of his rural nymph from memory—abandon his business to go in pursuit of her—spend weeks in her neighborhood without inquiring about her—and all the time be courting her under another name! I don't think Mary was consulted about *that*."[41] John Elihu's criticisms were no doubt deserved, but he failed to observe that Hall had attempted, and often achieved, unusual fidelity to scene. In fact, of the four tales in *Winter Evenings,* presumably all written by Americans, only Hall's story had its setting in the United States. And his thrilling description of the Battle of Bridgewater, with its convincing detail of color, sound, and emotion, was for its time a conspicuous American achievement in the realistic portrayal of warfare.[42]

IV

As early as 1818, when he was writing for the *Pittsburgh Gazette,* Hall had dreamed of a publication that would bring together the writings of Western authors. For the fulfillment of his ambition, the giftbook now seemed to be the ideal vehicle; and, by the spring of 1828, he had induced N. and G. Guilford of Cincinnati to publish a Western annual. Hall was to be editor. His prospectus described "A Western Souvenir" much like the Eastern annuals: "The only characteristic which it will attempt to assume as peculiar to itself will be its entire devotion to western literature. It will be written and published in the western country, by western men, embracing subjects connected with the history and character of the country which gives it birth." [43]

The Western Souvenir, a Christmas and New Year's Gift for 1829 appeared in November, 1828.[44] The volume did not come wearing garments of apology; it was bound in forest-green silk and was adorned with green end papers and neat gold lettering. Its subject matter was as redolent of the frontier as butternuts or buckskin. Through its stories glided Indians, keelboatmen, and hunters with their Kentucky rifles. Its pages celebrated the prairie, Indian mounds, the Ohio River, and an eighteenth-century French village on the Mississippi.

Yet for all *The Western Souvenir's* brave showing, an analysis of its authorship reveals the poverty of Western literature of the time. Of its 324 pages, Hall wrote 128, or two-fifths. "The rest I begged," he recalled a quarter of a century later, "all over the country, with infinite travail, and poor success." [45] He had the help of seventeen writers whose works in the *Souvenir* are signed. Two of these authors, Morgan Neville and Nathan Guilford, are represented by three pieces each; Otway Curry, S. S. Boyd, and H. D. Little each sent two contributions; and the remaining twelve

147

authors are represented by single productions. Apparently he could obtain no more contributions worth including, for he tried to conceal the preponderance of his own writings by printing some of them anonymously and signing others with his pen name, "Orlando."

Most of his nineteen poems in the little volume could have found nowhere a more fitting resting place than in the pages of a dainty giftbook. They bear the mark of hasty composition, as if they were the product of an hour's leisure seized during a lull in courtroom proceedings or during a shower that kept visitors from his office. Hall shows the influence of Scott especially in "The New Souvenir," beginning "OH a new SOUVENIR is come out of the west." Parodying Moore again in "The Plant of Havana," he avers that there is "something more exquisite yet" than the pleasure that he found in wine and cigars:

> 'Tis that round me choice spirits in high glee are seen,
> Who pour wit brightly out, as the wine they pour in. . . .

The main ingredients of the *Souvenir* poems are sighs, tears, dewy bowers, and broken hearts. In "Wedded Love's First Home," reminiscent of Burns's "John Anderson, My Jo," Hall no doubt appealed to the nostalgic sentiment of many an emigrant from the Eastern seaboard:

Far, far we left the sea-girt shore, endeared by childhood's dream,
To seek the humble cot, that smiled by fair Ohio's stream;
In vain the mountain cliff opposed, the mountain torrent roared,
For love unfurled her silken wing, and o'er each barrier soared;
And many a wide domain we passed, and many an ample dome,
But none so blessed, so dear to us, as wedded love's first home.

The sentiment continues in "La Belle Riviere"; but the scenery is specifically Western:

> Could I bear you, my dear, to the sycamore grove,
> By the graceful young cane could we stray,

148

Where the ever-green foliage resembles our love,
    Blooming fresh through each wintery day. . . .

In "The Shawanoe Warrior" and "The Forest Chief," Hall's
Indians are faithful and generous. In the former poem, the
grass-covered grave of the Shawanoe warrior is kept green
by an "enamoured, dark maiden," who waters it with her
tears. The idealization of the Indian is almost complete in
"The Forest Chief." In the beginning of the poem, a Spanish commandant is cursing the savages who have abducted
his only child. In the midst of his maledictions the Forest
Chief appears:

"Thy grief be hushed," the warrior said,
    And let thy terror cease;
My heart is good, my arm is strong,
    My feet are swift in chase.["]

Single-handed, the Forest Chief routs the offending tribe
and restores the boy to his father.

With transport and with dumb amaze
    The father clasps his boy;
The mother kissed his pallid cheek,
    And o'er him wept with joy.

In every eye that gazed on them,
    A generous tear-drop shone;
All turned to thank the Forest chief—
    The Forest chief was gone!

On the other hand, Hall's five prose tales—"The French
Village," "The Bachelors' Elysium," "The Billiard Table,"
"The Indian Hater," and "Pete Featherton"—as a body
surpass the work of any other author in the volume. Their
merit does not lie in their plots; indeed, some of them are

149

without memorable action. It was the creation of new characters and the accurate reproduction of fresh scenes that made the five tales significant early ventures in realistic American fiction. "So intent was I," Hall later recalled, "upon the faithful portraiture of western life, that I curbed my fancy and hardly did justice to my materials. . . . "[46]

His choice of Western subjects had a long foreground, stretching back to his boyhood in Philadelphia, where his imagination had been haunted by the vision of the Kentucky backwoodsman striding through the streets with saddlebags, bearskin, and dirk. As a young man in Pittsburgh, Hall had longed for a Western periodical which would be the product of Western writers and which "would yield us enjoyment at home, and respectability abroad." [47] When he took the keelboat for Shawneetown, "it was," he recalled afterward, "the search of adventure, rather than actions at law, that enticed him to the wilderness. The legends of the West . . . were more alluring than imaginary clients or prospective fees."[48] His inclination toward a sectional literature was no doubt strengthened by other Westerners who were beginning to urge a literature of their own. A community without literature, Timothy Flint wrote at Cincinnati in 1827, "is like a rude family without politeness, amenity and gentleness." "Amidst the freshness of an unspoiled nature, beneath the shade of the huge sycamores of the Miami, or cooling the forehead in the breeze of the beautiful Ohio," Flint believed, "a man might write as well, as in the dark dens of a city."[49]

The scene of "The Billiard Table" is Pittsburgh. The billiard table, the lights, the counters, and the spectators are described so faithfully that one can almost hear the clack of the balls. A flashily dressed river gambler, as much at home in Memphis as in New Orleans, is delineated with care. The setting of "The French Village," a Mississippi River town populated by descendants of the colonial French, is even more elaborately worked out. The people of the hamlet and their customs are painstakingly drawn, and Pierre Menou, the protagonist, is convincing even in his dialect. Of the characters, Hall wrote to Peter DuPonceau,

150

"I can vouch for their accuracy, as the whole picture is drawn from life."[50] "The French Village" may well be compared, for verisimilitude at least, with the work of George W. Cable, whose localized romances of the descendants of French colonists were to become popular a half century later.[51]

That Hall based "The Indian Hater" upon the life of Colonel John Moredock is made clear by an obituary account of Moredock in the *Illinois Intelligencer*.[52] Hall knew this elderly pioneer, whose residence was in nearby Monroe County, and he had often heard his story told "by those who were intimately conversant with all the events." Incidents in "The Indian Hater" are closely parallel to those in Moredock's life. The obituary sketch discloses that Moredock, after his mother and all of his brothers and sisters had been killed by Indians, "became emphatically an *Indian hater*," and devoted much of his life to vengeance.

The most striking and possibly the most influential of Hall's tales in *The Western Souvenir* was "Pete Featherton." Pete, who dwelt with his pretty wife in a log cabin on the Ohio River, was, when sober, a normal young man. But, like others in the backwoods where whisky was sold from the barrel, "he was a social man, who was liable to be 'overtaken.'" When he had had a glassful too many, there was no end to his boastfulness: "He . . . would slap his hands together, spring perpendicularly into the air, and after uttering a yell worthy of the stoutest Winnebago, swear that he was 'the best man in the country,' and 'could whip his weight in wild cats,' 'no two ways about it'—he was 'not afraid of no man, no way you could fix it;' and finally, after many other extravagancies, he would urge, with no gentle asseveration, his ability to 'ride through a crab-apple orchard on a streak of lightning.' "[53]

As Pete, one day, started hunting with his beloved rifle, "Brown Bess," he met some cronies, who persuaded him to go with them to the store. After drinking with them all morning, Pete resumed his hunting. As he crunched through the snow at noon, he could find no deer, though he knew they were usually plentiful in the neighborhood. The whole

151

woods seemed turned around; shadows fell in the wrong direction. When Pete stopped to drink from a spring, the water hissed and recoiled. Soon afterward he met a stranger, who later turned out to be the devil. The stranger, whose identity Pete suspected, told Pete that the deer belonged to him and that he was driving them home.

" 'Home—where is your home?' inquired Pete, at the same time casting an inquisitive glance at the stranger's feet.

"To this home question no reply was given, and Pete, fancying that he had got the best of the altercation, pushed his advantage,—adding sneeringly—

" 'Could'nt [sic] you take a pack or two of wolves along? We can spare you a small gang. It is mighty wolfy about here.' "[54] When Pete followed him, remonstrating, the devil, to stop him, blew his breath on Pete's rifle and made it useless. Later, an Indian doctor advised Pete to shoot a white fawn with a charmed bullet. Only by carrying out the prescription was Pete able to remove the curse from the weapon.

In the beginning of "Pete Featherton," Hall wrote that the story was one he "received from the lips" of Pete himself, who was "wonderfully addicted to the marvellous," and whose "imagination was a warm and fruitful soil." But the story contains elements as old as story telling, and Pete himself embodies the characteristics of the frontier folk-legend character classified by Constance Rourke as "the gamecock of the wilderness."[55] Although Hall apparently believed that he was drawing Pete's portrait from a living character, he was, to a large extent, making literary use of popular mythology, as Irving had done in "The Legend of Sleepy Hollow."[56] Hall, who, seven years earlier, had written a humorous sketch of a frontiersman in "The Bachelors' Elysium," drew Pete Featherton with sharper detail, warmer affection, and greater narrative skill. Droll, boastful, intemperate, exaggerative, happy-go-lucky, and, though illiterate, endowed with more than ample shrewdness, Pete had most of the characteristics that Bret Harte and Mark Twain were to exploit in their stories of frontiersmen forty years later. To Hall, now recognized as "the real pioneer of Western fiction," belongs also the credit for publicizing and perhaps originating, in print, the new Western humor.[57]

The work of one other author—"The Last of the Boat-men," by Morgan Neville—stood out from the sentimental matter in *The Western Souvenir.* "The Last of the Boat-men" was an account of Mike Fink; and Fink, like Pete Featherton, was scarcely the sort of character one would expect to find within the silken covers of a giftbook. Both were essentially wilderness gamecocks of the "half-horse, half-alligator" breed; both drank huge quantities of whisky; and both had a winning humor and openness of character.[58] Neville's account of Mike Fink, probably written at Hall's urging, is not fiction, but history.[59] The extraordinary Neville—whose acquaintances included King Louis-Philippe of France, General Lafayette, the Chevalier du Bac, Harman Blennerhassett, and Aaron Burr—appears to have set down the plain facts about another of his unusual friends, in this instance a scout whom he had known in his boyhood. Fink, finding his knowledge of the wilderness no longer in demand, had turned keelboatman. He lived gaily, careless of the morrow. Along the Ohio and the Mississippi he was famous for his ability to shoot a tin cup off his partner's head to win bets for whisky. He came to no sentimental end. He once shot for whisky when he "had corned too heavy. He elevated too low, and shot his companion through the head." Mike himself was then shot and killed by the dead man's friend. Neville's account of Fink, the first printed one of any length, immortalized this folk hero, who has become the subject of a shelf of tales by later romancers.

The Western Souvenir, appearing about the time of the English publication of *Letters from the West,* did much to earn recognition of Hall as the chief spokesman for the West. Appreciation of his efforts to achieve realism in his fiction came most clearly from England. There Mary Russell Mitford, who had gained fame for her stories of an English village, edited for Colburn a three-volume collection of tales which was published in 1830 as *Stories of American Life; by American Writers.* Of the twenty-four stories that she

153

selected for the collection, four were Hall's: "The French Village," "The Indian Hater," "Pete Featherton," and "The Captain's Lady." No other author was represented by so many. Miss Mitford wrote that, in choosing the tales, she never in her life worked harder. But she appears to have made her selections with some prejudice. In her preface she explained her omission of stories by Irving—who had then lived in Europe seventeen years—by characterizing his writings as "essentially European."[60] In a letter to a friend, however, she divulged a more vital objection to Irving's work. Forgettingly momentarily the excellence of Irving's two best tales in *The Sketch Book*, she predicted that the forthcoming *Stories of American Life* would be "really very good—characteristic, national, various, and healthy—as different from the 'Sketch Book' (which, in my mind, is a pack of maudlin trash) as anything you can imagine."[61]

V

On January 17, 1829, the *Illinois Intelligencer*, the eleven-year-old weekly newspaper published in Vandalia, announced that Hall had bought from Robert Blackwell (1796-1866) a half-interest in that newspaper and its printing establishment. Blackwell, who remained with the newspaper as Hall's partner, was then thirty-four. By good management he had built a large and prosperous press with a general printing business even more profitable than the newspaper. He was public printer to the state of Illinois;[62] and soon the partners, Hall and Blackwell, were publishing in neat volumes the laws of the General Assembly and the journals of its two branches.

The *Intelligencer*'s age, the strict regularity of its appearance, and the fact that it was published at the state capital had given it prestige. Unlike the *Illinois Gazette*, it was issued punctually every Saturday. Its printing was good; its advertisements did not run on indefinitely merely to fill space; and the owners did not trouble the public with mournful tales of sick compositors or the difficulties of getting supplies from St. Louis by river and wagon.

The burden of editing the *Intelligencer* was chiefly Hall's. To be sure, as a small-town paper, its news dealt with village affairs, but Hall often managed to treat these topics with a genial coffee-house urbanity. In reporting, for instance, the repeated theft of meat in the village, he commented, "Our own opinion is, that in so small a place as Vandalia, stealing ought not to be allowed, for there are so few to steal from, that it is oppressive. We do not make these remarks from any interested motive, for, thank fortune, all our fodder and corn were stolen long ago, and we think we know how to save our own bacon." But concerned as he was with the welfare of the village, he set out to make the *Intelligencer*, not merely a well-managed bulletin, but a major influence in Illinois. Although there can be little doubt that he bought his share partly for political purposes, under his guidance the *Intelligencer* became an outstanding newspaper, worthy of comparison with some of its metropolitan contemporaries. It had literary quality and an enlightened public policy. Signs of a new prosperity for the paper were evident soon after he became an owner. In his editorial of April 11, 1829, the paper's twelfth birthday, he stated with satisfaction, "Our list of subscribers is now larger than it has been at any former period."[63] On January 30, 1830, the partners proudly printed with new type.

As author and editor, Hall, during the six years of his residence in Vandalia, was the social and cultural leader of Illinois. The *Intelligencer*'s columns reveal that he was as tireless in devising and fostering cultural organizations for frontier Illinois as Franklin had been in performing similar services for Philadelphia ninety years earlier. In the execution of the purely mundane tasks necessary for social progress, Hall did his full share. He was, for example, one of a committee of five appointed to descend the Kaskaskia River to its mouth to determine the cost of removing the obstructions to navigation in the narrow stream.[64] He was one of six men commissioned to oversee the erection of an addition to the statehouse; he also labored for the rapid construction of the Cumberland Road westward from Terre Haute through Vandalia to St. Louis.[65]

He showed his greatest zeal in promoting public education for Illinois. In his Independence Day oration, delivered at Vandalia in 1830, according to the *Intelligencer* of July 10, he declared that "Illinois is destined to have wealth and strength, and it is important that she should also have intelligence, virtue, refinement, to enable her to direct her mighty energies to the noblest ends." Recognizing that a system of free education could not be achieved at once, he advocated as temporary substitutes the Bible Society and Sunday schools, which might teach the people at least to read and write. A little later he showed by example how frontier communities could form their own schools. At a meeting of Vandalia's citizens in the summer of 1829, he explained his plan for building a meeting house that could be used for both education and worship. He was elected one of the trustees of the building fund. Two weeks later he reported that enough money had been subscribed to construct an assembly hall that would "be adorned with a steeple and bell, and erected with a view to ornament as well as utility." He added that it would be finished by the first of November and would "be open to the use of different sects of Christians indiscriminately." He believed that the management of the school should rest in a board of trustees, who would collect the money and employ the teachers. He was probably the author of the school's constitution, which he presented for adoption at a public meeting held early in 1830. After the acceptance of the constitution, he printed it in the *Intelligencer* as a model for the guidance of other communities. In November, 1830, the Vandalia High School opened with classes in reading, writing, arithmetic, Latin, Greek, and French. Hall was one of the trustees.[66]

Probably from the time of its organization, he was a stockholder in Jacksonville Seminary. John Ellis, a missionary stationed at Kaskaskia, had drawn up a plan for the school. The prospectus fell into the hands of seven students at Yale College who had formed a compact to devote themselves to religion and education in the West.[67] The "Yale Band," as they were called later, suggested the formation of a college from the seminary. On December 18, 1830, Hall played a leading part in a meeting of the stockholders in the un-finished Seminary Hall in Jacksonville, then "a hamlet of log houses." As the stockholders "stood among the carpenter's chips and shavings," he made the motion to accept the offer of the Yale men and to establish the college. He then moved "that this institution shall hereafter be called and known by the name of ILLINOIS COLLEGE."[68] Four years later he wrote, "From this small beginning has arisen a valuable institution, having a faculty consisting of a President and four other gentlemen, and a list of eighty-two students." Today, Illinois College still flourishes under the name with which Hall christened it a century and a quarter ago.

During the college's formative years, his home at Vandalia was something like headquarters for the institution's officers and sponsors. Two members of the Yale Band, Theron Baldwin and Julian M. Sturtevant, met there in April, 1830.[69] Edward Beecher, the older brother of Henry Ward and Harriet Beecher, became the president in that year, and Hall became acquainted with him when Beecher was in Vandalia during the legislature's session of 1830-1831.[70] Hall welcomed these men to Illinois without any apparent trace of the prejudice against Yankees which he had expressed and was to express again. In fact, he seems to have been stimulated to increased civic and cultural activity by Beecher and his New England associates, whose names soon began to appear in the membership lists of a series of moral and intellectual enterprises in which Hall was a leader and an officer.

The Yale Band was influential in the organization, in 1831, of the Illinois Colonization Society, a branch of the American Colonization Society, which had been established in 1817 with the object of gradually eradicating slavery by transporting freed slaves to Africa. Although the Colonizationists were later denounced by the abolitionists for their gradualism and for the doctrine of Negro inferiority implicit in their colonization plan, many, and perhaps most, Colonizationists were, as a student of the movement has stated, "as truly opposed to slavery as Garrison himself," and they constituted "the most important unofficial organization in trying to bring about a peaceable settlement of the negro problem."[71]

Hall was from the beginning vice-president of the Illinois Colonization Society, in which, indeed, nearly every well-known Illinois politician held some office. At the first regular meeting of the group, he introduced a resolution which, in a tantalizingly ambiguous way, represented the strongest antislavery statement he is known to have made up to that time. "The permanent existence of the union of the American republic, and its prosperity, will be, in our opinion, greatly promoted," he proposed, "by the eradication of every vestige of domestic slavery, on terms which shall be equitable alike to all parts of the Union."[72] In evaluating this hedging resolution and its prompt approval by Hall's fellow Colonizationists, it is to be remembered that—in accordance with Hall's own recommendation in the *Illinois Gazette* of July 28, 1821—Illinois had enacted laws demanding of incoming colored people certificates of freedom and guarantees of self-sufficiency that amounted almost to the exclusion of free Negroes.[73] Moreover, probably a wide majority of the members of the Illinois Colonization Society had been reared in southern states.[74] Whether Hall offered his resolution in an unexpected seizure of antislavery enthusiasm, engendered possibly by some member of the Yale Band, or whether he presented it chiefly to insure the inclusion of the temporizing clause—"on terms which shall be equitable alike to all parts of the Union"—may never be surely determined.

During 1830 and 1831, he was an officer in two other societies in which there was possibly some leaven from the Yale Band. He was a director of the Fayette County Temperance Society, formed in the autumn of 1831; and he was a member of the executive committee of the State Temperance Society, established during the winter of that year.[75] Hall was temperate, but certainly no teetotaler, and was only mildly and temporarily interested in the temperance movement.

The development of lyceums was closer to his heart

because of his concern for education in the West. Cincinnati already had a lyceum, and proponents of education there recognized Hall's leadership in Western culture by inviting him to lecture before the Cincinnati lyceum on April 23, 1831. In his address, he pleaded for the study of the natural sciences because of their suitability for general diffusion. The lecture was described with considerable justice by one Cincinnati reviewer as "elegant but illogical."[76] However, Hall returned to Vandalia kindled with enthusiasm for the lyceum movement. There, on December 8, the Illinois State Lyceum was formed with Edward Beecher as president and Hall and Edward Coles as vice-presidents. Hall was one of the committee responsible for the drafting of the constitution, which stated that the purposes of the society were to form other lyceums "in towns and populous neighborhoods" and "to collect, preserve, and disseminate authentic information" on education and on the history, climate, topography, animals, minerals, and population of Illinois. Three of the twenty original members belonged to the Yale Band, and at least two were on the faculty of Illinois College. Annual meetings were held in Jacksonville, where it was probably hoped that the members, all of whom were pledged to writing or to some other intellectual exertion, would bring scientific specimens and rare books and manuscripts to be housed at the college. At the meeting held in August, 1832, Hall, though unable to be present, was again elected vice-president. He was out of the state at the time of the third annual meeting in October, 1833, which was attended by only ten members and was probably the last.[77] One of the principal aims of the Lyceum, the formation of branches, apparently met with little success. Under Hall's influence, however, Vandalia organized its own lyceum on February 14, 1832. He was elected president and delivered the first of the proposed weekly lectures.[78]

At a public meeting in Vandalia on December 8, 1827, only nine months after becoming a resident of the town, he had proposed the formation of the Antiquarian and Historical Society of Illinois.[79] With Edward Coles, Samuel McRoberts, John M. Robinson, and A. W. Cavarly, he was chosen to write the constitution, which was adopted two days later. He was the first president of the Society and was re-elected at least once. Twenty-five lawyers and judges, nearly all of them politicians, were the original members, but some ministers and doctors were admitted later. At the State House, four annual meetings were held, at which the chief business usually consisted of hearing Hall's presidential address. The Society's first three years' proceedings were neatly printed, and Hall proudly forwarded copies to General Lafayette.[80] A British traveler visiting Vandalia in 1830 noted with amazement and premature enthusiasm that the frontier state had already produced an historical society whose minutes were published by the Hall-Blackwell press with as much regularity and propriety "as if the seat of the society had been at Oxford or Cambridge."[81] In the end, possibly nothing contributed so much to the Society's dissolution as the well-meant action of one of the most learned and faithful members, former Governor Edward Coles. At the 1829 meeting, the Society innocently adopted his motion requiring that the members put themselves to the grueling labor of compiling a history of Illinois and requesting that they report at the next meeting. To accomplish the purpose of the motion, the membership was divided into ten committees assigned to research on such subjects as the aborigines, the first settlers, the lives of important pioneers, the French colonists, and the inhabitants before the Indians. The assignment was so formidable that no one but Coles appears to have been able to perform it, for there is no record that any "historian" except him made a report at the 1830 convocation. With that meeting the organization appears to have died of its members' unwillingness to submit to the rigors of research.

XI

The Illinois Monthly Magazine

FROM 1821 to 1830, Hall's political party served as his literary patron. He was indebted to his political friends for positions that gave him a settled income and some freedom to write. And during that period he earned this profitable patronage by being a militant champion of his party.

On December 20, 1828, he was elected state treasurer for a second term of two years; the vote was almost unanimous, only two members of the legislature dissenting.[1] By action of the legislature a few weeks later, the cashiership of the Illinois State Bank was added to his duties as treasurer.[2]

Hall's purchase of a half-interest in the *Illinois Intelligencer* on January 17, 1829, a month after his election as treasurer, probably signifies that he had already decided to repay his party by supporting William Kinney (1781-1843) against John Reynolds in the approaching contest for the governorship.

The state campaign of 1830 was a bitterly-fought struggle of "ins" versus "outs"—two more or less equally ill-assorted groups of former Adams supporters, Jacksonians, and Clay men fighting for offices. Issues were, to be sure, occasionally referred to—public education, state ownership of public lands, and Jacksonianism; but, as often happened, especially in Western politics, the most fiercely debated subjects were the personalities of the candidates and their supporters. With respect to the national scene, both candidates were Jacksonians: Kinney apparently a genuine one; Reynolds at least a vacillating one. Kinney, a straightforward and loyal man, was hampered by the fact that he was a practicing clergyman.[3] However, he was a good speaker, whose discourse was "couched in rustic metaphor which often rises to the height of epigram." Had he been well educated, he would have been, one historian believes, "the most remarkable man in the Illinois of his day."[4] Reynolds, on the other hand, appears to have been a clever politician who made so many promises that, according to one of his critics, it remained for him only to pledge "that the Mississippi run upstream one half the year and downstream the other for the special benefit of the river trade." His talent was for machination; he unhesitatingly abandoned old friends no longer useful to him. He was an ineffective speaker and writer, notable for "shambling phrases" and "mental slovenliness." In short, his character was so undistinguished that Governor Ninian Edwards—who appears to have been Reynolds's chief champion and strategist—felt compelled to make public apology for supporting him.[5]

Edwards was influential in the campaign strategy of the five newspapers—three or four of them established especially for the contest—which supported Reynolds. Edwards's editorial strategy was to attack Kinney through Hall. His articles, published over fictitious names, branded Kinney as an illiterate who was willing to be governor in name with the understanding that Hall was to be governor in fact. "We cannot believe," Edwards wrote, "that any man is fit to be Governor who is ignorant of the duties of that important office, & especially one who has never acquired the rudiments of a common & english [*sic*] education, or ever mastered the simple rule of three. As such a man could not discharge the duties of the office himself, he would therefore necessarily be dependent upon someone who owed no responsibility to the public, & hence we should have 'a power behind the Throne greater than the Throne itself,' than which, nothing could be more dangerous to the rights & liberties of the people—This however, might suit Mr Hall very well, as he no doubt calculates upon being the *actual* should Mr. Kinney have the good luck to become the *nominal* Governor." [6] Edwards attempted also to drive wedges between Hall and Blackwell and between Hall and McLean, then United States Senator. *"Oh Bobby Blackwell!!!"* he wrote. "Why have you let Hall make you disgrace yourself in this ridiculous manner? It is known that you have long been tired of him. You have had good reason to be so. Cut your connection then with him, & try by your future conduct to make atonement for the past, & to regain your former standing."[7] In another article, Edwards wrote that McLean, at the time of Hall's settlement in Illinois, had seen and "pitied" Hall, had sought "to save him from absolute want & confirmed despondency," and, in befriending Hall, had "warmed into animation a viper that would sting him to death!"[8] Throughout the campaign, Hall, as the editor of the only noteworthy paper supporting Kinney, remained the outstanding target of the Reynolds party; although he was not a candidate, perhaps as much as a third or a half of the campaign literature was directed against him.[9] Near the end of the struggle, he observed, with apparent accuracy, that more evil had been spoken of him during the contest than of either of the candidates. Even the literary quality of his short story "The Captain's Lady" was brought into the dispute; and he complained that the Springfield *Courier* had had the indecency "to invade my family circle."[10]

Under this barrage, he bore himself with the aplomb of a veteran controversialist. Nearly all of his writing is level-headed and good humored, and he appears to have enjoyed the conflict. Near the close of the campaign, he wrote proudly that the *Intelligencer* had not attacked private character. He printed many letters written by his political enemies. Although publication of anonymous or pseudony-mous letters was still a newspaper custom, he said that he was willing to provide the name of the author of any letter that he had printed.

One apparent exception to his ethical conduct of the campaign was his handling of a dispute with Singleton Kimmel. Kimmel had written a letter for the *Gazette* describing Hall and his friend Samuel McRoberts (1799-1843) as "two of the same batch of broken down Circuit Judges." "I heartily despise," Kimmel continued, "this puffing, toad-eating propensity in the Ex-Judge now Editor, it is despicable in itself and unworthy a man of his station. If he must puff a man or swell a toad let him do it *decently* and not in this open barefaced style."[11] McRoberts replied with an article in the *Intelligencer* relating the story of an old prosecution of Kimmel for forgery, of which he had been acquitted. Included in the McRoberts article was a letter of Hall's stating that he as prosecutor had prepared the case against Kimmel. "I had not then," Hall concluded, "nor have I yet, the smallest doubt of Kimmel's guilt; and I was well satisfied at that time, that could I have been permitted to bring before the Court the same witnesses who had appeared before the Grand Jury, and all of whom could have been had *in a few hours,* a verdict of guilty must have been rendered." For this single descent to the level of his enemies, Hall was amply punished. In his return blow, de-livered in the Kaskaskia *Democrat,* Kimmel asserted that, fourteen years earlier, Hall had been dismissed from the army in disgrace. Hall's eight-column rejoinder revealed the intensity of the pain inflicted by Kimmel's reopening of the old wound.[12]

164

But in all this rough-and-tumble newspaper fight, Hall won at least the respect of his enemies. From his blistering castigations, Alexander Grant, editor of the *Gazette,* reeled back whimpering, "The rhapsodies of poetry-enchanted gardens . . . constitute the proper field for your intellectual exercise, and you are then harmless, at least. . . . But touch not, handle not, reputations. . . . " Referring principally to Hall, Reynolds himself pleaded, "To the virtuous people of this State, then, I appeal for protection, to shield me from the assault of this band of desperate men. . . ."[13]

At the election in August, Kinney was decisively beaten. Hall, although he had made numerous enemies among the winning candidates, still had so many friends that he was almost able to hold his office. When the House and Senate met in joint session the following winter to elect a treasurer, his opponents were unable in eight ballots to secure a majority against him, and were forced to postpone the election. Had the powerful McLean not been taken from the scene by his sudden death in the previous October, Hall might well have retained the office for another term; for the friendship between the two former partners appears to have survived Edwards's assaults.[14] But when the legislature resumed its balloting, Hall was defeated on the twelfth ballot.[15] On February 14, 1831, he was out of office.

Not satisfied, his political enemies pursued him even further. On February 16, just two days after the end of his treasurership, the Finance Committee of the House, a majority of whom were Hall's opponents,[16] reported after a preliminary investigation that there was due to the state from Hall a considerable sum in cash. The committee also demanded all the papers and notes of the state bank, of which he had been appointed cashier a week after giving bond for his second term as treasurer.[17] Just before adjournment, the House moved to put his bond in suit if all the documents and money were not delivered by April 1.

Hall replied in the *Intelligencer* three days later, on February 19, 1831:

The resolution passed by the Legislature, relative to the

accounts of the late Treasurer, is as untrue, as it is unprecedented. They have not only assumed the functions of a court of justice, in attempting to pass upon the accounts of an officer, but they have acted without the slightest shadow of evidence, and without any fact before them to justify even a suspicion. Not satisfied with turning a gentleman out of office for his political opinions, they have attempted to blast his character. The fact is, that when that resolution passed, the State Treasurer had been but two days out of office—he had paid over and accounted for sixty thousand dollars within a few days, and was busily engaged in the settlement of his accounts. The public are requested to suspend any opinion upon the circumstances for the present.

In September, however, a complaint was filed in the circuit court at Vandalia to recover ten thousand dollars from Hall and his bondsmen. At the trial on October 21, the jury rendered a judgment of $1,450.48 against them.[18] Hall appealed to the state supreme court, which six months later upheld the lower court's award, but ruled that, since the cashiership had been added to his duties after he had given bond, he and his securities were not responsible for any shortage in the funds of the state bank.[19] Meanwhile Hall, who no doubt lacked the money to pay the judgment, made an agreement, probably drafted by himself, which the legislature approved as a private law on February 26, 1833. This act provided that as soon as he had paid the sum of $1,450.48, three trustees would receive his deed "for all the real estate owned by him in this state," that they would sell it, and that they would use the proceeds to settle his accounts with the state bank.[20] Apparently the terms of the agreement were eventually carried out, for, four years later, the trustees reported that the sale of his town lots and farms had yielded $2,350.32—$899.84 more than the amount of the judgment—which they had deposited in the treasury. The legislature then discharged its Committee on Public Accounts "from the further consideration of the subject."[21] The state of Illinois appears, therefore, to have become Hall's debtor, and possibly is in his debt to this day.

The exact nature and cause of Hall's shortage, if there really was one, may never be explained. Since both the

166

bank and treasury statements presented by him at the trial are in balance, and since the auditors had not before the trial allowed him credit for certain receipts that he held, the alleged discrepancy may have been due to a disagreement over accounting methods.[22] Moreover, he had been forced to conduct the affairs of the bank without possession of its books or papers, for these had been retained by the former cashier. There is no known explanation of the deficit by either Hall or his contemporaries; however, it is worth noting that, six months before he lost the election for treasurer, his political opponent Henry Eddy wrote to another of Hall's enemies that "it is not denied but that he [Hall] makes a good officer."[23] Hall's integrity is best confirmed by the fact that, five years after the trial, when he was being considered for the cashiership of perhaps the largest bank in the West, he searched out the Illinois State Bank records in the Treasury Department in Washington and submitted them to his prospective employers, who must have been completely satisfied.[24] The prosecution of Hall and his bondsmen was no doubt motivated by the desire of the Reynolds party for revenge against his sharp pen and perhaps by a more farsighted determination to destroy his fair prospects of some day becoming governor. But whatever the motive of his opponents, his downfall was complete. On the very day of the trial against him and his bondsmen, he was obliged to defend himself in two other suits for debts of one hundred dollars each.[25] After that day, the *Intelligencer* was scanty in news and broken in spirit. On Christmas Eve, 1831, he and Blackwell were compelled to offer their press for sale; and on March 3, 1832, Hall wrote his farewell editorial for the paper they had published more than three years.[26]

II

At the same time that Hall was being turned away from Illinois politics, his ties with his family in the East were being broken. The Hall family as a group of writers had been all but wiped out by the spring of 1830. James's brother Thomas Mifflin Hall, who had enlisted as a ship's doctor, was lost at sea in 1828. John Elihu Hall died on June 12, 1829, at the age of forty-five. His mother, surviving him less than a year, died on April 8, 1830. Since James's father had died in 1826, only James's brothers Harrison and Alexander and his sister Hannah—none of whom had significant literary ambitions—were left.

The summer following Sarah Hall's death marked the beginning of the period of James's greatest devotion to writing. His awareness of his trusteeship of the family's literary reputation may be inferred from his preface to *Selections from the Writings of Mrs. Sarah Hall,* a little memorial volume of her essays and poems which he and Harrison began preparing for the press soon after her death. If we are to believe him, he was content to be temporarily out of politics, for he observed that "the flowers of literature, and the bitter fruits of party dissention, can never be made to flourish upon the same tree. . . . "[27]

As late as February, 1830, Hall planned to publish *The Western Souvenir* annually.[28] But he failed to secure enough contributions for a second volume. A man less determined to foster Western literature might have given up. But the very next month he projected the most audacious venture of his literary career—nothing less than a monthly magazine to be published on his and Blackwell's press in the backwoods hamlet of Vandalia. The modest success of the magazine was due to his own courage and energy, for he was owner, publisher, editor, and chief contributor.[29] In March, 1830, he issued his prospectus for the *Illinois Monthly Magazine.* "The object of this work," he wrote,

will be to develope the character and resources of Illinois—to furnish accurate information upon subjects connected with its present state and future prospects—to awaken and cherish a taste for literature in our new country—to advance the cause of education—and to aid and advocate every plan for the moral improvement of our population. Its pages therefore shall be devoted to the publication of well written articles, original or selected, of the following description:
Statistics of Illinois—Descriptions of Scenery, Local Peculiarities, and Characteristic Manners in the Western States. — Essays on Rural Economy. —Scientific Papers. —Notices of

the Fine and Useful Arts. —Criticisms on New Books and Pamphlets. —Periodical Essays, after the manner of Johnson, Addison and Goldsmith. —Biography. —Tales. —Literary Intelligence. —Fugitive Poetry.[30]

It is clear that Hall, living in a clearing among perhaps six hundred souls, intended nothing less than a new, Western, *Port Folio*. The remarkable thing is not the grandiosity of his prospectus, but the fact that he came at all close to fulfilling it. A less ambitious man might have been deterred by the experience of his predecessors. The three magazines significant in frontier literary history before 1830 had lived respectively one, two, and three years.[31] Hall's immediate predecessor in magazine publishing, Timothy Flint, had begun his editorial work in the enthusiastic belief that the Westerners were "a scribbling and forth-putting people. Little as they have dreamed of the fact in the Atlantic country, we have our thousand orators and poets."[32] But upon the completion of the first volume, he was writing that "it would be useless for any one, to imagine the difficulties we have had to encounter."[33] At the end of three years, he was forced to yield to the indifference of the Western public, and his magazine came to an end.

Hall, in endeavoring to foster a Western literature by founding a magazine, was quite consciously motivated by loyalty to his country and especially to the West. As he himself explained, "It would not become us to disclaim selfish motives. . . . But we are sure the desire of doing good formed a prominent feature in our plan; to elevate the character and promote the interests of Illinois . . . the home of our adoption, the land in which our affections are centered."[34] By the establishment of a magazine, he thought, "We should find our literary institutions, and character, much improved by such means, and a taste for letters might be awakened *now,* which would be permanent. Those who reflect how slight are the moral causes which sometimes give impulse to national character, will see how important it may be, that in the infancy of our society, literature should be planted as one of its institutions."[35]

His patriotism and sectional loyalty were in accord with the temper of his generation. Patriotism manifesting itself in elated expansiveness was, of course, not a new thing in America nor peculiar to the West. It had pre-Revolutionary roots, going back at least to the Princeton commencement of 1771, when Philip Freneau and Hugh Henry Brackenridge had dreamed of the day

> When Britain's sons shall spread
> Dominion to the north and south and west
> Far from th' Atlantic to Pacific shores.[36]

As the United States began the vast and rapid expansion of its territory in the early nineteenth century, the vision of Freneau and Brackenridge seemed even more likely to materialize. In 1817, James K. Paulding, a New Yorker, predicted that Kentucky, Tennessee, and Ohio would become "the parents of new states, far in the wilderness," and that "the current of emigration will continue to flow, till it reaches the shores of another Atlantic in the West."[37]

In the West itself, where the pioneers could see the very face of the country changing before their eyes, untold possibilities seemed to lie ahead. As the emigrants streamed westward in 1827, Timothy Flint exulted in the "noble" roads that were being built, the hundreds of miles of canals that were being dug, and the steamboats—"fairy structures of oriental gorgeousness and splendor"—that were "rushing down the Mississippi, as on the wings of the wind, or plowing up[stream] between the forests." "The very thought" of such magnificent canals and steamboats, he believed, "would have been rejected, as moon shine speculation at the close of the revolutionary war." Cincinnati, he predicted, "will soon be the centre of the 'celestial empire.' . . . "[38] In view of all this improvement, a writer in the *Western Monthly Review,* probably Flint himself, essayed even higher flights of optimism: "It would be a proud anticipation for a Fourth of July orator, and not without *vraisemblance,* to predict, that we shall shortly make aerial

170

voyages to the moon, and get green peas and asparagus thence every month in the year. . . ."

Such expansiveness as Flint's and Paulding's was increasingly accompanied by a widespread anti-British feeling in which democracy was glorified and outworn British monarchical forms were ridiculed. British observers in America who pointed out the rawness and crudity of American manners and institutions were answered with vituperation. The Westerners, to most of whom Jacksonianism seemed to usher in the day of the common man, were especially sensitive to British criticism. They were prone to refer to Western colleges as "flourishing universities" and to the teachers as "distinguished professors"; and they spoke in comparable or stronger terms of their other institutions. In literature, however, they must have felt some deficiency. Without granting the defect, Flint assured his readers that there was "a rough shod energy of intellect diffused over all 'Old Kentucky,' which, when properly trained, will make her as fruitful in literature, as she is now in flour and tobacco."[39] By 1830, the demands for a Western literature were numerous, and they were to swell into a chorus within the next three decades.[40]

Hall undertook the task of defining the sought-after literature. In his prospectuses for *The Western Souvenir* and the *Illinois Monthly,* in the prefaces to his books, and in his literary criticism, he indicated that its principal function must be the faithful portrayal of Western scenery and manners. In the prospectus for *The Western Souvenir* he declared that "the work will be devoted exclusively to the higher species of polite literature." He would accept in the department of historical anecdotes only those "which possess some dramatic or picturesque attraction to recommend them, and are adorned with graceful beauties of wit." But in the prospectus for the *Illinois Monthly,* although he announced that he was still seeking essays "after the manner of Johnson, Addison and Goldsmith," he emphasized that he was soliciting articles describing Western localities. Two years later, in the preface to his first volume of tales, *Legends of the West,* he wrote, "The sole intention of the

171

tales comprised in the following pages is to convey accurate descriptions of the scenery and population of the country in which the author resides. The only merit claimed for them is fidelity." The stories, he maintained, "are entirely fictitious; but they are founded upon incidents which have been witnessed by the author during a long residence in the western states, or upon traditions preserved by the people, and have received but little artificial embellishment." Three years later, in the preface to his *Tales of the Border,* he again declared, "Although the garb of fiction has been assumed, as that which would afford the greatest freedom of description, the incidents which are related in these and other tales of the author are mostly such as have occurred; and he has only exercised his own invention in framing the plots, so as to bring together, in one sketch, the adventures which may not have occurred in the connection in which he has chosen to place them, or which may have happened to different individuals. In the descriptions of scenery he has not, in any instance, intentionally departed from nature, or exercised his own fancy in the creation of a landscape, or in the exaggeration of the features which he has attempted to draw. . . . "

In a critical notice, Hall praised Cooper's *The Pioneers* because "it abounds in fine description, and in correct delineations of American manners and scenery." But Cooper's *The Prairie,* he thought, "is a complete failure. Admirable as some of the scenes are, it was evidently written by one who had never seen *a prairie,* and had no knowledge of life as it is exhibited on the western frontier. The plot is improbable—we might say *impossible.* The language which is put into the mouths of the speakers, is not that of the western people, nor any thing like it; and the whole work wants that quality which English critics affectedly term *verisimilitude,* but which those who write in the English language, call *truth.*"[41]

By 1833, he had worked out, on the same principles, a definition of a national literature. "Our national literature," he observed, "according to the Dutch sage, is to be based upon 'stupendous mountains,' magnificent rivers, in-

172

terminable plains, 'a sun placed in a sky without a shadow, and without a cloud;' thunder, lightning, whirlwinds; and in short, the sublime and beautiful of nature. This we do not think. Even if there be more of the sublime and beautiful in America than elsewhere, it differs only in quantity, not in kind, from that of other lands; and the poets and writers of past times, have occupied, as it seems to us, the whole ground of natural description; for their portraitures are sufficiently caricatured to cover our reality; and if we go beyond them, we are absurd. Our national literature will rest upon our national character—upon our peculiar history, cultivation, and *moral* scenery, if such an expression is intelligible."[42]

The first number of the *Illinois Monthly* appeared in October, 1830. It was the West's only magazine, Flint's *Western Monthly Review* having expired the previous June. The new forty-eight-page journal was nearly, if not quite, as attractive as if it had been printed in Philadelphia rather than in a backwoods village. But it was never financially successful. At the end of its first year, Hall calculated, "The number of dollars actually received for that volume [the first], has not equalled the number of pages written for it, and of course has fallen far short of the expenses; thus making our own labor entirely gratuitous."[43] The income for the first year, then, was less than $576; and fewer than two hundred subscriptions had been paid for by the end of the year. The high paper costs incurred by long shipments by boat and wagon were in part offset by low publication costs in Vandalia. The *Illinois Monthly* may be regarded, therefore, as a moderately expensive luxury, a drain upon Hall's income from the treasurership and, later, from his private practice of law.

Even more distressing was the drain upon his energies. Once he fretted, "To be forced to write at all times, whether in the humour or not, is a hard task; but it is one which may be, and often is accomplished." Upon the completion of the first volume of the magazine, he complained, "The greatest obstacle to success has been found in the want of literary assistance; of the 576 pages . . . 350 have been

173

written by the editor, a very few have been contributed by two or three friends who have had the kindness to assist us occasionally, and the remainder have been selected."[44] This statement was perhaps less than just to his literary friends. Actually, a score of contributors had written about a hundred pages for the first volume.[45] The second year he had more aid; he selected more from other periodicals and wrote less himself. During the two years of the magazine's existence, twenty-eight writers, all Westerners, supported him, although only seven of them wrote three or more pieces.

Only five of the known contributors lived in Illinois, and only one of these—John Russell (1793-1863), a graduate of Middlebury College in the class of 1818 and a teacher in the Vandalia High School—had his home in Vandalia.[46] Others residing in the state were Thomas Lippincott (1791-1869)[47] and Arthur Bryant (born in 1803), one of William Cullen Bryant's younger brothers who had settled in Illinois.

Three contributors, Mrs. Anna P. Dinnies, her husband, John Dinnies, and the unidentified "Kelpie," lived in St. Louis. The writer living farthest west was J. Ormrod, of Boonville, Missouri, who sent to Hall from this lonely outpost 280 miles west of St. Louis "An Essay on the Sources of Genius," a remarkably learned article for the time.[48]

Fourteen of the *Illinois Monthly's* authors lived in Cincinnati, but only four of these were natives of the West. Among the latter were Morgan Neville, who had moved to the city about 1824, and Kentucky-born Benjamin Drake (1795-1841), a lawyer and the editor of the weekly *Cincinnati Chronicle and Literary Gazette*. Noteworthy Cincinnati contributors born in the East were James Handasyd Perkins; Frederick W. Thomas, later Poe's friend and correspondent; Gouverneur Morris (born in 1813),[49] nineteen-year-old son of his Revolutionary namesake; Salmon Portland Chase, a Dartmouth graduate destined to become Secretary of the Treasury under Lincoln; Timothy Walker, a lawyer who had been graduated from Harvard in 1826 as a first scholar; Hugh Peters (1807-1831),[50] of the Yale class of 1826, whose poetic promise was frustrated by his early death in 1831; and Isaac Appleton Jewett (1808-

1853), a graduate of Harvard in the class just below that of Oliver Wendell Holmes. Most of these men in the Cincinnati group were lawyers or law students. None of them was a professional writer.

The narratives by Perkins and Russell in the *Illinois Monthly* are undistinguished, but Neville's "Reminiscence of Pittsburgh" and "Reminiscence of the Scioto Valley"[51] have some appeal because of their apparent fidelity to history. Only an occasional poem in the magazine impresses the reader. One, "A Sketch,"[52] is fresh with views of the rivers, meadows, and wild flowers of the prairie, and is probably the work of John Howard Bryant (1809-1902), another of William Cullen Bryant's Illinois brothers. The descriptive essays, such as Perkins's praiseworthy history of his city, and "Porcellian Speculations," by Isaac Appleton Jewett, an article demonstrating an observer's knowledge of the pork-packing industry in Cincinnati, helped fulfil Hall's aim for the magazine.[53] Salmon Portland Chase's essay, "The State of the South,"[54] is a prophetic analysis of the conflict between the South and the North which, it is interesting to consider, was possibly read by the twenty-three-year-old Abraham Lincoln, whose home was then at New Salem.

It was, however, Hall's writing—constituting three-fifths of the first volume and half of the second—that gave the *Illinois Monthly* its distinctive Western character. Almost invariably his theme was the West; and it probably can be said more truly of him than of any other of the magazine's authors that he wrote not as an Easterner away from home but as a cultural pioneer in a region rich with promise.

III

There can be little doubt that, in "The Cottage," a poem printed in the *Illinois Monthly* for February, 1832, Hall was describing his and Mary's Vandalia home, where he appears to have done much of his writing:

175

The cottage by the prairie side, that dearest spot on earth,
Where cheerfulness and happy love sit smiling by the hearth,
Where brightest flowers bloom around, and cares nor crowds
    intrude,
With discord, or unhallowed mirth, to mar the solitude. . . .

Here rested first the blooming bride, whose heart confessed her
    mine;
The rose and vine our hands have trained, here sweetly intertwine;
The rose shall fade, the vine shall droop, the autumn sun shall sear
The verdant leaf with yellow tinge, on each revolving year;
But love, within its own blest home, smiles brightly as before,
Though penury, with haggard scowl, sits frowning at the door. . . .

Five months after these verses were printed, he forgot
his fears of failure long enough to write another idyllic
description of his situation as a village author. The forest
trees still grew along the village streets, he noted; and the
solitude of the country was all around him.

"Here we are seated in the hot month of July, at a south
window, which the morning sun has not yet reached. The
green and wooded slope of a hill is before us. A merry
colony of martins are chirping in their box, or whirling
swiftly and playfully about in the air. The bees are plying
their labor with industrious wing, as if determined to take
advantage of the pleasant coolness of the morning, while
their hum, mingling with other sounds, falls pleasantly on
the ear. There is a delicious calmness and fragrance in the
atmosphere; a gentle breeze, that barely ruffles the boughs,
comes wafted over broad plains, bringing no odor but that
of the wild flower. . . . A troop of children are trotting
by, to school . . . as clean as if it was Sunday morning,
and as happy as if it was Saturday afternoon. A distant
bell is heard at intervals, so indistinctly as scarcely to be
distinguished, yet mingling its tones so harmoniously with
the other notes that murmur almost inaudibly in the air,
that a real poet would be inspired—or lulled to sleep,—by
the gentle symphony."[55]

176

JAMES HALL

From a Portrait Owned by

Mrs. Elmer J. Rodenberg

Yet there was intellectual loneliness in his life as a frontier writer. Once asking his mother to correct a familiar quotation in a manuscript he had sent to her, he explained, "On such occasions I have no books to refer to." Like many other authors, he realized that good writing is in large part produced by the interplay of keen, well-stocked minds, and felt especially a need for a kind of advice which correspondence alone can not quite provide. "I am no judge of my own writings," he wrote to her on September 25, 1826, "and as I never hear of them except from you, who are of course partial—I often doubt whether their worth will be such as will warrant a further emission. These doubts create a depression which often induces me to throw aside my pen, for many days together. I am like a man shooting in the dark—I know that I expend a vast deal of ammunition, and that my gun cracks most excellently in my own ears, but am ignorant whether any execution is done—even the echo is lost in the vast distance. This is the disadvantage of writing from the insulated seclusion in which I live, works to be read in circles of which I seldom hear. My novel therefore goes on slowly."

He no doubt found compensations for this kind of loneliness. One was a relaxed mind engendered by a congenial family life. "I have been a light hearted and joyous person," he wrote in a summary of his life at the age of sixty-two.[56] After his death, his daughter Sarah also remembered his "rich fund of humor, that carried him through and raised him above all difficulties." Yet his gaiety was far from continuous frivolity. In the army and on the frontier judicial circuit, where one's dignity was constantly probed and threatened, he had conducted himself with an aplomb that commanded more than the respect usually accorded to dress and position. Joyous as he was, he could assume upon need a face of authority. In 1855, he himself noticed a stern cast in his face revealed by a daguerrotype that he sent to Evert Duyckinck and granted that it made him look like "an old revolutionary major." Disturbed by what the likeness had shown, he blamed the squinting necessitated by the photographer's intense light and said that the photograph would have to do, but he added that the picture did not present "the habitual expression of my countenance."[57] Perhaps his face revealed that he was quite without fear. His daughter observed that "he was the very coolest man in time of danger, or in any emergency that I have ever seen."[58]

It is true that in her letter to her parents written ten years after her marriage, Mary Hall referred to her husband as "Mr. Hall," and in his letters to close relatives he signed himself—as was not always the rule in intimate letters of the period—as James Hall. But the text of his letters to his friends is unfailingly amiable; and in those to his immediate family, solicitous and affectionate. Writing once to his mother that he was not sanguine about his chance of obtaining a political office, he added, "Nor indeed do I care much for any thing except it is to hear that you are all well, to enjoy my own fire-side and to bask in the smiles of my own Mary."[59] In 1830, he and Mary had three children— Sarah, six; John Posey, four; and Lucy Frances, two. With them he was gentle. "I never knew him to be so busy," Sarah remembered, "no matter what his occupation, and no matter how hurried he might be, as not to turn to one of his own little children kindly, patiently, courteously, to answer any of their questions, if they were ever so foreign to the subject of his thoughts."[60]

IV

His sixteen poems in the *Illinois Monthly* demonstrate an improved craftmanship learned, in some instances, from famous poems of his period. The mood and stanzaic form of "The Capuchin" apparently have a model in "The Rime of the Ancient Mariner," as does "The Crusader" in Coleridge's "Christabel." "The Indian Wife's Lament" and "The Isle of the Yellow Sands" are renderings in anapestic quatrains of legends of northern Indians, but in these poems the characters are as much Scott's border people as they are American aborigines.[61] The graceful pleasantry of the fourth stanza of "The Serenade" is, perhaps, a fair example of his skill during this period:

Moonlight nights were never made
To be lost in sleeping;
Who, when skies are thus arrayed,
Lighted for a serenade,
Would to bed be creeping?[62]

In his criticism, Hall is at the same time strengthened and severely limited by his strong patriotic and moralistic bias. With the citation of an overwhelmingly long list of American works, he refuted, in the issue for April, 1831, the London *Monthly Review's* assertion that the United States had "no history worth reading, not a canto of poetry, no memoirs, no collections of speeches, no miscellaneous works of amusement, very few travels, and not even a single good sermon."[63] He was irritated by his country's booksellers who smacked their lips "on the arrival of a fresh importation from the vintage of English bards and Scotch reviewers. . . . " "We are determined," he vowed, "to be no longer accessory to this suicidal neglect of our ingenious selves; we will no longer be tame spectators of our country's dishonour, but will on every suitable occasion, vindicate the claims of our 'talented' fellow citizens."[64] American writers and thinkers, he believed, should call a convention in which they "must agree to be no longer ashamed of each other's company."[65] Nearly all of his reviews dealt with the work of his countrymen and usually of his contemporaries.

Western authors almost always received his sympathetic consideration. Though he thought that the love story of Timothy Flint's novel *Francis Berrian* was "not worth a farthing; and we would advise all young ladies and gentlemen, who are connoisseurs in such matters, to pass it by . . . ," he gave high praise to "the descriptive and didactic parts." He remarked that, "as a describer of nature, he [Flint] has few equals. Few can sketch out with so masterly a hand, the gorgeous scenery of our western solitudes. He has the heart, and the eye, of the poet, for the beauties of the mountain, the forest, and the stream, and for the sublimities of the cataract and the storm." *The Shoshonee*

Valley, he observed tactfully, "has its defects, too, we dare say; but we leave the task of pointing these out, to those who may choose to take the trouble; being satisfied that if Mr. Flint has his faults as a writer, he has many excellent qualities to redeem them, and that his industry, his genius, and his zeal in the cause of letters, entitle him to the cordial support of the literary and the patriotic."[66] *A History of Literature* by Wilkins Tannehill, of Nashville, Tennessee, Hall observed, "is a work of great research, and is written in a style of classical purity, which speaks highly of the scholarship of its author."[67] He quoted generously from Benjamin Drake's address delivered before the Erodelphian Society of Miami University in 1831, and gave Drake credit, perhaps with some caution, for being "one of our most assiduous writers. His labors in the cause of literature have been considerable; but have been as unassuming as they are valuable."[68]

Hall demonstrated his stature as a critic of our national literature by being the first to notice the artistry of Hawthorne's short stories. His praise for the New England writer appeared in a remarkable review of *The Token* and *The Atlantic Souvenir* for 1832.[69] The stories in the two annuals were almost entirely the work of Eastern writers, Hall's own meritorious story, "My Cousin Lucy and the Village Teacher," being the only exception. In his review, however, Hall rose completely above sectionalism and self-interest. The two annuals, he thought, did not present "any favorable evidence of the state of our literature. They each contain articles written with elegance and power, but they contain also a vast deal that is very insipid." "The general character of the writing in both these volumes," he believed, "is dull, stately, and artificial." He indicated that the terror novel was not a salutary influence upon American fiction. In the two annuals he detected "a propensity for the meloncholy and the horrible—for tales that, as the young ladies say, end badly, which, in our opinion, is the result of perverted judgment. . . . It is marvellous to us, that any one should think of covering sorrowful tales, fit only for the nursery, under a beautiful exterior of embossed morocco!

Yet a great portion of these volumes, is as direful as Monk Lewis's tales of wonder and as stately as the Dutch Maiden in her stays!"

Had propriety and modesty permitted, Hall might, in justice to himself, have pointed out the merits of his own heart-stirring story "My Cousin Lucy and the Village Teacher." Instead, he mentioned, as exceptions to his criticism, a tale of Godfrey Wallace, two narratives by Paulding, and two anonymous stories now known as the work of Hawthorne, who was not to reveal his authorship until their publication in *Twice-Told Tales* in 1837. Hawthorne's two tales may have been somewhat hard to classify, for they leave the reader, if not melancholy, at least thoughtful. Nevertheless, he reserved for them the only extended praise, brief as it was, in his review. "The 'Wives of the Dead,' in the Token," he wrote, "though pathetic, has a touch of nature about it which goes to the heart, and a spirit which awakens interest. 'My Kinsman, Major Molineux,' is well told." This praise came when Hawthorne was most in need of it. After his graduation from Bowdoin, he had gone to his home in Salem a year before Hall had moved to Vandalia. More single-purposed than Hall, he had dedicated himself to learning the craft of writing. It was a trying period in his life, lasting twelve years. In his "lonely chamber" in Salem, as he later wrote to Sophia Peabody, he had sat year after year, hoping for recognition and sometimes experiencing a chill and numbness suggestive of the grave.[70] There is no evidence that Hawthorne ever heard of Hall's praise. It is interesting to conjecture that, if he had learned of it and had responded with an offer of anything approaching a literary alliance, the *Illinois Monthly* and its successor, the *Western Monthly*, might have become more national in character and have had even a more notable history than they did have. As it was, Hawthorne, apparently unaware of Hall's commendation, had to wait four years longer for the recognition he was seeking. Then, in what has heretofore been believed the first public notice of his tales, Park Benjamin published a half sentence of approval in the *New-England Magazine*.[71]

Hall's religion was fundamentalist, his morals somewhat puritan. The Bible, he asserted, contained "no historical misstatement, no false philosophy, nor any absurd reasoning," and Moses' writings were inspired "in direct sensible communications from the Deity."[72] He believed that Robert Owen, founder of the socialistic colony at New Harmony, Indiana, by destroying faith in the Bible, had trampled down the safeguards of virtue and the hopes of immortality and substituted nothing in their stead. Frances Wright's doctrines were to him "unsocial," and he described both her and Owen as "adventurers."[73]

"You ask why I tell you nothing about Mr Owen & his Harmonites—" he wrote in 1826. "Truly my dear mother, because I think Mr O. and his atheism, and Social system, and tag rag and bob tail of a society not worth any body's attention. Such a motley crew of bankrupts, vagabonds, and idlers, was never collected since the gathering at the cave of Abdulam—Mr Owen lectures them against government and religion, & M^r [Robert L.] Jennings his sub lecturer declaims against *mariage* [*sic*] and all such tyranical [*sic*] institutions as restrain people from obeying the dictates of nature—they have dances and concerts & military shews, and the girls wear pantaloons, Grecian drapes as they call [them], to shew their contempt of vulgar customs. It won't do. They are already quarelling among themselves and those of the Society who have young wives or pretty daughters, are prudently taking their leave of the Social System & Mr Owen. And yet Owen when he first came here enlisted the feelings of all good men on his side, and his friends say that those abuses which I have noticed are corruptions which crept in, in his absence, and which he is now determined to eradicate. This may be so—like many other anti-religious system makers, he is strictly moral in his own conduct—but it requires no great discernment to see that these abuses naturally grow out of his system—and of any system which rejects revelation, and contemns the civil regulations of society."[74]

Hall admitted that Fielding and Smollett "were men of genius," and that their works may be accurate pictures of

182

English society as far as they go, but, if so, they leave out, he thought, "all that was worth relating." "We cannot believe," he added, "that any man of delicacy ever read their novels without disgust, and we should be sorry to accuse any lady of having read them at all."[75] Yet he berated the prettiness of the annuals, their tinsel ornaments, their mawkish love stories, and their interminable succession of pictures "of pretty little boys and girls, with curly locks and bulbous cheeks! in naked beauty, or in phantastical apparel."[76] He pointed out the pitfall of imitating "bad foreign models" and upheld simplicity of style and fidelity to nature. "To adopt the fashionable style which prevails at present in the periodical writing of Great Britain," he declared, "would be to discard truth and nature, and array our literature in a foreign garb, which is only tolerable to those to whom it has become familiar."[77]

Although, as a conscious and dedicated proponent of Western literature, Hall wrote and fostered stories, poems, and critical articles, he was careful to provide his readers with a robust diet of solid information about the West. During the first half of the nineteenth century, the hunger for knowledge of the frontier was intense and world-wide. "There is no region of the earth respecting which accurate information is so eagerly sought," wrote the projectors of a new literary work in Cincinnati.[78] The need was met in part by practical guides for the traveler. Cramer's *The Navigator,* for instance, detailed for the river emigrant the channel of every mile of the Ohio. Descriptions of the frontier regions were written by travelers from the major countries of Europe; those written by British travelers alone constitute a voluminous literature.

In his *Illinois Monthly* articles concerned with the description, history, and improvement of the West, Hall sought to satisfy this craving for trustworthy intelligence. Almost none of his poems, reviews, or stories in the magazine was without some exposition or description of the West. His major work of a purely descriptive nature was "Notes on Illinois," a series of nine articles on the "Geology," "Surface," "Soil and Productions," "Timber," "Wild

Animals," "Constitution," "Laws," "Public Officers," and "French Settlements" of the state. He also wrote brief accounts of the new villages of Quincy and Danville and a vivid description of Vandalia.[79] He recorded encouragingly the progress of steamboats, canals, railroads, and agriculture as well as the signs of cultural growth. He wrote valuable biographical notes on Daniel Boone, Jo Daviess, and Jedediah Strong Smith.[80] His biographical sketch of his friend and war comrade Thomas Biddle and his "Reminiscence of the Last War" are significant documents in the history of the Niagara Campaign. The former, written just after Biddle's death in a bloody duel near St. Louis in 1831, is also a grim commentary on the fierceness of Western political feuds.[81]

His series of four articles "On the Intercourse of the American People with the Indians,"[82] shows his enthusiasm for the diffusion of knowledge, "like the solar light," throughout the whole of American society, not excluding the Indian. He warned, "The march of the mind will never penetrate into our forests, by the beat of the drum, nor will civilization be transmitted in bales of scarlet cloth and glass beads."[83] He would first force a cessation of the Indians' intertribal wars and then remove the causes of their perpetual hunger. "It is useless," he declared, "to attempt to operate on the mind, while the body is in a state of suffering."[84] "Let the Indians be settled in fixed residences, be secure, and begin to own property, and the rest will follow as certainly as cause and effect."[85] His humanitarianism must have seemed naive to those who approved of the brutal butchery of helpless Indian women and children in the Black Hawk War, which broke out a year after his series on Indian-white relations.

To read the *Illinois Monthly* articles favoring education is to be reminded that the achievement of a public school system in America was a democratic triumph. The most eloquent of the magazine's discourses on the question are "A Few Thoughts on Education" and "The General Diffusion of Knowledge."[86] By content and style, the first appears to be Hall's writing; the second certainly is. The author argued that education is necessary for national greatness; democracy, he emphasized, is unattainable without it.

> The rich man *will* educate his son, and if a school is not provided at his door, he is able to send him to a distance; while the poor man, who cannot send his child to an expensive boarding school, must be content to keep him at home in ignorance. Here, then, will be two classes of society, and all the odious features, and miserable distinctions, of aristocracy will be engrafted upon our free institutions. The only way to avoid these evils is, to have the education of the youth conducted under the direction of the state. . . . . [87]

The aims of the proponents of popular learning were clearly stated:

> The friends of education will never be satisfied, until every neighborhood shall have its school, at which all the children of the republic shall be educated, under the public care, and all shall be taught alike. We may talk of equality of rights, but this equality cannot exist, until the methods of acquiring knowledge, shall be brought within the reach of all, and the child of the poorest man, receive the same education as that of his wealthy neighbor—until the door of the schoolhouse, like that of the church, shall be open to all, and the blessings of education be disseminated as widely as the protection of law, and the principles of liberty.[88]

He declared, "Talents are not hereditary; they belong to no rank; and are as often found in the cottage of the husbandman, as in the palace of the proud aristocrat. The only difference is in the cultivation, and the opportunity."[89] He pleaded for simple expositions of scientific matter for the plain people.[90] In "Children's Books," in the June, 1831, issue of the magazine, he compiled a critical list of works for the education of children at home and urged writers to increase the production of books in simple language.

In the issue of March, 1831, he proposed that the intellectuals of the West meet in Cincinnati in the autumn of that year for a conference on education.[91] His summons was probably influential in the organization there the next year of the Western Literary Institute and College of Professional Teachers. He later was to become, for a time, a leader in the Institute,[92] which, by 1840, had auxiliary organizations in seventeen states and two territories.[93] In Vandalia, on February 13, 1833, he was the principal speaker at a meeting which organized the Illinois Institute on Education.[94] Illinois had to wait a generation for a public school system to be securely written into the constitution, but the Sunday schools that Hall encouraged as makeshifts were widespread in the state by 1833, and the lyceums in Vandalia and St. Louis were established by that year. Throughout the period of his residence in Illinois, he was the state's most powerful advocate of education.

Unlike other expansionists, he emphasized the extension of culture and dreamed of an American empire of enlightenment extending to the Pacific. In "Columbia River," in the number for January, 1832, he concluded his description of the fabulous wealth of the Oregon country with an enunciation of the doctrine of "manifest destiny," preceding by thirteen years John L. O'Sullivan's coining of the phrase:

Westward is the march of our power. Our population is spreading gradually towards the Rocky Mountains, with a force like that of an inundation, which can neither be directed nor repressed. Over these barriers it must go. It will carry with it our liberty, our laws, our language, our civilization, our religion. The college, the court-house, and the church, will adorn the shores of the Pacific. The toll of the bell will be heard over the silent lake, where the hunter now lurks for his prey. Then will a cultivated, a free, and a christian people, extend the salutary influence of their institutions over a whole continent, and no barrier less powerful than oceans restrain the expansion of a population, whose liberty is chastened by virtue, and whose industry is directed by intelligence.[95]

V

Twelve of Hall's short stories were published in the *Illinois Monthly,* and by the end of 1832, he had produced for *The Western Souvenir,* for other annuals, and for the magazine, twenty-five tales upon which his reputation as a story-teller chiefly rests. He gathered nearly all of these into two volumes: *Legends of the West,* published by his brother Harrison in the late summer of 1832; and *The Soldier's Bride and Other Tales,* published the following spring by Key and Biddle of Philadelphia.

As a writer of fiction, Hall was, for his time, unusually dedicated to "fidelity." As he stated in his preface to *Legends of the West,* his sole intention was "to convey accurate descriptions of the scenery and population of the country in which the author resides" or had resided. The scenes of "Empty Pockets," "The Captain's Lady," "The Dentist," and "My Cousin Lucy and the Village Teacher" are laid in the East. The last of these, probably modeled upon country-school experiences of Hall's own boyhood in Maryland, is a serious attempt to portray the painful jealousy of an adolescent boy who is hopelessly in love with a much older girl.

"Adventure of a Ranger" and "A Frontier Scene" are intended to recount factual Western episodes of an earlier period: the former, a Vandalia neighbor's experience in a battle with Indians in the War of 1812; and the latter, a fist fight between Daniel Morgan (later General Morgan) and a wagoner. "The Barrack-Master's Daughter" is a light love story related against the background of Colonel Scott's disastrous campaign against Fort Du Quesne in 1758. "Michel De Coucy" and "A Legend of Carondelet" depict the eighteenth-century French colonists in their settlements on the Mississippi. In these stories, Hall's close observation, obviously based upon careful study of the ruins,[96] results in a vivid picture of Fort Chartres and the villages Carondelet and Prairie de Rocher; and his use of dialect is effective in portraying the healthy, easy-going, and democratic French residents. "Michel De Coucy," the better of the two tales, reveals Hall's legal cleverness in devising a way for Captain De Val and the French priest to outwit a money-lender living in Spanish territory on the western bank of the Mississippi. In order to include the capture of a girl by the Indians, Hall also set "The Backwoodsman" in the previous century, but the description of the camp meeting in the story was probably drawn from one he had attended.

In most of his stories, Hall, faithful to his definition of a Western literature, portrayed his contemporary West. By intimate association he had learned to regard his fellow frontiersmen with esteem as well as affection. They stalk through his pages in rich variety—swapping their property, drunkenly cavorting in court-day crowds, drifting on flat-boats, pushing through forest traces to their new homes, worshiping at camp meetings, waiting in doctors' offices, fearfully watching prairie fires, conducting elections, or ferrying across rivers. There is Zedekiah Bangs, in "The Divining Rod," a traveling preacher scornful of pay for his services and distrustful of "school larning" and mechanical improvements. Bangs's friend Tom Johnson is a reformed gambler and horse racer. Logan, in "The Emigrants," was trained for the law in the best schools of Kentucky. In "The Philadelphia Dun," a drunken Tennesseean gallops his horse back and forth through a village and brags to a crowd of court followers: "All the time he was ranting and roaring in praise of himself, his horse, and the United States of America. He boasted that he was born in the woods, rocked in a sugar trough, and suckled by a buffalo; that he could tote a steamboat, and out-run a streak of lightning; that his wife was as handsome as a pet fawn, and his children *real roarers*."[97] Dr. Jeremy Geode, of "The Seventh Son," a story playing hard upon the frontier faith in seventh-son doctors, has few patients until he proclaims himself the seventh son of a celebrated Indian doctor and the possessor of the secret Hygeian Tablet or Kickapoo Panacea. Timothy Tompkinson, a quack doctor in "A Legend of Carondelet," builds a wheel which, upon being spun, registers the disease and its remedy. The characters of "The Silver Mine"—Uncle Mose, the trader; the French ferryman at St. Charles on the Missouri; and the post-master with his whole office in his hat—all move so convincingly that this is one of the most real of Hall's narratives.

Sometimes, perhaps at the expense of "fidelity," Hall was

fond of setting off his frontiersmen against unmanly products of older cultures. The quiet competence of Wilkinson in "The Village Musician" is enhanced by contrast with the inadequacy of Johnny Vanderbocker, of Herkimer, New York. Dandies bred in Philadelphia are easily worsted in matches of wits with backwoodsmen in "The Philadelphia Dun" and "The Useful Man." Logan's self-reliance and liberality are conspicuous in contrast with the stubborn narrowness of the Londoner in "The Emigrants."

Again, as might be expected from his comment on the works of Fielding and Smollett, his concern for propriety sometimes limited his selection of incidents and warped his treatment of them. Although he once wrote that the legal profession "above all others, opens to its members familiar views of the whole organization of society, and of much of all that passes in the business and bosoms of men,"[98] in his stories he rarely developed situations involving ugly emotions. He neglected some unattractive aspects of frontier life, such as the gross excesses of some camp meetings.[99] One may also point out instances of a lack of verisimilitude: the too-quickly accumulated fortune of Wilkinson in "The Village Musician"; the resetting of natural teeth in "The Dentist"; and the death scene in "The Missionaries," in which the spirit of the dying mother already "had begun to assume its celestial character." In some instances his backwoodsmen, after speaking a few phrases in their vernacular, fall into educated speech. Although his prose is often remarkable for grace and charm, his elegant, literary style in narratives of crude frontiersmen like Pete Featherton is sometimes grotesquely incongruous, however effective it may have been in portraying the romantic scenery of the West.

Yet the publication of these twenty-five stories was an important milestone in the development of the American short story. Hall's use of native materials set a wholesome example when the craft was still young in this country. In 1832, Irving was America's only acknowledged classic writer of short narratives; Poe's first short story was published in that year, and Hawthorne's only two years earlier. Irving, author of four volumes of tales, returned from Europe in that year to find the West "the subject of engrossing interest"[100] which Hall had done much to create.[101] That same year Irving started on his Western journey and early in the next year began to write *A Tour of the Prairies*.[102] Meanwhile, the popularity of Hall's *Legends of the West* evoked a second edition in 1833. By 1885, at least eight editions had been printed.

Unquestionably Hall, by demonstrating that rich narrative veins could be exploited through careful observation and recording of distinctive regional characteristics, was, after Irving—who, indeed, had no competitors—the next most significant of the American short story writers who published a large number of tales between 1820 and 1832. His "The Bachelor's Elysium" appeared in the *Port Folio* six years before William Leggett's "The Rifle," which has been considered the first story to call the attention of the East to the frontier as a background for tales, and he was the first to publish a body of Western stories in a single volume.[103] Among Western writers of short fiction of the period, he was supreme. But there were not, it appears, more than fourteen American authors besides Irving who produced a volume of short stories between 1820 and 1832, and only three of these can be regarded as Western writers.[104] The American short story, still in the process of its evolution out of the character sketch, was then in its awkward age. Generally, the authors tended to emphasize incident rather than character. With rare exceptions, they were unable to achieve the structure or the dramatic effect which we now expect. Moreover, they felt compelled to clothe their productions in an ornate, formal language. It was a period of gorgeous prose.[105]

These criticisms may be fairly made of the work of Catherine Maria Sedgwick and James Kirke Paulding, whom Fred Lewis Pattee regarded as the two authors, next to Irving, "of most import to the readers of the decade."[106] In addition to the general faults of the tales of the period, Miss Sedgwick's stories—for example "The Country Cousin" and "The Catholic Iroquois"—are infused with a kind of irritating moralization which Hall was usually able to avoid. Paulding's "The Little Dutch Sentinel of the Manhadoes" is unconvincing, and the events of "The Ghost" are incredible. His "The Azure Hose" and "The Politician" are marked by a didacticism rare in Hall's narratives. Both Paulding and Miss Sedgwick could have profited by attention to Hall's characterizations and to his fidelity to nature. And Hall had a better sense than either of them of the singleness of effect which it is the function of the story to create.

The decisive weakness in Hall's work—the common weakness of the period—is in the technique. In "The Backwoodsman," he wrote ten pages of description of the frontier before he introduced a character. Praiseworthy as the portrait of the genteel London shopkeeper is in "The Emigrants," the story is almost as much an emigrants' guide for living in the Western woods and prairies as a presentation of the kind of conflict that creates dramatic effect. But some of Hall's stories are relatively free of these faults. In spite of the fact that most of his heroines lack individuality,[107] his chief strength is in the diversity and reality of his characterizations of frontiersmen. In "The Divining Rod," a skillful portrait of an "ignorant and illiterate" frontier preacher, he develops an interesting conflict between the evangelist's hatred of trappings and his desire for wealth. He allows the events of the narrative to develop the character and reveals a certain expertness in the use of dialogue.

During the decade after the appearance of *The Western Souvenir,* several volumes of short fiction about frontiersmen, a large proportion of them influenced by Hall's stories, issued from the press. Less than a year after the publication of the *Souvenir,* William Leggett published *Tales and Sketches by a Country Schoolmaster* (1829), a collection of ten stories, of which three were Western tales. His work is marked by theatrically stilted dialogue and vague settings; and in each of the three Western narratives, the hero, accused of murder upon apparently overwhelming circumstantial evidence, is saved from hanging by new testimony rushed to the magistrates at the last moment. Within a few months of the publication of Leggett's volume, William Joseph Snelling published *Tales of the Northwest; or, Sketches of Indian Life and Character* (1830). His knowledge of Indians appears to have been gained chiefly from his association with them on the Northwestern frontier, though he did use Hall's *Illinois Intelligencer* account of the Indian hater John Moredock.[108] Snelling's portraits of aborigines, unlike Hall's Indian poems and some of his later Indian stories, are remarkably free from sentimentality, and his style is less self-conscious than Hall's, although his narratives show a grievous lack of form. Some of the sketches by Hall's friend Benjamin Drake, in *Tales of the Queen City* (1838), though undramatic, are notable for the precision with which the backgrounds and some of the characters are drawn. Drake had read Hall, and, in "The Novice of Cahokia," turned to the colonial French settlements on the Mississippi as a scene for romance, as Hall had done eleven years earlier in "The French Village." Charles Fenno Hoffman's "The Dead Clearing," a story in his *Wild Scenes in the Forest and Prairie* (1839), follows the pattern of Hall's Indian-hater relations,[109] just as the quack doctor in Hoffman's "The Major's Story" is reminiscent of Timothy Tompkinson in Hall's "A Legend of Carondelet."

In the South, also, about the time Hall was winning a place for himself as an exponent of Western life and character, a regionalistic literature was springing up. Four years after the publication of *The Western Souvenir*, John Pendleton Kennedy published *Swallow Barn* (1832), regarded by Jay B. Hubbell as "the first important fictional treatment of Virginia life." This series of sunny sketches of the life of two families of planters manifestly bears a strong resemblance to Irving's *Bracebridge Hall*. But one of Kennedy's minor characters, Mike Brown—who, fortified with substantial drafts of whisky taken at the village tavern, went home in the snow and had an encounter with the devil—bears a striking similarity to Hall's somewhat earlier Pete Featherton.[110] With a broader view of society than that presented in *Swallow Barn,* Augustus Baldwin Longstreet began, about 1832, to write his earthy narratives of life on the Georgia frontier. Published first in Georgia newspapers, the series was later collected in *Georgia Scenes* (1835).[111] Pete Featherton seems to turn up again in Longstreet's "The Horse-Swap" as a backwoodsman named Yellow Blossom. Yellow Blossom has all, or almost all, of the ebullition of the "cavorter" or "Ring-tail Roarer" whom Hall was apparently the first to describe in American fiction.[112] A boaster like Pete Featherton and the cavorter in Hall's "The Philadelphia Dun," he "galloped this way, then that, and then the other; spurred his horse to one group of citizens, then to another; then dashed off at half-speed, as if fleeing from danger; and, suddenly checking his horse, returned first in a pace, then in a trot, and then in a canter. [He] . . . fetched a whoop, and swore that 'he could out-swap any live man, woman, or child that ever walked these hills, or that ever straddled horseflesh since the days of old daddy Adam.' "[113] Longstreet, however, is more fortunate than Hall in his narrative style, which is more consonant with the raw action and speech of the frontiersmen. Longstreet's superiority in this respect is particularly evident in a comparison of his "The Fight" and Hall's "A Frontier Scene."[114] Both are apparently factual accounts of fights between backwoodsmen; but Longstreet describes the fight in the coarse idiom of the backwoods and without Hall's squeamishness about bloody details.

During the half century following the publication of Hall's "The Bachelors' Elysium," "Pete Featherton," and "The Philadelphia Dun," the cavorter of frontier fiction lost nothing in physical agility or extravagance of language. The most notable of the authors who exploited his talents was Mark Twain, who, in his "raftsmen passage," portrayed a pair of roarers. This section was originally drafted as part of the manuscript of *Huckleberry Finn,* but it was printed first in *Life on the Mississippi* (1883) and has been restored by some editors to the text of *Huckleberry Finn.* In the incident, Mark Twain brings together Bob and the Child of Calamity to compete in braggadocio:

193

" 'Look at me!' Bob shouted, 'I'm the man they call Sudden Death and General Desolation! Sired by a hurricane, dam'd by an earthquake, half-brother to the cholera, nearly related to the smallpox on my mother's side! Look at me! I take nineteen alligators and a bar'l of whiskey for breakfast when I'm in robust health. . . .' "

"When he got through, he jumped up and cracked his heels together three times, and let off a roaring, 'Whoo-oop! I'm the bloodiest son of a wildcat that lives.' "

"Then he [the Child of Calamity] straightened, and jumped up and cracked his heels together three times before he lit again . . . , and he began to shout like this:

" 'Whoo-oop! bow your neck and spread, for the kingdom of sorrow's a-coming. . . . I scratch my head with the lightning and purr myself with the thunder! When I'm cold, I bile the Gulf of Mexico and bathe in it; when I'm hot I fan myself with an equinoctial storm; when I'm thirsty I reach up and suck a cloud dry like a sponge; when I range the earth hungry, famine follows in my tracks! Whoo-oop.' "[115]

The characteristics of the cavorter are again apparent in the drunken Boggs, who appears in *Huckleberry Finn* (1885):

"Boggs comes a-tearing along on his horse, whooping and yelling like an Injun, and singing out—

" 'Cler the track, thar. I'm on the waw-path, and the price uv coffins is a-gwyne to raise.' " [116]

VI

So great were Hall's troubles and griefs in 1832 that the second volume of the magazine could hardly have been completed without the aid of his friends in Cincinnati. At least one subscriber received his copy of the February issue two months late.[117] Apparently this was the first of the issues that were printed in St. Louis after the sale of the Hall-Blackwell press. Hall went on doggedly. In June, Corey and Fairbank of Cincinnati took over the printing. On June 23, still lacking material for that month's number, Hall wrote to Salmon Portland Chase in Cincinnati and

194

pleaded, "Cannot you and my other friends, nib your pens and help me a little?"[118] Perkins, Gouverneur Morris, Chase, Jewett, Benjamin Drake, Charles D. Drake, and John P. Foote loyally met the emergency and helped complete the volume. Perkins, the most prolific of the group, wrote more than half of the July number.[119]

Chase and other Cincinnati intellectuals, however, had planned a new magazine to be called the *Western Quarterly Review*. Recognizing Hall's leadership in Western culture, Chase asked Hall to be the editor.[120] But by September, Hall had secured the enterprising firm of Corey and Fairbank as partners in the publication of his own magazine on the condition that it be moved to Cincinnati.[121] When September came, an epidemic of cholera was raging in the city; and the début of Hall's new periodical, to be known as the *Western Monthly Magazine,* was postponed until the first of the following year.[122] Chase and his group abandoned their plans for a journal and facilitated the removal of the *Illinois Monthly* to Cincinnati. When January, 1833, came and Hall's affairs still held him in Vandalia, his friends in Cincinnati superintended the publication of the *Western Monthly's* first three numbers.[123]

Hall's anxieties, arising from the loss of his press, the difficulty of printing his magazine, and his debts, had been increased in the spring of 1832 by the outbreak of the war against Black Hawk and, in August, by the death of his wife.

Mary Hall, in her only surviving letter—written on Wednesday, May 23, to her parents in Henderson, Kentucky—showed concern about the war.[124] Her brother John had gone to the front in northern Illinois with a company of Vandalia men, including Robert Blackwell, Hall's partner. Mary reported that Blackwell has ridden back into town on Sunday with a letter from Governor Reynolds asking for volunteers. "Mr Hall is one of them," she wrote, "but he has not entirely decided yet whether he will go. They will start next monday. . . . " Although she was expecting a baby in August, she continued, "I feel perfectly satisfied for Mr Hall to go—though I shall feel anxious about him just as I now do about John." It seems, however, that Hall

195

had no ardor for the war. "Mr Hall," Mary said, "does not believe there will be any more fighting & every one thinks those lives which are lost have just been foolishly thrown away. . . . " By remaining at home, he was able to be with Mary in her confinement.

Mary had gone to her parents' home in Henderson for the birth of Lucy Frances in 1828, and probably for the arrival of John Posey in 1826, but for this confinement she remained in Vandalia. The baby was born on August 10, and was named James. About midnight of the following day, she was attacked by a fever. Hall, in describing the tragic days that followed, noted, "From the first, she believed the disease to be fatal. For three days her pains and sufferings were exquisite. . . . Through the whole of a long melancholy week, while the hearts of those who loved her were broken with grief and alarm, she showed no impatience, nor gave way to the weakness of human nature. She submitted to every prescription, and received every attention that was rendered her with expressions of lively gratitude. Her native gentleness and kindness, to those around her, and her submission to God, were more than ever conspicuous. She was continually in prayer. She wished to be spared to her husband and children but was prepared to go to the bosom of her Redeemer, whenever it should be God's will."[125]

She died about one o'clock in the morning of August 18. Schooled though Hall was to the restraint of feeling, he poured out his grief in private. "For nine years," he wrote in his Bible, "she has been the most precious treasure, and the choicest blessing of a proud and happy husband, who prized nothing on earth so much as her love. . . . Her noble heart soared above every selfish feeling, and she lived only for those she loved. . . . In her last moments, he discovered noble qualities treasured in her heart, which were unknown even to him. It was then that she rose above human nature. In her life she was the pure, the lovely, the exalted woman, in death she was an angel. The only consolation of the broken heart that dictates these feeble lines, is that she *is happy*. If this book is true, if God is a faithful Creator, which I humbly believe, *she is happy*. May God enable her bereaved husband and children, to live as she lived, and die as she died!"

Carved on the flat stone that he later sent up from Cincinnati to be placed over her grave in the Vandalia cemetery are the words, "She was very lovely, and greatly beloved." His grief was intensified two months later, on October 15, by the death of the infant James.[126]

The next February, with plans already made to move to Cincinnati, Hall lingered in Vandalia for the legislature to pass the bill that would dispose of his property and settle his debt to the state.

On February 9, 1833, a few weeks before he left Illinois, his fellow citizens paid him high tribute at a public meeting in the State House. The purpose of the gathering was, appropriately, to advance the cause of education, and he had been invited to deliver the address. According to the newspaper account, there was that Saturday evening "a crowded assembly of ladies and gentlemen, consisting of the inhabitants of this town, the officers of the government, members of the legislature, and citizens of different parts of the State." After he had finished speaking, the meeting was organized with Sidney Breese as chairman. Three motions were unanimously approved. Benjamin Mills, a lawyer of Galena, moved that "the thanks of this meeting be presented" to Hall "for his able and eloquent address, upon a subject of most vital importance to our State—that we appreciate his literary labors while a fellow-citizen, and tender him our warmest wishes for his success in his new residence." William L. D. Ewing followed with a resolution on behalf of the citizens of Vandalia and Fayette County, stating "that as a scholar and a man of learning, we admire him; and as a gentleman and friend, we offer him our most unqualified respect, and best wishes for his prosperity and happiness wherever destiny may cast him." Finally, Jesse B. Thomas, of Edwardsville, undertook to speak for all of Illinois in resolving "That we have the highest confidence in the talents, integrity, and public services of our fellow-citizen" and "that we regret the loss that the State must sustain in his departure from it."[127]

Hall probably left Illinois immediately after February 26, 1833, when the legislature approved the law to clear his account with the state treasury. On March 6, he was in Kentucky at the home of Mary's parents,[128] with whom he arranged to leave his three children.[129] After a visit of a few weeks there, he arrived in Cincinnati in late March.[130]

XII

Cincinnati

AFTER LIVING in a remote town of four or five hundred people, Hall must have been somewhat excited by the opulence and bustle of the West's largest city when he arrived in the spring of 1833 to assume the direction of his magazine. The steamboat traveler approaching the wharf could see sloping above him a city lying in a noble amphitheater of green hills.[1] Once on shore, he found this grand panorama gradually broken up into details, some of them only modestly attractive and some even ugly. The houses were generally of brick. There were more than twenty churches (six of them Presbyterian), a medical college, a theological seminary, several common schools, a theater, a hospital, market houses, and two magnificent hotels. In the outskirts were the factories that converted the raw material brought by canal and river into steamboats, cotton gins, steam engines, whisky, flour, meat, soap, leather, hardware, furniture, paper, and books for the people of the West and of the South. The slaughter each winter of more than a hundred thousand hogs in the packing plants earned the city its nickname "Porkopolis."

Especially in the central area, a closer view revealed much rawness. The city's terrifying experiences with visitations of cholera are not surprising to us. A water tank on a hill supplied river water to the houses below, but there was no plumbing in the houses and no sewage system. Many unpaved streets were dusty or muddy, and most were dark at night. Garbage was thrown into the streets, where it was eaten by the homeless hogs that abounded there as they did in most cities, including New York. These outcasts, some crippled and lean, harassed and torn by dogs, pelted by boys and men, and sometimes even infected with hydrophobia, were complained of for at least fifteen more years.[2]

Although the founders of Cincinnati were mostly—like Hall himself—of Pennsylvania or New Jersey stock,[3] the city's population had become cosmopolitan by 1833. It was said that half of its thirty thousand people were then from New England.[4] In the streets the economist Michel Chevalier (1806-1879), who apparently visited Cincinnati in 1835, heard French accented as it was on the bank of the Rhine. There were already several thousands of Germans and Irish in the city, and three-fourths of the Germans still spoke their native language.[5] About three thousand free Negroes were reminders of slave territory lying just across the river.[6]

Only a half century removed from the wilderness, Cincinnati already offered many of the frivolities of longer established cities. The "first" society of the city, according to Isaac Appleton Jewett, cousin of Frances Appleton (who later became Longfellow's second wife), was made up chiefly of New Englanders, who were regarded by others

200

as the enterprising portion of the population. He considered the social circle as polished as the highest of Boston. The ladies, he thought, could even tie as tight a corset, flaunt as spacious a head piece, and talk of billets-doux with as much sophistication as their Broadway contemporaries. Jewett himself, dressed in the height of fashion, with excruciatingly tight trousers and an enormous breast pin, noted that most of the Cincinnati bucks spent their days weighing out iron or rolling tar barrels.[7]

In June, 1833, the beauty and fashion of the city filled the new theater's two thousand seats to see the tragedian Edwin Forrest; but Jewett thought that Cincinnati's dominant puritanism hindered the development of a vigorous popular drama there.[8] The renowned museums, however, flourished by catering to citizens with a relish for nerve-tingling frivolities. One of them circumvented piety with the presentation of a moral lesson, a representation of hell constructed by the ingenious artist Hiram Powers. This was really a dimly lighted chamber of horrors containing gigantic representations of Beelzebub, the serpent, a burning lake, corpses groaning on gallowses, lightning, and thunder. The unwary were shocked by electricity, and the accumulation of terrors set the children to crying and the women to wailing. The wise Chevalier perceived that those principally delighted were the younger Cincinnatians, especially ladies and young girls who went there "in pursuit of emotions that are denied them in their ordinary mode of life, which, though comfortable and tranquil, is cold and monotonous."[9] But the Western museum catered to an even more morbid taste with the following advertisement:

A DINNER,
    EXTRAORDINARY,—will be served up This Evening, June 6th, at 4 o'clock precisely, to one of the Great Serpents of India. The public are respectfully informed that the beautiful Embroydered Boa of Bengal will be fed with a live Rabit [*sic*]. . . .[10]

Those inclined to more relaxing diversions were appealed to by the Cincinnati Arcade Bath House, on Sycamore between Third and Fourth streets. The proprietors assured the wary public that "the practice of bathing needs no other recommendation than that which the experience of all enlightened ages has bestowed upon it. For while we view it as a luxury to those in good health, as a preventive to disease, or as a means of relief to the afflicted, it is entitled to a rank among the most rational enjoyments." Season tickets for a gentleman and his lady could be had for six dollars, and a capable female attended the ladies in their apartment.[11]

More than two hundred "coffee houses," or saloons, one for every 150 persons including women and children, supplied the people with liquor seven days a week.[12]

However, the truly distinctive feature of the city—and the particular pride of its citizens—was its diverse and genuine cultural life. In 1833, when Hall arrived to assume his editorial duties on the *Western Monthly,* Cincinnati seemed to be on the verge of becoming the publishing center of the United States. In inducing Calvin Stowe to leave his professorship at Dartmouth and join the faculty of the just-opening Lane Theological Seminary, President Lyman Beecher tried to convince him that he would not be burying himself in a frontier town by accepting, but that his talents for learning and literature would be used and appreciated. "I firmly believe," he wrote, "that there is, according to the number of her inhabitants, as much intellectual and literary ability here as in Boston. . . . "[13] He might have added as evidence that—besides printing several daily newspapers, three religious and two literary weeklies, and two magazines —Cincinnati's presses turned out nearly a half million volumes a year.[14] The Queen City was, by 1835, the foremost publishing center in the West and in the publication of books assumed soon afterward the fourth rank among the cities of the entire United States.[15]

Eighteen public schools and several private ones provided education for two-thirds of the city's children of the middle and upper classes. Outstanding institutions for the improvement of adults were the Lyceum and the Mechanics Institute, but the general public was admitted only to the latter.

The Lyceum's lecture subjects for the season of 1833-34 were heterogeneous: prairies, taxation, the life of Mahomet, the history of navigation, and domestic education.[16] Notable lecturers on both platforms were James H. Perkins, Salmon P. Chase, Calvin Stowe, Lyman Beecher, and Hall. Cultured people often attended the meetings of both societies. The Mechanics Institute, however, survives as a strong institution today, probably because of support from skilled workmen, who, in 1832, were already organized in unions which within a few years would be using the strike to obtain better working conditions.[17]

Many cultivated citizens could be found at the meetings of two significant intellectual and literary societies.[18] One met at the residence of Dr. Daniel Drake, on Vine Street, where the group was small enough for the doctor's parlor. He was the acknowledged chairman; and after the group had assembled, about seven-thirty, he rang a little bell and announced the subject for the evening. Averting any tendency to gossip, he encouraged even the timid to participate in the lively discussions of problems of society, religion, literature, and education.

The meetings of the Semi-Colon society at the elegant home of Samuel E. Foote, and at the adjoining residences of Charles Stetson and William Greene, were apparently larger and more literary. Some of the lecturers of the Lyceum and the Mechanics Institute, like Hall and other prominent men, attended the meetings of both societies. Calvin Stowe, who had accepted the professorship of biblical literature at Lane, was one. Among other Semi-Colons was Lyman Beecher's daughter, Catharine, who at thirty was already a successful and progressive educator, and, with her younger sister Harriet, was opening the Western Female Institute in Cincinnati. Their pupils were to be taught calisthenics; their prospectus scoffed at the mere *"technical acquisition of knowledge"* and proposed *"to teach them to think for themselves."*[19] Lyman Beecher's other daughter, Harriet, was twenty-one and attractive. Though few knew it, she had written a geography for children.[20] Twenty-two years afterward, she remembered the stimulation of these literary clubs and dedicated an edition of her book *The Mayflower, and Miscellaneous Writings* to the Semi-Colons, "for whose genial meetings many of these articles were prepared."[21] Caroline Lee Hentz, who had grown up in Lancaster, Massachusetts, had written plays and the novel *Lamorah, or the Western Wild.* Her shy French husband, painter of miniatures, former professor at the University of North Carolina, and an able entomologist, then conducted, with his wife's aid, a popular academy for girls on Third Street. Both Hall and his friend Benjamin Drake, the editor of the weekly *Chronicle and Literary Gazette,* appealed in verse to the members of the Semi-Colon for contributions to their journals.[22] Although some papers written for the society were juvenile, Hall found several good enough for the *Western Monthly.*[23]

Hall, of course, also moved in other social circles besides those of Dr. Drake's group and the Semi-Colons and was a friend of such Cincinnatians as General William Henry Harrison and Bishop John Purcell. General Harrison had been a soldier on the frontier, and he was soon to become, after his memorable "log-cabin and hard-cider" campaign, President of the United States for a single month. Bishop Purcell had been professor of moral philosophy and president of Mount St. Mary's College. Now bishop of the Cincinnati Catholic diocese, he was an intense friend of education.[24]

There were few who doubted the promise of Cincinnati. Gazing out upon the city and the surrounding country from Montgomery Road high in the Walnut Hills, Harriet Martineau in the summer of 1835 caught a view "of that melting beauty which dims the eyes and fills the heart— that magical combination of all elements—of hill, wood, lawn, river, with a picturesque city steeped in evening sunshine, the impression of which can never be lost nor ever communicated." Of all American cities, Cincinnati was to her the most beautiful to live in. Moreover, no city in the country, she thought, could provide a more beautiful setting for the buildings of the federal government. But Miss Martineau also probed beneath the outward beauty and doubted. She saw in the citizens themselves "a faith-lessness which manifests itself in illiberality." She saw Protestant mistrust of the Catholic minority, intolerance of the opinions and actions of the Abolitionists, and, most threatening of all, sectional prejudice. Easterners coolly assumed "the superiority of New-England over all other countries."[25] The feeling, to some degree reciprocated by native Westerners, was too strong to give way even in social gatherings. Events of the next two decades were to prove the shrewdness of her insight.

II

For three years, or perhaps four, Hall lived at the Pearl Street House, on the northeast corner of Pearl and Walnut streets.[26] Built in the grand style, the hotel was one that Charles Fenno Hoffman thought "would rival the best in New York."[27] One writer declared that "the table groans beneath the greatest possible variety of every species of luxurious living, from the most rare and substantial viands, to the nicest delicacies in fruit and pastry," and that "a goodly number of highly respectable boarders, both male and female, . . . greatly contribute to the agreeableness of the establishment."[28]

A severe epidemic of cholera broke out early in the summer of 1833, soon spread a gloom over the city, and "paralyzed all its business operations." In June, Hall was stricken, and for more than two months was incapable of any mental effort.[29] By early September, however, he had apparently recovered completely.

Hall was now forty and at the height of his powers. He had, in his long residence in Illinois, developed the convic-tion that the creation of a Western culture should not be left to slow, evolutionary processes, but that it should be advanced by conscious and determined effort.

From the beginning of his Cincinnati residence, he was prominent in educational enterprises. Within a few weeks after his arrival he was elected to the board of trustees of Catharine and Harriet Beecher's Western Female Institute, and the board made him its secretary.[30] In September, he became an examiner of Woodward High School, and later he was one of the examiners and inspectors of the city's schools.[31] Also in September, the Western Literary Institute and College of Professional Teachers appointed him, after he had made an address to the members assembled in Cincinnati, to the standing committee formed to advance the cause of education throughout the West.[32] About that time, he was also honored by an invitation to address the Erodelphian Society of Miami University during commencement week. The fine weather that autumn invited travel by gig, carriage, and canal boat; and a thousand people gathered in the village of Oxford for the examinations, the addresses, and the commencement ball.[33]

On Thursday evening, September 24, Hall spoke on education to this assembly. He wanted learning to be "useful," but his espousal of the liberal arts showed that he meant only to disavow esoteric learning. His peroration was a plea to the young gentlemen of the Erodelphian Society. "I conjure you," he said, "to devote your hearts to the great cause of popular education and national literature!"[34] Popular education he regarded as the next great step in the American revolution, and as one necessary for democracy's survival, for he believed that only learning could break down the distinction between rich and poor. "In any country," he said, "where a few are educated, and the great mass of the people ignorant, the uninstructed many will be governed by the enlightened minority." His address is interesting also because for the first time in his discourses, he urged, in the year of the founding of Oberlin, the first coeducational college in the United States, the inclusion of women in plans for education.

Insisting principally upon the education of the poor, he declared that Talent sought her favorites among the rich and the impoverished with an impartial eye, and that "it is a misfortune and a discredit to any people to bury the talent and smother the ambition of their children." As at least a partial solution to the problem, he said, "It is for the children of poverty I plead when I implore you to give your influence to the building up of nurseries of learning in your own land."

Soon after the Erodelphian address, Hall himself set about making a contribution to popular education and, during the latter part of 1833, was busy compiling a book of readings for school children. It was brought out the January following as *The Western Reader*.[35] In the preface he explained its novel plan: "This book is intended to take the place in our common schools, heretofore occupied by the English Reader, and other similar works. In adapting it to our own time and country, it has been thought proper to confine the selections exclusively to the works of American writers, for the double purpose of rendering the young reader familiar with the literature of his own land, and of placing before him topics of the most immediate interest. In accordance with the spirit of this plan, a large portion of the matter has been selected from Western writers, and treats of interesting subjects connected with this portion of the Union. It is a work of Western origin and manufacture; having been prepared in this city expressly for the use of our own schools, and published here by means of our own workmanship and materials."

Of *The Western Reader's* forty-nine authors who can be readily identified, twenty-three were Easterners, and twenty-six, more than half, had lived in the West. Among the Eastern writers were Benjamin Franklin, Thomas Jefferson, John Marshall, Noah Webster, John Pierpont, William Cullen Bryant, Washington Irving, and James Fenimore Cooper. The West was represented by such authors as John Audubon, Benjamin Drake, Dr. Daniel Drake, John Russell, Henry Clay, Lewis Cass, Timothy Flint, and Morgan Neville.

In the preface Hall promises that there is no sentiment in the *Reader* "which could be pernicious to young minds, nor any in which serious things are treated with unbecoming levity." Therefore one is not surprised to find a few selections inculcating reverence for God, respect for American heroes, inspiration to national morality, and encouragement of temperance. However, having acquired in boyhood a "deep-seated disgust against schools and schoolmasters, and school learning" and having become convinced ahead of his age that the schoolmaster should substitute friendliness for whipping, Hall has taken special pains to collect literature that would be entertaining to the children of the West. Most of the selections, he observes in the preface, had never before appeared in a textbook. He includes descriptions of Ohio River scenery, a hurricane, the prairie wolf, Niagara Falls, and the eggs of insects. There are also such narratives as Irving's "The Little Man in Black," Morgan Neville's "Reminiscence of the Scioto Valley," Cooper's account of a capture of a whale, from *The Pilot,* and, from Charles Brockden Brown's *Arthur Mervyn,* the relation of a patient's experiences in a Philadelphia hospital during the yellow fever epidemic of 1793. A stuffy schoolmaster would have had to be adroit to make the use of *The Western Reader* entirely dull to his pupils.

The book was a radical departure, published when there was much American dependence upon European culture. Yet it seems fair to ascribe the plan of *The Western Reader,* not to vainglorious patriotism, but to Hall's dream of building a culture with the materials at hand—a dream that had already led him to produce *The Western Souvenir,* to found the Historical and Antiquarian Society of Illinois, and to establish his magazine. Within two years, a hundred thousand or more copies of *The Western Reader* had been sold. It was adopted for use in the Cincinnati public schools, and for several years was part of the daily diet of boys and girls studying in the log schoolhouses of the West.[36]

Probably shortly before Hall had begun to compile *The Western Reader,* his only novel, *The Harpe's Head: A Legend of Kentucky,* was published in the autumn of 1833. The story, probably based on the westward migration of the families of Mary Hall's father and grandfather, is one of patrician family life in Virginia and Kentucky. Journeying over the wilderness trace with their slaves and livestock, the travelers of the story are beset by Indians and by the murderous Wiley and Micajah Harpe and their gang. The novel was apparently written in haste, probably

MARY HARRISON POSEY HALL

From a Portrait Owned by

Mrs. Elmer J. Rodenberg

in Illinois or Henderson, Kentucky. It was inadequately planned; although the narrative is rich in action and moves with considerable dispatch, the incidents are not well integrated and are related with little climactic effect. Yet *The Harpe's Head* is somewhat redeemed by the reproduction of certain frontier scenes and customs with which Hall was familiar. We see his patricians in their Eastern mansions and later in their log houses in Kentucky. There is apparent fidelity in his gentle satire of the aristocratic Virginians, with their high-bred horses in tattered harness, their crazy coaches, and their faded Revolutionary uniforms. The descriptions of the barbecue and of the coon hunt on the frontier are memorable and valuable. With the exception of the Indians, who are unconvincing, the uneducated characters speak with naturalness. One of these, Hark Short, a wild boy of the wilderness who turns out to be the son of Micajah Harpe, has an arresting vitality which suggests that he was drawn from life. Another unusual character portrayed with consistency and perhaps having an actual person as a prototype is George Lee, a dull-witted Virginia aristocrat who, disappointed in love, drinks himself into derangement.

The Harpe's Head, republished in London in 1834, was probably read with considerable interest by people who, living in cultivated societies, were curious about frontier life; and it appears to have had a strong influence upon other writers. The striking character Hark Short seems to have made a deep impression upon William Gilmore Simms, who appears to have used Hark as a model for Chub Williams in *Guy Rivers* (1835), and probably for Dick Stillyards in *Border Beagles* (1840).[37] The marked similarities between *The Harpe's Head* and Robert Montgomery Bird's *Nick of the Woods* (1837) leave little doubt that Bird was indebted to Hall's novel for incidents and characterization.[38]

On May 21, 1834, Volume I, approximately the first half, of Hall's *Sketches of History, Life, and Manners in the West* was published by Hubbard and Edmands, of Cincinnati; but the firm soon afterward went out of business, and the entire work was published in two volumes the next year by Harrison Hall.[39]

In writing *Sketches of History,* Hall aimed at a broad view of the development of the West from the time that the Indians reigned in undisputed possession of the land to the year of the book's publication. The work is divided into six parts: "Intercourse of the American People with the Indians," "History of the French Settlements [on the Wabash and the Mississippi]," "Early Settlements on the Ohio,"[40] "Events in the Early History of Kentucky," "Military Operations in the North-western Territory," and "Civil Institutions of the Territories and New States." Faced with a subject immense in both time and space, he drew a general view of the history of the region and focused sharply upon those scenes and events which he himself had witnessed or participated in, or of which he had intimate knowledge through records or manuscripts. His story is one of a region that for centuries was a rich prize in the struggles between Spain, France, Great Britain, and, later, the United States; but in its truer aspect his narrative is one of a hardy people who, with little regard for the designs of national governments, penetrated the wilderness, at first in little groups of two or three, faced the heavy odds of nature and savage tribes, and, after great suffering and bloodshed, established an orderly society. The hero of *Sketches of History* is the pioneer, whom Hall fondly clothes with valor, patience, and an ingrained spirit of independence.

He had been at work on sections of the book since 1830, and he included several of his articles from the *Illinois Monthly* and the *Western Monthly,* notably "On the Intercourse of the American People with the Indians," "The French Settlements"—in "Notes on Illinois"—and "Indian Hating." [41] The wonder is that so rich a history was written in a period of meager Western libraries, of primitive methods of travel and communication, and of widely scattered and elusive private and public documents. Nevertheless, the reader of "Intercourse of the American People with the Indians" and "History of the French Settlements" must be astonished at the wide range of books that Hall used— and cited—when he was writing in isolated Vandalia.

210

No less remarkable was his zeal in the collection of information from other sources. "To acquire an adequate knowledge of such a country, requires extensive personal observation," he wrote in the introduction. "It is necessary to examine things instead of books, to travel over this wide region, to become acquainted with the people, to learn their history from tradition and to become informed as to their manners and modes of thinking, by associating with them in the peculiar intercourse of business and domestic life." He had spent, the book revealed, a substantial portion of his eighteen years in the West in travel. Journeys by keelboat and steamboat throughout the whole navigable length of the Ohio and probably of the Illinois and the Mississippi had provided him with a panoramic view of the West. But his intimate knowledge of the region was the result of what must have been thousands of miles of travel on horseback. Wherever he went in the interior of Pennsylvania, Illinois, Missouri, or Kentucky, he talked with the frontier people, stayed in their cabins, and listened to their stories. He seems to have neglected few opportunities to examine the records in old churches or public buildings or to scramble through thickets to study the design of an old fort. Moreover, he collected old newspapers and a considerable body of manuscripts. For his chapters on the early history of Kentucky, he had acquired the papers of the Transylvania Company (many of which he reproduced in the appendix); he had access to the manuscripts of Judge Benjamin Sebastian, one of the leaders in the Spanish conspiracy; and he reproduced a letter written by Daniel Boone in 1775.[42]

Part of the book—such as the description of Kaskaskia and Fort Chartres in Part II, Chapter I, and of the construction of a log cabin in Part IV, Chapter V—are the enduring records of an eyewitness who wrote with precision of scenes now obliterated and of customs long since grown obsolete in American life. Few people can read *Sketches of History* today without increasing their knowledge of the West as a factor in world history or without enlarging their understanding of the frontiersman. The book is also conspicuous for its graceful and lucid prose.

In the title, the preface, and the concluding paragraph

of *Sketches of History,* Hall underlined his intention to write a popular, rather than a definitive, scholarly book. "Nothing further is attempted," he wrote in the preface, "than a collection of facts, . . . which are intended rather as examples and illustrations of topics connected with the western states, than as regular narrative history." But the book fell into the hands of his enemies. True, most of the reviewers took the work at its declared value and gave it commendatory notices;[43] but others, subjecting it to a closer, unfriendlier, scrutiny, were less favorably impressed. Unfortunately, Hall had stirred up jealousies—some of them sectional—by beginning his introduction with the remark that "but few of the writers who have treated of the western country, rank above mediocrity; and little of all that has been written on the subject is interesting or true." Such a statement could hardly have pleased Mann Butler, who had published his own *History of the Commonwealth of Kentucky* the year before Hall's two-volume edition appeared. Butler wrote a twelve-page review of Hall's work for the *Western Messenger* of May, 1836. He asserted, in his somewhat lumbering and sometimes obscure style, that Hall should have used original documents, some of them existing in several languages; that his book lacked chronological order; that he had made several statements contrary to fact; and that he had used the fruit of other men's labors, especially Butler's own, without acknowledgement. In the last charge he hinted strongly that Hall had plagiarized part of Butler's history, particularly in writing the account of the Treaty of Fort Stanwix.

Another and better known adverse criticism, appearing in the *North American Review,* has damaged Hall's reputation. This "so *very North* American" magazine, as Hall called it, had not taken notice of his work until, in July, 1836—two months after the appearance of Butler's review in the *Messenger*—it printed as the leading article a criticism dealing with both Hall's *Sketches of History* and Butler's history of Kentucky. The critic gave the bulk of his space and commendation to Butler's relation, which, he said, was "deserving of all praise." He admitted that Hall's work was valuable and praised it as "the most entertaining book on the subject," but he condemned it as inaccurate. The errors that he charged against Hall, except for one, were the very ones that Butler had alleged in the *Messenger*.

The critic then arraigned Hall's ability to write about the West at all. "He professes to be a western man"; the reviewer wrote, "the scene of his stories is generally in the west; his incidents are taken from western life; but of the western character he knows little, and of the western spirit he knows nothing. He wants the intellectual *openness* which would enable him to catch the spirit of society. His mind is shut up in its own ways of thinking and feeling, and his writings, in consequence, give no true reflection of western character. In this respect he is the exact antithesis of Timothy Flint, whose writings, though sometimes inaccurate in detail, are always charged full of a western spirit. Flint's 'Ten Years' Residence'[44] is one of our few genuine national works. It could have been written nowhere but in the Western Valley. It could have been written by no one, whose mind had not been moulded by a constant contact with western scenery and people. Judge Hall's books might all have been composed by one who had never been beyond the atmosphere of London, but who had heard a few anecdotes and read a few works about the western world."

It was not generally known until nearly a half century later, when a list of the authors of the *North American Review* was published, that Hall's harsh reviewer was the Transcendentalist James Freeman Clarke,[45] and apparently few of Hall's critics since that time have been aware of Clarke's authorship of the article. A graduate of Harvard in Oliver Wendell Holmes's class, Clarke was at twenty-six the minister of the Unitarian church in Louisville. There he was also the editor of the Unitarian magazine, the *Western Messenger*, eminently memorable as the first to publish some of the works of Emerson and Keats, but notable for the present purpose as the magazine in which Butler's review of *Sketches of History* had appeared.

At the end of the year, Hall devoted the preface of his next book, *Statistics of the West* (1836), to a reply, and two years later published the preface as a pamphlet entitled *Reply to Strictures on Sketches of the West*. A year later, Butler resumed the attack with a pamphlet of his own, *An Appeal from the Misrepresentations of James Hall Respecting the History of Kentucky and the West;* [46] and Clarke answered Hall in the *North American Review* for July, 1837. The *Western Messenger* also printed a carping review of Hall's next book.[47]

The *Reply to Strictures* is probably the best example of Hall's forensic skill, and it still makes entertaining reading. Since his two enemies and their reviews had an obvious and close relationship, he replied to both critics at once. His *Reply* is essentially a defense of *Sketches of History* as sketches. "Our offense seems to be, in their eyes," he said, "that of not compiling a history, from existing publications, instead of writing sketches from memory and observation." "We cheerfully admit," he continued, "that . . . a seasoning of 'original and native authorities,' might have earned us a reputation for scholarship, to which we have never aspired. But such was not our plan. . . . " In the *North American Review,* he pointed out, he had been blamed for a lack of Western spirit, yet all of the specific charges in that magazine had been directed at his scholarship. But he also defended his work as history, and he acquitted himself, this writer believes, of all charges except a few of factual error.

It is unrewarding to sift exhaustively the merits of all the charges, replies, and rejoinders of that part of the debate concerned with minor mistakes of date and fact. It is certainly true that Hall made errors in *Sketches of History.* He erred, as Butler asserted, in his contention that Judge Sebastian was innocent in the Spanish conspiracy. It is also true that he used other men's works; and he freely acknowledged his debt to many of them, including Butler. But Butler's charges were directed principally against those sections dealing with the history of Kentucky, and even if all alleged misstatements had been demonstrated—and they were not—they were minor errors, not likely to vitiate seriously the *Sketches'* usefulness in presenting the essential history of the frontier.

From a consideration of Butler's questionable, but at least specific, charges of factual error, one turns with vexation to the semantic traps in which Clarke couched his accusation that Hall was not by nature equipped to write about the West. One does not well know what to make of the charge that Hall lacked "intellectual *openness*," or that he provided an untrue "reflection of western character," or a tourist-like superficiality. Indeed, the whole attack, originating as it did in a magazine conducted by former New Englanders, reflecting a sensitivity to attack upon New England character, and elevating the New Englander Timothy Flint at Hall's expense, is, as Hall indicated, under suspicion of sectional bias.[48] Ranged beside Hall in this aspect of the controversy is no less a critic than Edgar Allan Poe, who had read both *Sketches of History* and Clarke's review of it in the *North American.* Writing to Harrison Hall about Clarke's review, he observed, "Some personal pique is at the bottom of it."[49]

Since it has become almost a fashion for modern literary historians to sum up their criticism of Hall's writings by quoting Clarke's charge that Hall was not "Western,"[50] it is only fair to record that, among either Eastern or Western critics of Hall's day and later, Clarke's criticism was discordant and, so far as is known, unique. Moreover, since Clarke had lived in the West only three years, he was hardly an authority on the "western spirit." Better qualified witnesses were Hall's Western contemporaries Benjamin Drake and William Gallagher. Drake, who had been born at Mays Lick, Kentucky, in 1795, spent his life on the frontier. A writer in his *Cincinnati Chronicle and Literary Gazette,* presumably Drake himself, praises Hall for his "accuracy of coloring, which renders the efforts of his pen in sketching backwoods life so captivating."[51] The *Cincinnati Mirror,* edited by Gallagher, who had spent his youth on a farm in southern Ohio, believed that Hall painted "true pictures of men and manners and things as they really move and exist in the 'far West' " and thought that his tales were the "very best delineations of western character that have been published."[52] William Gilmore Simms, in dedicating to Hall the novel *Charlemont* and its sequel *Beauchampe,* described him as "one of the ablest of our literary pioneers; a genuine representative of the great west; whose writings illustrate her history and genius." At Hall's death the *Nation* declared, "Nobody who would understand how the people of the great Valley became what they are should neglect Judge Hall."[53] This opinion is corroborated by a recent historian of the frontier, R. Carlyle Buley, who appraises Hall's writings as the "most valuable one-man historical output of the region."[54]

Before the end of 1834, Hall had sent to press *Tales of the Border,* the third volume of his short stories published within three years. Four of the volume's seven tales—"The French Village," "The Capuchin," "The Silver Mine," and "The Spy"—had appeared in the *Illinois Monthly* or *The Western Souvenir.*[55] The remaining narratives—"The Pioneer," "The Dark Maid of Illinois," and "The New Moon" —occupying more than half of *Tales of the Border,* had not been collected; and only "The Dark Maid of Illinois," which had appeared in the *Knickerbocker* for July, 1833, had been previously printed. The new volume marked Hall's abandonment of white backwoodsmen, such as the "Salt River roarers," as fictional characters, and his turn to narratives of Indian-white relations. In all three of the new stories, as he observed in the preface, the theme was the white man's inhumanity to the Indian.

Probably because in Cincinnati he was able for the first time in thirteen years to profit from association with other literary men like Benjamin Drake and Benjamin's brother Dr. Daniel Drake, the narratives in *Tales of the Border* are markedly superior in style and structure to those of his second collection, *The Soldier's Bride.* The improvement is apparent in the first story, "The Pioneer." In this tale, perhaps the swiftest and least self-conscious of all his narratives, he retold the account of John Moredock, the Indian hater, adding to that relation, however, an interesting conflict. In the beginning, the plot follows the earlier account. When the Indian hater was a child, Indians murdered his father, his mother, and his uncle. But to the earlier plot Hall added a new feature—the abduction of a sister by the Indians. As the Indian hater grew to manhood, he dedicated his life to revenge and relentlessly hunted down and killed the red men who had destroyed his family. But when he at last discovered his sister in the woods and learned that she was the contented wife of an Indian and the mother of Indian children, the avenging brother underwent a change of conscience, abandoned his career of revenge, and devoted himself to religion.

In "The New Moon," on the other hand, Menae, the beautiful and generous-spirited daughter of Blackbird, chief of the Omaha tribe, married a cold and mercenary white trader. Compelled to suffer the anguish of having her child torn from her to be sent to the settlements, and forced to endure the indignity of her husband's appearance at their cabin with a white wife, Menae took refuge with her tribe. In spite of the cruel treatment she had received, she nevertheless arranged for her husband's escape from her tribesmen who were bent upon killing him for his cruelty to her. Thereafter, having regained her children, she lived in retirement with her tribe and reared her children in Indian fashion, "continually advising them to avoid the society, the customs, and the vices of the whites." In "The Dark Maid of Illinois" a chief's daughter again is married to a white man, but in this instance to a shallow and garrulous French adventurer who, without any conception of her feelings, left her to be scorned and eventually die with grief.

These stories of racial intermarriage, particularly "The Dark Maid of Illinois" and "The New Moon," lose something in effectiveness because Hall, in his attitude toward Indian culture, was torn between idealization and condescension. He was influenced in part by the frontiersman's conventional hatred and loathing for the red man. The inconsistency was also partly due to Hall's having spent seventeen years outside the main intellectual current, which was predominantly romantic. Although the prevailing theme of "The Dark Maid of Illinois" is romantic, Hall, as an unconfirmed romanticist in whom the eighteenth-century inclinations toward rationalism and realism were strong, treated satirically the alleged casualness of the Indian marriage ceremony and the supposed indifference of Indian parents toward the marital happiness of their children.

Although in Illinois he had had at least a slight first-hand knowledge of Indian tribal life, he was as meagerly equipped as most writers of the period to develop amply the emotions of an Indian mother or wife in fiction.[56] In some instances he seems merely to have superimposed white mores upon Indian characters. Even so, he was sometimes moderately convincing, as, for example, in the love scene between Menae and Bolingbroke in "The New Moon." In this narrative he was sufficiently sympathetic toward the wronged Indian wife to move the reader; and the entire relation, as one critic observed, "would require but few changes to make it a really effective modern short story."[57]

In spite of the discrepancies of the three stories, the reader is swept along by the charm of Hall's style and is frequently entertained by his humor, which one may in some instances fairly characterize as "delightful," as one modern critic has done.[58] The publication of *Tales of the Border* established Hall as one of the most prolific American short-story writers of the decade and as the most important contributor to "the Western tributary" of early nineteenth-century American fiction.

That his interest in the general subject of Indian-white relations went deeper than a mere search for fictional material is demonstrated by one of his articles written during this period. In "Indian Hating" (1833)[59] he took up the Moredock story again, this time in an attempt to explain this curious aspect of frontier life. For twelve years he had witnessed the day-to-day animosity of the frontiersman toward the Indian; he had written down his troubled feelings about it in his "On the Intercourse of the American People with the Indians"; and he had seen a mixture of fear and fury mount until it broke out in the atrocities of the Black Hawk War. In "Indian Hating" he tried to show how the frontiersman from his birth onward was taught to fear the Indian by reminders of some relative or friend slain by the red men. The article is objective and offers no moralization or attempt at solution.

Hall was preceded in his first portrayal of the Indian-hater by James McHenry, author of *The Spectre of the Forest* (1823) and by N. M. Hentz, author of *Tadeskund, the Last King of the Lenape* (1825).[60] Hall may have read these novels and he may have heard of Indian-haters from story tellers gathered about hearths and camp fires in Illinois. But he said that he was acquainted with John Moredock,[61] and the similarity between Moredock and Samuel Monson, in Hall's first fiction on the subject—"The Indian Hater," published in *The Western Souvenir* in November, 1828—clearly indicates that Moredock was his model for Monson in the story. Nearly a year later, Hall's biographical sketch of Moredock appeared in the *Illinois Intelligencer*. Apparently perplexed by the wide divergence between the literary view of the Indian as a noble savage and the frontiersman's hatred of him as a detestable "var-ment," Hall wrote, in all, five different accounts of the Indian-hater.[62] In his earliest narration, his frontiersman was possessed by an unswerving monomania for vengeance; in the last story, "The Pioneer," he was capable of assent to the "unnatural union" of his sister's marriage to an Indian. Altogether, Hall's stories constitute, one student of early American fiction has said, an "almost definitive" treatment of this phenomenal character.[63] Hall was followed in his studies of the type by Timothy Flint, James Kirke Paulding, Robert Montgomery Bird, William Gilmore Simms, William Joseph Snelling, and Charles Fenno Hoffman,[64] some of whom, if not all, based their descriptions on Hall's stories. The Indian-hater became—along with the scout, the bee-hunter, and the white renegade—one of the bizarre charac-ters which the frontier contributed to American fiction.

A very strange use of Hall's study of the Indian-hater was made by the most important novelist that employed it. Herman Melville made Hall's "Indian Hating" the basis of Chapters XXV-XXVII of *The Confidence-Man,* published in 1857, when Hall was sixty-four and no longer an active writer. A character in Melville's novel, Charles Noble, traveling on a Mississippi River steamboat, tells a corrupted version of Hall's account of Colonel John Moredock. In his recital, Noble not only pretends "to render you the judge [Hall] upon the colonel almost word for word" but to impersonate Hall, from whom, he alleges, he had heard Moredock's history "again and again." Noble, as Melville's mouthpiece, reshapes Hall's account and portrays Hall as one who has himself become a proponent of hatred as a doctrine. As Noble described him, Hall, when he told the story of Moredock, would light a fresh cigar, rise, and request the company to smoke "in deep silence" to Moredock's memory. Melville's narrator then expands and embroiders Hall's explanation of Indian-hating so that the explanation becomes a defense of hatred, even so far as to make Hall say that "Indian hating may be regarded as not wholly without the efficacy of a devout sentiment." Though there is still disagreement among scholars about Melville's meaning,[65] Hall, if he ever read or heard of *The Confidence-Man,*[66] could hardly have felt flattered by Melville's portrait of him or been pleased by Melville's changes in the sketch of Moredock. It is even more likely—since Hall showed little taste for metaphysics or for symbolic writing—that he, like some modern readers, would have been puzzled by Melville's chapters on Indian-hating.

XIII
The Western Monthly Magazine

THE WESTERN MONTHLY MAGAZINE throve from its beginning in January, 1833. Starting with fewer than five hundred subscribers, Hall reported in April that, even though seven hundred extra copies had been printed, the impression of the first and second numbers had been used up and a second edition was necessary. By June, there were 2,100 names on the list, and the *Chronicle* announced that three thousand copies would be printed thenceforth. In September, Hall put the number of subscribers at "nearly three thousand." Before 1836, that number was reached and perhaps exceeded. No Western magazine had had patronage so great, and Hall believed that few if any Eastern ones had succeeded so well.[1] Hall enlarged the journal from fifty to fifty-six pages at the beginning of 1834, and to seventy-two pages in March, 1835. In printing and art it compared favorably with most Eastern magazines of the period. Colored engravings—for example, "The Vast, Illimitable, Changing West," in yellow and blue, and the "Burning of the French Missionaries," in red, green, and aquamarine—embellished several numbers for 1834; and perhaps, if complete files were extant, it would be found that such adornments were a regular feature of the magazine.[2] Hall announced in the autumn of 1833 that he would award fifty dollars to winners of short-story and essay contests and, in May, 1834, that he would pay a dollar a page for accepted articles.[3] The magazine's prompt appearance for nearly three years, usually on the first day of the month, is further indication of its prosperity.[4]

Hall kept a share of the ownership, apparently a half, as long as he was editor. His statements about the magazine's finances are ambiguous. Once he declared that the income from subscriptions never exceeded the disbursements, but presumably his salary as editor was included in the expenses. The chief financial difficulty arose from the quixotic custom of allowing the subscribers to defer payment until the end of the yearly subscription. At the close of the magazine's second year, "several thousand" of them were delinquent, and a year later Hall complained that they still owed from seven to ten thousand dollars. The collection of these debts cost more than printing the magazine. But even while he was discussing what his subscribers owed, he considered the magazine prosperous and profitable.[5]

Throughout Hall's active editorship, the circulation of the *Western Monthly* exceeded that of any previous or contemporary Western magazine, and its subscription list would have been considered healthy anywhere in the United States during the period of the magazine's publication. Timothy Flint's *Western Monthly Review*, published at Cincinnati from 1827 to 1830, had fewer than a thousand subscribers in 1827.[6] The *Western Messenger*, published at

Cincinnati and Louisville from 1835 to 1841, probably never reached a circulation of a thousand copies.[7] In the South or the East, few magazines of quality published between 1833 and 1837 had a larger circulation than the *Western Monthly*. The *Southern Literary Messenger*, published at Richmond (1834-1845), probably had not obtained a thousand subscribers at the completion of the first volume in 1835. The list of subscribers to the *Knickerbocker*, published in New York (1833-1865), had fewer than a thousand names in May, 1834, although the number was increased, by 1837, to more than five thousand. Even the well established *North American Review* had only about three thousand subscribers in 1826.[8]

Hall's offer of a dollar a page for accepted and printed articles was liberal. The *North American Review* and the *New-England Magazine* paid the same rate. Although the *Whig Review* paid two dollars per page, and the *Knickerbocker*, after it became well established, is said to have paid five dollars per page, such rates were exceptional in the United States.

Perhaps following the example of Dennie's editorship of the *Port Folio*, Hall appears to have expected the intellectual community to furnish most of the writing for his magazine without much direct solicitation on his part. In fact, the aid of a group of intellectuals in Cincinnati was apparently offered him as an inducement to establish his magazine in their city. In any event, he appears not to have been as zealous as he might have been in securing the nation's best talent. No letter in which he sought contributions from major authors is known to have survived. As a result, the magazine was interesting, but with more enterprise on his part it could perhaps have been distinguished. Other regional magazines developed major authors. The *Southern Literary Messenger*, which Hall praised, began to publish Poe's tales in 1835. The *New-England Magazine*, which Hall admired and whose very young editor, Edwin Buckingham, was Hall's friend,[9] was publishing Holmes's essays, Whittier's poems, and Hawthorne's stories. Yet there is no evidence to indicate that Hall, who had been the first to publish a laudatory notice of Hawthorne, made any effort to secure an occasional story from him.

Even so, an abundance of contributions flowed in from every quarter, enabling Hall to publish a journal entirely of original matter. There were thirty-seven known contributors to the volume for 1834. "Of these," Hall wrote, "four reside in Kentucky, two in Indiana, four in Illinois, one in Missouri, one in Tennessee, two in Alabama, one in Michigan, one in Mississippi, one in Pennsylvania, one in New York, one in Massachusetts, and the remainder in Ohio. Of these, six are ladies. . . . "

Hall himself did not know the names of all of his authors, and many of them remain unidentified. Most of those who are known lived in Cincinnati.[10] Two young men, James H. Perkins and Isaac Appleton Jewett, stand out because they wrote more for the magazine than any other known contributor except Hall and because they appear to have aided him in his editorial duties. Both were born and reared in New England. Perkins, who was twenty-three in 1833, and who was at least tinged with transcendentalist opinions,[11] was probably one of the "cabinet of gentlemen" who conducted the magazine during the first three months; and, when Hall was ill with cholera during the summer following, Perkins edited the numbers for July and August.[12] Jewett, like Perkins, studied law in Cincinnati and was admitted to the bar in 1833, when he was twenty-five. He despaired when the "outrageous principles" of President Jackson were upheld in the election of 1832. He regarded Ohioans generally as "tabernacles of flesh" without vision, and in his letters to Joseph Willard, son of the Harvard president, he sighed for "the electricity of Harvard wit and mirth." [13] He wrote at least ten essays and two poems for the *Western Monthly* and won the magazine's essay contest with his "Themes for Western Fiction." [14] The frequency of his contributions in the number for August, 1835, indicates that he probably was "the friend" to whose hands Hall entrusted the editorship while he was absent in the East. Among the other Cincinnati contributors were Charles A. Jones; William D. Gallagher; Ephraim Peabody; H. J.

Groesbeck; U. T. Howe; Edward D. Mansfield; Charles D. Drake, son of Dr. Daniel Drake; and Edward P. Cranch, Perkins's law partner and brother of the transcendentalist poet Christopher P. Cranch. Apparently most of the authors living outside of Cincinnati sent Hall only one contribution apiece. Notable exceptions were John Russell, who wrote three stories, and Hannah Flagg Gould of Newburyport, Massachusetts, who sent Hall nine poems for first publication in his magazine. The names of most of the *Western Monthly's* known authors are now familiar only to students of regional history.

Of all Hall's identified authors, only the women achieved wide acclaim in literature, and the magazine will be remembered partly because it helped to develop the talents of two ladies who lived in Cincinnati. One was Caroline Lee Hentz, who wrote five stories signed with her name or initials. The best of these tales is "Thanksgiving Day," in which she exhibits skill in characterization and narrative structure.[15] But veins of sentiment and piety run through all her stories in the *Western Monthly,* and they reflect the West but little. Long after she left Cincinnati in 1834, she wrote in the 1850's eleven novels that had an amazing popularity.

The magazine performed perhaps its greatest service to American letters by recognizing and fostering the talent of Harriet Beecher. She was only twenty-one when she excitedly wrote to a friend that the men of the Semi-Colon society had taken a fancy to her essay "Modern Uses of Language."[16] She timidly permitted them to print it in the *Western Monthly* for March, 1833, with the signature B. The lively story "Isabelle and Her Sister Kate, and Their Cousin," signed May and appearing the next February, may now be added to the list of her known works.[17] Hall's praise of this tale was probably the first favorable notice of her work to appear in print. "We hope," Hall remarked, "that one who writes with so much ease and gracefulness, will frequently exercise her powers of pleasing for the benefit of our readers."[18] Soon afterward he awarded her the *Western Monthly's* short-story prize for "A New England Sketch."

Hall may have persuaded her to enter the contest. He had announced that fifty dollars would be awarded to the authors of the best story and the best essay submitted by November 10, 1833. In the December number, however, he printed only the winning essay, observing that "the competition for the best Tale, was not such as to render it desirable, that an award should be made at the appointed time. It has therefore been determined," he continued, "to defer the decision of that prize until the first of February, in order that all who are competent, may have an opportunity of entering into the competition."[19] Accordingly, the result of the fiction contest was not disclosed until the publication of Harriet's prize story in April, 1834.

From these circumstances, a biographer of Harriet reasons that Hall had put off the closing date of the story contest in order to accommodate her. He argued that Hall, at a Semi-Colon meeting, had heard someone read her story, was impressed, and after ferreting out the name of the author, persuaded her to revise the manuscript and submit it in the competition. He then postponed the close of the contest to give her time for revision, and in due time awarded her the prize.[20]

The theory is plausible; however, it is likely that Hall knew of Harriet's literary ambitions and encouraged them earlier than has been thought. It should be remembered that in Illinois he had become known as a powerful friend of the Presbyterian church and of Presbyterian education in the West. He had been an important factor in bringing Harriet's brother Edward to the presidency of Illinois College, and he had known Edward and probably entertained him as a guest at his Vandalia home, which was always open to officers of the college and to western Presbyterian ministers. When Hall went to Cincinnati, he was, for a time, a friend of Harriet's father and attended his church.[21] He probably became acquainted with Harriet soon after his arrival. He must have seen and talked with her at her father's church, at Dr. Drake's intellectual soirees, at the Semi-Colon parties, and at her and her sister's school, of which he was a stockholder, secretary of the board of trustees, and a member of the board's executive committee.[22] Given an abundance of occasions on which he was thrown into Harriet's company, it is hard to believe he would not have known something of her talents and ambitions. Her first contribution to the *Western Monthly* appeared in March, 1833, about the time he had arrived in Cincinnati and a year earlier than her biographer places her "debut" in the magazine. Since Hall's editorial cabinet appears to have known her as the author of this contribution,[23] it is unlikely that Hall himself was uninformed; he did know the name of the author of every contribution to the number published the next month.[24] He appears to have known that she was the author of "Isabelle and Her Sister Kate, and Their Cousin," which was printed two months before the appearance of the prize-winning story.[25]

The prize story, "A New England Sketch," is remarkable for the way in which it brings to life the people and the spirit of a region, a quality superbly evidenced in such stories as *Oldtown Folks* (1869) and *Poganuc People* (1878), published during the later period of her world-wide popularity. The degree of Hall's influence upon her narratives remains a matter of conjecture. However, it can be said that earlier accounts of her first ventures into authorship have probably overemphasized her shyness. Her use of pseudonyms, while it might conceivably indicate a retiring nature as Forrest Wilson believed,[26] more likely indicates simply her awareness of literary etiquette and her desire to conform to it; it should be noted that almost no contribution to the *Western Monthly*, especially those written by women, appeared with the author's real name. Moreover, it is hard to imagine an eager girl with literary ambitions who would not seek the criticism of an author who had published several books and who was the editor of a magazine which had printed her earliest efforts. The evidence suggests that Hall met Harriet soon after his arrival, that he encouraged her and urged her to develop her talents, that she replied— as beginning authors so frequently do—that she did not know what to write about, and that Hall, who had himself risen to prominence as a writer of regionalistic fiction, advised her to write about the people and the region she knew best.

Her sketches "Frankness, by a Lady" and "Aunt Mary" appeared in the May and July issues following the publication of the prize tale. The religious preoccupation of her stories is out of fashion, but they have rapid movement, skillful characterization, and fidelity to the New England scene. Of the prize tale, written when Harriet was only twenty-two, John Erskine has said, "The heroic flame already burns in it."[27]

Relieved of the necessity that in Vandalia had driven him to provide stories and poems to give variety to his magazine, Hall in Cincinnati wrote few of either. Seven poems in the *Western Monthly* bear his pen name AIO; but he is known to have written only three narratives for his new journal, and since they had been printed by April, 1833, even these probably had been composed in Vandalia or Henderson, Kentucky. His "Hunting Exploits," in the February, 1833, number, is a brief relation of extraordinary experiences of western hunters. The events of his unfinished "Travels of a Student" and of "The Spy, a Tale of the Revolution" take place on the eastern seaboard.[28] Of the three narratives, only "The Spy" can be regarded as more than a trifle. It is tempting, however, to ascribe to Hall two tales of unknown authorship, "Circumstantial Evidence" and "Le Rouge, or the Red Tavern."[29] The latter is an interesting story of a murder committed on the shore of the St. Lawrence during the War of 1812.

Most of the *Western Monthly's* writers did not attempt to appease the general hunger for knowledge of the West. Instead, they sent Hall articles dealing with abstractions, with Europe and Europeans, or with homesick reminiscences of New England. As a result, the *Western Monthly* did not contain as large a proportion of Western articles and stories as its Vandalia predecessor or as Flint's earlier *Western Monthly Review,* although it did exceed in that respect the nearly contemporary *Western Messenger,* a predominantly religious magazine. Since Hall was unable, as he had been in conducting the *Illinois Monthly,* to depend upon his contributors for Western matter, he himself wrote most of the articles that gave the new journal its Western character. And his descriptions of the West, his criticisms, his essays on education, and his controversial articles stamped the magazine with his vigorous personality.

The most poetic of all his descriptive writings is "Western Scenery," in which he portrays the grand expanse between the Alleghenies and the Mississippi but especially the prairies in their various seasonal beauties.[30] With a sweep comparable with that of his "The Public Domain," he conveys his enthusiasm for the gaiety of the humble prairie flowers as well as for the magnificence of the Western rivers and forests. Equally interesting is his "Travels in Hot Weather," a series of six articles that describe his passage to the East by steamboat and his leisurely journey, chiefly on horseback, through central Kentucky.[31] On the latter excursion, which he made in 1834, he visited Henry Clay at Ashland, stopped at Harrodsburg Springs, went on to Mammoth Cave, and there turned north and rode to Cloverport on the Ohio. He describes the countryside, the inns, and his first railroad ride over the fifteen miles of track between Frankfort and Lexington. In his account of the following summer's travels, he notes the throngs of wayfarers and the gamblers and drunken profanity that he encountered on the Western steamboats.

True to his promise in the first issue, Hall printed more than a score of articles devoted entirely or in part to the promotion of Western education; he probably wrote most of them himself. Nearly all were radically democratic and rooted in his faith in the intelligence and good sense of the backwoodsmen. The author, probably Hall, of "On the Formation of National Character" repeated again and again the conviction that "the people are the strength of our country," and stated that the very founding of our republic was due more to the intelligence and education of our forefathers than to their arms.[32]

Since the principle of public education was already widely

accepted, the magazine urged the improvement of instruction. With a wisdom often lacking among the educational reformers of our own generation, the *Western Monthly's* proposals for improvement began with the teacher, whom the magazine regarded as more important than the lawyer or the clergyman. "Why," asked the author of "Education," "has it been the prerogative of the man who could do nothing else, to keep school? Why are men, at this day, laughed at by their fellow-students, because they propose to become teachers?"[33] The magazine advocated an increase in the public school teacher's wages to at least the level of those of the day laborer; the establishment of normal schools and departments of education to train and test the teacher in his art; the extension of the requirements for teaching appointments beyond the customary requisites of ability to read, write, and multiply by three; the appointment of female teachers; and the replacement of whipping and terror by friendliness and professional skill.[34] If these proposals seem commonplace, it should be remembered that even so progressive an educator as Hall's friend Dr. Daniel Drake considered whipping an indispensable aid to instruction.

Except when he was out of town, Hall appears to have written nearly all of the *Western Monthly's* literary criticism. His critical tests applied in the *Illinois Monthly*— truthfulness of detail, patriotism, religious orthodoxy, and reverence for women — were also his criteria in the new periodical.

Probably no magazine could have lived long in the pioneer West without upholding, or at least acquiescing in, a stern moral code and a literal interpretation of the Bible. The pioneer's concern for the world to come is illustrated by an account book of the postmaster at Jacksonville, Illinois, which lists 153 religious journals received by patrons of that post office in 1831 and 1832, against seventeen copies of the state's only literary magazine, the *Illinois Monthly*.[35] Cincinnati's religious papers sometimes laid a heavy hand on the novel; and, through propagation by the clergy, these periodicals enjoyed an influence even beyond

230

their wide circulation. Soon after Hall arrived in the city, the Presbyterian *Journal,* edited by Rev. Thomas Brainerd and having a subscription list as large as the *Western Monthly*'s, rebuked an agent who was soliciting subscriptions for a Bible commentary and the works of Scott. That author's novels, the *Journal* contended, "have exerted and are now exerting a pernicious influence on the cause of morality and religion. We could by no means recommend them to the rising generation. . . . The excitement caused by his glowing details leaves nothing salutary behind it. The reader wakes from his fascinations, with no new purposes of virtuous conduct, with no new relish for the sober enjoyments of life, and with no new light to guide him to his home in heaven." Two weeks after this warning, the *Journal* was able to relieve the anxiety of the parents of the jeopardized children by announcing that the agent had undertaken his work without reflection, and "so soon as judicious christians advised him of the evil tendencies of the above works [Scott's], he desisted altogether."[36]

Hall had been christened in the Presbyterian church, and he and Mary had joined the Presbyterian congregation in Vandalia.[37] Even though he believed in a strict interpretation of the Bible, he was also a cultivated man of the world, and in his Mechanics Institute address, printed in the magazine as "On Novel Writing," he rebelled against the pietistic detractors of fiction. He admitted that the deficiencies of novels were great, but, he countered, "may not the same objection be applied to every other department of literature? Is all history true? Are all moral treatises safe guides? Are scientific works universally accurate? Are all sermons orthodox?" It is an obvious fact, he declared, that "rational minds engaged in the highest and holiest purposes of benevolence have deemed it expedient to address the intellect through the imagination," and some novelists "have probably been among the greatest benefactors of the age."[38]

In this lecture he did, however, turn a satirical searchlight upon the heroine of sentimental fiction: "Intoxicated with the perfume of a lilly [*sic*], fainting in ecstasy at the murmurs of an eolian harp, mourning in elegy over a dying linnet, and weeping over the untimely demise of a fallen leaf; she can yet feed for a month together on bread and water, lest some horrible soporific should be mingled in her food; lies down in her clothes, which never require washing or mending in spite of being made to do double duty; watches through long nights and weeps through weary days, without the least diminution of the lustre of the eye, or the slightest symptoms of catarrhal affection; and after all this, she has the resolution to hold a loaded pistol at the head of the persevering baronet; to jump out of windows, scale walls, scramble through thicket, forest, fence, and swamp; sleep in barns, without a night-cap, and put up at inns without a penny in her pocket—her fear, famine, delicacy, loveliness, and satin slippers, to the contrary notwithstanding."[39]

But Hall favored fidelity to nature only if it did not violate propriety. "I have always held and imposed as a rule on myself," he wrote twenty years later, "that a writer should not put on paper that which he would be unwilling to speak or read in good society, and when writing he should imagine a modest woman, or a sober-minded well bred gentleman to be looking over his shoulder."[40] Thus the *Western Monthly* frowned upon Richardson and Frances Burney because they used the theme of seduction; upon Mrs. Jameson's *The Beauties of the Court of Charles the Second* because she made the famous adulteresses attractive; and upon Bulwer's *The Last Days of Pompeii* because Bulwer exhibited sensuality and vice in disgusting detail.[41]

Hall tried to conduct a genial magazine; he praised more works than he condemned. But his salutary insistence upon truth in descriptive and scientific works kept him in hot water. With devastating humor he exposed, in the issue for June, 1833, Timothy Flint's *Lectures upon Natural History,* a work soberly avowing that dogs have almost useless eyes, that horses' eyes magnify children into colossi, and that horse hairs turn into snakes.[42] Many sensible people like Hall's friend John Pierpont—poet, liberal pastor

of the Hollis Street Unitarian Church in Boston, and grandfather of John Pierpont Morgan—no doubt relished Hall's
review of Flint's book. But in Cincinnati the article aroused
a storm of anger among those who were loyal to Flint
because he was a New Englander, because to some Westerners he was a venerable champion of their region, or
because as a minister he was considered an unfair target
for ridicule. The review marked the beginning of long-
continued abuse of Hall by Flint's friend Charles Hammond
in his powerful *Daily Gazette* as well as the beginning of
ill-natured notices of Hall and his magazine in two of the
less influential literary newspapers of Cincinnati.[43] Flint,
whose retirement to the East that same summer left Hall
as the leading spokesman for the West, retaliated in the
Knickerbocker with a bilious review of Hall's *The Harpe's
Head*.[44] Two years later—in his "Sketches of the Literature
of the United States," in the London *Athenæum* for October, 1835—he revealed his resentment by dismissing Hall's
work with a brief, derisive paragraph, in which he accused
him of "self-complacency," and said "he wants learning."

More durable damage to Hall's reputation was wrought
by a response to his review of John Audubon's *Ornitho-
logical Biography,* in which he praised Audubon as an artist
but took exception to some of his statements on natural
history. A critic in the *American Quarterly Review* accused
Hall of deriding Audubon's book and praising Alexander
Wilson's *American Ornithology* because his brother Harrison was Wilson's publisher.[45] Hall was hurt by this charge
of venality and refuted it by explaining that, when he wrote
the review, Harrison had no interest in Wilson's work and
did not intend to have any.[46] But the *Quarterly's* accusation has been repeated even in modern biographies of
Audubon by Constance Rourke and Francis Herrick, neither
of whom appears to have read Hall's refutation.[47]

But Hall's most partial critic could hardly justify the
vituperation he hurled at William Gallagher, Thomas
Shreve, and James Perkins, editors of the *Cincinnati Mirror,*
a weekly literary newspaper. These young men—the oldest
was twenty-seven—had, to be sure, annoyed Hall by reveal-

ing the real names of some of the *Western Monthly*'s anonymous authors. The *Mirror* had committed a more serious offense in printing, sometimes even without clear credit, as much as half of its matter from the articles Hall had paid for and published in the *Western Monthly*.[48] Such careless use of literary property was general, and it discouraged the profession of letters in America perhaps as much as did the lack of an international copyright agreement. Hall was silent a long time, but in July, 1835, he poured forth at the young editors a torrent of deplorable, petty rage.[49] One hopes that he had this diatribe in mind when he wrote his farewell editorial, in which he acknowledged "those errors from which it is not the lot of any to be exempt."

Although some of these critical clashes incurred the resentment of influential persons, his stand on the burning questions of slavery and religious toleration was of greater significance, both for the duration of his magazine and for Western culture.

II

The population of Cincinnati in the 1830's had so many diverse elements that an editor who took a firm stand on any vital question was likely to incur the resentment of a considerable section of the people. Heterogeneous in nationality, religion, culture, and even in race, the people had had little time to learn to live together in harmony; and the city was so situated, both geographically and economically, that it was particularly subject to passionate conflict.

The sectionalism of the native American settlers in Cincinnati appears to have been one of the greatest single causes of unrest. The natives of the West and the settlers from New Jersey, New York, Pennsylvania, and the southern states appear to have dwelt together in amity. But toward the East generally, and toward New England in particular, the Westerner was traditionally resentful. He regarded the East as the seat of capital, of credit, and of manufacturing—the region which year after year drained off his scanty supply of currency. He had to pay high transportation costs on the finished goods that came from the East, and in the East his bank notes were discounted. In the West, where Jacksonianism was strong, the East was remembered as the seat of the Hartford Convention and was associated with an uncompromising Federalism. The Westerner was also jealous of the established culture and commerce of the East, and he was quick to defend his own accomplishments.[50]

The New Englanders, constituting a large segment of the population of Cincinnati, appear to have provoked the strongest sectional antagonism. Many of them came to the West conscious of their culture, especially of their religion, and were intent upon grafting their superior stock upon the inferior culture of the West.[51] They soon assumed power in the Protestant churches of Cincinnati, especially in the Unitarian and Presbyterian denominations, of which the latter, with six churches, was the most numerous and powerful sect in the city.[52] Through Lyman Beecher, leader of the "New School" Presbyterians, they soon gained an important part in the control of the city's Presbyterian organization and of its newspaper, the widely circulated *Cincinnati Journal*.[53] From New England they brought a puritanism to which may be traced much of the opposition in Cincinnati to gambling, horse-racing, the drama, and to novels which did not rather definitely point out the reader's path to heaven.[54] The thoroughness, the minuteness even, of this scrutiny must have been irksome to the easy-going Westerner. One can imagine the irritation of Hall, a conscientious Mason, when Beecher complained of a Sunday parade of Masons dressed "in habiliments as black as superstition itself." [55] Since the Westerner was especially thinskinned about his culture, he found especially galling the New Englander's declaration that he had come as a missionary to raise his Western brother from a quasi-barbarism; and he was prone to retaliate with exaggerated descriptions of his colleges, his literature, and his mechanical achievements. In the literary criticism of the Cincinnati journals there was frequently a petty sectionalism detrimental to the growth of a Western literature. Some New Englanders appear even to have tried to form in the city an upper-class society from which Westerners were to have been excluded.[56] Harriet Martineau, noting in 1835 the prevalence of sectional prejudices throughout the United States—a feeling for which " 'hatred' is not too strong a term"—found "the most mortifying instance" of it in Cincinnati, where it did not give away even in social intercourse.[57]

Such divisions among the native-born Americans augured ill for a city which had to assimilate a large foreign population and deal with the vexatious problems of slavery and Catholicism. There were in Cincinnati people of many nationalities, but the Irish and the Germans were present in such large blocks as to make their absorption difficult. The Irish, who were settling in the city while the great canals were being built, were poor and uneducated; in a predominantly Protestant city most of them clung to their Catholic religion. The Germans were even more numerous. Calvin Stowe, in a paper prepared for the 1835 meeting of the Western Literary Institute and College of Professional Teachers, stated that there were "not less than 10,000 Germans in Cincinnati, and its immediate vicinity, including those only, who live so near the city as to attend church here on the Sabbath." Of these more than 7,000 were Catholic and not more than a fourth could speak English well. There were, Stowe said, between 1,200 and 1,500 German children of school age, many of whom were deterred from attending the public schools "because their foreign garb and accent expose them to the ridicule of the native scholars."[58] The foreign problem might not have been so hazardous in Cincinnati had there not arisen, in the early 1830's, a national anti-Catholic "crusade" which by 1835 was in full swing. Anti-Catholic feeling had reached the riot stage in Boston by August, 1834;[59] and in Cincinnati, in 1834, Bishop John Purcell was writing in his journal, "Bigots growing fierce in their opposition to Popery. . . . Why do not Catholics awake? . . . We must descend sometimes into the Plain & fight the Philistines with their own arms."[60] In 1835, the flames were fanned higher by the

236

publication of such "revelations" as Rebecca Reed's *Six Months in a Convent* and the *Journal of Frances Anne Butler*.

Even more inflammatory than the problems of nationality and religion was the slavery question. Lying on the border between North and South, Cincinnati was destined to feel the outbreak of hostility sooner and more violently than most of the other Northern cities. The conflict was exacerbated by the three thousand Negroes in the city, nearly all of whom were free, although some, it is said, were slaves hired to Cincinnatians as household servants.[61] The free Negroes, living in the worst slum section, were subject to the assaults of rioters living in Cincinnati or across the river in Kentucky.[62] The existence of this Negro population in the city undoubtedly intensified the abolitionist controversy and influenced the opinion of many Cincinnatians toward the entire slavery question. But the people of the Queen City could decide against slavery only at great cost, for the manufacturing and wholesaling economy of the city was closely linked to the economy and principles of the non-manufacturing South, which was, apparently, the city's best customer.[63] Cincinnati was, in short, an explosive spot, destined to face in the 1830's the burning questions of abolitionism and Catholicism. As it happened, abolitionism was the first to threaten the peace of the city.

In Walnut Hills, two miles above Cincinnati, Lane Theological Seminary admitted its first class in 1833.[64] The president was Lyman Beecher, who had been brought from the pastorate of the Bowdoin Street church in Boston to build a stronghold of Presbyterianism in the West. Powerful as Lyman Beecher was, the strongest figure in the Seminary at that time was a student, Theodore Weld. Then in his thirtieth year, Weld had already achieved proficiency in oratory by preaching and lecturing far and wide in the West in favor of temperance and of manual-labor colleges. He had helped secure an important part of Lane's endowment, and he had provided the bulk of her students.[65] His selfless devotion to his fellow students stricken in the cholera epidemic of 1833 had earned for him the love and

237

admiration of the whole student body. "In the estimation of his class," Lyman Beecher remembered later, "he was president. He took the lead of the whole institution. The young men had, many of them, been under his care, and they thought he was a god."[66] Of his oratory, Beecher is reported to have said that Weld was "logic on fire," as "eloquent as an angel and powerful as thunder."[67]

This young man, regarded by one student of the anti-slavery movement as the greatest of the abolitionists,[68] was made an agent of the American Anti-Slavery Society soon after it was founded in December, 1833.[69] Under his leadership, the students soberly discussed slavery in a series of eighteen evening meetings held during their first winter at Lane. On the first nine evenings the question was, "Ought the people of the Slaveholding States to abolish Slavery immediately?" The students' answer was that slavery was a sin, and should be abolished. The remaining evenings were devoted to debate on whether the doctrines and tendencies of the American Colonization Society "render it worthy of the support of the Christian public." Their answer to this question was in the negative.[70] On March 10, 1834, they formed the Anti-Slavery Society of Lane Seminary and, on March 28, printed the Society's constitution in the Presbyterian newspaper, the *Cincinnati Journal*. The uncompromising nature of the Anti-Slavery group, as contrasted with the moderation of the older Colonization Society, was manifested in its denunciation of slaveholding as a sin and by its denial of the doctrine of Negro inferiority. Members of the Lane Society began at once to carry out their beliefs by conducting Sabbath schools, day schools, and lyceums among Cincinnati's large population of free Negroes. On Sundays the Lane students taught religion, and on week days they lectured on science.[71]

Since at that time the Colonization Society was recognized as the leading antislavery organization, the Lane reformers were impelled to proclaim their disagreement with the older association. Many of the Lane students had been members of the Colonization Society and could plead the authority of experience. Their position was neatly summed up by John Rankin, a Presbyterian minister in nearby Ripley, Ohio: "The tendency of its [the Colonization Society's] doctrines is to perpetuate slavery. . . . Let the doctrine prevail that the people of color cannot be free among us, and that they ought not to be liberated until they can be removed to Africa, and the society may go on for a thousand generations, but it will never carry off so much as the increase."[72] James Thome, a Lane student who had been born and reared in Kentucky, "reverenced" many colonizationists but believed that the dogma of colonization was pernicious. "I *know* its evils," he said, "and can lay my finger on them one by one. I *know* the individual slaves who are now in bondage by its influence *alone*. I *know* the masters whose only plea for continuing in the sin, is drawn from *its* doctrines. . . . " He believed that abolitionism, on the other hand, "seizes the conscience with an authoritarian grasp; it runs across every path of the guilty, haunts him, goads him, and rings in his ear the cry of blood. . . . It writes 'thou art the man' upon the forehead of every oppressor."[73]

Hall had been a member of the Colonization Society for three years. He believed that slavery was an evil and that some day the slaves should be freed. But partly because he was a scion of a Maryland family of slaveholding planters and had married the daughter of a Kentucky slaveowning family—with whom his children were then living—he thought, as did some of the abolitionists, that the uncompromising doctrine of the Anti-Slavery Society would lead to national calamity.[74] He believed that the Colonization Society, on the other hand, since it advocated that the Northerner share with the Southerner the burden of the slavery problem, furnished a peaceable solution.[75] As a lover of law and order who had probably been informed of the bloody race riots that Cincinnati had endured four years earlier, he knew also that the people of the North would not then tolerate the dissemination of radical abolitionist principles.[76] In 1834, his view was probably shared by most people interested in emancipation. It had been the position of William Lloyd Garrison in 1828; it was the position of the faculty and twenty-one of the twenty-five trustees of Lane in 1834; and it was to be the position of Abraham Lincoln.[77]

For the *Western Monthly* for May, 1834, Hall wrote "Education and Slavery," the first significant reaction to the Lane movement.[78] To him the new society was the terrible swift sword that would cleave the nation asunder. "Upon the abstract question [of slavery], all good men are agreed, in viewing it as a national misfortune—all are willing to see it gradually melt away, until no trace of its existence shall be left; but no honest and reflecting man is willing to see it broken up, like the snows of the spring, by a sudden change, which shall inundate the land, and spread devastation and distress over the whole country."[79]

He then turned to the objects of the new society—"the immediate emancipation of the whole colored race within the United States" and the elevation of the Negro "to an intellectual, moral, and political equality with the whites"— and he was filled with consternation. He observed that even the patriots of the Revolution who had braved "the armies of the most powerful empire in the world" had "shrunk with pious horror from the contest with each other, which would have convulsed and torn asunder the whole of the newly-erected political fabric." Now, Hall argued, here were students like schoolboys "wearing paper caps, flourishing wooden swords, and fancying themselves for the moment endued with the prowess of Hector and Achilles" blithely setting out to dispose of a question from "which sages and patriots grown grey in their country's service" had recoiled. "The calm wisdom of the nation," he said, "has long since settled down in the opinion that this subject should be left to the providence of God, to the matured decision of time and public sentiment. . . ."[80]

In the remainder of the article, Hall, by demanding that students avoid controversial subjects, precipitated one of America's memorable struggles for academic freedom. He argued that the usefulness of any college is diminished by being "perverted to party purposes." Moreover, he believed that students should not reach voting age with prejudices;

they should be left "unprepossessed, and free to act according to the unbiassed judgment of their minds and the dictates of their consciences." He approved of college literary societies, which "afford an agreeable recreation, and promote friendly intercourse, while they exercise and improve the mind. But any thing beyond this is, in our judgment, inadmissible." In short, nothing in a college should be allowed "to prevent the most amicable intercourse among its members, or to distract the attention of the pupil from his main purpose, which is the acquisition of knowledge."[81]

He saw clearly the danger to the colonization movement in the abolitionists' training of a band of ministers who, with evangelistic fervor, would traverse the land emphasizing the "sinfulness" of slavery and urging immediate action. It was, he said, "a cunningly devised scheme, which would have been creditable to a college of Jesuits." The only flaw in this plot, he predicted, was that "the indignation of the public will put it down, and the united voice of all moderate and reflecting men, who prize the ornament of a meek and quiet spirit, who love peace, and who desire to see the schools of our country kept free from all irritating causes, vain disputings, and heresies, will be raised to admonish these gentlemen, to mind their own business, and their books."[82]

It is easier to understand Hall's antipathy to immediate abolition than his denial of the students' right to discuss it. Certainly if he had been in the place of the students and if, after eighteen evenings of prayerful discussion, he had felt compelled to embrace the most explosive cause of his day, he would never have submitted to any restraint. Indeed, less than two years later he was raging against interference with his own editorial discussion of hot public questions and against those who would strait-jacket him into being merely "literary."[83]

Apparently Weld called on Hall and asked him to print a correction of "Education and Slavery." Upon Hall's refusal, Weld wrote a reply addressed to Hall and printed it in the *Journal* of May 30.[84] (Hall probably did not know until six months later that it had first been read to Lyman

Beecher and that it was printed with his "hearty approval.")[85] The letter was crushing. Weld first cut the ground from under Hall's feet by showing that nine-tenths of Lane's students were over twenty-one years old and then went on to an excellent defense of academic freedom. Had the question been decided on the basis of reason, Weld would have had an easy victory. Extra copies of his letter were printed, and news of the new college society spread rapidly.[86]

Hall may have instigated the Cincinnati Colonization Society's series of evening meetings that began five days after the publication of Weld's letter and were designed, Weld's men believed, to woo them back to that organization.[87] For a moment, Hall and Beecher acted in concert. At the first meeting, Beecher pleaded with the abolitionists to work with the colonizationists. The two antislavery groups, he said, must not risk delaying emancipation by quarreling with each other or by antagonizing the slaveholder. Calvin Stowe, speaking on June 9, admitted preference for colonization but acknowledged that other anti-slavery weapons were needed. Of Hall's speech at the final meeting, we know only that he advocated colonization "with great energy." Beecher and Stowe then went to the East for the summer vacation, which Beecher spent in raising money for the Seminary. Weld and many other Lane abolitionists, however, remained in town and continued their work in the Negro schools and lyceums.[88]

Perhaps no other Northern city would have been more hostile than Cincinnati to the benevolent labors of the Lane students. A determined effort to elevate the Negro "to an intellectual, moral, and political equality with the whites" would have been shocking in any American city then, as it would be in many communities today. Cincinnati's nearness to slave territory made the citizens especially sensitive. Moreover, the continued prosperity of the city depended, many leading citizens believed, upon its development of Southern trade; and a year later, they were to urge the construction of a railroad from Cincinnati through the South.[89] The students, however, worked diligently and with "the most flattering prospects." "The [Negro] Sabbath schools," John Rankin observed, "were crowded. Multitudes manifested a desire to hear the word of life." But the success of the students' enterprise precipitated its defeat. Some Negroes began to attend Cincinnati churches. Immediately a writer to the *Journal* protested against this mingling with white people. One of the city's periodicals reported that the Lane students were fraternizing with the Negroes. Exaggerated rumors of the familiarities of the Lane students with their Negro friends then began to fly. These tales, Rankin thought, "if not invented, were retailed by the more respectable classes of the citizens, even in public prints, until the rabble of the city were excited, and the mob preparing to tear down Lane Seminary."[90]

The opposition soon crystallized. In the *Journal* of June 27, "A Ruling Elder" wrote that he had not yet paid the whole of his subscription to Lane and felt no obligation to do so unless rules were adopted "to prevent interference with any and every political question, and confine the student to his proper duties." About two months later, the executive committee of the trustees proposed legislation to abolish the Seminary's troublesome society and to discountenance even informal student discussions of slavery.[91] The *Western Monthly*'s October issue, distributed a few days before the meeting of the entire board of trustees,[92] contained "Efficient Discipline Necessary to the Permanent Prosperity of Our Literary Institutions," almost certainly written by Hall. The article attempted to justify the proposed academic gag. The author contended that the government of a college is like that of a family. "When a person becomes an inmate of my house," he asked, "must I be charged with anti-republicanism . . . for requiring him to submit to the family regulations which he had no influence in establishing?"[93]

Hall's theory that "efficient discipline" was necessary for the prosperity of colleges was immediately put to the test. At their October meeting the Lane trustees passed the gag rule.[94] When the fall term opened, nearly all of the students seceded from the Seminary and many of them entered

Oberlin College; from the secessionists Weld trained a band of speakers that later became the backbone of the anti-slavery movement.[95] After the exodus, the Seminary that had begun with such high hope withered and never flourished again.[96]

III

Surveying his almost vacant classrooms in the autumn of 1834, Lyman Beecher would have welcomed the least possible further interference from the *Western Monthly Magazine*. He had come to Cincinnati, according to a letter he had written to his daughter Catharine in 1830, in the belief that "the moral destiny of our nation, and all our institutions and hopes, and the world's hopes, turns [*sic*] on the character of the West, and the competition now is for that of preoccupancy in the education of the rising generation, in which Catholics and infidels have got the start of us." He had come with the hope of "consecrating all my children to God in that region who are willing to go."[97] But to Hall, Beecher's idealism in practice was irritating. Hall had lived in the West for eighteen years; he had identified himself with the West and had embraced its causes. Although he found the vagaries of a few of the pioneers humorously fantastic, he trusted the good sense of the Western people as a whole, and had become their partisan. To him it seemed that Beecher had come to the West with a feeling of superiority, in the spirit of a missionary rather than of a fellow citizen, and with an inclination to drive rather than to lead the Western people. Beecher, even before leaving the East, had taken a position which, when he confirmed it later as a citizen of the West, could only rouse Hall's antagonism. The ensuing conflict impaired the work of both men.

In Boston as early as 1830, Beecher had preached a series of anti-Catholic sermons that swelled a wave of intolerance.[98] Later, in Cincinnati, Hall probably regarded him as partly responsible for the militant anti-Catholicism of the Presbyterian *Journal*, for its editor was Beecher's associate pastor of the Second Church, Thomas Brainerd.[99] In a lecture delivered repeatedly in the East during the summer of 1834, while the abolitionist activities of his students were creating a crisis for his seminary, Beecher appealed for money for Lane by drawing a frightening picture of national danger arising from an increasing Catholic population, especially threatening in the West.[100] He spoke in Boston on August 10, when Protestant excitement was at fever pitch there.[101] The next night a mob burned the Ursuline convent in adjacent Charlestown.

Hall may not have known fully the nature of Beecher's Eastern lectures until later, but he did read a newspaper account of the address delivered at Lowell. The Lane president was reported to have spoken there of the Westerners' "limited means of education, and of the importance of introducing social and religious principles of New England among them—New England principles, the matchless bounty of a bountiful Providence!—He dwelt upon the importance of . . . sowing the seeds of virtue before vice had taken root among them . . . and called upon New England's sons to go among them—not in a mass, to excite an envious feeling —but to mix with them as *leaven* in the loaf, and thus produce a saving and enduring influence."[102]

Hall's reply to this condescending expression of Yankee benevolence appeared in the *Western Monthly* for December and was satirically entitled "The March of Intellect." Beginning with mock humbleness, he said, "We are a young people, and have much to learn. We are a modest people, and listen with humility to the instructions of those who are wiser than ourselves." With arch sweetness he acknowledged even more: "Of the vast importance of introducing the 'social and religious principles of New England,' into our country, we do not presume to entertain a moment's doubt; for we cannot hesitate to believe that any thing which is to be brought so far, must be very good." But he went on to exhibit what he had thought was progress in the West since Daniel Boone's time. He mentioned steamboats, churches, schools, colleges that were more numerous in proportion than in the East, people who read Greek, Latin, and Hebrew, and a citizenry that believed the same Bible that

the New Englanders believed. "What a fine thing it is to
have learning!" he sighed. "We might have vegetated here
forever, without being aware that we were degenerating so
fast, that our race would soon become wholly corrupt,
unless a cross should be introduced from a purer stock."[103]
From such icy satire, he turned to soberness in his conclusion: "*We* hold to the doctrine of equality—and believing
that there is no very marked difference as to intellect or
intelligence, between any of the different parts of the United
States . . . we think that those who emigrate to this land
from any other, should be welcomed with kindness as friends
and fellow citizens. . . . "

Probably Hall's essay brought chuckles from many Westerners. But James H. Perkins, reared in New England and
then editor of the *Cincinnati Chronicle and Literary Gazette,*
deplored the use of satire against a doctor of divinity.[104]
He might have added that Beecher was the most prominent
anti-Catholic minister in the country and that to disagree
with him at that time of nationalist and religious tension
required courage. Beecher's eastern lecture, which was soon
printed, was a leading factor in the origin of America's first
political nativistic movement. In Cincinnati the *Journal,*
under his influence if not under his domination, poured
forth a steady stream of anti-Catholicism from the time of
Beecher's arrival in the city until the demise of the paper
in 1836. His doctrines, released in Cincinnati, with its large
foreign population, were probably no small influence in the
formation there by 1835 of a branch of one of the first
American nativistic parties—dedicated to opposition to the
Catholic church, to office-holding by foreigners, and to the
immigration of paupers and criminals.[105] The effects of such
agitation soon became apparent. By February, 1835, there
was a scuffle between Protestants and Catholics in the
streets of Cincinnati.[106] In August, Edward King, a prominent Cincinnatian writing to his wife about Beecher's
nativistic doctrine, said, "You of course hear if you do not
see, the spirit of mobocracy, that is abroad in the land—One
or two more years of such lawless proceedings, and the
necessity of a standing army and a military hero, will be-

come apparent to all who are attached to good order & sobriety."[107]

Beecher's lecture was published in April, 1835, as *A Plea for the West* without the original version's odious comparison of Eastern and Western culture which had offended Hall.[108] The published address, however, was still preponderantly a warning against the growth of Catholic influence in the West. In the first forty-nine pages Beecher pointed out the duty of Easterners to contribute money to Western education and explained that Western colleges were necessary for the preservation of American democracy. In the remaining 132 pages—seven-tenths of the entire work—he subtly insinuated the existence of an international plot to destroy American freedom. If the potentates of Europe had no designs upon our liberties, why, Beecher asked, were they paying the passage of "such floods of pauper emigrants —the contents of the poor house and the sweepings of the streets?" To possible wealthy donors to his Seminary, he spoke of the danger of radical democratic mobs in the West. "Our intelligence and virtue," he said, "will falter and fall back into a dark minded, vicious populace—a poor, uneducated, reckless mass of infuriated animalism, to push on resistless as the tornado, or to burn as if set on fire of hell." He declared that even "half a million of unprincipled, reckless voters, in the hands of demagogues, may, in our balanced elections, overrule all the property, and wisdom, and moral principle of the nation."[109]

Hall promptly reviewed *A Plea for the West* in the number for May. One of his most distinguished writings, his discussion, though fearless, was temperate and reasonable. He explained Beecher's dishonesty in both misquoting and misrepresenting Bishop Fenwick, who had tried to quiet the Boston Catholics after the riots.[110] On the main question, Hall wrote, "Dr. Beecher attempts seriously to show that 'this emigration, self-moved and slow in the beginning, is now rolling its broad tide, at the bidding of the powers of Europe, hostile to free institutions, and associated in holy alliance to arrest and put them down.' The evidence should be ample, indeed, upon which a christian minister undertakes thus to denounce a whole class of laborious foreigners, who have chosen our country as their home, and have quietly submitted themselves to our laws. It is a charge of conspiracy against our liberties, which includes in its denunciation, the whole body of catholics in the United States, whether native-born or foreign. It is a charge made without the support of a single tittle of testimony—without the production of a single overt act of hostility, towards our government, on the part of the Roman Catholics. It is a charge made against a body, in which were numbered many of the patriots of the revolution, and of those who, at a later period, have participated in the counsels of the nation, or have bared their breasts in battle to the enemies of our country, and among whom are found thousands of reputable, industrious citizens, whose integrity is above suspicion, and whose love of country is too pure and elevated to be tainted by the breath of a calumny so gratuitous and unfounded."

The evidence indicates that Hall wrote from principle and not, as Brainerd asserted, from spite. Hall had attended, and presumably still attended, Beecher's church,[111] and the two had been friends.[112] Moreover, in the same issue of the magazine Hall had used equal space in praising Beecher's *Sermons on Scepticism,* which he had heard the author deliver at the Second Church, because in that work Beecher had assumed nothing as a theologian or as a sectarian, but had relied solely upon reasonable argument. Still more compelling evidence that Hall was not impelled by rancor is the fact that he had defended the Catholics against intolerance six years earlier, in the *Illinois Intelligencer.*[113]

Hall followed his review of *A Plea for the West* with "The Catholic Question" in the June number, in which with understanding, good humor, and logic he tried to bring an excited public to its senses. He spelled out the necessity of settling the question only upon the evidence. He showed that Catholics were democratic and loyal citizens, and tried to allay fear by demonstrating that there were twenty-three times as many Protestants as Catholics in the country. He was perfectly willing, he wrote, to see a dispute over theo-

248

logical principle: "Those who believe this form of belief [Catholicism] to be unscriptural, to be pernicious in its tendencies, to be inefficient in its code of morality, or to be unsafe as a guide to salvation, have an undoubted right to erect a barrier of moral antagonism against it, and to oppose it with all the weapons which may be used consistently with truth and fairness. . . . but it is not allowable to oppose even error, by artifice or injustice, by violating private right, or disturbing the public peace. . . .

"We have not the slightest partiality for their form of belief, their mode of worship, or the practical operation of their system. We like our own faith and practice better. But these questions are not material to the issue now under discussion. However wrong they may be, they have a right to be considered as being conscientiously wrong, and to be treated with kindness."[114]

He concluded by proposing a treaty reminscent of Franklin's good-humored tact. Let the religious papers on both sides, he suggested, cease to treat the subject except as a theological question. Let the Protestants use toward Catholics the same arts of friendly persuasion that they use toward others. Let Metternich and the Emperor of Austria be turned over to the politicians. "Any literary peccadillos which may be committed under the auspices of the pope, will be punctually attended to, by some of the numerous literary journals which deal with such matters. . . . We hardly know how to include the nuns, who are noncombattants [sic], in any regular treaty, but we recommend, when any convent, in future, shall be taken by assault, that the garrison, if not consisting of more than half a dozen females, shall be permitted to march out with the honors of war, with colors flying. . . . "[115]

Although "The Catholic Question" and the brilliant review of A Plea for the West have suffered undeserved neglect by succeeding generations, the hard-pressed Catholics of 1836 recognized the effectiveness of these two essays and at once reprinted them as a tract, which they distributed by thousands. There was a second printing within four months, and perhaps many more, for one copy of 1838 survives.[116]

At the close of his editorship, when he looked back over his conduct of the magazine, Hall found mistakes that he regretted, but he took justifiable pride in having faced a mounting hatred with these appeals to reason.[117]

But Beecher and Brainerd were incensed. Beecher is said to have considered nothing less than a libel suit against Hall for his mild and reasonable review;[118] and in the *Journal*, Thomas Brainerd retorted to "The Catholic Question" only with vituperation. The article, he fumed, was "pernicious," "false in its assumptions, incorrect . . . and sarcastic"; and Hall was a "stanch [*sic*] advocate of catholicism."[119] Hall wrote a rejoinder asking Brainerd either to substantiate the charges or stand guilty of having borne false witness against his neighbor; and, after correcting the proof sheets, Hall sent the article to the printer for publication in the August number.[120] Apparently unaware that the dispute had reached the ignition point, he then turned over the editorship to a substitute and left for a journey of several months in the East. Brainerd somehow procured the proof sheets, and having read them, knew that he was cornered. He and a group of Presbyterian lawyers persuaded Hall's perhaps already disaffected publisher, Eli Taylor, to suppress the article on the ground that it was libelous.[121]

When Hall returned, probably in December, he found his magazine in danger of ruin. He broke his partnership with Taylor, whom he accused not only of suppressing the article but of sabotaging the magazine by predicting its early death, by delaying its publication, and by insulting subscribers. He formed a new publishing alliance with Flash, Ryder, and Company; but Taylor, who was near bankruptcy, clung to Hall's share of the profits and to half of the subscription list, from which many anti-Catholics had already withdrawn.[122] Hall thought it necessary to go to court against Taylor, and had to begin rebuilding the magazine almost from the ground.[123] The establishment in Cincinnati in June, 1835, of the *Western Messenger*, a well-edited magazine under Unitarian influence, had not made his task easier.

The episode illustrates one phase of the repression of

Western literature by religious denominations. Hall was denounced by Western Protestant papers; he was threatened with mob action; and he believed that certain Presbyterian leaders of Cincinnati had formed a cabal that wished not only to injure his magazine but to throttle discussion generally.[124]

Two letters written by Edward King, an attorney of Cincinnati and a son of Rufus King, the senator and minister to Great Britain, demonstrate that the struggle involved more than religion. As early as December 24, 1834, King had written to his wife that the "Yankee" element in Cincinnati society, particularly the Beechers, was trying to "shake off Hall & Drake" by attempting to dictate to Cincinnati hostesses whom they should invite to dinner. He cautioned her that, to the Beechers, "Hall is a sore thorn & Drake does not court them."[125] Nine months later, on August 12, 1835, King reported to his wife a conversation with his cousin Catharine Beecher, who had just concluded a visit to Chillicothe, Ohio. "On the whole, she did not add much to her reputation as a learned or well mannered lady—as we rode down, she broached the everlasting subject of the Western Society—& as she thought highly improper attempt to draw a line of distinction between the emigrants and the settlers—and she feared that Judge Hall would bring me into difficulty, that he quarreled with every body & had no friends—As she began the matter, I gave her my opinion very freely & told her that, the difficulty had begun with them, in endeavouring exclusively to assume all the society, intelligence & literature of the city, and that for one I should promote the Western society, untill [sic] the emigrants thought proper to yield to the customs & habits of the people amidst whom they might come & not endeavor to establish their own rules for the regulation of society— that as to Hall—as far as I knew him he was a gentleman, and that I did not blame him, after he had been assaulted & pecked at by all the jackdaws of literature, for pulling out their feathers & exhibiting their baldness—That the plan of putting him down & passing the review into the hands of those who would be the more favorable to the views of M^r

251

Brainerd &c was understood—but that it would not succeed —That the course pursued by the Mirror &c—towards Hall & Worthington, was such as deserved severe castigation—"[126]

It seems, then, that Beecher and Brainerd had tried to wrest control of the *Western Monthly* from Hall. The two Presbyterian leaders were close and powerful. As editor of the *Journal*, Brainerd owed his appointment and support to Cincinnati's Presbyterian Pastoral Association, in which Beecher was the dominant figure.[127] In a statement concerning Hall's suppressed rebuttal, Brainerd admitted that he had been "unwilling to have it published." He remained bitter toward Hall. As a parting shot, he announced to a religious public that Hall was not a member of any Presbyterian church in the city.[128]

Perhaps Hall had never transferred his membership from the Vandalia church that he and Mary had joined, but he may also have resigned a Cincinnati membership in disgust.[129] Not long afterward he did join the Episcopal Christ Church, in which he was a leading member the rest of his life.[130]

In any event, the often repeated statement that Hall was driven from the editorship by the enemies of religious tolerance seems invalid. His retirement from the magazine occurred "at a very favorable time for him," Eli Taylor wrote.[131] During the first six months after Hall had reestablished his magazine with Flash, Ryder, and Company, it was well printed and reasonably interesting. Moreover, it is apparent that for more than a year Hall had not found in the editorship sufficient satisfaction for his restless ambitions. In January, 1835, he had begun the serial publication of his "Sketch of the Life of General Harrison" in the *Western Monthly*. The early appearance of this work— which was republished the next year as part of a campaign biography—indicates that he was an originator of the movement to elect his friend Harrison to the presidency.[132] On May 26, he announced the formation of a law partnership with Edward King, who, though ill, was one of the city's ablest attorneys.[133] Finally, Hall probably made his journeys to the East that summer and the following winter with the purpose of forming a connection with the Commercial Bank, a Cincinnati institution owned largely by Philadelphians.[134] By February, 1836, he had been elected to the Commercial's board of directors; and, on May 12, he was elected cashier.[135] With business more than double that of any other Ohio bank, the Commercial was one of the great financial houses of the Middle West.[136] Because of his new responsibility, Hall announced his resignation as editor of the *Western Monthly* in the June number of 1836. "We consider the work to be now so well established," he wrote in his farewell editorial, "that we feel a confidence in leaving it, that with the careful attention of those in whose hands it is now placed, it must be a permanent and valuable work."[137] But under far less able direction the magazine lived only eleven months longer and succumbed to the panic of 1837.

XIV

Cincinnati Gentleman, 1836-68

We have only a few glimpses of Hall in the first three years after he became cashier of the Commercial Bank, but these indicate an increasing prosperity. He lived until about 1838 at the Pearl Street House and then moved into a house at the southwest corner of Broadway and Fourth Street.[1] It was probably about this time that he brought his children from Henderson to live with him.[2] He was forty-three in 1836, vigorous and good looking; his hair was black and his still youthful face revealed a capacity for good humor. Probably he was often in society. Harriet Martineau records meeting "Judge Hall, the popular writer" at a party at Nicholas Longworth's in the summer of 1835.[3] In 1838, he was prominent in planning a great ball to pay for the building for the Mechanics Institute, and was one of the managers assigned to wait upon the ladies in the refreshment room.[4] Early in 1839, we find him at a hotel, sipping champagne with Benjamin Drake and discussing a letter from John Pendleton Kennedy, whose writing both Cincinnatians admired.[5]

In accepting direction of the bank, Hall had no intention of forsaking all ambition as a writer. After all, one who had edited and written most of a magazine while he was treasurer of a commonwealth, an active attorney, and a civic leader of a state could scarcely have been content merely to fatten on a cashiership. On December 16, only six months after his appointment, he published his *Statistics of the West* through J. A. James and Company of Cincinnati.[6]

The title is a misnomer, for only a few of the book's pages are devoted to figures. It is really a collection of some of Hall's best descriptive writing, retrieved chiefly from magazines, and includes the brilliant "Western Scenery" and "The Public Domain" as well as his "Notes on Illinois."[7] All is skillfully woven into an orderly work describing the Middle West. There are chapters on the Ohio and Mississippi rivers and on the topography of the region. Four chapters are devoted to the formation, the appearance, and the products of the prairies. One deals with wild animals, another with Western steamboats, and one with the region's trade and commerce.

Statistics of the West is sometimes discursive, but few books with so formidable a title are so readable. The earlier *Letters from the West* has perhaps more youthful exuberance and is memorable, of course, for its sharply etched descriptions of emigrants; but the greater simplicity and directness of the *Statistics* win for it a higher place. It also has vividness and great richness of detail. Much of it was written in the wilderness which it describes, in sight of the prairie flowers and within the sound of deep-woods birds.

Western reviewers generally vouched for the book's reliability.[8] A critic in the *New England Galaxy*, after praising Hall's fresh and vigorous language, declared that the volume should be read by every emigrant and by those who, staying at home, had any curiosity about the West.[9] In the *Western Messenger,* however, James Freeman Clarke, whom Hall had so sharply taken to task in the Preface, scoffed at the book as a fraud because it did not fulfill the promise of the title with series of tabulations.[10] To each of two subsequent editions of the work Hall gave a different name: *Notes on the Western States* (1838) and *The West: Its Soil, Surface, and Productions* (1847).[11]

He had already committed himself to a much more rigorous literary task. Late in 1835, more than a year before the publication of *Statistics of the West,* he had allied himself with Thomas L. McKenney in a vast enterprise that was to require much of his energy during the next seven years.[12] Hall told the story of this opus in an autobiographical sketch which he wrote as a letter to Evert Duyckinck eight years after the completion of the book.

"About the time I came to Cincinnati," he recalled, "I was invited to unite with Col. Thomas L. McKenney, in editing & writing 'A History and Biography of the Indians of N. America,' to be published in 20 numbers, on large folio paper at $6:00 per number."[13] McKenney appears in Hall's account to have been a charming person, radiating a contagious optimism. He had been superintendent of Indian trade under President Madison and, from 1826 to 1830, had been in charge of the bureau of Indian affairs. McKenney spoke expansively of his "vast hoard of official correspondence, and other documents." And he no doubt glowingly described a collection of portraits of Indian chiefs painted by Charles King and hung in the corridors of the War Department in Washington, where it was the custom to honor visiting Indian chiefs by having them sit for their likenesses. To these portraits he had access, and he conceived the idea of publishing a *magnum opus* which would consist of color-plate reproductions of the portraits, each to be accompanied by a biography of the portrayed chief, and of a history of the various tribes of North American Indians. McKenney threw out expectations of enormous profits.

Hall entered into partnership with McKenney to produce the work. "I became editor," Hall related to Duyckinck, "and set to work, with my usual ardor and energy (which were not small)." But he was soon disappointed. He found the first number partly written, he said, and "I had to begin there in the middle of that N° and finish it." McKenney, Hall informed Duyckinck confidentially, "was as lazy a man as ever lived, and as unreliable a mortal as ever made big promises. This hoard of materials dwindled down to almost nothing, and after exhausting them, I could neither get him to furnish more, or to aid in writing. I went on alone. The labor was Herculean." Hall was confronted with "a long list of Indian heroes, to be supplied with biographies—of whom he knew nothing but the names."

"I was compromised to the work," Hall wrote, "and I determined to do it. . . . " He corresponded with men who had been stationed among the Indians, and he went "several times" to St. Louis, where "men were still living who had spent their lives on the frontier" and where he talked to Indian agents, traders, and military men. He also paid several visits to Washington "when Indian delegations were there," interviewed federal officers and employees, and called upon superintendents of Indian affairs and former territorial governors, such as William Henry Harrison and Lewis Cass.

For about eight years, Hall devoted to the work much of the time that he could spare from his banking duties. In his letter to Duyckinck, he remembered his Indian history as one of originality. With the exception of a few facts from the accounts of the expeditions of Stephen H. Long, Zebulon M. Pike, and Henry Rowe Schoolcraft, "nothing was complied from books—all was collected from original sources— mostly from living and highly respectable individuals, whose testimony was examined carefully, and compared one with another."

McKenney's side of the story is lacking. He may have been remiss in providing some of the expected materials; but Hall's notes in the completed work show that McKenney contributed, either from his published writings or with new information, somewhat more than Hall indicated in his letter to Duyckinck. But McKenney's letter to Jared Sparks of November 24, 1836, which states that "the history that you read will be continued by Judge Hall," and Hall's earlier statement that "my part of the work is to do the writing"[14] leave little doubt about that part of their agreement. The business arrangements appear to have been chiefly in the hands of McKenney.

The publication of the *History of the Indian Tribes* was beset with difficulties. The first publishers went bankrupt. Their assignees produced a few numbers, another company printed a few more, and the work was finally completed, six years after the appearance of the first volume, by Rice and Clarke of Philadelphia. The subscription list of more than a thousand names is reproduced in facsimile at the end of the third volume. An interesting roster of wealthy and notable Americans of the time, it contains also the signatures of some famous Europeans, including members of several royal families. McKenney once thought the list represented a value of $200,000;[15] but according to Hall's recollection, he and McKenney, who "were to have had half the profits, . . . got little or nothing."

Although some copies of the first volume of the *History of the Indian Tribes of North America* bear the date 1836, it apparently was not distributed until 1838. The second volume appeared in 1842, and the third in 1844. A separate edition, said to have been produced from new plates, was published simultaneously in London by Campbell & Burns.[16] The whole work was one of the most elegant printing achievements of a period remarkable for its ambitious illustrated books. The specially made type and paper are handsome; the colored portraits by King and others are magnificent.

The first two volumes consist of biographical sketches of the portrayed Indians; the third contains general histories of Indian-white relations in America, with a proposal for civilizing the red man. There is no evidence to refute Hall's avowal of the authorship of nearly all of the first two volumes.[17] In the third McKenney appears to have written the "History of the Indian Tribes of North America," taking up the first quarter of the volume. The remaining three-quarters, an "Essay on the History of the North American Indians," is by Hall and is an expansion, to three times its original length, of his "On the Intercourse of the American People with the Indians," which appeared first in the *Illinois Monthly* of 1831. McKenney has had more credit for the authorship of the *History* than he deserved; probably Hall was the author of approximately eleven-twelfths of the entire work.

The only first-hand experiences that Hall is known to have had with Indians were the uncomfortably close relations with them in the War of 1812; an interview with Black Hawk during a visit to the Indian village of Black Rock, Illinois, in 1829; and his attendance at Indian councils in Washington.[18] Perhaps, too, he had occasionally met Indians at Shawneetown, in Vandalia, or on journeys on the Illinois frontier. Evidently he was self-conscious of his lack of an intimate knowledge of the red men; his citations in the *History of the Indian Tribes* reveal his laborious search for printed information beyond the records of the travels of Pike, Schoolcraft, and Long, to say nothing of his determined efforts to secure data through interviews with men who had known the various Indians of his biographical sketches. His labor was often unfruitful; many of the biographies suffer from a lack of information. But many are still interesting in spite of the authors' sometimes rambling style and tendency to repetitiveness; and they contain much history. In his concluding "Essay," Hall appears to have sloughed off his earlier bias against Negroes, for he even asserted that the golden rule was intended to apply to all races. After presenting ample evidence that the Indians were capable of being civilized, he advanced his plan for their uplift. "Our system [of dealing with the Indians] is not only inefficient," he wrote, "but it is positively malicious. Its direct tendency is to retard the civilization of the Indian." He came out with the flat demand that the Indians be granted "*equality with ourselves*" and that they be assured of their rights to ultimate full citizenship and of the eventual admission of their territories to statehood.[19] But his plan was too advanced. Helen Hunt Jackson's *A Century of Dishonor* (1881) shows how tragically the succeeding generation ignored Hall's plea for justice.

To Duyckinck, Hall conceded that the *History of the Indian Tribes* "is not known in the literature of the country, nor has it gained me any reputation." Nevertheless, he believed that it was "the most authentic work on the subject" and that the day would come "when some scholar whose studies shall be directed into that channel, will discover, and recognize the value of my labors."

That the *History of the Indian Tribes* brought Hall little fame can hardly be denied. Perhaps because of the expensiveness of the work, only three magazines are known to have noticed it, and these, basing their remarks upon the first few numbers or the first volume, restricted their sparse comments to the artistic and historical aspects. The *Western Monthly* for February, 1837, only briefly mentioned the appearance of the first number of the *History*.[20] The London *Athenæum* believed that "as a work of mere art, it will take at once a high rank among publications of the same order" and praised the "valuable and interesting accompaniments [to the portraits], both biographical and historical."[21] Jared Sparks and C. C. Felton, writing in the *North American Review*, regarded the work as "second only to that of Audubon," and, like the *Athenæum*, filled out the review with extracts from the *History*.[22] The leading scientific magazine in the United States, the *American Journal of Science and Arts*, so far as can be discovered, did not mention it. When the *History of the Indian Tribes* was published by John Grant in Edinburgh nearly a century later (1933-1934), no magazine, so far as is now known, mentioned even that edition.

In spite of this almost phenomenal silence, Hall's prediction that his labors would be of benefit to some future scholar has been fulfilled. Since nearly all of the Indian portraits executed by Charles King, as well as those by George Catlin, were destroyed by a fire at the Smithsonian Institution in 1865, the Hall-McKenney volumes have become a work of permanent value, without which, writes the modern ethnologist Frederick Webb Hodge, "comparatively little would now be extant to illustrate the appearance of the Indians as they were three-quarters of a century ago, when they were in a condition that has passed forever." The value of the reproduction of these paintings made from life and showing the Indians' ornaments, clothing, and painting, Hodge believes, "cannot be overestimated." The accompanying biographies, written during the lifetime of many of the Indians, also preserve much history that was rapidly disappearing when Hall wrote, and many of the data "are now," Hodge observes, "the only source of information respecting them."[23]

The third volume, comprising a general history of the North American Indians, has, however, not sustained the high approval won by the portraits and the biographical sketches. The ethnologists Hodge and H. J. Braunholz regard part of this section as unsound; Hodge characterizing it as "unscientific and untrustworthy" and Braunholz objecting to the low estimate of Indian culture, now overthrown—criticisms that are comparatively minor in a work so largely biographical. On the other hand, Braunholz upholds the authors' theory of the Asiatic origin of the North American Indian and acknowledges that much valuable information is recorded in the reprinted source material of the volume.[24] The *History* went through at least twelve editions before 1875. Its republication as late as 1934 and its use by twentieth-century specialists in Indian ethnology attest its vitality.[25]

II

On September 3, 1839, in Chillicothe at the mansion since enshrined as the one-time residence of General Duncan McArthur (1772-1839) and other notable persons, Hall was married to Mary Louisa Anderson Alexander, the thirty-year-old widowed daughter of the Revolutionary War general Richard Clough Anderson.[26] In Cincinnati, two months before the wedding, he had bought a fashionable three-story brick house—number 507, the third building east of Lawrence Street on the south side of Third—which was their residence from about 1842 until the end of his life.[27] Between 1840 and 1850, he and Louisa (as he called her) had five children, all of whom lived to maturity except the first, a daughter who died at the age of five.[28]

After 1838, we see little of Hall as a controversialist. Rather, he emerges as an affable man of affairs, fond of his family and friends and known in many states with respect, if not with affection, as "Judge Hall." In his fashionable neighborhood he lived near such friends as his brother-in-law Larz Anderson; Robert Buchanan, a banker and gentleman farmer; and Nicholas Longworth, the millionaire landowner and horticulturist.[29] He was on friendly terms with William Henry Harrison. Hall devoted much of his time and talent to the nearby Episcopal Christ Church, which he had probably begun to attend soon after his dispute with the Presbyterians. His daughter was baptized there in 1841, and he and Louisa were confirmed there three years later. Serving seven years as vestryman and four years as warden, Hall was present at most of the monthly meetings of the wardens and vestry until 1860.[30] He continued to speak before the Young Men's Mercantile Library Association. For the Cincinnati Society for the Promotion of Useful Knowledge, he delivered a series of popular lectures on early American history.[31] He was the city's live author for exhibition to traveling celebrities such as Charles Dickens, who, after his visit in Cincinnati in 1842, asked especially to be remembered to Hall and the same day asked his American publishers to buy for him two sets of Hall's and McKenney's *History of the Indian Tribes*.[32] A considerable traveler, he frequently set forth on such steamboats as the "Telegraph" or the "John Simpson" for long business journeys, on which he still found time to collect data about the West. To Louisa, he wrote back genial and sometimes humorous letters, once recording that a landlord ("selecting me no doubt as the best looking of the company") put two pretty girls in his charge for a stagecoach journey.[33]

Meanwhile, Cincinnati was fast becoming a metropolis. Its population of thirty thousand in 1830 had doubled by

1840 and redoubled by 1850. During the same twenty years, pork production tripled, and river traffic increased sevenfold; even in 1846, Hall was able to boast that his city was "the greatest provision market in the world."[34] The swiftly accelerating growth of manufacturing, of population, and of wealth brought luxuries. Steel pens, postage stamps, experiments with chloroform and ether in childbirth, gas lights, the telegraph, and the railroad came to Cincinnati in the 1840's.[35] As a result of the steamboat and the railway, well-to-do Cincinnatians were able to enjoy at their banquets choice foods that might have been the envy of wealthy Londoners or Parisians.

However, there is evidence to indicate that the city was becoming impoverished in more significant respects. Some of Cincinnati's prominent cultural institutions—with which Hall was associated—were withering; the Semi-Colon and the Lyceum died before 1840; the Mechanics Institute survived; but the Lyceum's successor, the Cincinnati Society for the Promotion of Useful Knowledge, proved a feeble plant of short life. An author in the *Western Monthly*, probably Hall, argued that laboring men and farmers had greater opportunity for cultural self-advancement than professional men.[36] Yet no great number of any of these three groups flocked to the city's institutions of higher learning. Lane had only a handful of students, its entering classes from 1836 to 1840 averaging only five members. In 1836, when Hall was a trustee of Cincinnati College and the able William Holmes McGuffey was its president, an attempt to revive that institution's literary department failed; in 1840, the census taker counted only eighty college students in the city.[37] No less disturbing than the decay of these institutions were the overt attacks on other organizations. The Anti-Slavery Society and the Colonization Society were suppressed at Lane in 1834. In 1836, a mob inspired by a meeting called and held by some of the city's leaders of business and industry (Hall's name is not on the newspaper lists of the conveners or of those present) blackened Cincinnati's reputation by destroying the press of the *Philanthropist*, the West's principal antislavery newspaper; its

263

editor, James Birney, was soon afterward prosecuted on a flimsy charge of harboring a slave.[38]

During this period, Cincinnati endured the stresses of the business cycle and other social misfortunes without developing effective public means to soften their effects. The business panic that began in 1837 was relieved by relative prosperity between 1844 and 1848, and then hard times again enervated the city. Especially in the 1840's, social maladjustments multiplied as the industrial revolution progressed. In 1842, mobs broke into two banks that had failed. Three soup houses for the poor were established in 1843, one of them feeding as many as 413 persons in a single day. Large numbers of children sold matches or begged. Vagrant boys idled about the theater and slept in shops and stables.[39] In the streets, "females" were not infrequently seen "reeling with rum"; and by 1849, James H. Perkins had written a verified account of an actual starvation in the Queen City.[40] Census-taker Charles Cist believed that the city missionary Horace Bushnell was wild in his 1850 estimate of a thousand grogshops, four thousand prostitutes, and a thousand houses of prostitution in Cincinnati; but Cist's own estimate of "not more than" five hundred prostitutes (in a city of 115,000) makes an odd kind of defense.[41] The climax of this convulsive decade was the cholera epidemic of 1849, which, in Cincinnati, carried off 4,377 persons in six weeks, an average of more than a hundred people a day.[42]

These raw social sores provoked some restlessness for reform. True, the *Gazette* probably reflected the prevailing attitude when at the death of John Jacob Astor it pointed to the vast fortune he had accumulated by "industry and perseverance," without an education and in spite of a humble birth. "Think of that boys," it moralized, "and be encouraged to move on without despondency." Others, however, distrusted the social structure. James H. Perkins believed that the only true way to cure the evils of pauperism was "to extend religious instruction."[43] Acting more directly, the bricklayers, molders, and journeyman tailors learned to strike peacefully and avoid the sheriff's posse sent out to put down their "mobocracy." Workingmen of both political parties united to bring out an independent ticket for the state legislature. The radical Horace Greeley, editor of the *New York Tribune*, spoke in Cincinnati before the Young Men's Mercantile Library Association and to a large audience at the Universalist Church on the "Organization of Labor."[44]

In a lecture delivered in the city in 1846, six years before the publication of *Uncle Tom's Cabin*, Thomas H. Shreve lyrically and even prophetically described the role of literature in the movement. Shreve had possibly been stirred by Emerson's welcome to "the literature of the poor," his confidence in "the unsearched might of man," and his exhortation to the American scholar to break the spell of "the courtly muse of Europe."[45] Addressing an audience at College Hall, Shreve exceeded the enthusiasm for democracy voiced in Emerson's "The American Scholar": "A great movement is in progress, which will overthrow a thousand venerable prejudices and hoary iniquities. This revolution will effect a general establishment of the truth that this world, with its beauties and its sublimities, its birds, blossoms, and sunbeams, its shining valleys and heaven-kissing hills, was not made for the few alone, but was designed by an impartial Providence equally to bless the millions on whose sullen brows stand the big drops of sweat wrung from them by exhausting labor. . . . [America's literature] must speak *to* and FOR, the masses. It must strike off manacles wherever or by whomsoever worn. . . . The Literature of the world has already felt the influence of the breeze that heralds the storm, and is now speaking to the poor and the humble as well as to the rich and the proud. . . . American Literature must sympathize with this grand movement, and those authors who do not feel and acknowledge a universal brotherhood will be swept away by the tide of oblivion."[46]

When Hall himself spoke before the Young Men's Mercantile Library Association on April 18 of the same year, he showed an awareness of this social ferment, but was silent about reform. Nor did he sound like the same man who, twelve years earlier, had pleaded so fervently for universal free education lest "the uninstructed many . . . be governed by the enlightened minority." Now, he lamented, "Under the influence of that fell spirit of demagoguism which has swept over our land, it has become fashionable to flatter the agricultural and laboring classes, because they are the most numerous, and wield the greatest power at the ballot boxes. . . . " He deplored what he thought was a systematic effort "to decry the merchant and the banker, and to stigmatize their business as inimical to the liberty and prosperity of the country." He conceded to labor "a vast amount of power, utility, and consequent influence"; but he believed that "this country has grown rich through the money of banks, and the enterprise of merchants." Bluntly he added, "The resources of this country are controled [*sic*] chiefly by . . . 'the business community.'" He mentioned no need for social adjustment, but placed his faith in commerce as "the most efficient agent of national prosperity," and pointed to the need for the extension of the facilities for commerce, such as the improvement of waterways. He concluded, however, that businessmen must accept the responsibility that goes with power. He deplored making money for its own sake; indeed, he cautioned the merchant to "guard his heart against the seductive influence of money" and urged that it be sought as a defense against poverty and an instrument of parental love and public interest. He held up the ideal of the scrupulously honest businessman who was also "a patron of the arts, a promoter of education, a friend to literature and science, an active agent in all public improvements."[47]

No doubt Hall's address was disappointing to the more liberal few; but, as a civic leader during the 1840's, he demonstrated that the principles that he did avow were more than empty words. At public meetings in Cincinnati, he was authorized to write two pamphlets significant in the development of Western commerce and in America's understanding of her hinterland. The first, printed in 1841, presented the merits of Cincinnati as the site for a proposed national armory.[48] The second, broader in its appeal and consequences, was his *Memorial* on the Western rivers, printed in 1843 and enlarged and republished the year following.[49] Still valuable as a description of the West of the period, this interesting document avoids both statistical dullness and the inflated optimism of a Colonel Sellers. A sober statement of the progress already achieved in the West, it also provokes visions of a vast inland domain unified and enriched by a network of canals and improved rivers. The pamphlet brought Hall a new prominence.

In the *Memorial* he again had scope for the gift for panoramic description that he had displayed in "The Public Domain." With affectionate pride he described the great rivers with twenty-four thousand miles of shore line extending through eighteen degrees of latitude. He showed the wealth of the plains moving over a vast system of canals, lakes, and rivers, of which the Mississippi and the Ohio, bordering on nine states and two territories, were the great arteries. Two-thirds of the steamboats of the United States, he calculated, plied the Western waters; and the steamboat tonnage of the West exceeded that of Great Britain. The care and improvement of interior waterways, vital to the prosperity of the nation and invaluable for defense in war, he thought, should be the responsibility of the federal government rather than of the states along their banks and shores: "As well might the states on the seaboard be required to erect light houses, and to improve the harbors of the seacoast, as the Western States be left to open the navigation of those giant rivers, which separate States, that are declared by the supreme law of the Union to be public highways for all the States, and upon which no single State nor combination of States, can place an obstruction, or collect a toll."[50]

Hall, like many Westerners aware of their dependence upon transportation by water, tended to regard the West and South as a geographic and economic unit knitted together by the Mississippi and its tributaries. In this inland empire Cincinnati was the principal manufacturing city and the greatest depot of finished goods, supplying, it has been said, a seventh of the produce that found its way to New Orleans.[51] But as early as the 1830's, it was evident that the Mississippi river system did not provide adequate transportation for Cincinnati's development. In seasons of ice and low water especially, merchandise accumulated in the city's warehouses. A railroad was needed to carry her freight swiftly to an Atlantic port and to tap the markets of the agricultural South, just as the Ohio and Miami canals, linking the Ohio River with Lake Erie, had enabled Cincinnati to profit from trade with the agricultural North. Far-seeing Cincinnatians energetically set out to solve their transportation problems. Their efforts reflected the struggle whose outcome was to determine whether, in the conflict which was to begin in 1861, the West would be allied with the South or with the North.

Within two years after his arrival in Cincinnati, Hall had been in the forefront of a movement to build a railroad from his city to the Atlantic port of Charleston, South Carolina. At a meeting of interested citizens on August 15, 1835, he was elected, with Dr. Daniel Drake, General Harrison, and others, to a committee charged with the task of promoting the enterprise.[52] This project, however, was frustrated by the business depression of 1837. In 1845, Hall led a meeting of citizens assembled to choose delegates to a great convention in Memphis, and his name headed the list of Cincinnati representatives elected and instructed to urge at this gathering the improvement of Western waterways and the construction of Western railroads.[53]

The Memphis meeting was perhaps the most notable of the twelve or more Southern commercial conventions held annually during the two decades before the Civil War.[54] Of the nearly six hundred delegates that assembled in Memphis in November, more than five hundred were Southern. The object of the leaders was to arouse and consolidate sentiment for a closer union of the South and West by means of new and improved systems of transportation to be financed, many hoped, by the national government. In the opening address, John C. Calhoun, president of the convention and a leader whose political party had for twenty years opposed federal legislation for internal improvements, altered his position and argued that "the invention of Fulton has in reality . . . converted the Mississippi with its great tributaries into an inland sea." Therefore, he said, the federal government owed to this system of communication a concern equal to her interest in "the Gulf and Atlantic coast, the Chesapeake and Delaware Bays, and the Lakes.[55] The Memphis convention concluded with the almost unanimous approval of Calhoun's view embodied in eighteen resolutions.

Hall, who, in his armory report and in his *Memorial*, had anticipated, if not actually influenced, Calhoun's stand, probably was in sympathy also with the convention's attempt to bind the South and the West. He continued to urge a Southern railway outlet for Cincinnati; and as late as 1854, although unable to attend the commercial convention of that year in Charleston, he sent to the meeting his hearty endorsement of the plan for a Cincinnati-Charleston railroad.[56] But the attempt at Memphis to unify the whole Mississippi Valley by federal development of Calhoun's "inland sea" was severely rebuffed when President Polk vetoed the Whig rivers-and-harbors bill of 1846. So vehement was Polk's message to Congress that there was no further river-and-harbor legislation until 1854.[57]

Polk's stand against internal improvements probably did much to turn Hall and other Cincinnatians northward in their search for allies. Hall made his own views clear when he publicly said that federal funds had been withheld from Western improvements "with a degree of injustice which has scarcely a parallel in the annals of civilized legislation."[58] But his principal revisions in the second edition of the *Memorial* show that, as early as 1844, he had already been awakened to the importance of the northern outlet for Western products. In this edition he declared that the "most obvious and direct connection" of the Western river system was "with the great northern lakes, a vast chain of inland seas . . . already whitened by the sails of a most valuable commerce." The Great Lakes, he pointed out, were soon to be joined to the Mississippi by the Illinois-Michigan Canal and were already linked with the Atlantic by the Erie Canal and the railway between Buffalo and the Hudson River.[59] Other events that doubtless played a part in Hall's shift of interest to the North were the assembly, at the confluence of the Kansas and Missouri Rivers in May, 1843, of a thousand settlers who pushed their way through to Oregon before the end of the year;[60] a convention held in Cincinnati July 3-5, 1843, to urge "immediate occupation of the Oregon Territory by the arms and laws of the Republic";[61] and Asa Whitney's request, laid before Congress in 1845 and before the citizens of Cincinnati a year later, for a vast grant of land to enable him to construct a railroad between Lake Michigan and the Pacific.

In 1846, Hall was elected to represent his city in a convention to be held in St. Louis for the promotion of Western navigation. A year later, a municipal committee which he headed was asked to draft resolutions favoring a railroad between Cincinnati and St. Louis.[62] The meeting that was to have convened in St. Louis in 1846 was postponed in favor of a more comprehensive one to be held in Chicago in July, 1847. On June 22, two weeks before the Chicago convention was to open, Hall, then in Philadelphia, wrote to his Cincinnati friend Robert Buchanan and asked him to bring to the convention a copy of the *Memorial* and to make sure of Hall's election as an official delegate.[63] Hall himself journeyed westward to Chicago by way of Cleveland and the lakes.

On July 5, representatives from seventeen states, as well as a throng of pleasure seekers, crowded into the booming town of sixteen thousand people to make this gathering probably the largest commercial convention of the period. The official list of delegates contained about 2,500 names. However, Horace Greeley, attending as delegate and reporter, estimated the crowd at twenty thousand people, of whom ten thousand, he thought, were members of the convention. Only six of the representatives were from Southern states. The fifteen resolutions adopted by the meeting were almost entirely concerned with a legal justification of the use of federal funds for the improvement of Western navigation. The few strict-constructionists were enthusiastically overridden.

At the meetings, which lasted three days, Hall had an opportunity to hear Abraham Lincoln, a minor speaker at

270

the convention, then thirty-six years old and notable chiefly as the only Whig Congressman from Illinois. But Hall's greatest gratification must have come from the recognition of his own work, evinced by his election to the convention's permanent committee. After the adjournment of the Chicago Rivers-and-Harbors Convention, the delegates formed themselves into a committee of the whole with Greeley as chairman, and unanimously adopted resolutions favoring the federal construction of a railroad from Lake Michigan to the Pacific. At the close of the Chicago meetings, Hall, as well as the six Southern delegates, could hardly have been unimpressed by the convention's portentous demonstration of Northern economic power.

Starting homeward, Hall joined a party of more than a hundred delegates, chiefly from the East, who had chartered the steamboat "St. Louis" to make their return journey a gay and leisurely excursion on the Great Lakes. Hall, no doubt, became acquainted with such of his fellow passengers as Philip Hone and his daughter Margaret, of New York, and Thurlow Weed and his wife, of Albany.[64]

In the promotion of commercial prosperity, Hall did not forget his ideal of the businessman friendly to learning and art. He contributed money to the founding of the Cincinnati Observatory;[65] he was one of the founders of the Western Art Union, served as director and treasurer, and, since his name stands first on the committee to draw up the constitution, he may have developed this unusual organization's plan for the encouragement of American artists and the dissemination of their works.[66] Flourishing between 1847 and 1851, the Union had more than four thousand members, each of whom, for an annual fee of five dollars, had a chance to obtain one of the pictures distributed by lottery.[67] A little gallery was established in the city, and the Union aided such American artists as Joseph Eaton, William Sonntag, and Rembrandt Peale.[68]

It is true that Hall did not accomplish in his influential later life the good works for Western culture, particularly for education, that his earlier enthusiasm had promised. But neither did he succumb to the too common spirit of greed.

271

In spite of his unusual opportunities, his wealth was modest: in 1860, he had property worth about seventy thousand dollars; at his death, after the Civil War had inflated prices, it was valued at $103,000.[69]

His labors in national politics were intermittent. In spite of Salmon Portland Chase's belief in 1835 that Hall had been "formerly attached to the Jackson party," he had not been a very outspoken or confirmed Democrat while in Illinois or Cincinnati, if he had been one at all. His prominent political work in Cincinnati favored the Whigs. His part in the movement to elect his fellow townsman William Henry Harrison to the Presidency was, at first, conspicuous. In January, 1835, he was elected chairman of the Committee of Correspondence for the promotion of Harrison's candidacy. He wrote a biography of the General, was elected a delegate to the Ohio convention, and, according to Charles Hammond, editor of the *Cincinnati Daily Gazette,* "placed himself at the head of a newspaper."[70] Hall apparently worked actively in the Harrison cause until near the end of the year, when he went on a two-month journey to the East, probably to urge the stockholders of the Commercial Bank to elect him to the cashiership of that institution.[71] While he was away, he was made a director of the Commercial. On May 12, about two months after his return, he was elected cashier.[72] Near the time of his Eastern journey, he dropped at least his public activity in Harrison's behalf.

The reason for this sudden change may never be known. However, two years later, Hammond, who had an aversion for Hall that might be called hatred if one could be sure that his editorials were written in complete sobriety, explained that Hall had "entered the Presidential battlefield, armed cap-a-pie for Harrison," taken charge of a newspaper, and written a biography. "Fuse! Flash in the pan!" Hammond scoffed, "the literary champion in president making, was suddenly installed cashier of the Commercial Bank of Cincinnati and converted to the support of Martin Van Buren!!"[73] In spite of Hammond's antipathy to Hall— dating back to Hall's crushing review of Flint's *Lectures upon Natural History*—his implied accusation of Hall is at least interesting. The Commercial was a "pet" bank, into which the Democratic administration had deposited federal funds.[74] These deposits were profitable to the Commercial and would be naturally an influence in the politics of the twelve directors, at least five of whom, including the president and the cashier who preceded Hall, were Democrats.[75] Hammond's editorship sometimes rose to greatness; but he could hardly have discussed the Bank of the United States or Jackson's "pet" banks without bias, for he was one of the influential persons to whom the Bank of the United States had lent large sums, ostensibly in return for support of the Bank. Although Hammond's explanation of Hall's withdrawal from the Harrison campaign is temptingly neat, Hall usually acted upon principle, and the real reason for his change of position is still in doubt. In Harrison's successful campaign four years later, Hall's name does not appear on the newpaper lists of the General's advocates. But upon Harrison's death a month after the inauguration, Hall was elected chairman of the predominantly Whig committee formed in Cincinnati to make arrangements for the public funeral.[76]

However firm or feeble his attachment to the Democratic cause may have been in 1836 or 1840, Hall returned to the Whig position in 1844, probably, and certainly in 1848. In the latter year, he was made chairman of the Cincinnati Executive Committee which was elected to advance General Zachary Taylor's candidacy. The committee pointed out, however, that Taylor, though a Whig, was not an "ultra" Whig.[77] Taylor was elected, and afterwards Hall was on close enough terms with the President to have dinner with him at Bedford Springs, Pennsylvania, in 1849.[78] Shortly after the inauguration, Hall was restored to his position as pension agent for Ohio, an office which he had held earlier, but from which he had been removed by President Polk.[79] Hall's public participation in politics seems to have ended in March, 1854, with his chairmanship of a meeting in Cincinnati of more than a thousand men gathered at the Mechanics Institute to oppose the Nebraska Bill. In his prefatory remarks, according to the *Daily Atlas* of March 8, he appealed to the audience to act "not as Whigs, or Democrats, or Freesoilers, but as Americans."

III

Hall's last volume of short stories, *The Wilderness and the War Path*, was published in 1846, when he was fifty-three. Of the book's eight tales, all but three—"The War Belt," "The Black Steed of the Prairies," and "The Red Sky of the Morning"—were selected from his earlier volumes. "The War Belt," published first in the *Knickerbocker*,[80] relates a tense episode in George Rogers Clarke's negotiation, in 1786, of a treaty with hostile Indians.[81] "The Black Steed of the Prairies" and "The Red Sky of the Morning" are tales of the far-western Chippewa and Omaha tribes. The latter story, especially, is long drawn out. Although the footnotes accompanying these narratives demonstrate Hall's striving for fidelity, both tales suffer from the meagerness of his first-hand knowledge of Indian life; his citations show his reliance upon Schoolcraft, Long, and Tanner. The first shipment of *The Wilderness and the War Path* to one Cincinnati bookseller—who advertised it along with Dickens' *Italian Travels*—was said to have been exhausted within "a very few days,"[82] but the volume's popularity must have been due in part to the inclusion of Hall's earlier and better stories, "The Indian Hater" and "Pete Featherton."

In his appendix to "The Black Steed of the Prairies," Hall explains that in his source, the legend that circulated among traders and Indians of the plains, the horse was white. "Travellers speak of the existence of this fine creature as an admitted fact; and we tell the tale as it was told to us; but as others may have used the same tale, and we have no ambition to acquire fame as a taker of other men's horses, we have made ours a horse of a different colour."[83]

In his story and the appendix, Hall describes "a remarkably fleet, strong and beautiful horse. . . . He was the leader of a herd, and . . . as he swept gracefully over the plain, outstripped his fellows in swiftness, as much as he excelled them in beauty." Should one "see him among a thousand, he will remark his small head carried high above all others, his slender ear pointing forwards, his large eye full of fire and courage, his fine limbs, and a tail that trails like that of a fox." "The extraordinary beauty of this noble steed, and the exquisite gracefulness of his movements, as he plays round the grazing drove, or scours the prairie before the eager pursuers, have rendered him an object of intense interest to the wild hunters."

In Chapter XLII of *Moby-Dick*, Herman Melville describes several white animals, one of which is a wild, white horse of the Western plains which Melville seems to have derived from Hall's story. His stallion has mystical grandeur: "Most famous in our Western annals and Indian traditions is that of the White Steed of the Prairies; a magnificent milkwhite charger, large-eyed, small headed, bluff-chested, and with the dignity of a thousand monarchs in his lofty, overscorning carriage. He was the elected Xerxes of vast herds of wild horses, whose pastures in those days were only fenced by the Rocky Mountains and the Alleghanies. At their flaming head he westward trooped it like that chosen star which every evening leads on the hosts of light. The flaming cascade of his mane, the curving comet of his tail, invested him with housings more resplendent than gold and silverbeaters could have furnished him. . . . Always to the bravest Indians he was the object of trembling reverence and awe. . . . It was his spiritual whiteness chiefly, which so clothed him with divineness; and . . . this divineness had that in it which, though commanding worship, at the same time enforced a certain nameless terror."[84]

With the publication of *The Wilderness and the War Path*, Hall entered upon a period of modest prestige, for the volume was brought out by the important New York firm of Wiley and Putnam as one of their "Library of American Books." Earlier he had had to guarantee the publication cost of some of his works, especially those published by Harrison Hall.[85] But Hall was dismayed when he learned that Wiley and Putnam intended to bring out his stories and Caroline Kirkland's *Western Clearings* in a single volume. He wrote to them protesting against "a destiny for my poor little volume as unexpected as it would be to me to

275

find myself under the same cover with the author of that work." "I beg you," he continued—with injustice to Caroline Kirkland's work—"not to inflict so great an injury upon me, and so great a disgrace upon my book. The Western Clearings is a wretched imposition—a vile piece of humbug. If the authoress ever was in the West, she has failed to convey the slightest idea of the country or its people."[86]

His protest had little effect.[87] Several years later, Wiley and Putnam planned to publish Hall's work in four volumes uniform with their edition of Irving's writings, but, so far as is known, they issued only one additional volume, *Legends of the West*, in 1853.

On November 3, 1835, Jared Sparks had asked Hall to write a biography of Daniel Boone for the "Library of American Biography," a series that Sparks was editing. Hall had for several years collected information about Boone, had spent fifty dollars in 1834 to visit several old men who had been Boone's companions, and had paid thirty dollars for a collection of letters and a diary dated about 1775. It is astonishing to learn from Hall's reply that Sparks had offered him for the work less than he had already spent for the journey and documents. He regretfully declined the undertaking.[88] Yet he wished to appear in the company of scholarly historians writing for Sparks's series; and in 1845, he sent Sparks the *Memoir of Thomas Posey, Major-General, and Governor of Indiana,* a relation of forty pages which Sparks printed almost without change the next year.[89] Based upon manuscripts held by the Posey family, the carefully wrought *Memoir* is restrained and sober. After this work and almost to the time of his death, Hall made occasional revisions of his writings for new editions. As late as 1847, he was busy in compiling from his earlier publications a book about Western trade and its river highways. Preponderantly a combination of his *Address before the Young Men's Mercantile Library Association,* the *Memorial* on the Western rivers, the "Western Armory Report," and Chapter XII of *Statistics of the West,* the work was published in 1848 as *The West: Its Commerce and Navigation.* But his real literary work was done.

IV

In 1849, Hall became ill and went to Bedford Springs in Pennsylvania to recuperate. He was not bedridden and was able to dine with President Taylor, but he complained of a constant severe headache.[90] Three years later, he made his will.[91] But he was to live sixteen years longer and to see not only his Illinois-born children grow up, but his younger ones as well.

In 1854, he bought for a summer home a farm of 181 acres on the Little Miami River, a mile from Loveland, Ohio, twenty miles northeast of Cincinnati.[92] He named the place Mount Welcome, after the old family estate in Maryland. His house, which once stood high above the river, is gone now, although some of his great cucumber trees may still be seen on the lawn.

Two remaining writings, one of which was delivered as a speech, were devoted to reminiscence and summation. The next year (1855) he wrote a brief account of his own life, as well as sketches of his old literary friends Dr. Daniel Drake and Benjamin Drake, for Evert and George Duyckinck, who were preparing their *Cyclopædia of American Literature*.[93]

The reader of Hall's sketch of his own life senses that Hall knew that his contribution to Western culture had been his extraordinary faith, for ever since that warm spring day in 1820 when his keelboat had slipped away from the landing at Pittsburgh, he had, with uncommon insight, been aware that the movement of which he was a part was of epic proportions and of consequence to world history. One feels his just pride in having led the frontier people in the paths of order and culture; in having portrayed with his pen the fast-disappearing forests, prairies, and frontier societies; in having suggested the direction for the production of a native literature that would be worthy of the new land; and in having established, at great cost in labor and money, first an annual and then a magazine for the advancement of knowledge and the development of Western writers.

In 1854, thirty-eight years after his own emigration, in response to a toast at a sumptuous banquet of the press at the Spencer House in Cincinnati, Hall again glanced back over the history of Western literature. "The subject," he said, "has long been dear to my heart. But I fear you have assigned me a district, which, however honorable in name and associations, is of narrow limits, and slender productiveness. Literature is a plant of slow growth. It is not a flower of the wilderness—it comes not even with the first advance of civilization, but follows in the train of industry, enterprise, and refinement. We have therefore in the West, no distinctive literature. . . . The field is an inviting one, and there have been generous and patriotic men who have labored nobly in it—but none have earned in it a subsistence, nor have any gathered from it as yet, the bright rewards of literary success. In Cincinnati we have had some devoted men . . . such as Louis R. Noble, Morgan Neville, Timothy Flint, Charles Hammond, James H. Perkins, Daniel Drake, Thomas H. Shreve—all of whom have passed away from among us, but all of whose names deserve to be freshly remembered on occasions like the present when we assemble to call up the genial and generous associations connected with the press and its productions.

"But gentlemen, we shall have a Western literature. We have the elements and the materials of a literature, and room and verge enough for its growth. We cannot look abroad over our wide land, and behold its magnificent dimensions, its productive plains, its long rivers, its progress, its wealth, without a conviction that we shall soon also be blessed with all the refinements and luxuries of life. The west is fast ceasing to be a border, and is becoming the center of a great nation—and so will be the center of all that is symbolic of national pride and power."[94]

It is not difficult to detect in Hall's speech his regret that his literary movement had not flourished. He had made a brave beginning. Only enthusiasm and a robust energy could have accomplished so much in "the first advance of civilization." Yet there were, during the last three years of his life, unmistakable signs that a distinctive Western literature was taking root. Lacking the perspective that time could give, Hall, if he was aware of these early shoots of the movement, may not have recognized their significance or necessarily approved the direction of their growth, even though he had probably done more than any other Western author to prepare their seedbed. Two early events in the movement especially stand out: In 1866, Samuel Clemens was astonished that his "villainous backwoods sketch" about a frog was being printed up and down the land and making the name of Mark Twain famous; on a tour of the Holy Land two years later, the same frontier-bred author sent back to an eager American public the irreverent descriptions that gave strength to a new, if somewhat brash, spirit of American cultural independence.[95]

By 1853, Hall was a principal stockholder in the bank and in that year became its president. Two years later, he wrote in his autobiographical sketch, "My circumstances are quite easy—thanks to banking—not to authorship." He said that he owed "no man any thing," and added, "I have been married twice, am happy in my domestic relations, and am a father and grandfather." Although he could go from his country place to the city in an hour by train, he probably went only occasionally during the summers. In his last known letter, written from his country home in 1862, he exhibited his old-school hospitality in welcoming a visit from the son of his former law partner Edward King.[96] But to Evert Duyckinck, in 1855, Hall had mentioned a sensitiveness of his eyes, which, in the photographer's intense light, compelled him to squint so much that in the picture he had enclosed he looked fierce.[97] Four years later, he wrote to a friend, "I must be brief, as I write with pain, owing to a trouble in my eyes."[98] His son Harrison, a cadet at West Point, referred to his father's illness in letters written in 1862 and 1864.[99] But during these years, Hall had vigor enough to be about, to maintain an interest in politics, and to write to his son exhorting him to cherish a good military record.[100] After the death of his sister, Catherine Hannah, in Philadelphia in 1865, Harrison, then eighty, journeyed to Cincinnati to spend his last days with his brother James, but lived only five months longer.[101] At his country home on Sunday, July 5, 1868, in his seventy-sixth year, James Hall himself died, and the following Wednesday was buried in Cincinnati's Spring Grove Cemetery, a place of uncommon beauty, provided for the city largely through his efforts twenty-four years before.[102]

NOTES

Chapter I

1. MS records in Sarah Hall's Bible (owned by Mary Posey Foote) and the MS records of the First Presbyterian Church of Philadelphia (owned by the Historical Society of Pennsylvania) give July 29 as the day of James Hall's birth. The date on his tombstone is August 19, and Hall himself, in his MS autobiographical sketch (owned by the New York Public Library), says he was born August 19. His mother and the church records appear to be the best authorities.

Hall's short autobiography will be referred to hereafter as "autobiographical sketch." David Donald has edited the document in the *Ohio State Archaeological and Historical Society Quarterly,* LVI (July, 1947), 295–304.

2. MS records of the First Presbyterian Church, Philadelphia. Hall was baptized by his grandfather, Dr. John Ewing.

3. *Tales of the Border* (Philadelphia, 1835), pp. 130–31, 10.

4. For the account of James Hall's ancestors from the first known Hall in America to James Hall's father's generation, I am indebted, unless I have stated otherwise, to Christopher Johnston's "Hall Family of Calvert County," *Maryland Historical Magazine,* VIII (September and December, 1913), 291–301, 381–82. My examination of some of Mr. Johnston's sources convinces me that his account of these early generations is correct, but that there are errors in his statements about later ones.

5. Mrs. Juliet R. Frazier, of Garrison-on-Hudson, New York, gave me a photograph of this portrait.

6. *Tales of the Border,* p. 131. See also MS records in Sarah Hall's Bible. These records are the principal source for my statements about the genealogy of the Hall and Ewing families beginning with the generation of James Hall's grandfathers.

7. John Hall to Thomas Jefferson, March 7, 1801 (MS in the files of the Department of State, National Archives) and D. Lenox's statement of Hall's services (MS owned by the Historical and Philosophical Society of Ohio).

8. N. G. Goodman, *Benjamin Rush, Physician and Citizen* (Philadelphia, 1934), pp. 66, 62.

9. MS records in Sarah Hall's Bible.

10. *Ibid.;* MS records of the First Presbyterian Church, Philadelphia.

11. *Selections from the Writings of Mrs. Sarah Hall* (Philadelphia, 1833), "Memoir," pp. xiii–xiv, xxx. James Hall was the author of the "Memoir" (E. A. and G. L. Duyckinck, *Cyclopædia of American Literature,*

New York, 1856, p. 147). Sarah Hall's work is referred to hereinafter as *Selections.*

12. *Pennsylvania Archives,* Series 9, II, 1794.

13. *Ibid.,* pp. 932–33, 993–94.

14. *Extracts from the Diary of Jacob Hiltzheimer,* ed. J. C. Parsons (Philadelphia, 1893), pp. 221, 236, 228.

15. *Pennsylvania Archives,* Series 9, II, 1145.

16. "Life of John Ewing, D. D. Late Provost of the University of Pennsylvania," *Port Folio,* I (March, 1813), 216. Princeton's name until 1896 was the College of New Jersey. I use the modern name throughout.

17. A. H. Smyth, *The Philadelphia Magazines and Their Contributors 1741–1850* (Philadelphia, 1892), p. 137.

18. MS records in Sarah Hall's Bible; E. L. Halfield, "Jonathan Dickinson Sergeant," *Pennsylvania Magazine of History and Biography,* II, No. 4, (1878), 438–42.

19. February 20, 1774. Miss Alice Hall, of Dayton, Ohio, gave me a typed copy of Ewing's letters from London.

20. W. J. Maxwell (comp.), *General Alumni Catalog of the University of Pennsylvania* (Philadelphia, 1922), pp. 9–11.

21. Sarah Hall, *Selections,* pp. x–xiii.

22. *Ibid.*

23. James Hall, *Letters from the West* (London, 1828), p. 5. This work is hereinafter referred to as *Letters.*

24. See the Philadelphia city directories, 1796–1802.

25. *Letters,* p. 5.

26. The birth and death dates of John and Sarah Hall's children are as follows: John Elihu, 1783–1829; Harrison, 1785–1866; Sergeant, 1788–?; Edward, 1791–1814; James, 1793–1868; Catherine Hannah, 1796–1865; Thomas Mifflin, 1798–(*ca.*)1828; Alexander, 1802–1845; Charles, 1804–1806; and William, b. 1807, died an infant (MS records in Sarah Hall's Bible).

27. Sarah Hall, *Selections,* pp. xii, xv.

28. James Hall, "The Academy," *Western Monthly Review,* I (November, 1827), 380. The article is anonymous, and it is proper to question its authenticity. It is signed "Orlando," Hall's pen name. A poem known to be Hall's, "The Indian Maid's Death Song," in the same magazine two months earlier (p. 271), is also signed "Orlando" and is dated "Vandalia, September, 1827." Hall was living in Vandalia at that time. His poem "To a Coquette" appears in the same number as "The Academy," and it, too, is signed "Orlando" (I, 394). In the *Review* for June, 1828 (II, 19–20), the editor, Timothy Flint, states that some of Hall's writings "have adorned the pages of this journal." These circumstances, added to those of the style and the substance of "The Academy," constitute for me conclusive proof of Hall's authorship. It seems incredible that some author besides Hall would sign "Orlando" to a contribution, send it to the same magazine at the same time or nearly the same time that Hall sent his, and yet fail to evoke from the editor, in his two mentions of those contributions (I, 310, 376), any comment upon differences in handwriting or postmark.

29. *Letters,* pp. 339–40.

30. Sarah Hall, *Selections*, pp. xix–xx.

31. J. E. Hall (ed.), *The Philadelphia Souvenir* (Philadelphia, 1826), p. 89.

32. For a list of contributions of these authors, see my article "Authors of the *Port Folio* Revealed by the Hall Files," *American Literature*, XI (January, 1940), 379–416.

33. S. L. Knapp, *Female Biography* (New York, 1834), pp. 268–69.

34. Sarah Hall, *Selections*, pp. xv–xvii.

35. J. E. Hall (ed.), *The Philadelphia Souvenir*, p. 90.

36. H. M. Ellis, *Joseph Dennie and His Circle* (Austin, 1915), pp. 183, 107.

37. For a summary of Dennie's criticism of Godwin and Southey, see Ellis, pp. 125, 189.

38. J. E. Hall (ed.), *The Philadelphia Souvenir*, p. 5.

39. Joseph Anderson to Thomas Jefferson, March 1, 1801 (MS in the files of the Department of State, National Archives).

40. *Pennsylvania Archives*, Series 9, II, 1565.

41. Letter book of United States Marshal John Smith (MS owned by the Historical Society of Pennsylvania) ; *Poulson's American Daily Advertiser* (Philadelphia), April 10, 28, 1801. Joseph Anderson's letter to Thomas Jefferson, March 1, 1801, contains, as enclosures, the MS statements of Peters and Rawle. See also W.W.H. Davis, *The Fries Rebellion 1798–99* (Doylestown, Pa., 1899), pp. 137–38.

42. Sarah Hall, *Selections*, pp. xxx–xxxi.

43. Maxwell, p. 12; James Hall's sketch of the life of John Elihu Hall (MS owned by the Historical and Philosophical Society of Ohio).

44. Mrs. Harry J. Wright, Jr., of Princeton University, secured for me, from the Princeton faculty minutes of 1801, the information about John Elihu's attendance. See also James Hall's MS sketch of the life of John Elihu Hall.

45. See my "Authors of the *Port Folio* revealed by the Hall Files," pp. 400–401.

46. *Western Monthly Review*, I (November, 1827), 377–84.

47. James Hall to Sarah Hall, September 25, 1824 (MS in the Charles Roberts Autograph Collection, Haverford College).

48. Sarah Hall, *Selections*, pp. xxx–xxxi.

49. J. E. Hall to Timothy Pickering, April 27, 1805 (MS owned by the Massachusetts Historical Society).

50. Sarah Hall, *Selections*, xxx–xxxi.

51. See George Johnston, *The Poets and Poetry of Cecil County, Maryland* (Elkton, 1887), p. 189; and, by the same author, *The History of Cecil County, Maryland* (Elkton, 1881), p. 482. See also the MS biographical sketch of James Hall and the Hall family by James Hall's daughter Sarah Hall Foote (copy owned by Mr. Nicholas Van Antwerp, of Cincinnati). The house mentioned by Mr. Johnston was once the residence of Mr. Arthur Hale.

52. "Sketch of a Landscape in Cecil County," *Port Folio*, VIII (July, 1819), 81–83.

53. Sarah Hall Foote, MS biographical sketch of James Hall and the Hall family.

54. Sarah Hall, *Selections*, pp. xxx–xxxi.

55. *Poulson's American Daily Advertiser*, March 11, 1814.

56. Sarah Hall, *Selections*, p. xxviii.

57. R. W. Griswold, *The Prose Writers of America* (3rd ed.; Philadelphia, 1849), p. 228. Hall wrote an account of his life for Griswold's work (Hall to E. A. Duyckinck, March 9, 1855 [MS owned by the New York Public Library]).

58. "A Merchant's Complaint," III, (May, 1814) 489–90. The poem is like Hall's verse and is signed J. H., as is his poem "To Miss M." (*ibid.*, VIII [November, 1812] 547).

59. James Hall's MS autobiographical sketch.

60. For accounts of Ewing, see the *Port Folio*, XX, (December, 1825), 441–45; and H. Simpson, *The Lives of Eminent Philadelphians, Now Deceased* (Philadelphia, 1859), pp. 356–57.

61. L. E. L. Ewing, *Dr. John Ewing and Some of His Noted Connections* (Philadelphia, 1924), pp. 53–55.

62. The friendship of Irving for Ewing and John Elihu Hall is indicated by Irving's letter to John Elihu Hall, June 30, 1822 (MS owned by the New York Public Library).

63. III (March, 1814), 258; II (November, 1813), 436.

64. The portrait is owned by Mrs. Elmer J. Rodenberg, of Henderson, Kentucky.

65. R. Gratz, *Letters of Rebecca Gratz*, ed. D. Philipson (Philadelphia, 1929), p. 208. The "James Hale" of the letter cited here is surely James Hall.

66. James Hall, "Biographical Sketch of Maj. Thomas Biddle," *Illinois Monthly Magazine*, I, (September, 1831), 552.

67. Pleasants' MS diary is owned by the Historical Society of Pennsylvania. The muster roll of the Washington Guards reveals some of James Hall's acquaintances (*Pennsylvania Archives*, Series 6, VIII, 286–90). Joseph Gratz died in 1858, and Benjamin Gratz in 1884.

68. James Hall, MS sketch of the life of John Elihu Hall; Ellis, p. 163.

69. J. E. Hall to Charles Prentiss, November 4, 1819 (MS owned by the American Antiquarian Society).

70. *Poulson's American Daily Advertiser*, August 14, 29, 1812. For an account of the riots in Baltimore, see T. Boyd, *Light Horse Harry Lee* (New York, 1931), pp. 307–27.

71. "The Narrative of John E. Hall," in *Interesting Papers Illustrative of the Recent Riots at Baltimore* (1812). The Philadelphia Library Company's copy of this pamphlet is a gift of John Elihu's brother, Harrison Hall.

72. In his journal (MS owned by the Historical and Philosophical Society of Ohio), James Hall dated the poem 1812. See also the *Port Folio*, III, (May, 1817) 442–44.

73. See James Hall's MS journal in which this poem is dated "May, 1812."

74. "To Miss M.," *Port Folio*, VIII (November, 1812), 547. See also the version in Hall's MS journal, which I have quoted here.

CHAPTER II

1. Henry Adams, *History of the United States* (New York, 1921), VI, 336, 358, 359.

2. W. Powell, *A History of Delaware* (Boston, 1928), pp. 207–9.

3. J. T. Scharf and T. Westcott, *History of Philadelphia* (Philadelphia, 1884), I, 563.

4. Griswold, p. 289. See also the copies of the muster rolls in *Pennsylvania Archives,* Series 6, VIII, 286–90.

5. J. F. Meline, "Biography of the Late Judge Hall, of Cincinnati," *Cincinnati Commercial,* October 16, 1868.

6. *Poulson's American Daily Advertiser,* March 29, April 8, 13, 1813.

7. Scharf and Westcott, I, 565. For the date of the mustering out, see the MS records in the War Department.

8. James Hall, "Biographical Sketch of Maj. Thomas Biddle," *Illinois Monthly Magazine,* I, 552.

9. Hall to John Armstrong, Philadelphia, April 13, 1814 (MS in the War Department).

10. MS records in the War Department.

11. James Hall, "Biographical Sketch of Maj. Thomas Biddle," 552.

12. "The Soldier's Bride," in James Hall's *The Soldier's Bride and Other Tales* (Philadephia, 1833), pp. 15–23.

13. James Hall, "Biographical Sketch of Maj. Thomas Biddle," 552.

14. Adams, VIII, 28. Chapters II, III, and IV of Volume VIII are the source for my account of Brown's campaign except when I have stated otherwise.

15. James Hall, "Biographical Sketch of Maj. Thomas Biddle," 553.

16. "The Soldier's Bride," pp. 33–39.

17. Hindman's report of July 7, 1814 (MS in the War Department).

18. James Hall, "Reminiscence of the Last War," *Illinois Monthly Magazine,* II (February, 1832), 202–7.

19. *Ibid.,* p. 204.

20. Adams, VIII, map facing page 56; B. J. Lossing, *The Pictorial Field Book of the War of 1812* (New York, 1869), p. 824 n.

21. James Hall, "Biographical Sketch of Maj. Thomas Biddle," pp. 555–56.

22. MS records in the War Department state that the muster roll for August (the original now unavailable) lists Hall as having been detained since August 5 by the enemy, to whom he had been sent with a flag of truce. Hall's own accounts of the episode are in "The Wanderer, No. 8," *Pittsburgh Gazette,* July 14, 1818, and "A Reminiscence," in *Knickerbocker,* VI (July, 1835), 10–19. See also Griswold, p. 289. In the *Illinois Intelligencer,* July 10, 1830, Hall wrote, "I was taken prisoner and remained for a short period in the hands of the enemy." J. E. Hall, in an introduction to one of James's poems in the *Port Folio* (I [June, 1816], 527), refers to one of James's confidential missions. Meline states that Hall "was employed twice on separate and confidential service by General Brown. . . . "

23. See Sarah Hall Foote, MS biographical sketch of James Hall and the Hall family.

24. "A Reminiscence," p. 11.

25. E. A. Cruikshank (ed.), *The Documentary History of the Campaign upon the Niagara Frontier* (Welland, Ont., 1896–1908), VIII, frontispiece.

26. J. Carnochan, *Inscriptions and Graves in the Niagara Peninsula* (2d ed.; "Niagara Historical Society Publications," No. 19, 1910), pp. 47–48, 50.

27. James Hall, "The Wanderer, No. 8."

28. J. P. Merritt, *Biography of the Hon. W. H. Merritt* (St. Catharines, 1875), p. 41; Carnochan, p. 48.

29. Sarah Hall Foote, MS biographical sketch of James Hall and the Hall family; S. Ewing to J. E. Hall, September 29, 1814.

30. James Hall, "Biographical Sketch of Maj. Thomas Biddle," pp. 556–59.

31. *Port Folio,* XX (September, 1825), 200–208. The internal evidence of "The Bearer of Despatches" indicates very strongly that Hall was the courier whose expedition is related. He fits the description of the messenger, and the sharpness of detail in regard to events and places makes the narrative seem the work of one who had had the experience. Moreover, Meline, who knew Hall, says Hall was twice employed on confidential missions by General Brown ("Biography of the Late Judge Hall, of Cincinnati"). The affair of the flag of truce (see note 22, above) is the only other confidential mission Hall ever related. Also, John Elihu wrote of James, "At an eventful crisis, we might follow his dangerous and devious path through the wilderness, the confidential channel of important communication between two divisions of our army. . . . " (*Port Folio,* I [June, 1816], 527).

However, a summary of the original records in the War Department (the originals are unavailable) states in the monthly return for October that Hall was "reported sick at Williamsville since September 22." Yet, I doubt that this summary record excludes the possibility of Hall's meeting with Izard because, first, the monthly return does not always state the whole truth (e.g., the monthly return for July reports Hall sick at Buffalo, whereas he is known to have been fighting with the army during nearly all of July); second, there is a possibility of error in making the return or in making the summary, particularly strong in the latter instance because there were other soldiers in the army named James Hall, at least one of whom was an officer. With me, John Elihu's statement and the internal evidence of "The Bearer of Despatches" weigh more heavily than the summary of the record.

32. See Izard to the Secretary of War, September 29, 1814 (Cruikshank, I, 213).

33. Adams, VIII, 34.

34. J. E. Hall [to the Secretary of War], January 6, 1816; E. W. Ripley, memorandum dated Wise's Tavern, Pa., January 4, 1816 (MSS in the War Department).

35. Hall's MS journal.

36. Colonel A. Eustis to Lieutenant Hall, June 15, 1817; statement of Major A. S. Brooks and nine others, June 11, 1817 (MSS in the War Department).

37. Statement of J. Bates, October 27, 1814 (MS in the War Department).

38. Izard to the Secretary of War, November 8, 1814 (MS in the War Department).

39. "Empty Pockets," in *The Soldier's Bride*, p. 84.

40. The documents pertaining to Hall's leave are: T. Biddle to Lieutenant J. Hall, Fort Erie, October 29, 1814; J. Bates, *op. cit.*; James Hall to Colonel C. K. Gardner, Williamsville, October 31, 1814; "Post Revolutionary War Records," XXI, 54 (MSS in the War Department).

41. "Empty Pockets," in *The Soldier's Bride*, p. 84. See the entire narrative for a description of this visit to New York.

CHAPTER III

1. MS records in the War Department.

2. P. H. Musser, *James Nelson Barker* (Philadelphia, 1929), pp. 57–58; Simpson, p. 28.

3. Barker's handwritten name is on the Library of Congress copy of *Trial and Defence of First Lieutenant James Hall* (Pittsburgh, 1820). This publication is referred to hereafter as *Trial and Defence.*

4. See Plates XIII and XIV, by H. A. Ogden and the accompanying text (unpaginated) by H. L. Nelson in the Quartermaster General's *The Army of the United States* (New York, [1886]).

5. *Poulson's American Daily Advertiser,* January 26, 1815.

6. *Ibid.,* February 13, 1815.

7. MS records in the War Department.

8. James Hall, journal (MS owned by the Historical and Philosophical Society of Ohio). Hall notes that the poem was published in the *Telegraph* in February.

9. James Hall, autobiographical sketch.

10. "Stanzas," dated "Washington City March 1815" (Hall's MS journal).

11. James Hall, MS autobiographical sketch.

12. B. W. Crowninshield to S. Decatur, May 10, 1815 (MS in the Navy Department).

13. Hall to Crowninshield, May 23, 1815 (MS in the Navy Department).

14. S. T. Williams, *The Life of Washington Irving* (New York, 1935), I, 135, 144.

15. Hall to Crowninshield, May 23, 1815.

16. James Hall, MS journal.

17. See "To Mr. D. S . . . . tt," *ibid.;* F. B. Heitman, *Historical Register and Dictionary of the United States Army* (Washington, 1903), I, 856; C. H. Weygant, *The Sacketts of America* (Newburgh, New York, 1907), pp. 165, 262.

18. Except when I state otherwise, Hall's MS journal is the source for my account of the voyage. The log for this expedition is missing from the "Enterprise's" logbooks in the National Archives.

19. *Childe Harold's Pilgrimage,* Canto II, stanza XXII.

20. See G. W. Allen, *Our Navy and the Barbary Corsairs* (Boston, 1905), pp. 291–95.

21. I. Anthony, *Decatur* (New York, 1931), pp. 115, 261.

22. *Poulson's American Daily Advertiser,* November 24, 1815.

23. MS records in the War Department.

24. Hall to Brown, Newport, December 4, 1815 (MS owned by the Massachusetts Historical Society).

25. J. E. Hall [to the Secretary of War?], Philadelphia, January 6, 1816; J. E. Hall to General Ripley, January 6, 1816 (MSS in the War Department).

26. *Port Folio,* I (June, 1816), 527.

27. Ripley to W. H. Crawford, Wise's Tavern, Pa., [1816?] (MS in the War Department).

28. Hall to D. Parker, January 13, 1816 (MS in the Navy Department).

29. Eustis to Parker, November 30, 1816 (MS in the Navy Department).

30. Ripley to Crawford, February 8, 1816 (MS in the Navy Department).

31. MS records in the Navy Department.

32. See the poems marked "Newport" in Hall's MS journal.

33. "Proceedings of a General Court Martial, Held at Pittsburgh, Penn., on the 11th of September, 1817" (MSS in the Judge Advocate General's Office). Hereinafter these manuscripts are referred to as "Proceedings of a General Court Martial, Held at Pittsburgh."

34. Heitman, I, 744.

35. *Western Sun* (Vincennes), October 12, 26, 1816.

36. "Book 448, Old Number" (MS in the War Department).

CHAPTER IV

1. Carnegie Library (comp.), *Pittsburgh in 1816* (Pittsburgh, 1916), pp. 20, frontispiece; James Hall, *Letters,* pp. 22–24, 28–30.

2. James Hall, *Letters,* pp. 315, 35, 63.

3. *Pittsburgh Gazette,* December 8, 1818.

4. S. H. Killikelly, *The History of Pittsburgh* (Pittsburgh, 1906), pp. 150–51.

5. Heitman, I, 1060.

6. Woolley's testimony in "Proceedings of a General Court Martial, Held at Pittsburgh" (MSS in the Judge Advocate General's Office). This unpaginated record is the source of my account of Hall's military life in Pittsburgh except when I have indicated other sources.

7. *Ibid.,* Hall to Woolley, n. d., Woolley's testimony.

8. *Ibid.,* Woolley to Hall, December 16, 1816.

9. *Ibid.,* Hall to Woolley, December 17, 1816.

10. *Ibid.,* Woolley's testimony and Hall's defense.

11. *Ibid.,* Catlett's testimony.

12. *Ibid.,* Woolley's testimony.

13. *Ibid.,* Hall to Woolley, December 27, 1816.

14. *Ibid.,* Woolley to Hall, December 27, 1816.

15. *Ibid.,* Hall's defense.

16. *Ibid.* My relation of Saturday's events is condensed from Hall's account, most of which is corroborated by other testimony.

17. *Ibid.,* Hall to Woolley, December 29, 1816.

18. *Ibid.,* Hall's defense.

19. *Ibid.,* Hall to Woolley, December 29, 1816.

20. *Ibid.,* Catlett's testimony.

21. *Illinois Intelligencer,* July 10, 1830.

22. M. James, *The Life of Andrew Jackson* (Indianapolis, 1938), pp. 115–18.

23. Heitman, I, 432; Killikelly, p. 151.

24. M. Foster, *My Brother Stephen* (Indianapolis, 1932), p. 19.

25. R. Walters, *Stephen Foster* (Princeton, 1936), p. 29. Mr. Walters almost certainly intended to refer to James Hall, not James C. Hall.

26. "Proceedings of a General Court Martial, Held at Pittsburgh." Both letters are dated at the Arsenal, January 7, 1817.

27. *Ibid.,* Wadsworth to Woolley, January 25, 1817; Hall to Parker, February 10, 1817.

28. *Pittsburgh Gazette,* February 14, 1817; Hall's MS journal, quoted here. See also in the journal, "Can sorrow e'er depress the heart."

29. "The American Lounger," *Port Folio,* IV (October, 1817), 321–25.

30. C. B. Todd, *Life and Letters of Joel Barlow* (New York, 1886), pp. 216, 234.

31. *Pittsburgh Gazette,* April 15, 1817. I am informed that the court records of the trial are not extant.

32. Barlow's second testimony in "Proceedings of a General Court Martial, Held at Pittsburgh." Hall later charged that Woolley employed Barlow to follow Hall, draw him into controversy, and take notes of what he said (*Trial and Defence,* Preface, p. ix). Barlow, Baldwin, and Colonel George Bomford, a high official of the Ordnance in Washington, were relatives.

33. "Proceedings of a General Court Martial, Held at Pittsburgh," Barlow's second testimony.

34. *Ibid.,* J. I. Scull's testimony.

35. Hall to Rush, May 12, 1817; Rush to Hall, May 20, 1817 (*Trial and Defence,* p. 93).

36. "Proceedings of a General Court Martial, Held at Pittsburgh," Parker to Woolley, July 11, 1817.

37. *Ibid.,* Hall's defense.

38. *Ibid.*

39. D. Agnew, "Address to the Allegheny County Bar Association," *Pennsylvania Magazine of History and Biography,* XIII, No. 1 (1889), 58.

40. *Trial and Defence,* p. vii.

41. "General and Special Orders," II, 86 (MS in the War Department).

42. J. Morton to Hall, December 9, 1817 (*Trial and Defence,* p. 93).

43. Hall to Parker, February 3, 1818 (MS in the War Department).

44. *Trial and Defence,* p. iii.

45. Hall to Parker, June 10, 1818 (MS in the War Department).

Chapter V

1. Griswold, p. 289.

2. H. M. Brackenridge, *Recollections of Persons and Places in the West* (Philadelphia, 1865), pp. 98–99; Agnew, p. 4; *Letters,* p. 44; Z. Cramer, *The Navigator* (Pittsburgh, 1821), p. 45.

3. Anon., *The Twentieth Century Bench and Bar of Pennsylvania* (Chicago, 1903), II, 819.

4. *Pittsburgh Gazette,* June 23, 1817; *Pittsburgh Directory, 1819,* p. 56.

5. *Pittsburgh Gazette,* July 24, 1818; January 5, 1820.

6. Anon., *History of Gallatin, Saline, Hamilton, Franklin, and Williamson Counties, Illinois* (Chicago, 1887) pp. 538–39 (hereinafter cited as *History of Gallatin . . .*); *Pittsburgh Gazette,* January 7, 1820; Agnew, p. 33.

7. *Trial and Defence,* p. xiv; *Letters,* p. 37; "The Ladies—dear creatures," "Sleighing," and "Goodby ———," (Hall's MS journal).

8. MS in the Charles Roberts Autograph Collection, owned by Haverford College; *Letters,* p. 37; *Pittsburgh Gazette,* January 14, 1817, October 26, 1819; *Pittsburgh Commonwealth,* January 13, 1819.

9. *Pittsburgh Gazette,* July 2, 9, 30, 1819.

10. *Ibid.,* June 27, 1817; January 1, 1819; January 7, 1820; *Letters,* p. 38.

11. I am indebted to Mr. Matthew Galt, Jr., Grand Secretary of the Grand Lodge of Pennsylvania, for data from Hall's early Masonic record.

12. James Hall, *An Oration Delivered in Commemoration of the Festival of St. John the Baptist* (Pittsburgh, 1818), p. 13. The libraries of the American Philosophical Society and Western Reserve University own copies.

13. J. C. Andrews, *Pittsburgh's Post-Gazette* (Boston, 1936), p. 57.

14. H. Blackburn and W. H. Welfley, *History of Bedford and Somerset Counties, Pennsylvania* (New York, 1906), III, 19–20; Anon., *The Twentieth Century Bench and Bar of Pennsylvania,* II, 815.

15. *Pittsburgh Gazette,* December 19, 1817.

16. *Ibid.,* December 24, 1816; June 13, March 11, November 25, 1817.

17. Andrews, pp. 60–62.

18. Heitman, I, 744.

19. *Pittsburgh Gazette,* September 11, 1820; May 19, June 23, December 18, 1818; *Pittsburgh Directory, 1819; Letters,* p. 153.

20. *The Western Souvenir* (Cincinnati, [1828]), pp. 107–22.

21. *Letters,* pp. 143–53; W. H. Egle, *Pennsylvania Genealogies* (Harrisburg, 1886), pp. 480–83.

22. Brackenridge, p. 55; [Morgan Neville], "Reminiscences of Pittsburgh," *Illinois Monthly Magazine,* I (February, 1831), 233–38, reprinted from the *Cincinnati Chronicle and Literary Gazette,* January 8, 1831.

23. *The Western Souvenir,* pp. 108–9; Agnew, p. 19.

24. E. O. Randall and D. J. Ryan, *History of Ohio* (New York, 1912), III, 236, 246–47; W. H. Safford, *The Life of Harman Blennerhassett* (Cincinnati, 1859), pp. 110-16; *The Blennerhassett Papers,* ed. W. H. Safford (Cincinnati, 1864), pp. 193–97, 274, 277, 279, 408; *Reports of the Trials of Aaron Burr,* compiled by D. Robertson (Philadelphia, 1808), I, 360, 362.

25. *Pittsburgh Gazette,* November 29, 1816; April 10, 1818; July 23, 1819.

26. *Port Folio,* VII (May, 1819), 442.

27. M. R. Watson, "The Essay Tradition and the Magazine Serials (1731–1820)" (Doctoral dissertation, Johns Hopkins University, 1944), p. 34; W. Graham, *English Literary Periodicals* (New York, 1930), p. 144.

28. Ellis, p. 51.

29. Ellis, pp. 91, 153, 157 ff.

30. Watson, pp. 106–10.

31. See my "Authors of the *Port Folio* Revealed by the Hall Files."

32. Watson, p. 63.

33. Apparently essays Nos. 11–15 are misnumbered, and only fourteen essays actually appeared.

34. Nos. 6 and 11.

35. Hall listed in his MS journal the periodicals in which some of the poems appeared.

36. *Pittsburgh Gazette,* April 6, 1819; Hall's MS journal.

37. *Port Folio,* VII (January, 1819), 81; Hall's MS journal.

38. Compare the following of Moore's poems (for which pages are cited from his *Poetical Works,* ed. Godley [London, 1810]), and Hall's poems (for which dates of the *Pittsburgh Gazette* are cited) : "In the Morning of Life," pp. 211–12, with "Parody," June 24, 1817; "Oh! Think Not My Spirits Are Always As Light," p. 183, with "Parody," October 27, 1818; "The Meeting of the Waters," pp. 184–85, with "Parody," November 6, 1818; "Go Where Glory Waits Thee," p. 180, with "A Pittsburgh Merchant to His Correspondent in the West," July 16, 1819; and "Love's Young Dream," p. 195, with "Oh! there were days when blissful dreams," April 13, 1819.

39. *Pittsburgh Gazette,* October, 1, 1819; "All Hail to the 'Man in the Moon,'" September 24, 1819.

40. *Ibid.,* December 7, 17, 1819; "A New Song to an Old Tune," *ibid.,* December 31, 1819; *Mercury,* January 7, 1820.

41. J. Dennie, *The Lay Preacher,* ed. J. E. Hall (Philadelphia, 1817), p. v.

42. Hopkinson to Hall, December 21, 1815 (MS owned by the Historical Society of Pennsylvania).

43. F. L. Mott, *A History of American Magazines, 1741–1850* (New York, 1930), p. 154.

44. *Port Folio,* IV (July, 1814), 109; VI (November, 1815), 518–19;

American Philosophical Society, *Early Proceedings* (Philadelphia, 1884), p. 443.

45. *Port Folio,* II (October, 1816), 353–54; XX (August, 1825), 146–50; Sarah Hall, *Selections,* p. xxxi.

46. Vol. I, front cover.

47. See above, Chapter II.

48. All were signed "J.H." except "To Miss —— ——," I (June, 1816), 528. This poem is in Hall's MS journal.

49. III (March, 1817), 242–47.

50. IV (October, 1817), 321–25. All the prose mentioned here, except the biographical sketch of Presley Neville, appeared in the "American Lounger" section.

51. *Trial and Defence,* p. 95. For Hall's account of this second dispute, see the Preface. Woolley's case is stated in the manuscripts in the files of Hall's letters in the War Department.

52. Hall to Parker, May 24, July 22, 1818; Woolley to Bomford, May 10, 1818 (MSS in the War Department).

53. *Trial and Defence,* pp. 96, 95, 97, v.

54. August 31, 1816 (*ibid.,* p. vi).

55. The publication date on the title page is incorrect (*Pittsburgh Gazette,* December 31, 1819).

56. MSS in the Woolley files, War Department.

57. James Hall, MS autobiographical sketch.

58. S. E. Morison and H. S. Commager, *The Growth of the American Republic* (New York, 1937), I, 337.

59. *Pittsburgh Gazette,* January 11, 1820; July 30, 1819. Part of the decline of Pittsburgh's shipping was due to the completion of the National Road to Wheeling in 1818. Hall may have feared that Pittsburgh's commercial supremacy was therefore doomed (*Letters,* p. 35).

60. *Pittsburgh Gazette,* July 30, 1819; December 8, 1818. The latter article is signed "H."

61. *Letters,* pp. 310, 315.

62. *Pittsburgh Gazette,* October 22, September 7, November 5, 1819.

63. *Letters,* pp. 47–48.

Chapter VI

1. In *Letters,* page 78, Hall indicates that the journey from Wheeling to Marietta occupied April 18. Wheeling is ninety-eight miles from Pittsburgh by the river—approximately one day's journey (Cramer, p. 71). Hall describes the towns between Pittsburgh and Wheeling as if he had passed them in the daytime (*Letters,* pp. 49, 50, 56).

2. The first steamboat on Western waters was launched in 1811 (Rusk, I, 24). Seven years later, a writer in the *Pittsburgh Gazette* of April 2,

1819, listed forty steamboats that had been built and twenty-seven that were then in construction.

3. *Letters*, pp. 322–23, 47–48, 111–12, 182.

4. James Hall, *Legends of the West* (Cincinnati, 1869), p. xiii. (This work is hereinafter cited as *Legends*.)

5. *Letters*, pp. 154, 186–87, 82–83.

6. *Ibid.*, pp. 91, 94.

7. *Ibid.*, pp. 87, 138–40, 141–42.

8. In 1820, New Orleans was the only Western city whose population exceeded Cincinnati's (Anon., *Statistical Abstracts of the United States* [Washington, D. C., 1911], p. 50).

9. *Letters*, pp. 156–58, 184–92.

Chapter VII

1. For an analysis of the settlement of Illinois in 1820, see *Illinois Census Returns 1810, 1818*, ed. M. C. Norton (Springfield, 1935), pp. xv–xvi; T. C. Pease, *The Frontier State* (Springfield, 1918), pp. 1–5; S. J. Buck, *Illinois in 1818* (Springfield, 1917), chap. iii; and James Hall, *Legends* (Cincinnati, 1869), p. vii.

2. Buck, pp. 58, 69.

3. See the following descriptions of Shawneetown written by people who were there between 1817 and 1826: *Letters from the West*, pp. 215–33; C. H. Tillson, *A Woman's Story of Pioneer Illinois*, ed. M. M. Quaife (Chicago, 1919), pp. 46–51; Bernhard, Duke of Saxe-Weimar Eisenach, *Travels through North America* (Philadelphia, 1828), II, 105; W. Owen, *Diary of William Owen from November 10, 1824 to April 20, 1825*, ed. J. W. Hiatt (Indianapolis, 1906); M. Birkbeck, *Notes on a Journey in America* (London, 1818), pp. 119, 130; J. Woods, *Two Years Residence in the Settlement on the English Prairie* (London, 1822), pp. 129–32; H. B. Fearon, *Sketches of America* (London, 1819), p. 258; T. Nuttall, *A Journal of Travels into the Arkansa Territory during the Year 1819* (Philadelphia, 1821), p. 40. For photographs of some of the pioneer buildings which survive, see C. J. Small, "River Stay Away from My Door; New Deal Is Moving Illinois' Oldest Town Bodily," *Saturday Evening Post*, CCXIII (December 7, 1940), 16–17.

4. Woods, pp. 132–33.

5. *Audubon's America*, ed. D. C. Peattie (Boston, 1940), p. 139.

6. *Illinois Gazette*, May 5, December 8, 1821; November 30, 1822.

7. *Letters*, p. 215.

8. Birkbeck, p. 119.

9. Sarah Weed to A. F. Grant, March 11, 1829 (MS in the Eddy Papers, owned by Mr. Eugene Carroll).

10. *Illinois Gazette*, May 27, 1820; January 31, 1824.

11. *Legends* (1869), p. xiii; *Letters*, p. 220.

12. *Legends* (1869), p. ix.

13. *Illinois Gazette,* September 9, May 27, July 22, 1820.

14. Historians of the *Gazette* who have claimed that Eddy and Allen Kimmel founded the newspaper seem not to have been aware of Eddy's statement in his letter to William Orr, February 16, 1827: "I gave $1000 to Kimmel for half [of the *Gazette*] in 1818. . . . " (MS in the Eddy Papers.)

Peter Kimmel (1771–1843) was born in Somerset County, Pennsylvania. In 1813, he moved to Pittsburgh. In 1820, he emigrated first to Jackson County and later to Union County, Illinois. He died at Jonesboro.

Allen W. Kimmel (1799–1867) was the son of Peter Kimmel and his second wife, Mary Weaver Kimmel. He was born in Somerset County; learned the printer's trade, probably in Pittsburgh; and died near Jonesboro. (Dr. Harry Kimmel Stoner, of Berlin, Pennsylvania, has generously provided me with these facts about the Kimmels.)

15. Eddy's tombstone, Shawneetown; Heitman, II, 307; *History of Gallatin* . . . , pp. 538–39.

16. H. A. Kurtz to Henry Eddy, November 27, 1823 (MS in the Eddy Papers); *History of Gallatin* . . . , p. 539.

17. U. F. Linder, *Reminiscences of the Early Bench and Bar of Illinois* (Chicago, 1879), p. 52.

18. See Eddy's announcements in the *Illinois Gazette,* July 8, 1820; July 17, 1824. See also Eddy to William Gatewood, January 6, 1835 (MS in the Eddy Papers).

19. C. S. Brigham, "Bibliography of American Newspapers," American Antiquarian Society *Proceedings,* N.S. XXIII (October, 1913), 395, 397.

20. *Illinois Gazette,* May 27, 1820.

21. T. Ford, *A History of Illinois* (Chicago, 1854), p. 74; Pease, pp. 92–93.

22. *Illinois Gazette,* May 27, 1820.

23. Pease, pp. 73–74, 82; *Illinois Gazette,* July 8, 1820.

24. J. Reynolds, *The Pioneer History of Illinois* (Chicago, 1887), pp. 391–93.

25. Ford, pp. 46, 47.

26. See the statements of John McLernand and John Eddy in J. H. Burnham, "Hon. John McLean," Illinois Historical Society, *Transactions,* No. 8 (1903), pp. 198–201.

27. There is a gap of twelve weeks between the surviving issues of Vol. III, No. 4 (December 2, 1820) and No. 9 (March 3, 1821).

28. *Journal of the House of Representives* [*sic*] *of the Second General Assembly* (Vandalia, 1821), pp. 170–71.

29. "Executive Record," I, 36, 38 (MS in the Archives Division, Springfield).

30. [James Hall?], "John's Elegy in a Country Town," *Port Folio,* XVII (April, 1824), 347–48.

31. See, for examples, T. T. Tucker to Eddy and Kimmel, July 13, 1819; J. McLean to Hall and Eddy, November 27, 1822 (MSS in the Eddy Papers).

32. S. H. Kimmel to A. F. Grant, December 20, 1829 (MS in the Eddy Papers).

33. Eddy to Orr, February 16, 1827; Orr to Eddy, February 21, 1827 (MSS in the Eddy Papers).

34. Pease, p. 189.

35. Eddy to Kimmel [January 4, 1822?] (MS in the Eddy Papers). It is possible that this letter was not sent.

36. W. J. Wilcher and T. Jent to Eddy, February 22, 1825 (MS in the Eddy Papers); *History of Gallatin . . .* , p. 113.

37. In 1822, Eddy paid Hall that sum for the same consideration (Eddy to Orr, February 16, 1827).

38. P. and A. W. Kimmel to Eddy, February 15, 1819; J. H. Lambdin to Eddy, February 11, 1819 (MSS in the Eddy Papers).

39. Woods, pp. 130–31.

40. The court records of Johnson County, Illinois, show that Hall was at court at Vienna in September, 1821. See also the *Illinois Gazette,* August 25, 1821.

41. *Illinois Gazette,* February 16, 1822.

42. Edward Patchett to Hall, September 4, 1823 (MS in the Eddy Papers).

43. *Illinois Gazette,* July 6, 1822.

44. *Pittsburgh Gazette,* July 30, 1819; *Letters,* p. 48; *Illinois Gazette,* June 3, July 1, 1820; December 29, 1821; January 5, 1822.

45. Hall's notice helps to establish the date of the first issue of this magazine. See Rusk, I, 201 n.

46. *Illinois Gazette,* December 2, September 9, 1820. I know of no extant copy of Drake's address.

47. *Ibid.,* July 14, 1821.

48. *Ibid.,* July 28, December 8, 15, May 5, June 2, 1821.

49. *Ibid.,* May 12, 1821.

50. *Ibid.,* April 6, August 3, 1822.

51. Quoted from the *Port Folio,* XV (January, 1823), 58–60.

52. Watson, pp. 187, 166–83.

53. *Port Folio,* XVI (November, 1823), 362–74.

54. I have found no extended study devoted solely to the genesis of the frontiersman in American fiction. See, however, W. H. Willer, "Native Themes in American Short Prose Fiction, 1770–1835" (Doctoral dissertation, University of Minnesota, 1944), chap. viii. Dr. Willer mentions no short story of the type before Hall's appeared in 1821–22; however, he does not include the newspapers in his study. See also Harold Blaine, "The Frontiersman in American Prose Fiction (1800–1860)" (Doctoral dissertation, Western Reserve University, 1936), p. 66. Paulding, in his *Letters from the South* (1817), relates a fight between a boatman and a wagoner. This account was probably influential; however, it occurs as an apparently factual relation in a book of travels, and, according to Paulding's statement for a later edition of the book, "may be depended upon" ([New York, 1835], II, 73 n.). Paulding's *The Lion of the West* (1831) was the "first drama to introduce a raw and uncouth frontiersman as its leading character" (N. F. Adkins, "James K. Paulding's *Lion of the West,*" *American Literature,* III [November, 1931], 249). See also W. T. Conklin, *Paulding's Prose Treatment of Types and Frontier Lore before Cooper* ("University of Texas Studies in English," 1939), pp. 163–71; and H. E. Hall, "James Kirke

Paulding: A Pioneer in American Fiction" (Doctoral dissertation, University of Pennsylvania, 1953), pp. 163–70.

55. For a synopsis of *The Lion of the West,* the text of which is lost, see Adkins, pp. 257–58.

56. For a discussion of the uncouthness of Leather Stocking in *The Pioneers,* see J. Grossman, *James Fenimore Cooper* ([New York], 1949), p. 33.

57. Sarah Hall, *Selections,* p. xxiii.

58. Probably Mary Posey, of Henderson, Kentucky, later Hall's wife.

59. Probably John Foliart, aged about seventeen in 1822 (*Illinois Gazette,* February 11, 1826).

60. Since the poem is not in the *Gazette* of January 5, 1822, it must have been a broadside. See the *Port Folio,* II (August, 1822), 168–71.

61. N. W. Edwards, *History of Illinois* (Springfield, Ill., 1870), p. 268.

62. Pease, pp. 103–4.

63. The genuineness of Cook's quotation is questionable. Although I have not found the *Gazette* containing "Letter I," there is no such language in Hall's extant "Letters II, III, IV." For Cook's "Reply to Brutus," see the *Illinois Gazette,* July 27, 1822.

64. Pease, pp. 103–4.

65. *Illinois Gazette,* September 19, 1829; July 3, 1830.

66. See Eddy to A. F. Grant, December 22, 24, 1828; Eddy to Grant, December 19, 1830; Hall to Eddy, October 22, 1831; Eddy to G. Ewing, February 8, 1831; Hall to Eddy, March 6, 1833 (MSS in the Eddy Papers).

67. Eddy to Orr, February 16, 1827; *Illinois Gazette,* November 9, 1822.

68. Eddy to N. Edwards, July 28, 1829 (MS in the Eddy Papers).

CHAPTER VIII

1. *Illinois Gazette,* April 21, July 7, 1821.

2. For a map of the early counties, see Buck, *op. cit.,* p. 59; for court dates, see the *Illinois Gazette,* March 3, 1821.

3. *Legends* (1869), pp. viii, xii.

4. Court Record No. 3, p. 132 (MS in the courthouse at Vienna).

5. *History of Gallatin . . . ,* pp. 69–70; Order Book B, pp. 123, 118–19 (MS in the courthouse at Jonesboro).

6. See, for examples, the Union County Order Book B and the Judge's Docket 1821–1840 (MSS in the Jonesboro courthouse); also the records in the box marked "Indictments Disposed 1825–1829," and in another box marked "Court Papers 1825" (MSS in the courthouse at Golconda).

7. O. A. Rothert, *The Outlaws of Cave-in-Rock* (Cleveland, 1924), pp. 174–76, 91–94.

8. *Sketches of History, Life, and Manners, in the West* (Philadelphia, 1835), II, 89. This work is hereinafter referred to as *Sketches of History.*

9. *Illinois Gazette,* January 1, 1820.

10. *Sketches of History,* II, 89, 90.

11. Hall's part in the expedition is revealed by W. H. Venable, who, in writing his *Beginnings of Literary Culture in the Ohio Valley* (Cincinnati, 1891), had the aid of Hall's daughter Mrs. Sarah Hall Foote (pp. v, 368–70). The *Gazette* records the expedition (July 6, 1822), but does not name any of the posse.

12. MS in the box marked "Indictments Disposed 1825–1829" (Golconda courthouse).

13. *Sketches of History,* II, 90–91.

14. *History of Gallatin . . . ,* pp. 69–70.

15. *Legends* (1869), p. xi.

<h2 style="text-align:center">CHAPTER IX</h2>

1. MS record in Mary Posey Hall's prayer book (owned by Miss Mary Posey Foote).

2. T. P. Hughes, *et. al., American Ancestry* (Albany, 1887–1898), VIII, 146.

3. Gravestones in the Shawneetown cemetery.

4. "The Seventh Son," in *Legends.*

5. In 1947, the portrait was owned by Miss Mary Posey Foote.

6. James Hall to Sarah Hall, October 8, 1824 (MS owned by the Chicago Historical Society).

7. James Hall to Sarah Hall, September 25, 1824 (MS in the Charles Roberts Autograph Collection, owned by Haverford College).

8. J. E. Hall to James Hall, September 13, 1827 (MS owned by the Historical and Philosophical Society of Ohio).

9. James Hall's autograph record in his Bible (owned by Mr. Francis Hall Kent). See also Hall's account book (MS owned by the Historical and Philosophical Society of Ohio).

10. After nine weeks, Hall appears to have given up keeping the account. He copied some of his poems in the rest of the pages of the book.

11. *Illinois Monthly Magazine,* I, (October, 1831), 9.

12. Johnson County (Illinois) Circuit Court fee book, entries for 1825 (MS in the courthouse at Vienna).

13. *Legends* (1869), p. ix.; James Hall's MS autobiographical sketch.

14. MS record in James Hall's Bible.

15. MS owned by the Chicago Historical Society.

16. Conversation with Miss Mary Posey Foote.

17. *Western Sun* (Vincennes), October 25, 1816; February 8, March 18, June 21, 1817.

18. Brigham, N. S. XXVI (April, 1916), 94.

19. *Illinois Gazette,* July 7, 1821; February 2, 1822; July 19, 1823.

20. For accounts of the Independence Day celebrations, see the *Illinois Gazette,* July 8, 1820; July 7, 1821; July 6, 1822; July 9, 1825.

21. *Ibid.,* July 21, 1821; "Executive Record," I, 36, 44, 97 (MS in the Archives Division, Springfield, Illinois) ; *Governors' Letter Books,* ed. E. B. Greene and C. W. Alford (Springfield, 1909), p. 56.

22. Mr. A. E. Orton, Grand Secretary of the Grand Lodge of Kentucky, graciously informed me of Hall's Masonic record in the Shawneetown lodge. For a history of his services in the Grand Lodge of Illinois, I am indebted to Mr. R. C. Davenport, Grand Secretary. See also the *Illinois Gazette,* July 19, 1823, and J. C. Reynolds, *History of the M. W. Grand Lodge of Illinois* (Springfield, 1869), pp. 74–104.

23. XVIII, 524.

24. Street to N. Edwards, July 28, 1827, *Edwards Papers,* ed. E. B. Washburne (Chicago, 1884), p. 295.

25. *Legends* (Philadelphia, 1832), pp. 8–11.

26. *Illinois Gazette,* November 30, 1822.

27. *Ibid.,* July 21, 28, 1821; July 15, 1826.

28. My account of Lafayette's visit is derived from the relation in the *Illinois Gazette* of May 14, 1825, which contains Hall's speech. Other histories of the event are based on the relations of the *Illinois Intelligencer,* May 27, 1825, and of A. Levasseur (Lafayette's secretary), in his *Lafayette en Amérique, en 1824 et 1825* (Paris, 1829), II, 346–47. These accounts, clearly mistaken, date the visit May 14 and May 8, respectively.

29. XVII, 524.

30. *Illinois Gazette,* May 14, 1824; November 27, 1824.

31. *Journal of the House of Representatives* (Vandalia, 1824), p. 171.

32. J. E. Hall to C. Prentiss, March 20, 1819; November 4, 1819 (MSS owned by the American Antiquarian Society).

33. *Port Folio,* XVII (April, 1824), 269.

34. Street to N. Edwards, March 30, 1827 (*Edwards Papers,* p. 274).

35. For this and other contributions discussed here, see XX, 116–28, 94–103, 200–208; II, 527.

36. MS records in Sarah Hall's Bible.

37. F. L. Mott, *A History of American Magazines 1741–1850* (New York, 1930), pp. 245–46.

Chapter X

1. *Illinois Gazette,* September 2, 1826.

2. *Illinois Intelligencer,* January 6, 7, 1827; Hall to Sloo, January 15, 1827 (MS owned by the Historical and Philosophical Society of Ohio).

3. Hall to Sloo, *ibid.*

4. *Journal of the Senate of the Fifth General Assembly of the State of Illinois* (Vandalia, 1826), p. 258.

5. In the *Illinois Intelligencer* of March 3, 1827, Hall announces the opening of his law office in Vandalia.

6. W. E. Baringer, *Lincoln's Vandalia: A Pioneer Portrait* (New Brunswick, 1949), p. 4. This work contains a detailed history of early Vandalia. Although the focus of the book is upon the period of 1834–39, much of the description of the town applies to the period of Hall's residence there, 1827–33.

7. *Illinois Intelligencer,* January 3, 1829.

8. [James Hall?], "Missionary Adventure," *Western Monthly Magazine,* I (May, 1833), 228–29.

9. *Illinois Intelligencer,* November 27, December 4, 18, 1830.

10. "Vandalia," *Illinois Monthly Magazine,* II (January, 1832), 173, 176.

11. *Illinois Intelligencer,* July 26, 1828.

12. "Vandalia," II, 175.

13. "Critical Notices," *Western Monthly Magazine,* II (December, 1834), 662.

14. "Vandalia," II, 173, 176.

15. James Hall, "Notes on Illinois," *Illinois Monthly Magazine,* I (December, 1830), 129–31.

16. *Ibid.,* I (October, 1831), 8–11.

17. I, 271.

18. I, 394; I, 377–84. In Chapter I, I have quoted extensively from the article.

19. Frontier poets had begun to relate their idealized Indians to distant tribes apparently as early as 1819 (Rusk, I, 344).

20. "Notes on Illinois," II (June, 1828), 19-20, 71; I (January, 1828), 563.

21. "Popular Superstitions," "Shawnee Town and Its Vicinity," and "Tales of Travellers," in James Hall's *Letters from the West,* pp. 215–33, 326–46 ff.

22. He also enlarged and included "General Presley Neville" from the *Port Folio,* VII (March, 1819), 263–64.

23. Irving to J. E. Hall, June 30, 1822.

24. MS autobiographical sketch.

25. M. W. Rosa, *The Silver-Fork School* (New York, 1936), p. 190.

26. Sabin lists a second edition of *Letters from the West* published in 1830, but I have not found a copy of this edition listed in catalogues of American or foreign libraries or any notice of it except Sabin's.

27. XXIV (December, 1828), 518–19.

28. *Letters,* pp. 327, 219, 322, 378, 138.

29. XXXIX (April, 1829), 345, 348, 356. M. F. Brightfield reveals the authorship of the review in "Lockhart's *Quarterly* Contributors," *Publications of the Modern Language Association,* LIX (June, 1944), 494.

30. Quoted in the *Illinois Gazette,* March 21, 1829.

31. P. 93.

32. P. 84.

33. Pp. 232–33.

34. See Chapter VI, above.

35. Pp. 311–13.

36. For my account of the history of the Hugh Glass story in oral tradition and in literature, I am indebted to Professor Edgeley W. Todd, "James Hall and the Hugh Glass Legend," *American Quarterly*, VII (Winter, 1955), 362–70.

37. W. Irving, *A Tour on the Prairies* (Philadelphia: Carey, Lea, & Blanchard, 1835), pp. 200–202.

38. G. F. Ruxton, *Ruxton of the Rockies*, ed. L. R. Hafen (Norman, Okla., 1950), pp. 253–55.

39. *Port Folio*, XVII (June, 1824), 518; XIX (January, 1825), 25–29. For an account of the origin of the giftbook, see R. Thompson, *American Literary Annuals and Gift Books, 1825–1865* (New York, 1936), pp. 2, 148, 156.

40. Two of the other three tales in *Winter Evenings* had appeared in the *Port Folio.* These are "An Account of An Attempt to Liberate M. De Lafayette," II (August, 1816), 93–112, and Robert Rose's "A Voyage to Italy," II (September, 1822), 207-36. See my article "Authors of the *Port Folio* Revealed by the Hall Files," *American Literature*, XI (January, 1940), 415, 406, for confirmation of Rose's authorship of the second relation. Although all of the narratives in *Winter Evenings* have several times been ascribed to Hall, there is no evidence that he wrote any except "The Soldier's Bride."

41. J. E. Hall to James Hall, September 13, 1827.

42. In Chapter II, I have quoted extensively from the description.

43. The prospectus, dated April 17, 1828, appeared in the *Illinois Intelligencer* of May 10.

44. *Liberty Hall and Cincinnati Gazette*, November 25, 1828.

45. MS autobiographical sketch.

46. *Ibid.*

47. *Pittsburgh Gazette*, September 29, 1818.

48. *Legends* (1869), p. lx.

49. *Western Monthly Review*, I (May, 1827), 9, 10. David Donald and Frederick A. Palmer, in "Toward a Western Literature, 1820–1860," *Mississippi Valley Historical Review*, XXXV (December, 1948), 413–28, show that such sentiment was widespread in the West between 1830 and 1860. However, since only two of their examples of a demand for a Western literature are drawn from works published before 1830, and none were drawn from those published before 1820 (the beginning date of their article's scope), Hall's 1818 call for a Western periodical was a very early one in the movement.

50. March 21, 1829.

51. C. S. Baldwin has pointed out the similarity in *American Short Stories* (New York, 1906), p. 5.

52. October 31, November 7, 1829. Hall was then editor of the *Intelligencer*. He wrote another account of Moredock in "Indian Hating" (*Western Monthly Magazine*, I [September, 1833], 403–8), and in fiction returned to the theme in "The Pioneer" (*Tales of the Border* [Philadelphia, 1835], pp. 13–101).

53. For the original, see *The Western Souvenir,* p. 306. I have quoted from the revised version in James Hall, *The Wilderness and the War Path* (New York, 1846), pp. 155–56.

54. *The Wilderness and the War Path,* p. 162. For the original, see p. 314.

55. *American Humor: A Study of the National Character* (New York, 1931), pp. 33–76.

56. D. G. Hoffman, "Irving's Use of American Folklore in 'The Legend of Sleepy Hollow,'" *Publications of the Modern Language Association,* LXVIII (June, 1953), 425–35.

57. F. L. Pattee, *The Development of the American Short Story* (New York, 1923), p. 55.

58. Miss Rourke has pointed out the relation in folklore of the boatman to the gamecock (*op. cit.,* p. 42).

59. Hall describes Fink as a real person (*Statistics of the West* [Cincinnati, 1836], p. 220).

60. Vol. I, p. iv. M. R. Mitford to W. Harness, January 24, 1830 (*The Life of Mary Russell Mitford,* ed. A. G. L'Estrange [London, 1870], II, 296–97).

61. M. R. Mitford to W. Harness, January 24, 1830 (L'Estrange, II, 296–97).

62. *Journal of the Senate of the Fifth General Assembly of the State of Illinois,* p. 258.

63. *Illinois Intelligencer,* April 11, 25, 1829.

64. *Ibid.,* March 1, 1828.

65. *Ibid.,* January 28, 1832; July 26, 1828; December 17, 1831.

66. *Ibid.,* January 30, December 5, 12, August 1, 1829; February 6, August 28, November 6, 1830.

67. J. M. Sturtevant, *An Autobiography* (New York, 1896), pp. 135–42.

68. For accounts of this meeting, see the *Illinois Gazette,* January 16, 1830, and the *Western Monthly Magazine,* II (April, 1834), 220. For a detailed relation of the founding of Illinois College, see C. H. Rammelkamp, *Illinois College: A Centennial History* (New Haven, 1928), chaps. i–iii. Rammelkamp, however, omits mentioning that it was Hall who made the motion to create Illinois College by accepting the terms of the Yale Band.

69. Sturtevant, p. 174.

70. *Ibid.,* p. 178; *Illinois Intelligencer,* January 1, 1831.

71. E. L. Fox, *The American Colonization Society 1817–1840* (Baltimore, 1919), pp. 125, 150.

72. The organization and first meeting of the Society were reported in the *Illinois Intelligencer* of March 19, 1831.

73. Hall to J. E. Worcester, June 7, 1831 (MS owned by the Massachusetts Historical Society).

74. There was apparently a preponderance of Southern white settlers in the state; more than two-thirds of the members of the legislature of 1828–29 had been born in Slave States (*Illinois Intelligencer,* December 20, 1828).

75. *Ibid.,* October 29, November 12, December 17, 1831.

76. *Cincinnati Chronicle and Literary Gazette,* April 23, May 28, 1831. The address was printed in the *Illinois Monthly Magazine,* I (April, 1831), 315–30.

77. "Records of the Illinois State Lyceum" (MS owned by the Illinois State Historical Library); *Illinois Intelligencer,* December 10, 1831; November 14, 1832.

78. *Illinois Intelligencer,* February 18, 1832. A lecture on astronomy was announced for the second weekly meeting, but I was unable to find in the *Intelligencer* a report of any meeting except the first.

79. My account of the Society is derived from the *Illinois Intelligencer,* December 22, 1827; December 22, 1828; January 3, February 14, November 14, 1829; January 16, 1830.

80. Hall to Peter DuPonceau, March 21, 1829.

81. J. Stuart, *Three Years in North America* (Edinburgh, 1833), II, 364. The first year's proceedings were printed by R. K. Fleming at Edwardsville; those for 1829 were printed by Robert Blackwell at Vandalia. The Library of the American Philosophical Society has copies of the proceedings for these two years.

CHAPTER XI

1. *Journal of the Senate of the Sixth General Assembly* (Kaskaskia, Ill., 1829), p. 104. The dissenters were Singleton Kimmel and George Churchill (1789–1872).

2. *Vandalia Whig and Illinois Intelligencer,* April 17, 1833.

3. Josephine Louise Harper, "John Reynolds, 'The Old Ranger' of Illinois" (Doctoral dissertation, University of Illinois, 1949), pp. 69, 70.

4. Pease, pp. 129–31.

5. *Illinois Gazette,* July 10, 1830; Harper, p. 75.

6. See Edwards's campaign piece, "James Hall Editor of the Illinois Intelligencer" (Edwards Transcripts, owned by the Illinois Historical Survey, Urbana).

7. Edwards to the editors of the *Illinois Gazette,* July 22, 1830.

8. "James Hall Editor of the Illinois Intelligencer" (Edwards Transcripts).

9. Harper, pp. 73–74.

10. *Illinois Intelligencer,* July 10, March 13, April 3, 1830.

11. *Illinois Gazette,* August 15, 1829.

12. *Illinois Intelligencer,* April 24, July 10, 1830.

13. *Illinois Gazette,* September 19, 1829; July 31, 1830.

14. *Illinois Intelligencer,* July 10, 1830.

15. *Journal of the House of Representatives of the Seventh General Assembly* (Vandalia, 1831), pp. 391–93, 437–39.

16. Of the five members of the Finance Committee, Churchill, Mundy,

and Stewart had voted against Hall for treasurer (*ibid.*, pp. 391–93). See also the *Illinois Intelligencer,* December 11, 1830.

17. *Illinois Intelligencer,* February 19, 1831; *Whig and Illinois Intelligencer,* April 17, 1833. Throughout his term, Hall had tried unsuccessfully to secure from the ousted cashier, James M. Duncan, the bank's money and its books. Hall, the bank's board of directors, and the legislature had all tried to bring about an accounting with Duncan; and the directors had asked the state's attorney to sue for this property (Hall's reports to the House, January 3, December 11, 20, 27, 1830 [MSS in the Archives Division, Springfield]; *Journal of the Senate* [Vandalia, 1831], pp. 172–84). Nevertheless, in the campaign of 1830, Hall had been accused of shielding Duncan (N. Edwards to editors of the *Illinois Gazette,* July 22, 1830 [Eddy Transcripts]).

18. "File No. 386, Circuit Court, Fayette County, Illinois, 1821–1875" (MSS in the courthouse at Vandalia). See also "Circuit Court Record 1821–32, 2A," pp. 278–79 (MS in the courthouse at Vandalia).

19. *Whig and Illinois Intelligencer,* April 17, 1833.

20. *Laws of a Private Nature* (Kaskaskia, Ill., 1833), p. 123.

21. *Journal of the House of Representatives* (Vandalia, 1836), pp. 193, 139.

22. See the receipts and the pleadings in "File No. 386," cited in note 18, above.

23. Eddy to A. F. Grant, December 19, 1830.

24. Hall to J. S. Armstrong, March 2, 1836 (MS owned by the Boston Public Library).

25. "Circuit Court Record 1821–32, 2A," pp. 277–79, 291, 296.

26. *Illinois Intelligencer,* December 24, 1831.

27. Philadelphia, 1833, p. xvii.

28. *Illinois Intelligencer,* February 20, 1830.

29. Hall to E. A. Duyckinck, March 9, 1855.

30. *Illinois Gazette,* March 20, 1830.

31. They were the *Medley, or Monthly Miscellany,* Lexington, 1803; the *Western Review and Miscellaneous Magazine,* Lexington, 1819–21; and the *Western Monthly Review,* Cincinnati, 1827–30 (Rusk, I, 164–68).

32. "Editor's Address," *Western Monthly Review,* I (May, 1827), 9.

33. "Advertisement," *ibid.,* I, iii.

34. "The Editor's Message," *Illinois Monthly Magazine,* I (December, 1831), 104.

35. *Illinois Intelligencer,* May 1, 1830.

36. *The Poems of Philip Freneau,* ed. F. L. Pattee (Princeton, 1902–1907), I, 73 n.

37. *Letters from the South, Written during an Excursion in the Summer of 1816* (New York, 1817), I, 87.

38. "Progress of the West," *Western Monthly Review,* I (May, 1827), 25–26.

39. "Cincinnati in 1826," *ibid.,* I, 64, 63.

40. D. Donald and F. A. Palmer, "Toward a Western Literature, 1820–1860," pp. 413–28.

41. *Illinois Monthly Magazine,* II (October, 1831), 23.

42. *Western Monthly Magazine,* I (August, 1833), 384.

43. *Illinois Monthly Magazine,* II (December, 1831), 105.

44. *Ibid.,* I (April, 1831), 334.

45. Mr. William T. Christian, of Indio, California, transcribed for me the handwritten names of authors in Hall's copy of the magazine now owned by the Henry E. Huntington Library. The file of the magazine at the Historical and Philosophical Society of Ohio also contains a few authors' names, probably written by James H. Perkins. Mr. James A. McMillen, Director of Libraries at Louisiana State University, searched his library's files and facilitated my borrowing of Volume II.

I have in preparation an article on the authorship of the *Illinois Monthly* and the *Western Monthly.*

46. S. G. Russell, "John Russell, of Bluffdale, Illinois," Illinois State Historical Society, *Transactions* (1901), pp. 103–7.

47. *Ibid.,* p. 105. See also N. Bateman and P. Selby, *Biographical and Memorial Edition of the National Encyclopedia of Illinois* (Chicago, 1915), II, 339.

48. II (April, 1832), 300–311.

49. *The Diary and Letters of Gouverneur Morris,* ed. A. C. Morris (New York, 1888), II, 582. I have not learned the date of Morris's death.

50. *The Poets of Connecticut,* ed. C. W. Everest (Hartford, 1844), pp. 349–50.

51. I (February, 1831), 233–38; I (May, 1831), 370–74.

52. I (September, 1831), 562.

53. "Cincinnati," II (July, 1832), 459–68; II (June, 1832), 427–32.

54. II (July, 1832), 469–74.

55. *Ibid.,* p. 474.

56. James Hall, MS autobiographical sketch.

57. Hall to Duyckinck, April 26, 1855.

58. Sarah Hall Foote, MS biographical sketch of James Hall and the Hall family (MS owned by Mary Posey Foote).

59. James Hall to Sarah Hall, September 25, 1824.

60. Sarah Hall Foote, MS biographical sketch of James Hall and the Hall family.

61. II (October, 1831), 46; II (February, 1832), 238–39; I (October, 1830), 17–19; I (March, 1831), 261–62.

62. I (January, 1831), 192. According to the headnote, this poem was "Translated from the Spanish." The not uncommon sentiment of the quoted stanza is expressed also by Byron in *Childe Harold's Pilgrimage,* Canto III, xciii.

63. "English Opinions of American Books," I (August, 1831), 524–25.

64. "American Poetry," I (March, 1831), 262–63.

65. "Periodicals," I (April, 1831), 304.

66. "Literary Intelligence," I (December, 1830), 142–43.

67. *Ibid.*, p. 144.

68. "Literary Intelligence," II (June, 1832), 166.

69. "The Annuals," II (November, 1831), 56–58.

70. R. Stewart, *Nathaniel Hawthorne: A Biography* (New Haven, 1948), p. 36.

71. B. Faust, *Hawthorne's Contemporaneous Reputation: A Study of Literary Opinion in America and England 1824–1864* (Philadelphia, 1939), pp. 15–16; and Stewart, p. 34. Both writers believed that Benjamin's notice was the first.

72. I (July, 1831), 435–36.

73. II (June, 1832), 405.

74. James Hall to Sarah Hall, June 12, 1826.

75. "Novel Writing," II (October, 1831), 21.

76. "The Annuals," I (January, 1831), 172–79.

77. "Literary Intelligence," I (October, 1830), 48; "Children's Books," I (June, 1831), 408.

78. *Cincinnati Chronicle and Literary Gazette,* April 7, 1832.

79. II (January, March, July, 1832), 172–76, 260–61, 456–57.

80. I (February, 1831), 202–8; II (June, 1832), 401–2; I (March, 1831), 279–82; II (June, 1832), 393–98. "The Patriot's Grave" is ascribed to Hall by the *Cincinnati Daily Gazette,* June 9, 1843.

81. I (September, 1831), 549–61; "Reminiscence of the Last War," II (February, 1832), 202–7.

82. I (May, June, July, August, 1831), 352–68, 385–98, 463–72, 509–18.

83. I (July, 1831), 469.

84. I (August, 1831), 514–15.

85. I (August, 1831), 516.

86. I (December, 1830), 111–22; II (May, August, 1832), 337–48, 481–88.

87. I (December, 1830), 112–13.

88. II (May, 1832), 343.

89. I (December, 1830), 119.

90. II (May, 1832), 346.

91. "Mr. Bell's Address," I (March, 1831), 277.

92. *Chronicle and Literary Gazette,* September 21, 1833.

93. E. P. Cubberley, *Public Education in the United States* (Boston, 1834), p. 169.

94. *Whig and Illinois Intelligencer,* February 20, 1833.

95. II (January, 1832), 154.

96. "Notes on Illinois," *Illinois Monthly Magazine,* II (August, 1832), 498–99.

97. *Ibid.,* I (November, 1830), 71.

98. *Legends* (1869), p. xi.

99. Rusk, I, 274–82, 46–48.

100. Williams, II, 36.

101. Hall's recognition, in 1832, by the *New York Mirror* as one of the "bold, powerful intellects" of the West and as the editor of a magazine "of great excellence" is one indication of the effect of his work in the East (quoted in the [Vandalia] *Whig and Illinois Intelligencer,* March 28, 1832).

102. Williams, II, 73.

103. That is, in *The Western Souvenir* (1828). See Pattee, *The Development of the American Short Story,* p. 54. On page 66, Pattee lists as the first collection of Western stories *Tales from [sic] the West, by the Author of Letters from the East* (1828). Possibly he had not seen this work, for he does not name the author or the publisher or mention the book elsewhere in his study. Apparently, he was referring to John Carne's *Tales of the West. By the Author of Letters from the East* (London, 1828), a collection of Cornish stories.

104. Pattee, *The Development of the American Short Story,* pp. 47–51, 66–68, 88.

105. *Ibid.,* pp. 26–51; A. H. Quinn, *American Fiction: An Historical and Critical Survey* (New York, 1936), p. 1.

106. Pattee, *The Development of the American Short Story,* p. 39.

107. A notable exception is Mrs. Flowerby, in "The Dentist."

108. Compare "The Devoted," pp. 39–51, with the obituary account of Moredock in the *Intelligencer,* November 7, 1829.

109. For an account of Hall's Indian-hater stories and a discussion of their place in American fiction, see Chapter XII, below.

110. J. P. Kennedy, *Swallow Barn, or a Sojourn in the Old Dominion,* ed. J. B. Hubbell (New York, 1929), pp. xxv, 221–47.

111. J. D. Wade, *August Baldwin Longstreet: A Study of the Development of Culture in the South* (New York, 1924), pp. 149, 384.

112. The "ring-tailed roarer's" boast was recorded as early as 1808 by Christian Schultz, Jr., in *Travels on an Inland Voyage* (1810), see W. Blair, *Native American Humor 1800–1900* (New York, 1937), pp. 29–30. It was also described by Paulding in *Letters from the South, Written during the Summer of 1816* (New York, 1817), II, 249–50, 90–91. But I have found no characterization of the cavorter in fiction earlier than Hall's "Pete Featherton" (1828). See F. C. Watkins, "James Kirke Paulding's Early Ring-Tailed Roarer," *Southern Folklore Quarterly,* XV (September, 1951), 183–87, and V. L. O. Chittick (ed.), *"Ring-Tailed Roarers" Tall Tales of the American Frontier 1830–1860* (Caldwell, Idaho, 1941), pp. 15–16. See also W. H. Willer, "Native Themes in American Short Prose Fiction, 1770–1835" (Doctoral dissertation, University of Minnesota, 1944), pp. 535–37.

113. *Georgia Scenes Characters, Incidents, Etc., in the First Half-Century of the Republic, by a Native Georgian* (New York, 1897), pp. 22–23.

114. *Illinois Monthly Magazine,* I (July, 1831), 454–56.

115. *Life on the Mississippi* (Boston, 1883), pp. 42–46.

116. *Adventures of Huckleberry Finn* (New York, 1885), p. 184.

117. *Whig and Illinois Intelligencer,* April 4, July 25, 1832.

118. Hall to Chase (MS in the Library of Congress).

119. See the authors' names written in the files of the magazine at the library of the Historical and Philosophical Society of Ohio.

120. R. B. Warden, *An Account of the Private Life and Public Services of Salmon Portland Chase* (Cincinnati, 1874), p. 218.

121. *Cincinnati Journal,* September 28, 1832.

122. *Chronicle and Literary Gazette,* November 10, 1832.

123. *Cincinnati Mirror and Ladies' Parterre,* March 30, 1833.

124. The letter is in the possession of Miss Margaret Yost Kent, who has kindly permitted me to quote from it and other manuscripts.

125. This relation is in Hall's handwriting; the Bible is owned by Miss Kent.

126. *Whig and Illinois Intelligencer,* October 17, 1832.

127. The *Chronicle and Literary Gazette* of March 2, 1833, quotes the account of the meeting from the *Illinois Advocate* of February 16.

128. Hall to Eddy, March 6, 1833 (MS in the Eddy Papers, owned by Mr. Eugene Carroll).

129. Miss Mary Posey Foote so informed me.

130. *Mirror and Ladies' Parterre,* March 30, 1833.

Chapter XII

1. Besides the Cincinnati newspapers, the chief sources of my description of the city are: Michel Chevalier, "Letters from France" and "Letters on America," *Western Monthly Magazine,* IV (November, December, 1835), 317–23, 404–14; C. F. Hoffman, *A Winter in the West* (New York, 1835), II, 129–40; Anon., "Hiram Powers," *Western Monthly Magazine,* III (April, 1835), 245; [Benjamin Drake], "Cincinnati at the Close of 1835," *ibid.,* V (January, 1836), 26–31; and the letters of I. A. Jewett to Joseph Willard, May 8, 1831, March 20, 1832, August 16, 1832, October 25, 1832, and November 18, 1833 (MSS owned by the Rosenbach Company, Philadelphia). In addition, through the kindness of Professor Daniel Aaron, I have used his "Cincinnati 1818–1839: A Study of Attitudes in the Urban West" (Doctoral dissertation, Harvard University, 1942).

2. *Daily Gazette,* October 31, 1845; June 28, 1849.

3. Chevalier, "Letters on America," IV (December, 1835), 404.

4. L. Beecher, *Autobiography, Correspondence, Etc.,* ed. C. Beecher (New York, 1864), II, 268.

5. Aaron, p. 329.

6. T. D. Weld to L. Tappan, March 18, 1834, in *Letters of Theodore Dwight Weld, Angelina Grimké Weld, and Sarah Grimké, 1822–1844,* ed. G. H. Barnes and D. L. Dumond (New York, 1934), I, 134. This work will be referred to hereinafter as *Letters of Theodore Dwight Weld.*

7. Jewett to Willard, May 8, 1831; November 18, 1833.

8. *Ibid.*, August 16, 1832; *Daily Gazette,* June 28, 1833.

9. Chevalier, "Letters from France," IV (November, 1835), 319 n.

10. *Daily Gazette,* June 6, 1833.

11. *Ibid.*, April 14, 1834.

12. *Western Monthly Magazine,* III (March, 1835), 183.

13. L. Beecher, *A Plea for the West* (Cincinnati, 1835), pp. 26–27 n.

14. "The March of Mind," *Illinois Monthly Magazine,* I (April, 1831), 330–31.

15. W. Sutton, *The Western Book Trade: Cincinnati as a Nineteenth-Century Publishing and Book-Trade Center* (Columbus, O., 1961), p. 67.

16. *Daily Gazette,* December 13, 1833.

17. Jewett to Willard, August 16, 1832; *Daily Gazette,* July 8, 1845, August 6, 1846, October 13, 1846, March 22, 1849.

18. E. D. Mansfield, *Memoirs of the Life and Services of Daniel Drake, M.D.* (Cincinnati, 1855), pp. 223–27, and *Personal Memories, Social Political and Literary* (Cincinnati, 1879), pp. 261–67; J. P. Foote, *Memoirs of the Life of Samuel E. Foote* (Cincinnati, 1860), pp. 176–83.

19. *Daily Gazette,* April 8, 1833.

20. F. Wilson, *Crusader in Crinoline: The Life of Harriet Beecher Stowe* (Philadelphia, 1941), pp. 112–14.

21. Boston, 1855, p. 4.

22. The poem is reprinted in Foote, pp. 258–61.

23. The Historical and Philosophical Society of Ohio owns a file of papers written for discussion in the Semi-Colon society.

24. The late Miss Mary Posey Foote informed me of Hall's friendship with Bishop Purcell.

25. See her *Society in America* (London, 1837), I, 186–87, 191–93; and her *Retrospect of Western Travel* (Cincinnati, 1838), II, 42, 48–49, 55–57.

26. The Cincinnati directories for 1834 and for 1836–37.

27. Hoffman, II, 134.

28. *Daily Gazette,* March 30, 1833.

29. James Hall, "The Budget," *Western Monthly Magazine,* I (September, 1833), 428–29.

30. *Daily Gazette,* April 17, 18, 1833.

31. *Ibid.*, September 14, 1833; the Cincinnati directory for 1836–37.

32. *Chronicle and Literary Gazette,* September 21, 1833; *The Annual Register of the Proceedings of the Western Literary Institute and College of Professional Teachers* (n. p., 1833), pp. 8–9. The annual *Proceedings* of the Institute for 1834–40 do not mention Hall or record any action on his proposal.

33. *Chronicle and Literary Gazette,* September 24, October 5, 1833; *Journal,* October 4, 1833.

34. James Hall, *An Address Delivered before the Erodelphian Society of Miami University* (Cincinnati, 1833). The passages I quote are on pages 32, 18, 24, 21–22.

35. *Journal,* March 14, 1834. The Preface is dated December, 1833.

36. *Ibid.,* April 4, 1834; *Daily Gazette,* August 6, 1834, October 26, 1835, February 20, 1837.

37. H. M. Jarrell, "William Gilmore Simms: Realistic Romancer" (Doctoral dissertation, Duke University, 1932), p. 132 n.

38. The characters, the locale, and the incidents of the two books have a general resemblance. There is, moreover, a striking similarity in some details. For example, in *Nick of the Woods* Nathan Slaughter's pious revulsion from the killing of Indians is very like that of Colonel Hendrickson in *The Harpe's Head* (pp. 204–6). The relation of an Indian captivity in the two books is similar. In both stories, also, an important part of the plot is a lost will. In both novels the loss of the will injures the heroine; and in both stories the will, lost in the East, is recovered on the frontier.

39. *Daily Gazette,* May 21, December 22, 1834.

40. The title of this section, used here for descriptive purposes, is in Hall's handwriting, as are a few other revisions, in the copy formerly owned by the late Mary Posey Foote.

41. "Retrospective Reviews," in the *Western Monthly Magazine,* IV (July, 1835), 24–34, is the same as *Sketches of History,* I, 216–32. "Travels in Hot Weather," from the *Western Monthly,* II (December, 1834), 637–39, is in *Sketches of History,* II, 56–59. "Indian Hating," in the *Western Monthly,* I (September, 1833), 403–8, is the same as *Sketches of History,* II, 74–82. For Chapter IV of Part II of *Sketches of History,* Hall used a part of Joseph Doddridge's *Notes on the Settlement and Indian Wars, of the Western Parts of Virginia and Pennsylvania* (Wellsburgh, 1824).

42. *Sketches of History,* II, 34, 221–76. For Boone's letter, see I, 254–55.

43. See, for examples, the *Southern Literary Messenger,* II (December, 1835), 67–68, and the *Mirror and Western Gazette,* May 24, 1834.

44. Timothy Flint, *Recollections of the Last Ten Years, Passed in Occasional Residences and Journeyings in the Valley of the Mississippi* (Boston, 1826).

45. W. Cushing, *Index to the "North American Review," Volumes, I-CXXV, 1815–1877* (Cambridge, 1878), p. 47.

46. Frankfort, Ky., 1837.

47. III (February, 1837), 497–99.

48. The *Messenger* was established in Cincinnati in January, 1835, and probably the entire first volume was published there. It was an organ of the Unitarian church and was strongly influenced by New Englanders (see Rusk, I, 183–84, 184 n). Hall's adverse review of Timothy Flint's *Lectures upon Natural History,* in the *Western Monthly* for June, 1833, apparently raised against Hall the antipathy of New Englanders.

49. E. A. Poe to Harrison Hall, September 2, 1836 (*The Letters of Edgar Allan Poe,* ed. J. W. Ostrom [Cambridge, 1948], I, 103–4).

50. F. L. Pattee, *The Development of the American Short Story,* p. 58; Rusk, I, 282; A. Cowie, *The Rise of the American Novel* (New York, 1948), p. 224; N. W. Yates, *William T. Porter and the "Spirit of the Times"* (Baton Rouge, La., 1957), p. 89.

51. December 22, 1832.

52. September 15, 1832; November 24, 1834.

53. VII (November 12, 1868), 394.

54. *The Old Northwest Pioneer Period 1815–1840* (Indianapolis, 1950), II, 644.

55. These stories are treated in Chapters X and XI, above, and in Chapter XIII, below.

56. Hall's first-hand acquaintance with Indian life is described in Chapter XIV, Section I, below.

57. Pattee, p. 57.

58. A. H. Quinn, *American Fiction: An Historical and Critical Survey,* p. 98.

59. *Western Monthly Magazine,* I (September, 1833), 403–8.

60. For a history of Indian-hater stories, see G. H. Orians, "The Indian Hater in Early American Fiction," *Journal of American History,* XXVII, No. 1 (1933), 34–44.
In every known literary account of him, the Indian-hater was the only survivor of a family that had been killed by the savages, and usually he forsook white settlements and disappeared into the forest to pursue his vengeance until he died. One historical Indian-hater, Tom Quick, some twenty years older than John Moredock, sought his revenge on the Pennsylvania and New York frontiers and died in 1795 or 1796, somewhat short of his goal of the destruction of a hundred Indians (H. W. Thompson, *Body, Boots & Britches* [Philadelphia, 1940], pp. 48–56).

61. Obituary sketch of Moredock, *Illinois Intelligencer,* November 7, 1829.

62. These are "The Indian Hater" (1828); the obituary account of Moredock (1829); *The Harpe's Head* (1833); "Indian Hating" (1833); and "The Pioneer" (1835). The Kentucky hunter in "The Backwoodsman," in *Legends of the West* (1832), has some characteristics of the Indian-hater.

63. Orians, p. 35.

64. Professor Orians lists the first three authors. Simms's use of the Indian-hater theme has been discussed earlier in this chapter. Hoffman's story is "The Dead Clearing," in *Wild Scenes in the Forest and Prairie* (London, 1839), II, 1–18. Snelling, in his *Tales of the Northwest* (1830), pp. 39–51, sketches the life of Moredock from Hall's *Intelligencer* account and then relates Moredock's killing of one Indian.

65. See J. W. Schroeder, "Sources and Symbols for Melville's *Confidence-Man," Publications of the Modern Language Association,* LXVI (June, 1951), 376–79; and R. H. Pearce, "Melville's Indian-Hater: A Note on a Meaning of *The Confidence-Man,*" *ibid.,* LXVII (December, 1952), 942–48. Since Melville alludes to Hall's advocacy of free schools and since the *Western Monthly* (Vol. I) contains several editorials favoring public education, it seems that Melville used "Indian Hating" in the *Western Monthly* rather than the same text in *Sketches of History,* II, 74–82, which Mr. Schroeder and Mr. Pearce regarded as Melville's source.

66. Several months after its publication, barely a third of the English edition of a thousand copies had been sold. The bankruptcy of the American publishers perhaps prevented the sale of even this many copies of the American edition (L. Howard, *Herman Melville: A Biography* [Berkeley, 1951], pp. 255–56).

Chapter XIII

1. For statements in the *Western Monthly* about its circulation, see I (April, September, 1833), 191–92, 428; V (January, June, 1836), 2, 371. See also the *Chronicle and Literary Gazette,* June 29, 1833, and the *Daily Gazette,* January 3, 1835.

2. See the files of the *Western Monthly* owned by the Indiana University Library.

3. *Western Monthly Magazine,* I (September, 1833), 429; II (May, 1834), 280.

4. *Ibid.,* III (February, 1835), 94. For notices of the appearance of each issue, see also the *Mirror* and the *Chronicle and Literary Gazette.*

5. *Western Monthly Magazine,* II (May, 1834), 280; V (January, 1836), 8; III (February, 1835), 92, 93; V (January, 1836), 8.

6. *Western Monthly Review,* I (October, 1827), 376.

7. Rusk, I, 184.

8. F. L. Mott, *A History of American Magazines 1741–1850,* pp. 630, 607, 514, 505–6.

9. *Western Monthly Magazine,* III (February, March, 1835), 94–95, 175.

10. My attributions of authorship are based in large part upon a study of the handwritten authors' names in the files of the *Western Monthly* at the Yale University Library, the Grand Rapids Public Library, the library of the Historical and Philosophical Society of Ohio, the Indiana University Library, the library of the American Antiquarian Society, the Widener Library of Harvard University, and the Boston Public Library. Other bases for my attributions are cited separately. Employees of those libraries containing the files listed in the *Union List of Serials* (1943) have graciously searched for manuscript authors' names in their libraries' copies of the *Western Monthly.*

11. See his "To a Flower," *Western Monthly,* I (January, 1833), 32.

12. *Ibid.,* I, 428; *Daily Gazette,* July 10, 1835; *Mirror and Chronicle,* July 11, 1835.

13. Jewett's letters to Willard, October 25, 1832; August 4, 1831; November 18, 1833 (MSS owned by the Rosenbach Company).

14. *Western Monthly Magazine,* I (December, 1833), 574–88.

15. II (December, 1834), 625–34.

16. C. E. Stowe, *Life of Harriet Beecher Stowe* (London, 1889), p. 69.

17. The story is reprinted and ascribed to her in the *Cincinnati Chronicle,* September 28, 1839.

18. *Western Monthly Magazine,* I (February, 1834), 112.

19. I, 592.

20. F. Wilson, *Crusader in Crinoline: The Life of Harriet Beecher Stowe,* pp. 125–26.

21. L. Beecher, *A Plea for the West* (Cincinnati, 1835), p. 18 n; *Cross and Baptist Journal* (Cincinnati), May 8, 1835.

22. *Daily Gazette,* April 17, 1833.

23. C. E. Stowe, p. 69.

24. See Hall's autograph annotations of authors' names on the title page in the copy owned by the American Antiquarian Society.

25. *Western Monthly Magazine,* I (February, 1834), 112.

26. Wilson, pp. 125–26.

27. J. Erskine, *Leading American Novelists* (New York, 1910), p. 280.

28. I (April, 1833), 145–51, 160–69.

29. II (December, 1834), 647–54; IV (July, 1835), 44–57.

30. II (July, 1834), 354–62.

31. The series is ascribed to Hall in the *Chronicle and Literary Gazette,* January 3, 1835.

32. I (August, 1833), 348–49.

33. I (January, 1833), 13–14.

34. Anonymous review of the *Transactions* of the Western Literary Institute and College of Teachers, III (May, 1835), 261, 263, 265, 266; Anon., "The Condition of Common Schools," III (March, 1835), 165–67; Anon., "Biblical Literature," II (April, 1834), 205.

35. F. J. Heinl, "Newspapers and Periodicals in the Lincoln-Douglas Country," Illinois State Historical Society *Journal,* XXIII (October, 1930), 371–438.

36. *Cincinnati Journal,* May 3, 17, 1833.

37. N. C. Gochenour, "One Hundredth Anniversary of Presbyterian Church of Vandalia, Illinois," Illinois State Historical Society *Journal,* XXI (January, 1929), 549.

38. The *Daily Gazette,* February 25, 1834, and the *Chronicle and Literary Gazette,* March 1, 1834, notice the address. These quotations are from the *Western Monthly Magazine,* II (April, May, 1834), 193–94, 227–30.

39. *Western Monthly Magazine,* II (May, 1834), 229.

40. Hall's MS autobiographical sketch.

41. I (July, 1833), 289–94; III (April, 1835), 248–53; III (March, 1835), 169–70.

42. Boston and Cincinnati, 1833, pp. 150, 49.

43. For Pierpont's reaction to the review, see John Pierpont to Hall, June 20, 1833 (MS owned by the Historical and Philosophical Society of Ohio). For the attacks upon Hall, see Anon., "Meridies Atticae," *Mirror and Chronicle,* June 27, August 1, 1835; Anon., "Literature," *Chronicle and Literary Gazette,* July 19, 1834; Anon., "Western Monthly Magazine," *Mirror and Western Gazette,* November 9, 1833; *Daily Gazette,* June 11, August 7, 1833; October 1, 1834; January 22, August 10, 1838.

44. II (October, 1833), 310.

45. Anon., "Audubon's Ornithology," XVIII (September, 1835), 59.

46. *Western Monthly Magazine,* IV (December, 1835), 398, 400.

47. C. Rourke, *Audubon* (New York, 1936), p. 290; F. H. Herrick, *Audubon the Naturalist* (2d ed.; New York, 1938), I, 329 n; II, 98 n.

48. *Mirror,* April 13, May 11, December 14, 1833.

49. *Western Monthly Magazine,* review of the *Mirror and Chronicle,* IV (July, 1835), 59–63.

50. For a summary of the spirit of sectionalism in Cincinnati in the 1830's, see Aaron, pp. 203–18; and Sutton, pp. 46–47, 65.

51. See, for examples, L. Beecher, *A Plea for the West,* p. 18; *Journal,* December 26, 1834. See also Aaron, p. 204.

52. Aaron, pp. 88, 256, 271.

53. The editor, Thomas Brainerd, who was for a time Beecher's associate pastor at the Second Church, owed his appointment to the Presbyterian Pastoral Association of Cincinnati, in which Beecher was the dominant figure. Beecher's son Henry Ward Beecher was editor during part of 1836 (M. Brainerd, *Life of Rev. Thomas Brainerd* [Philadelphia, 1870], pp. 79, 81).

54. Aaron, p. 415; *Journal,* May 3, 17, 1833.

55. Aaron, p. 171.

56. See Edward King to Mrs. Edward King, December 4, 1834, and August 12, 1835 (letters cited in this chapter are, unless otherwise noted, owned by the Historical and Philosophical Society of Ohio). See also H. Martineau, *Society in America,* I, 142.

57. Martineau, *Society in America,* I, 137–39, 186–87, 191–93.

58. Western Literary Institute and College of Professional Teachers, *Proceedings* (1835), pp. 61–63.

59. R. A. Billington, *The Protestant Crusade 1800–1860* (New York, 1938), pp. 72–73.

60. "Bishop Purcell's Journal, 1833–1836," ed. Sister Mary Agnes McCann, *Catholic Historical Review,* V (July–October, 1919), 247.

61. Aaron, p. 458.

62. *Ibid.,* pp. 61, 455; G. H. Barnes, *The Antislavery Impulse 1830–1834* (New York, 1933), p. 70.

63. Aaron, pp. 456, 447, 463, 213, 217.

64. Anon., *A Statement of the Reasons Which Induced the Students of Lane Seminary To Dissolve Their Connection with That Institution* (Cincinnati, 1834), p. 3. This pamphlet will be hereinafter cited as *A Statement of the Reasons.*

65. Barnes, pp. 41, 215.

66. Lyman Beecher, *Autobiography, Correspondence, Etc.,* II, 321.

67. J. Monroe, *Oberlin Thursday Lectures Addresses and Essays* (Oberlin, 1897), p. 55; T. C. Smith, *The Liberty and Free Soil Parties in the Northwest* (New York, 1897), p. 11.

68. See Gilbert Hobbs Barnes's appraisal of Weld in the *Dictionary of American Biography.*

69. *Letters of Theodore Dwight Weld,* I, 121–30.

70. H. B. Stanton to [?] Leavitt, March 10, 1834, in Anon., *Debate at the Lane Seminary* (Boston, 1834), pp. 3–7.

71. John Rankin, *A Review of the Statement of the Faculty of Lane*

Seminary, in Relation to the Recent Difficulties in That Institution (Ripley, O., 1835), p. 7.

72. *Ibid.*, p. 5.

73. See Thome's speech at the 1834 meeting of the American Anti-Slavery Society, in *Debate at the Lane Seminary*, pp. 10, 7.

74. For the evidence that the Abolitionists were aware of the divisive tendency of their doctrine, see E. L. Fox, *The American Colonization Society* (Baltimore, 1919), p. 146. John Posey speaks of his slaves in his letter to Frances Hall Whiteman, September 10, 1851 (MS owned by Miss Margaret Y. Kent).

75. Fox, p. 150.

76. W. R. Keagy, "The Lane Seminary Rebellion," *Bulletin of the Historical and Philosophical Society of Ohio*, IX (April, 1951), 152.

77. L. Swift, *William Lloyd Garrison* (Philadelphia, 1911), p. 64; *A Statement of the Reasons*, p. 21; Fox, p. 145.

78. R. S. Fletcher, *A History of Oberlin College from Its Foundation through the Civil War* (Oberlin, 1943), I, 156. For a narrative of the Lane revolt, see Chapters VI and XIII of this work.

79. II, 268.

80. II, 268–69.

81. II, 271.

82. II, 272–73.

83. "Letter from the Editor *de Jure* to the Editor *de Facto*," *Western Monthly Magazine*, IV (August, 1835), 130–33; "An Essay on Criticism," *ibid.*, V (January, 1836), 13–14.

84. "An Essay on Criticism," V, 13–14; *Journal*, May 30, 1834.

85. *A Statement of the Reasons*, p. 7.

86. *Journal*, June 20, August 29, 1834.

87. My discussion of the meetings is based on reports of them in the *Journal*, June 13, 20, 27, July 4, 1834. See also *A Statement of the Reasons*, pp. 21–22, and *Debate at the Lane Seminary*, pp. 3–7. The Colonization Society's ineffectiveness is described by D. L. Dumond in *Antislavery Origins of the Civil War in the United States* (Ann Arbor, 1939), pp. 14–19.

88. Barnes, pp. 68–70; A. Mahan, *Autobiography, Intellectual, Moral, and Spiritual* (London, 1882), p. 176.

89. See D. Drake and Others, *Rail-road from the Banks of the Ohio River to the Tide Waters of the Carolinas and Georgia* (Cincinnati, 1835).

90. Rankin, p. 7. For a discussion of the charges of fraternization, see also *A Statement of the Reasons*, pp. 24–26; and the *Fifth Annual Report of Lane Seminary* (Cincinnati, 1834), pp. 36 ff.

91. Mahan, pp. 176–82; Fletcher, I, 158.

92. *Letters of Theodore Dwight Weld*, I, 172–73 n; Fletcher, I, 160.

93. II, 542.

94. *Letters of Theodore Dwight Weld*, I, 172–73 n.

95. Barnes, 104–8.

96. See the class lists in the *Lane Theological Seminary General Catalog*

(Cincinnati, 1899) ; L. Beecher, *Autobiography, Correspondence, Etc.,* II, 407.

97. Beecher, *Autobiography, Correspondence, Etc.,* II, 224.

98. Billington, p. 70.

99. Brainerd, pp. 82, 123.

100. L. Beecher, *A Plea for the West,* p. 5.

101. Billington, pp. 72–75.

102. *Lowell* (Mass.) *Journal,* September 10, 1834. This was the account that Hall read and quoted in the *Western Monthly Magazine,* II (December, 1834), 655.

103. *Western Monthly Magazine,* II (December, 1834), 655–57.

104. *Chronicle and Literary Gazette,* December 6, 1834.

105. Billington, pp. 70, 130–31.

106. *Journal,* February 6, 1835; *Daily Gazette,* January 26, May 4, 1835, and *passim.*

107. King to Mrs. King, August 20, 1835.

108. *Daily Gazette,* April 7, 1835. On the revisions, see Beecher, *Autobiography, Correspondence, Etc.,* II, 333. Though Beecher said in a foreword to *A Plea for the West* that he had made only a few enlargements, the revisions were extensive.

109. *A Plea for the West,* pp. 52, 37, 49.

110. *Western Monthly Magazine,* III (May, 1835), 322–23, 325–26. See also Billington, p. 75.

111. Review of *Lectures on Scepticism,* in *Western Monthly Magazine,* III (May, 1835), 317; *Cross and Baptist Journal* (Cincinnati), May 8, 1835.

112. *Chronicle and Literary Gazette,* December 6, 1834. Brainerd said that Beecher "had excited his [Hall's] dislike" (*Journal,* June 19, 1835). Joshua L. Wilson, in his prosecution of Beecher for heresy on November 11, 1834, cites Hall as one of the witnesses to be used against Beecher. However, Hall did not appear as a witness at the trial ("Records of the Presbytery of Cincinnati," I, 450; II, 20–59 [MS owned by the Presbytery of Cincinnati and held by the Historical and Philosophical Society of Ohio]).

113. See the editorial for May 2, 1829.

114. III, 382.

115. III, 389–90.

116. *Journal and Western Luminary,* October 5, 1835 (the Western Reserve Historical Society has a copy).

117. "Editorial Remarks," *Western Monthly Magazine,* V (April, 1836), 239; "Editorial," *ibid.,* V (June, 1836), 370.

118. Wilson, p. 153. Probably this is the contemplated suit referred to in "Editorial Remarks," V, 243.

119. *Journal,* June 12, 19, 1835.

120. "An Essay on Criticism," *Western Monthly Magazine,* V (January, 1836), 20.

121. "Editorial Remarks," V (January, 1836), 7–8.

122. *Ibid.,* V (January, 1836), 8; "Editorial Remarks," V (April, 1836), 240.

123. "Editorial Remarks," V, 7–8. The court records for this period are lost.

124. "Editorial Remarks," V, 9; "Editorial Remarks," V (April, 1836), 239; "Editorial," V (June, 1836), 370.

125. King to Mrs. Edward King, December 24, 1834.

126. King to Mrs. Edward King, August 12, 1835.

127. M. Brainerd, p. 79. Brainerd was appointed editor of the *Journal* and associate pastor of Beecher's Second Church at the same time (*Ibid.,* p. 123; *Dictionary of American Biography*).

128. *Journal,* February 11, 1836.

129. Gochenour, XXI, 549. I cannot find Hall listed in the *Catalogue of the Members of the Second Presbyterian Church, in Cincinnati* (Cincinnati, 1835). Nor does his name appear in the minutes of the Second Church's "Sessional Records, No. 3 1832–1855," or in the "Church Register 1833–1842" of the First Church (MSS owned by the Presbytery of Cincinnati). However, there were in Cincinnati four other Presbyterian churches whose records are not known to be extant.

130. Hall was confirmed April 10, 1844, but he had been connected with the church earlier. See "Parish Record, No. I, 1818–1851," pp. 104, 84, 98 (MS owned by Christ Church).

131. Taylor to John Russell, July 8, 1836 (MS owned by the Illinois State Historical Society). In the same letter Taylor does say, "One year ago it [the magazine] had over 2000 subscribers—now it falls short of 800. and is fast decreasing." But Taylor reveals strong feeling against Hall, was no longer the publisher, and may have been repeating rumor. The *Daily Gazette* of January 3, 1835, stated that the *Western Monthly* had "about 3000" subscribers.

132. See the *Western Monthly,* III (January, February, March, 1835), 82–90, 113–28, 221–31; James Hall, *A Memoir of the Life and Public Services of William Henry Harrison of Ohio* (Philadelphia, 1836). In his MS autobiographical sketch, written nearly twenty years later, Hall stated that his biography of Harrison "was not written with any reference to the election. I had the materials prepared, and was writing out the matter for my Sketches of the West, when I was requested to prepare that memoir, and I selected that *time* for publishing, and that *form,* in reference to the then position of Gen. H." But in his letter to Orlando Brown, October 10, 1835, Hall wrote, "I have nearly completed a biography of the General and hope to have it out in a few weeks. . . . I hope [it] will help the cause [the election of Harrison]. I am writing it for that purpose solely" (MS owned by the Filson Club, Louisville). It is probably true that he had collected information pertaining to Harrison for use in *Sketches of History;* but his acceptance of the chairmanship of the Executive Committee of Correspondence shows that he was, at least no later than a month after the publication of the first installment of Harrison's life, deeply committed to the General's candidacy.

133. *Cincinnati Republican and Commercial Register,* May 26, 1835.

134. *Daily Gazette,* February 26, 1879 (in Robert Buchanan's scrapbook, owned by the Historical and Philosophical Society of Ohio).

135. *Republican and Commercial Register,* March 4, May 12, 1836.

136. See the state auditor's report in the *Daily Gazette,* March 16, 1837.

137. *Western Monthly Magazine,* V (June, 1836), 371.

CHAPTER XIV

1. Cincinnati directories for 1836–37, 1839–40, 1842, 1843, and later.

2. Miss Mary Posey Foote informed me of the event, but did not remember the exact date.

3. See her *Retrospect of Western Travel,* II, 51.

4. *Daily Gazette,* December 24, 1838; *Cincinnati Chronicle,* February 23, March 2, 1839.

5. See Hall to Kennedy, February 1, 1839, and B. Drake to Kennedy, May 2, 1839 (MSS owned by the Peabody Institute).

6. *Daily Gazette,* December 16, 1836.

7. Chapter II, pages 24–25, of *Statistics of the West* is from *Letters from the West,* pp. 175–77, 187–90. Chapter III is from "Notes on Illinois," *Illinois Monthly Magazine,* I (November, 1830), 65–70. Chapters IV and V are from "Western Scenery," *Western Monthly Magazine,* II (July, 1834), 354–62. Chapters VI through X include "Notes on Illinois" from the *Illinois Monthly Magazine,* I (December, 1830; March, July, 1831), 123–30, 254–60, 448–54, and from the *Western Monthly Magazine,* I (February, 1833), 90–92. Chapter XI is "The Public Domain" from the *American Quarterly Review,* VI (December, 1829), 263–68.

8. *Daily Gazette,* December 28, 1836; October 22, 1838

9. Quoted in the *Chronicle,* March 23, 1839.

10. *Western Messenger,* III (February, 1837), 497–99.

11. For the publication date, see the *Daily Gazette,* December 18, 1847.

12. *Buckeye and Cincinnati Mirror,* November 21, 1835. McKenney first offered the partnership to Jared Sparks (McKenney to Sparks, October 26, 1829; April 11, 20, 1833 [MSS owned by the library of Harvard University]).

13. Except where I have indicated otherwise, my account of the production of the Hall-McKenney work is derived from Hall's manuscript autobiographical sketch.

14. Hall to G. Catlin, February 12, 1836, in T. L. McKenney and J. Hall, *The Indian Tribes of North America,* ed. F. W. Hodge (Edinburgh, 1933–34), I, xxxi.

15. McKenney to J. Sparks, May 11, 1838 (MS owned by the library of Harvard University).

16. (London) *Athenæum,* April 14, 1838, p. 265. I have not seen a copy of this edition.

17. Internal evidence indicates McKenney's authorship of three sketches, all in Volume I, pp. iii–iv, 25–30, 127–28.

18. *Life of Ma-ka-tai-me-ahe-kia-kiah or Black Hawk, Dictated by Himself* (Cincinnati, 1833), pp. 91–93; *History of the Indian Tribes of North*

America, II, 37, 66, 77–79. See also [James Hall], "Letter from a Traveler," *Western Monthly Magazine,* I (September, 1833), 408–12.

19. *History of the Indian Tribes of North America,* III, 124, 108, 184.

20. *Western Monthly Magazine,* N.S. I (February, 1837), 73.

21. April 14, 1838, p. 265.

22. XLVII (July, 1838), 148.

23. *The Indian Tribes of North America,* ed. Hodge, I, xiv, lxi.

24. *Ibid.,* pp. xiii–xv. See also J. N. Larned (ed.), *The Literature of American History* (Boston, 1902), p. 46.

25. For examples, see E. H. Blair (ed.), *The Indian Tribes of the Upper Mississippi Valley and the Great Lakes* (Cleveland, 1911), and C. J. Milling, *Red Carolinians* (Chapel Hill, N. C., 1940).

26. *Chronicle,* September 14, 1839; Venable, p. 383; W. P. Anderson, *Anderson Family Records* (Cincinnati, 1936), p. 67.

27. See the record of the deed (MS in the Hamilton County Courthouse, Cincinnati).

28. Anderson, p. 76. See also the Hall family tombstones in Spring Grove Cemetery, Cincinnati.

29. Cincinnati directory for 1842.

30. "Parish Record No. I," pp. 84, 104; "Wardens and Vestry," II, 101, 106, and *passim* (MSS in the office of Christ Church, Cincinnati).

31. *Daily Gazette,* November 14, 16, 21, 28, December 1, 1842.

32. Dickens to T. Walker, April 13, 1842 (MS owned by the Historical and Philosophical Society of Ohio); Dickens to Lee and Blanchard, April 13, 1842, in E. L. Bradsher, *Mathew Carey: Editor, Author, and Publisher* (New York, 1912), pp. 133–34.

33. June 27, 1847 (MS owned by the Historical and Philosophical Society of Ohio).

34. United States census; James Hall, *Address before the Young Men's Mercantile Library Association* (Cincinnati, 1846), p. 25; James Hall, *Memorial of the Citizens of Cincinnati to the Congress of the United States* (Cincinnati, 1843), pp. 23–25.

35. *Daily Gazette,* January 18, December 18, 1843; August 8, 21, 1847; January 15, 1848.

36. II (January, 1834), 31.

37. *Daily Chronicle,* November 2, 1840. See also L. Beecher, *Autobiography, Correspondence, Etc.,* II, 407; *Daily Cincinnati Republican and Ohio Commercial Register,* March 29, 1836.

38. *Ibid.,* August 2, 1836; anonymous, *Narrative of the Late Riotous Proceedings against the Liberty of the Press in Cincinnati* (Cincinnati, 1836); W. Birney, *James G. Birney and His Times* (New York, 1890), p. 265.

39. *Daily Gazette,* January 12, 1842; March 6, 24, 1843; May 17, 1844; February 28, April 2, 1845.

40. *Ibid.,* August 4, 1847. Perkins's story, "Charity in the Counting House and Out of It," is in the *Gazette* for March 17, 1849.

41. *Cist's Weekly Advertiser,* April 3, 1850; January 31, 1851.

42. *Daily Gazette,* July 31, 1849; April 5, 1848.

43. *Chronicle,* April 25, 1840.

44. These labor movements are described in the *Daily Gazette,* September 24, 1844; July 8, 1845; August 6, October 13, 1846; March 22, November 29, 1849.

45. R. W. Emerson, *Works* (Boston, 1921), pp. 110–11, 114.

46. *Daily Gazette,* November 26, 30, 1846.

47. *Address before the Young Men's Mercantile Library Association,* pp. 7, 6, 13, 10, 28.

48. The report was published as a pamphlet, but I have not seen a copy. It was printed also in the *Daily Gazette,* November 10, 1841. See also the *Daily Gazette* for October 4, November 3, 1841.

49. *Memorial of the Citizens of Cincinnati, to the Congress of the United States, Relative to the Navigation of the Ohio and Mississippi Rivers* (Cincinnati, 1843). This work will be referred to hereinafter as the *Memorial.* The *Daily Gazette* of January 13, 1843, ascribes the authorship to Hall.

50. *Memorial* (1844), pp. 18, 32.

51. *Ibid.,* pp. 19, 22. R. S. Cotterill states that Cincinnati supplied half the Western produce that was sent to New Orleans ("Southern Railroads and Western Trade," *Mississippi Valley Historical Review,* III [March, 1917], 435).

52. *Rail-Road from the Banks of the Ohio River to the Tide Waters of the Carolinas and Georgia* (Cincinnati, 1835), p. 13.

53. *Daily Gazette,* October 27, 29, 1845.

54. For an account of these conventions, see H. Wender, *Southern Commercial Conventions 1837–1859* (Baltimore, 1930).

55. *Journal of the Proceedings of the South-Western Convention Began [sic] and Held at the City of Memphis, on the 12th Day of November, 1845* (Memphis, 1845), p. 11.

56. Wender, p. 133.

57. E. R. Johnson, "River and Harbor Bills," *Annals of the American Academy of Political Science,* II (May, 1892), 789–90.

58. *Address before the Young Men's Mercantile Library Association,* p. 17.

59. *Memorial* (1844), pp. 9, 12, 45.

60. "Settlement of Oregon—Emigrants of 1843," Senate Document No. 306, 29 Cong., 1 Sess., Report of the Committee on the Post Office and Post Roads (April 30, 1846), pp. 39–40.

61. J. C. Bell, *Opening a Highway to the Pacific 1838–1846* (New York, 1921), pp. 111–12.

62. *Daily Gazette,* October 31, November 16, 1846; February 6, 1847.

63. James Hall to Louisa Hall, June 27, 1847; Hall to Robert Buchanan, June 22, 1847 (MSS owned by the Historical and Philosophical Society of Ohio).

64. R. Fergus (comp.), *Chicago River-and-Harbor Convention* ("Fergus Historical Series," No. 18 [Chicago, 1882]), pp. 52–68, 88, 161–70, and *passim.*

65. Inventory of James Hall's estate (MS in the Warren County probate-court records, Lebanon, Ohio).

66. *Daily Gazette,* January 23, 25, February 8, 1847; November 17, 1848; December 11, 1849; Western Art Union, *Transactions for 1847,* p. 6.

67. Western Art Union, *Transactions for 1850,* p. 70; *Daily Gazette,* November 15, 1848.

68. Probably William H. Beard (1824–1900). See D. T. Mallett, *Mallett's Index of Artists* (New York, 1935).

69. MS inventory of James Hall's estate.

70. *Daily Gazette,* February 3, 21, November 10, 1835; August 10, 1838; Warden, pp. 246–47. I have been unable to identify the newspaper.

71. Hall's letter to Orlando Brown, October 10, 1835 (MS owned by the Filson Club, Louisville) shows Hall working for Harrison's election. On February 12, 1836, Hall was in Philadelphia, where he expected to remain ten days longer (Hall to Catlin, February 12, 1836, in *The Indian Tribes of North America,* ed. Hodge, I, xxix–xxxii). On March 2, he was in Washington. There he wrote to J. S. Armstrong, president of the Commercial Bank, that he had found in the Treasury Department some statements furnished "by the Ill. Bank" and that he was sending copies to Armstrong. He expected to leave for home "the day after tomorrow" (Hall to Armstrong, MS owned by the Boston Public Library).
The *Daily Gazette* of May 10, 1833, stated that the stock of the Commercial Bank was "almost exclusively owned in Philadelphia."

72. *Daily Cincinnati Republican and Commercial Register,* March 4, May 12, 1836.

73. *Daily Gazette,* August 10, 1838.

74. *Ibid.,* July 18, 1838; Hall's MS autobiographical sketch.

75. *Daily Cincinnati Republican and Commercial Register,* March 24, 1836.

76. *Daily Chronicle,* April 9, 12, 1841; M. James, *The Life of Andrew Jackson,* p. 658; *Daily Gazette,* July 2, 5, 1841.

77. *Daily Gazette,* February 2, 3, March 15, 1848.

78. Hall to Louisa Hall, August 18, 1849.

79. *Daily Gazette,* April 18, 19, 21, 1849.

80. XVI (November, 1840), 401–7.

81. Hall to W. H. Denny, January 22, 1859 (MS owned by the Historical Society of Pennsylvania).

82. *Daily Gazette,* May 16, 1846.

83. *The Wilderness and the War Path,* pp. 17–18, 169–70.

84. *Moby-Dick; or the Whale* (New York, 1851), pp. 210–11.

85. Hall to Mathew Carey, April 17, 1839 (MS owned by the Historical Society of Pennsylvania).

86. Hall to Wiley and Putnam, April 20, 1846 (MS owned by the New York Public Library).

87. I have found one copy bound separately and several bound with Mrs. Kirkland's *Western Clearings.*

88. Hall's negotiation with Sparks is detailed in Hall to Sparks, November 12, 1835 (MS owned by the library of Harvard University). The diary and the letters that Hall bought may have been those once owned by Phillip Lee Anthony, husband of Boone's granddaughter (*Daily Gazette,* May 21, 1833).

89. Hall to Sparks, October 16, 1845. This letter and the manuscript of the *Memoir of Thomas Posey* are owned by the library of Harvard University.

90. James Hall to Louisa Hall, August 18, 1849.

91. Hall's autograph will is dated July 22, 1852 (MS in the Warren County probate court records, Lebanon, Ohio).

92. "Deed Record No. 34," p. 51; "General Index, Virginia Military Surveys" (MSS in the Warren County Recorder's Office, Lebanon, Ohio).

93. Hall to E. A. Duyckinck, March 20, 1855 (MS owned by the New York Public Library).

94. The speech is preserved in an undated clipping from the *Columbian,* in Robert Buchanan's scrapbook, owned by the Historical and Philosophical Society of Ohio.

95. A. B. Paine, *Mark Twain: A Biography* (New York 1912), I, 278, 341–42.

96. Hall to Rufus King, August 29, 1862 (MS owned by the Historical and Philosophical Society of Ohio).

97. Hall to Duyckinck, March 20, 1855.

98. Hall to W. H. Denny, January 22, 1859.

99. Harrison Hall to James Hall, February 2, 1862; May 15, 1864 (MSS in the possession of Misses Alice, Agnes, and Eliza Hall, of Dayton, Ohio).

100. *Ibid.,* November 9, 1862; December 11, 1864. Hall was a pallbearer at Nicholas Longworth's funeral in February, 1863 (Robert Buchanan's scrapbook, owned by the Historical and Philosophical Society of Ohio).

101. My informant is Miss Mary Posey Foote. See also the Hall family tombstone in Spring Grove Cemetery, Cincinnati.

102. *Daily Gazette,* May 1, 14, 1844.

BIBLIOGRAPHY

I. MANUSCRIPTS

THE LARGEST COLLECTION of Hall's papers is owned by the Historical and Philosophical Society of Ohio. Other papers are or were in the possession of Hall's descendants: Miss Margaret Yost Kent and Mr. Francis Hall Kent, of Philadelphia; Misses Alice, Agnes, and Eliza Hall, of Dayton, Ohio; and Miss Mary Posey Foote. The papers owned by Miss Foote, who gave me permission to use them and whom I mention often in my notes and bibliography, were inherited after her death by Hall's great-granddaughter Mrs. Elmer J. Rodenberg, of Henderson, Kentucky. Still other groups of Hall manuscripts are to be found in the Duyckinck Collection of the New York Public Library; the Hall files of the War and Navy Departments in Washington; and the Charles Roberts Autograph Collection of the Haverford College Library.

Auxiliary manuscript collections are the Henry Eddy papers owned by Mr. Eugene Carroll, of Chicago; the Jewett letters in the possession of the Rosenbach Company, of Philadelphia; the Sparks collection in the Houghton Library of Harvard University; and letters of Hooper Warren to Ninian Edwards in the library of the Chicago Historical Society; the Edwards transcripts (typewritten copies of certain papers of Ninian Edwards), held by the Illinois Historical Survey, at Urbana; letters of Edward King to his wife, owned by the Historical and Philosophical Society of Ohio; and letters of John Ewing to his wife, typewritten copies of which were provided for me by Miss Alice Hall.

KEY TO THE LOCATION OF MANUSCRIPTS AND OF RARE EDITIONS OF HALL'S WORKS

AAEH   Harrison Hall [Hall's son] Papers, owned by Misses Alice, Agnes, and Eliza Hall, Dayton, Ohio

AmAS   American Antiquarian Society, Worcester, Massachusetts

AmPS   American Philosophical Society, Philadelphia

ADS   Archives Division, Illinois State Library, Springfield

BPL   Boston Public Library

CHS   Chicago Historical Society

EP   Henry Eddy Papers, owned by Mr. Eugene Carroll, Chicago

ET   Eddy Transcripts, Illinois Historical Survey, Urbana

FC   Filson Club, Louisville, Kentucky

HC   Haverford College Library

HPSO Historical and Philosophical Society of Ohio, Cincinnati

HSP   Historical Society of Pennsylvania, Philadelphia

HU   Widener Library, Harvard University

ISHL Illinois State Historical Library, Springfield

InUL   Lilly Library, Indiana University, Bloomington

LC   Library of Congress, Washington

MHS Massachusetts Historical Society, Boston

NL   Navy Library, Washington

NYPL New York Public Library

PI   Peabody Institute, Baltimore

UC   University of Chicago

WD   War Department, Washington

WRHS Western Reserve Historical Society, Cleveland

WRU Western Reserve University, Cleveland

WSHS Wisconsin State Historical Society, Madison

Y   Yale University Library

A. LETTERS

1. *Letters Written by or to Hall*

April 13, 1814. Hall to John Armstrong. WD
Oct. 29, 1814. Thomas Biddle to Hall. WD
Oct. 31, 1814. Hall to Col. C. K. Gardner. WD
May 23, 1815. Hall to B. W. Crowninshield. NL
Dec. 4, 1815. Hall to General Brown. MHS
Jan. 13, 1816. Hall to Brig. Gen. D. Parker. WD
Jan. 7, 1817. Hall to Col. Decius Wadsworth. WD
May 12, 1817. Hall to Richard Rush. WD
June 15, 1817. Abraham Eustis to Hall. WD
Feb. 3, 1818. Hall to Brig. Gen. D. Parker. WD

324

May 7, 1818. Hall to A. R. Woolley. WD
May 24, 1818. Hall to Brig. Gen. D. Parker. WD
June 10, 1818. Hall to Brig. Gen. D. Parker. WD
July 22, 1818. Hall to Brig. Gen. D. Parker. WD
Dec. 7, 1818. Hall to Mrs. Sarah Hall. HC
Sept. 25, 1819. Hall to Brig. Gen. D. Parker. HSP
Nov. 27, 1822. John McLean to Hall and Eddy. EP
Sept. 4, 1823. Edward Patchett to Hall. EP
Sept. 25, 1824. Hall to Mrs. Sarah Hall. HC
Oct. 8, 1824. Hall to Mrs. Sarah Hall. CHS
Nov. 30, 1824. Hall to John Foliart. EP
June 12, 1826. Hall to Mrs. Sarah Hall. HC
Jan. 15, 1827. Hall to Thomas Sloo, Jr. HPSO
June 3, 1827. Hall to Thomas Sloo, Jr. HPSO
Sept. 23, 1827. John E. Hall to Hall. HPSO
March 21, 1829. Hall to Peter S. DuPonceau. HSP
Dec. 20, 1830. Hall to the Speaker of the House. ADS
Dec. 27, 1830. Hall [to Mr. Speaker?]. ADS
Jan. 3, 1831. Hall to the House of Representatives. ADS
June 1, 1831. Hall to Dr. Joseph E. Worcester. MHS
Oct. 22, 1831. Hall to Henry Eddy. EP
May 2, 1832. Hall to S. P. Chase. LC
Feb. 10, 1833. Hall to Messrs. Stimson and Clapp. MHS
March 6, 1833. Hall to Henry Eddy. EP
June 20, 1833. John Pierpont to Hall. HPSO
No date [1835?]. Hall to Mr. [Mathew?] Carey. HSP
Oct. 10, 1835. Hall to Orlando Brown. FC
Nov. 12, 1835. Hall to Dr. Jared Sparks. HU
March 2, 1836. Hall to J. S. Armstrong. BPL
May 5, 1836. Hall to Rev. Dr. Joshua L. Wilson. UC
June 6, 1836. Hall to Orlando Brown. FC
Oct. 14, 1837. Hall to Robert Buchanan. HPSO
Oct. 21, 18[3? 5?]7. N. P. Stewart to Hall. HPSO
March 2, 1838. Hall to Lewis J. Cist. HSP
Feb. 1, 1839. Hall to J. P. Kennedy. PI
April 17, 1839. Hall to Mathew Carey. HSP
May 31, 1840. Hall to Harrison Hall. Miss Mary Posey Foote
Sept. 3, 1840. Hall to Robert Buchanan. HPSO
Jan. 22, 1841. Hall to Robert Buchanan. HPSO
Feb. 1, 1841. Hall to Robert Buchanan. HPSO
March 6, 1841. Hall to Robert Buchanan. HPSO
June 16, 1841. Hall to Rev. C. C. Beatty. HSP
Dec. 9, 1841. Hall to W. Rianhard. ISHL
March 13, 1842. Hall to Robert Buchanan. HPSO
Dec. 10, 1842. Hall to Robert Buchanan. HPSO
Jan. 27, 1845. Hall to Robert Buchanan. HPSO
June 21, 1845. Hall to Messrs. Wiley and Putnam. NYPL

325

July 9, 1845. Hall to Harrison Hall. Miss Mary Posey Foote
Oct. 2, 1845. Hall to Messrs. Wiley and Putnam. NYPL
Oct. 16, 1845. Hall to Professor Jared Sparks. HU
Oct. 25, 1845. Hall to Messrs. Wiley and Putnam. NYPL
April 20, 1846. Hall to Messrs. Wiley and Putnam. NYPL
June 22, 1847. Hall to Robert Buchanan. HPSO
June 27, 1847. Hall to Mrs. Hall. HPSO
Aug. 18, 1849. Hall to Mrs. Hall. HPSO
Oct. 27, 1849. Hall to R. W. Griswold. BPL
Aug. 8, 1851. Hall to Rev. Dr. William B. Stevens. HC
April 5, 1852. Hall to Mrs. Hall. Mr. Nicholas VanAntwerp, Cincinnati
March 9, 1853. Hall to Mrs. Hall. HPSO
Dec. 27, 1853. Hall to George P. Morris. Y
Feb. 12, 1854. Hall to Mrs. Hall. AAEH
March 9, 1855. Hall to E. A. Duyckinck. NYPL
March 20, 1855. Hall to E. A. Duyckinck. NYPL
April 26, 1855. Hall to E. A. Duyckinck. NYPL
Dec. 22, 1856. Hall to Harrison Hall [son of James Hall]. AAEH
March 5, 1857. Hall to Messrs. Childs & Peterson. InUL
Nov. 18, 1857. Hall to Mrs. Hall. HPSO
Jan. 17, 1859. Hall and Bellamy Storer to Rev. Joshua Peterkin. "Wardens
    and Vestry," II, Christ Church, Cincinnati
Jan. 17, 1859. Hall and Bellamy Storer to C. M. Butler. "Wardens and
    Vestry," II, Christ Church, Cincinnati
Jan. 22, 1859. Hall to W. H. Denny. HSP
Jan. 8, 1862. Harrison Hall [son of J. H.] to Hall. AAEH
Jan. 19, 1862. Harrison Hall [Hall's son] to Hall. AAEH
Feb. 2, 1862. Harrison Hall [Hall's son] to Hall. AAEH
June 9, 1862. Hall to Lyman C. Draper. WSHS
Aug. 29, 1862. Hall to Rufus King. HPSO
Oct. 21, 1862. Harrison Hall [Hall's son] to Hall. AAEH
Nov. 9, 1862. Harrison Hall [Hall's son] to Hall. AAEH
Dec. 14, [1863?]. Harrison Hall [Hall's son] to Hall. AAEH
May 15, 1864. Harrison Hall [Hall's son] to Hall. AAEH
Dec. 11, 1864. Harrison Hall [Hall's son] to Hall. AAEH

2. Other Letters Pertaining to Hall

Space does not permit a complete list of these letters. All that are used directly are cited in the chapter notes.

March 1, 1801. Joseph Anderson to Thomas Jefferson. National Archives,
    Files of the Department of State
March 7, 1801. John Hall to Thomas Jefferson. National Archives, Files
    of the Department of State
April 27, 1805. John E. Hall to Timothy Pickering. MHS
Oct. 27, 1814. J. Bates's certificate of Hall's illness. WD

Sept. 29, 1814. S. Ewing to J. E. Hall. Miss Mary Posey Foote
May 10, 1815. B. W. Crowninshield to Stephen Decatur. NL
Dec. 21, 1815. Joseph Hopkinson to J. E. Hall. HSP
Jan. 6, 1816. J. E. Hall [to the Secretary of War?]. WD
Jan. 6, 1816. J. E. Hall to General Ripley. WD
June 11, 1817. Capt. W. F. Hobart, Col. Abraham Eustis, and others, statement of Hall's character. WD
Sept. 1, 1817. J. H. Wilkins' certificate of Hall's character. WD
March 20, 1819. John E. Hall to Charles Prentiss. AmAS
Nov. 4, 1819. John E. Hall to Charles Prentiss. AmAS
June 30, 1822. Washington Irving to J. E. Hall. NYPL
May 11, 1838. Thomas L. McKenney to Jared Sparks. HU
May 2, 1839. Benjamin Drake to John P. Kennedy. PI
April 13, 1842. Charles Dickens to Timothy Walker. HPSO

B.   GENEALOGICAL AND CHURCH RECORDS

Record of the First Presbyterian Church, Philadelphia
    Owned by HSP.
[Sarah E. Hall's Bible]
    Containing MS genealogical data of the Halls and Ewings. Owned by Miss Mary Posey Foote.
[Mary Posey Hall's Prayerbook]
    Containing MS genealogical data of the Posey family. Owned by Miss Mary Posey Foote.
[James Hall's Bible]
    Containing genealogical data of Hall's family and an account of the death of Mary Posey Hall. Owned by Francis Hall Kent.
[Sarah Hall Foote's Biographical Sketch of James Hall and the Hall Family]
    Owned by Miss Mary Posey Foote. Mr. Nicholas VanAntwerp and the Historical and Philosophical Society of Ohio own MS copies.
Parish Record No. 1, 1818–1851
    Owned by Christ Church, Cincinnati.
Wardens and Vestry
    Owned by Christ Church, Cincinnati.

C.   JOURNALS AND ACCOUNT BOOKS

[Hall's Journal]
    Aug. 6–Sept. 16, 1815. Containing an account of Hall's voyage to the Mediterranean and seventy-eight poems. Owned by HPSO.
[Hall's Household Account Book]
    Feb. 18–April 30, 1823. Containing also nine of his poems. Owned by HPSO.

D. MISCELLANEOUS MANUSCRIPTS BY HALL

Life of Thomas Posey, Major-General and Governor of Indiana
Owned by HU.

[Sketch of the Life of Benjamin Drake]
Enclosed with Hall's letter to R. W. Griswold, Oct. 27, 1849. Owned by BPL.

[Biographical Sketch of John E. Hall]
Incomplete. Owned by HPSO.

[Hall's Autobiographical Sketch]
Inclosed in Hall's letter to E. A. Duyckinck, March 20, 1855. Owned by NYPL.

[Revisions in a copy of *The West: Its Commerce and Navigation* (Cincinnati, 1848)]
Owned by Misses Alice, Agnes, and Eliza Hall.

E. PUBLIC RECORDS

[Major Jacob Hindman's Report of July 7, 1814]
In WD.

Proceedings of a General Court Martial,—Held at Pittsburgh Penn. on the 17th of September 1817
Containing copies of twenty-eight letters to or from Hall or directly concerned with him. Hall's defense, consisting of sixty-five pages, is in his own handwriting. In Judge Advocate General's Office, WD.

Executive Record [of the governor of], Illinois
Volume I, 1818–1832; Vol. II, 1832–1837. In ADS.

[Hall's Reports to the House of Representatives]
Jan. 3, Dec. 11, 20, 27, 1830. In ADS.

Circuit Court Record 1821–1832 2A
In Fayette County Court House, Vandalia, Illinois.

Record 1, 1827–1840. Fayette County Circuit Court
In Fayette County Court House, Vandalia, Illinois.

File No. 386, Circuit Court, Fayette County, Illinois
In Fayette County Court House, Vandalia, Illinois.

[Hall's Will]
Autograph. In records of the Warren County Probate Court, Lebanon, Ohio.

[Miscellaneous Entries in the Court Records of Fayette, Pope, Union, Alexander, Johnson, and Gallatin Counties, Illinois; and of Hamilton and Warren Counties, Ohio]
In the courthouses of the respective counties.

328

II. PRINTED WORKS BY HALL

A. CONTRIBUTIONS TO PERIODICALS AND GIFTBOOKS

Hall's periodical and giftbook publications are chronologically arranged below under the names of the periodicals or giftbooks in which they appeared. Sometimes reissues are listed under a first citation. The pieces are identified principally by Hall's own signature, by the signature "O" or "Orlando," by the endorsement of Hall's name beside the contributions in surviving periodical files, or by the inclusion of the pieces in his MS Journal, MS Household Account Book, or later publications.

1. *In the "Analectic Magazine"*

Friendship
    III, 258 (March, 1814).

2. *In the "Pittsburgh Gazette"*

[Eugenius]
    Dec. 24, 1816.
The Captive
    Feb. 14, 1817. Verse.
Sleighing
    Feb. 18, 1817. Verse.
Major Andre
    March 11, 1817.
Parody
    June 24, 1817. Verse. Reprinted in *Port Folio,* VI, 63 (July, 1818); in *The Poetry of the Port Folio* (Philadelphia, 1818), pp. 68–69; and in the *Illinois Gazette,* July 6, 1822.
Extracts from a Journal of a Voyage to the Mediterranean
    Oct. 31, Nov. 4, 7, 14, 21, 1817.
The Wanderer, by Edward Ennui
    1818: No. 1, May 22; No. 2, May 29; No. 3, June 5; No. 4, June 12; No. 5, June 19; No. 6, June 30; No. 7, July 7; No. 8, July 14, No. 9, July 21; No. 11, Sept. 29; No. 12, Nov. 3; No. 13, Nov. 13; No. 14, Nov. 20; No. 15, Dec. 1.
To the Moon
    May 22, 1818. Verse. Reprinted as "Night Thoughts" in *Port Folio,* VII, 81 (Jan., 1819), and in *The Poetry of the Port Folio,* p. 130.
Epigram
    June 2, 1818. Verse.

Lines Occasioned by the Death of a Young Lady
> June 9, 1818. Verse. Reprinted as "On the Death of Miss M" in *Port Folio,* VI, 157 (Aug., 1818), and in *The Poetry of the Port Folio,* p. 71.

[A Report of an Examination of a School for Young Ladies]
> July 28, 1818.

["My love so quick the moments fly"]
> Aug. 18, 1818. Verse.

Parody
> Oct. 27, 1818. Verse. Reprinted as "The Banks" in *Port Folio,* VII, 262 (March, 1819) and in *The Poetry of the Port Folio,* pp. 108–9.

Parody
> Nov. 6, 1818. Verse. Reprinted in *The Philadelphia Souvenir* (Philadelphia, 1826), pp. 155–7.

[Biography of General Presley Neville]
> Dec. 18, 1818. Reprinted in *Port Folio,* VIII, 263–64 (March, 1819).

Parody
> Feb. 9, 1819. Verse. Reprinted in *Port Folio,* VII, 525 (June, 1819).

Sentimental Agonies
> March 2, 1819. Verse. Reprinted in *Port Folio,* VII, 525 (June, 1819).

The Smile of Love
> March 30, 1819. Verse.

["Lady, the rose"]
> April 6, 1819. Verse. Reprinted as "The Captive" in Illinois *Gazette,* Sept. 9, 1820.

["Oh! there were days when blissful dreams"]
> April 13, 1819. Verse. Reprinted in *Port Folio,* VII, 439–40 (May, 1819), and in *The Poetry of the Port Folio,* p. 135.

Lover's Vows
> April 20, 1819. Verse.

A Pittsburgh Merchant to His Correspondent in the West
> July 16, 1819. Verse. Reprinted in *Port Folio,* VIII, 238–39 (Sept., 1819).

["Ah who would consent through this wide world to roam"]
> Aug. 3, 1819. Verse. Reprinted in *Port Folio,* IX, 513 (Sept., 1820), and in the *Illinois Gazette,* Aug. 26, 1820.

["All hail to the 'Man in the Moon'"]
> Sept. 24, 1819. Verse.

Love
> Oct. 22, 1819. Verse.

To the Editor of the Statesman
> Dec. 7, 1819.

Woman
> Dec. 10, 1819. Verse.

To the Editor of the Mercury
> Dec. 17, 1819.

A New Song to an Old Tune
> Dec. 31, 1819. Verse.

["He has crossed the blue mountains to lands far away"]
> Jan. 4, 1820. Verse.

To a Lady
>Jan. 4, 1820. Verse.
["Fanny my love, if hope could tear"]
>Feb. 1, 1820. Verse.
["Sweetly purling, gently gliding"]
>Feb. 8, 1820. Verse.
["Oh say not the heart is unfruitful and cold"]
>March 30, 1820.

3. *In "The Poetry of the Port Folio" (Philadelphia, 1818)*

See under the *Pittsburgh Gazette* and *Port Folio* for titles of Hall's works in this publication.

4. *In the "Illinois Gazette"*

Letters from the West
>July 15, Sept. 2, 9, 30, Oct. 7, 14, 1820. The first number is untitled. Reprinted in *Port Folio*, XII, 66–82 (Sept., 1821); I, 178–80 (March, 1822); II, 94–99 (Aug., 1822); and in *Letters from the West* (London, 1828).
The Bachelor's Soliloquy
>Sept. 9, 1820. Verse.
Parody
>Oct. 7, 1820. Verse. Reprinted in *Port Folio,* II, 526 (Dec., 1822).
Epigram
>Oct. 7, 1820. Verse.
[Verses]
>**May 12, 1821.**
["Oh! bid me not, Lady"]
>May 19, 1821. Reprinted in *Port Folio,* II, 527 (Dec., 1822).
["All the world's a court house"]
>June 2, 1821. Verse.
["Lady, 'thy vows were traced in sand'"]
>June 16, 1821. Verse. Reprinted in *Port Folio,* XVII, 515 (June, 1824).
["Young Harry wooed as fair a maid"]
>June 30, 1821. Verse.
Cool Reflections, by a Village Beau
>Dec. 22, 1821. Reprinted in *Port Folio,* XV, 58–60 (Jan., 1823).
Christmas Gambols, by a Village Beau
>Dec. 29, 1821. Reprinted as "The Bachelor's Elysium" in *Port Folio,* II, 449–57 (Dec., 1822); in *The Western Souvenir* (Cincinnati, 1828), 133–54; and in *The Soldier's Bride and Other Tales* (Philadelphia, 1833), pp. 209 ff.
Fiddlers' Green, by a Village Beau
>Jan. 5, 1822. Reprinted as "The Bachelor's Elysium" in *Port Folio,* XVI, 362–74 (Nov., 1823); and in *The Soldier's Bride and Other Tales,* pp. 209 ff.

Dreams
    Feb. 2, 1822. Verse. Reprinted in *Port Folio,* I, 175–76 (Feb., 1822).
A Sublime and Pathetick Ode to Honour
    May 25, 1822. Verse. Reprinted in *Port Folio,* I, 346–47 (April, 1822).
[Letters Nos. II and III, signed Brutus]
    June 29, 1822.
To Mr. Cook, No. IV
    July 6, 1822.
To the Public
    July 27, 1822.
To the People of Illinois
    Aug. 3, 1822.
[Address of Welcome to General Lafayette]
    May 14, 1825.

5. *In the "Port Folio"*

To Miss M
    VIII, 547 (Nov., 1812).   Verse.
Description of St. Michael's Cave, in the Rock of Gibraltar
    I, 298–302 (April, 1816).
Extracts from the Journal of One of the Officers of the Army, Engaged in
    the Late Expedition against Algiers
    I, 507–10 (Jan., 1816) ; II, 284–90 (Oct., 1816).
Stanzas Written at Fort Erie
    I, 527 (June, 1816). Verse.
To a Young Lady Who Mended the Author's Stockings
    I, 528 (June, 1816). Verse.
To Miss —— ——
    I, 528–29 (June, 1816). Verse.
The Soldier's Invitation
    II, 260–61 (Sept., 1816). Verse.
Love and Glory
    II, 261–62 (Sept., 1816). Verse.
Epigram
    II, 262 (Sept., 1816). Verse.
The Power of Madeira
    II, 353 (Oct., 1816). Verse.
To Miss ——
    II, 354 (Oct., 1816). Verse.
To —— ——
    II, 355 (Oct., 1816). Verse.
The Smile
    II, 533–34 (Dec., 1816). Verse.
The Hermit Mouse
    III, 171–72 (Feb., 1817). Verse.
Evening
    III, 178 (Feb., 1817). Verse.

The American Lounger
      III, 242–47 (March, 1817).
Othello
      III, 442–44 (May, 1817). Verse. Reprinted in the Pittsburgh *Gazette,*
June 13, 1817.
Song
      III, 527 (June, 1817). Verse.
The Dream
      III, 527–28 (June, 1817). Verse.
Epigram
      IV, 57 (July, 1817). Verse.
The American Lounger
      IV, 60–62 (July, 1817).
On a Bad Poet
      IV, 88 (July, 1817). Verse.
Love
      IV, 154–55 (Aug., 1817). Verse.
The American Lounger
      IV, 321–25 (Oct., 1817).
Good-by to Capt. ——
      V, 84–85 (Jan., 1818). Verse. Reprinted in *The Poetry of the Port
Folio,* pp. 36–77.
Fancy and Sense
      V, 162 (Feb., 1818). Verse. Reprinted in *The Poetry of the Port
Folio,* pp. 44–45.
Song
      V, 396 (May, 1818).
To ——
      VI, 233 (Sept., 1818). Verse. Reprinted in *The Poetry of the Port
Folio,* p. 77.
Love and Hope
      VI, 325 (Oct., 1818). Verse. Reprinted in *The Poetry of the Port
Folio,* p. 89.
["Ye merchants, bankers, lawyers, all"]
      VIII, 239–40 (Sept., 1819). Verse.
To My Glass
      VIII, 237 (Sept., 1819). Verse. Reprinted in *The Philadelphia
Souvenir* (Philadelphia, 1826), p. 155.
A Woman's Love
      VI, 396 (Nov., 1818). Verse. Reprinted in *The Poetry of the Port
Folio,* pp. 86–87, and in the *Illinois Gazette,* Nov. 11, 1820.
["There's nothing true but heaven"]
      VIII, 237 (Sept., 1819). Verse. Reprinted in *The Philadelphia
Souvenir,* p. 156.
Epigram
      IX, No. 2 (1820), 513. Verse.
To Anna
      IX, No. 2 (1820), 514–15. Verse.
Letters from the West
      XII, 440–52 (Dec., 1821) ; I, 118–26 (Feb., 1822) ; I, 383–88 (May,

1822); XVI, 121–25, 182–93, 277–81 (Aug., Sept., Oct., 1823); XVII, 265–74 (April, 1824); XVIII, 136–43, 193–97 (Aug., Sept., 1824); XIX, 214–19 (March, 1825). Reprinted in *Letters from the West* (London, 1828).

A New Prologue to the Point of Honour
    XII, 495–96 (Dec. 1821). Verse.

Fanny
    I, 172 (Feb., 1822). Verse.

Lines Written on the Banks of the Wabash
    I, 174–75 (Feb., 1822). Verse.

To a Lady
    I, 348–49 (April, 1822). Verse.

To Fanny
    II, 527 (Dec., 1822). Verse.

Empty Pockets, by a Village Beau
    XVI, 284–88 (Oct., 1823). Reprinted in *The Soldier's Bride and Other Tales* (Philadelphia, 1833), pp. 81–90.

Major General Thomas Posey
    XVIII, 281–93 (Oct., 1824).

Fashionable Watering Places
    XX, 94–103 (Aug., 1825). Reprinted in *The Soldier's Bride and Other Tales,* pp. 159–74.

The Story of the Harps
    XX, 116–28 (Aug., 1825).

The Bearer of Despatches
    XX, 200–208 (Sept., 1825). Reprinted in *The Soldier's Bride and Other Tales,* pp. 117–31.

6. *In "The Philadelphia Souvenir," ed. J. E. Hall (Philadelphia, 1826)*

For titles in this collection, see under the *Port Folio.*

7. *In the "Western Monthly Review"*

The Academy
    I, 377–84 (Nov., 1827).

To a Coquette
    I, 394 (Nov., 1827). Verse.

The Indian Maid's Death Song
    I, 271 (Sept., 1827). Verse.

8. *In "The Western Souvenir, a Christmas and New Year's Gift for 1829"*
    (Cincinnati, [1828])

The New Souvenir
    Pp. 10–11. Verse.

Wedded Love's First Home
    P. 15. Verse.
Love in the Dew
    Pp. 17–18. Verse.
The French Village
    Pp. 37–61. Reprinted in *Stories of American Life,* ed. M. R. Mitford
    (London, 1830), I, 69–96; in *Tales of the Border,* pp. 102–28; and in
    American Short Stories, ed. C. S. Baldwin (New York, 1904), pp. 99–112.
The Bachelor's Elysium
    Pp. 133–54.
La Belle Riviere
    P. 155. Verse.
The Plant of Havana
    P. 167. Verse.
The Forest Chief
    P. 168. Verse.
To Mary
    P. 193. Verse.
The Billiard Table
    Pp. 194–211. Reprinted in *The Soldier's Bride and Other Tales,* pp.
    255–72.
The Parting
    P. 214. Verse.
Love's Smile
    P. 239. Verse.
The Shawanoe Warrior
    Pp. 251–52. Verse.
The Indian Hater
    Pp. 256–72. Reprinted in *Stories of American Life,* ed. M. R. Mitford,
    I, 340–58; in *Legends of the West,* pp. 247–62; and in *The Wilderness
    and the War Path* (New York, 1846), pp. 138–51.
Life's Twilight
    P. 273. Verse.
The Star of Love
    P. 275. Verse.
Repeat the Strain
    P. 279. Verse.
The Rose
    P. 279. Verse.
The Indian Maid's Death Song
    P. 280. Verse.
Can Years of Suffering
    P. 281. Verse.
The Massacre
    Pp. 296–97. Verse.
To a Young Lady
    P. 299. Verse.
Pete Featherton
    Pp. 301–21. Reprinted in *Stories of American Life,* ed. M. R. Mitford,

II, 1–23; in *The Soldier's Bride and Other Tales,* pp. 13–56; and in *The Wilderness and the War Path,* pp. 152–68.

The Gift
P. 324. Verse.

9. *In the "Illinois Monthly Magazine"*

The Missionaries. A Tale
I, 5–9 (Oct., 1830).

The Indian Wife's Lament
I, 17–19 (Oct., 1830). Verse.

Geology of Illinois
I, 43–46 (Oct., 1830).

American Silk
I, 46–47 (Oct., 1830).

Notes on Illinois. Surface of the Country
I, 55–70 (Nov., 1830).

The Philadelphia Dun
I, 70–76 (Nov., 1830).

Adventure of a Ranger
I, 76–81 (Nov., 1830).

A Legend of Carondelet; or Fifty Years Ago
I, 97–109 (Dec., 1830). Reprinted in *Legends of the West,* pp. 109–30.

The First Bell
I, 109–11 (Dec., 1830).

Notes on Illinois. Soil and Productions
I, 123–31 (Dec., 1830).

Literary Intelligence
I, 142–44 (Dec., 1830).

The Village Musician
I, 158–72 (Jan., 1831).

The Annuals
I, 172–79 (Jan., 1831).

Serenade
I, 192 (Jan., 1831). Verse.

The Intestate, or Jerry Smith's Widow
I, 193–202 (Feb., 1831). Reprinted in *Legends of the West,* pp. 131–46.

Daniel Boon
I, 202–8 (Feb., 1831).

Notes on Illinois. Timber
I, 254–60 (March, 1831).

The Isle of the Yellow Sands
I, 261–62 (March, 1831). Verse.

The Patriot's Grave
I, 279–82 (March, 1831).

Cupid's Courtship
I, 305 (April, 1831). Verse.

The Wedding Day
I, 305 (April, 1831). Verse.

On the Study of the Natural Sciences
I, 315–30 (April, 1831).
Traveller's Troubles
I, 333–34 (April, 1831). Verse.
Michel De Coucy, a Tale of Fort Chartres
I, 337–50 (May, 1831). Reprinted in *Legends of the West,* pp. 147–70.
On the Intercourse of the American People with the Indians
I, 352–68, 385–98, 463–72, 509–18 (May, June, July, Aug., 1831).
Obituary Sketch of Louis R. Noble
I, 375–77 (May, 1831).
Children's Books
I, 403–15 (June, 1831).
[Review]
I, 423–26 (June, 1831).
Review
I, 433–43 (July, 1831).
Notes on Illinois. Wild Animals
I, 448–54 (July, 1831).
A Frontier Scene
I, 454–56 (July, 1831).
English Periodicals
I, 456–58 (July, 1831).
An Essay on Dunning
I, 477–80 (July, 1831).
Review
I, 498–508 (Aug., 1831).
English Opinions of American Books
I, 524–28 (Aug., 1831).
American Tales
I, 529–35 (Sept., 1831).
[Letter to the Editor]
I, 537–40 (Sept., 1831).
Notes on Illinois. Constitution and Laws
I, 542–48 (Sept., 1831).
Biographical Sketch of Maj. Thomas Biddle
I, 549–61 (Sept., 1831).
The Prairie
I, 570–71 (Sept., 1831). Verse.
Notes on Illinois. Public Officers
II, 8–11 (Oct., 1831).
Review
II, 11–15 (Oct., 1831).
A New Work
II, 15–17 (Oct., 1831).
Novel Writing
II, 18–25 (Oct., 1831).
The Capuchin
II, 46 (Oct., 1831).

337

Hints to Emigrants
II, 49–55 (Nov., 1831).
The Annuals
II, 56–58 (Nov., 1831).
Inundations of the Mississippi
II, 58–63, 105–10, 249–55 (Nov., Dec., 1831; March, 1832).
Books
II, 64–66 (Nov., 1831).
Lines
II, 96 (Nov., 1831). Verse.
The Editor's Message
II, 97–105 (Dec., 1831).
Thoughts on Phrenology
II, 110–12 (Dec., 1831).
Remarks
II, 115–22 (Dec., 1831).
Passages in the Life of the Late Stephen Hempstead of St. Louis
II, 122–36 (Dec., 1831).
[Introduction to "Audubon's Sketches"]
II, 136–42 (Dec., 1831).
["Where is the heart that has not felt"]
II, 142 (Dec., 1831). Verse.
Why Weep
II, 144 (Dec., 1831). Verse.
Columbia River
II, 145–54 (Jan., 1832).
The Dentist
II, 155–65 (Jan., 1832). Reprinted in *The Soldier's Bride and Other Tales*, pp. 190–208.
Mr. Drake's Address
II, 166–72 (Jan., 1832).
Vandalia
II, 172–76 (Jan., 1832).
The Useful Man
II, 193–201 (Feb., 1832). Reprinted in *The Soldier's Bride and Other Tales*, pp. 175–89.
The Cottage
II, 201 (Feb., 1832). Verse.
Reminiscence of the Last War
II, 202–7 (Feb., 1832).
Try Me
II, 211 (Feb., 1832). Verse.
Quincy
II, 212–13 (Feb., 1832).
Cobbett and Corn
II, 213–15 (Feb., 1832).
Webster's Dictionary
II, 215–16 (Feb., 1832).

338

Transylvania University
    II, 217–18 (Feb., 1832)
My Cousin Lucy and the Village Teacher
    II, 218–31 (Feb., 1832).
The Crusader
    II, 238–39 (Feb., 1832). Verse.
The Indian Maid's Fountain
    II, 239–40 (Feb., 1832). Verse.
Notes on Illinois. Laws
    II, 241–49 (March, 1832).
Recollections of a Voyage
    II, 255–58 (March, 1832).
Alton
    II, 258–60 (March, 1832).
Rushville
    II, 260–61 (March, 1832).
Holbrook's Tracts
    II, 264 (March, 1832).
Epigram
    II, 264 (March, 1832). Verse.
Winter
    II, 287–88 (March, 1832). Verse.
The General Diffusion of Knowledge
    II, 337–48 (May, 1832).
A Journey over the Rocky Mountains
    II, 348–55 (May, 1832).
The Silver Mine
    II, 365–74 (May, 1832). Reprinted in *Tales of the Border,* pp. 157–76.
[Review of Reports of the Supreme Court of Illinois]
    II, 383 (May, 1832).
Peck's Guide to Emigrants
    II, 403 (June, 1832).
Western Quarterly Review
    II, 403–5 (June, 1832).
American Conchology
    II, 405–6 (June, 1832). A review.
Havana
    II, 406–7 (June, 1832).
American Stories for Children
    II, 407–8 (June, 1832).
Blackford's Reports
    II, 408-9 (June, 1832).
Danville
    II, 456–57 (July, 1832).
Town or Country; or, Which Is Best?
    II, 474–78 (July, 1832).
On the General Diffusion of Knowledge
    II, 481–88 (Aug., 1832).

339

Notes on Illinois. The French Settlements
    II, 488–99 (Aug., 1832).
Scenes in the Last War
    II, 502–5 (Aug., 1832).

10. *In the "American Quarterly Review"*

The Public Domain of the United States
    VI, 263–88 (Dec., 1829).
Annual Report of the Treasury Department, at the Opening of the First
    Session of the Twenty-second Congress
    XI, 265–84 (June, 1832).

11. *In "Winter Evenings. A Series of American Tales" (Philadelphia, 1829)*

The Soldier's Bride
    Pp. 1–47. Reprinted in *The Soldier's Bride and Other Tales,* pp. 13–56.

12. *In "The Token" (Boston, 1830, 1831, 1832, 1835)*

The Captain's Lady
    In the volume for 1830, pp. 197–210. Reprinted in *Stories of American Life,* ed. M. R. Mitford, III, 92–107; and in *The Soldier's Bride and Other Tales,* pp. 91–116.
The Village Musician
    In the volume for 1831, pp. 219–46. Reprinted in *The Soldier's Bride and Other Tales,* pp. 132–58.
My Cousin Lucy and the Village Teacher
    In the volume for 1832, pp. 41–61. Reprinted in *The Soldier's Bride and Other Tales,* pp. 57–80.
A Legend of the Prairies
    In the volume for 1835, pp. 303–14.

13. *In the "Western Monthly Magazine"*

To the Reader
    I, 1–5 (Jan., 1833).
American Literature
    I, 5–9 (Jan., 1833).
On Western Character
    I, 49–55 (Feb., 1833).
Hunting Exploits
    I, 90–92 (Feb., 1833).
Travels of a Student
    I, 145–51 (April, 1833).

Waldie's Select Circulating Library
    I, 151–55 (April, 1833).
Domestic Poetry
    I, 155–56 (April, 1833).
Ruin
    I, 156–60 (April, 1833.)
The Spy. A Tale of the Revolution
    I, 160–69 (April, 1833). Reprinted in *Tales of the Border,* pp. 129–150.
Wit and Wisdom
    I, 172–76 (April, 1833).
American Literature
    I, 184–88 (April, 1833).
The Budget
    I, 189–91 (April, 1833).
To Subscribers
    I, 191 (April, 1833).
Missionary Adventure
    I, 226–31 (May, 1833).
Flint on the Natural Sciences
    I, 262–73 (June, 1833).
Indian Hating
    I, 403–8 (Sept., 1833).
Letter from a Traveller No. I
    I, 408–12 (Sept., 1833).
The Song Bird
    I, 513 (Nov., 1833). Verse.
Literature and Religion
    I, 545–52 (Dec., 1833).
Winter
    I, 560 (Dec., 1833).
Letter from a Young Gentleman, Whose Education Has Been Neglected
    II, 75–83 (Feb., 1834).
On Novel Writing
    II, 193–201, 225–37 (April, May, 1834).
Education and Slavery
    II, 266–73 (May, 1834).
American Ornithology
    II, 337–50 (July, 1834).
Western Scenery
    II, 354–62 (July, 1834).
Critical Notices
    II, 375–87 (July, 1834).
Travels in Hot Weather
    II, 486–92, 589–96, 637–46; III, 29–40, IV, 85–90 (Sept., Nov., Dec., 1834; Jan., Aug., 1835).
The March of Intellect
    II, 655–60 (Dec., 1834).
Critical Notices
    III, 41–55 (Jan., 1835).

341

Sketch of the Life of General Harrison
    III, 82–90, 113–28, 221–31 (Feb., March, April, 1835).
Review of the *New England Magazine*
    III, 105–10 (Feb., 1835).
[Review of *A Plea for the West,* by Lyman Beecher]
    III, 320–27 (May, 1835).
Retrospective Review
    III, 368–75 (June, 1835).
The Catholic Question
    III, 375–90 (June, 1835).
Retrospective Review
    IV, 24–34 (July, 1835).
The Night Bird
    IV, 34–35 (July, 1835). Verse.
Stanzas
    IV, 35 (July, 1835). Verse.
Critical Notices
    IV, 59–65 (July, 1835).
Letter from the Editor *De Jure* to the Editor *De Facto*
    IV, 130–33 (Aug., 1835).
To ———
    IV, 272 (Oct., 1835). Verse.
Retrospective Reviews
    IV, 309–17 (Nov., 1835).
The Reason Why
    IV, 336 (Nov., 1835).
The American Quarterly Review No. XXXV. Sept., 1835
    IV, 392–03 (Dec., 1835).
To Sleep
    IV, 418 (Dec., 1835).
The Silent Lover
    IV, 419 (Dec., 1835).
Editorial Remarks
    V, 1–10 (Jan., 1836).
An Essay on Criticism
    V, 10–24 (Jan., 1836).
Editorial Remarks
    V, 239–43 (April, 1836).
Editorial
    V, 369–75 (June, 1836).

14. *In "Knickerbocker"*

The Dark Maid of Illinois
    II, 17–28 (July, 1833). Reprinted in *Tales of the Border,* pp. 177–212;
    and in *The Wilderness and the War Path,* pp. 117–37.
A Reminiscence
    VI, 10–19 (July, 1835).

The War Belt
    XVI, 401–7 (Nov., 1840). Reprinted in *The Wilderness and the War Path*, pp. 32–42.
The Single Combat
    XVII, 22–28 (Jan., 1841).

15. *In the "Cincinnati Weekly Chronicle"*

The Life of Benjamin Drake
    April 10, 1841.

B. WRITINGS IN NON-PERIODICAL WORKS WRITTEN OR EDITED BY OTHERS

1. *In "Stories of American Life," ed. M. R. Mitford (London, 1830)*

For titles in this collection, see under *The Western Souvenir* and *The Token*.

2. *In "Memorial of James Fenimore Cooper" (New York, 1852)*

Letter to Rev. Rufus W. Griswold and others, dated Feb. 14, 1852
    Pp. 29–30.

3. *In "Selections from the Writings of Mrs. Sarah Hall," ed. H. Hall (Philadelphia. 1833)*

Memoir
    Pp. ix–xxxiv.

C. BOOKS AND PAMPHLETS BY HALL

An Oration Delivered in Commemoration of the Festival of St. John the Baptist, 24th. June 1818 before Lodges Nos. 45, and 113, Ancient York Masons Held in the City of Pittsburgh. By James Hall Esq. *Secretary of Ohio Lodge No.* 113. With an introductory Prayer by the *Reverend Abiel Carter.* Pastor of Trinity Church. Pittsburgh, Published by Request Ohio Lodge No. 113. *Butler & Lambdin Printers.* 1818.
    Copy in WRU.
Trial and Defence of First Lieutenant James Hall, of the Ordnance Department, United States' [*sic*] Army. Published by Himself. Eichbaum and Johnson, Printers, Pittsburgh. 1820.
    Actually published in 1819. Copy in LC.

Proceedings of the Antiquarian and Historical Society of Illinois, at Its First Session, in December 1827: with an Address, Delivered by the Hon. James Hall, President of the Society. Published by Order of the Committee of Correspondence. Edwardsville: Printed by Robert K. Fleming, at the Office of the Illinois Corrector. 1828.
Copy in AmPS.

Letters from the West; Containing Sketches of Scenery, Manners, and Customs; and Anecdotes Connected with the First Settlements of the Western Sections of the United States. By the Hon. Judge Hall. London: Henry Colburn, New Burlington Street. 1828.
Reviews: (London) *New Monthly Magazine*, XXIV, 518–19 (Dec. 1, 1828); (London) *Quarterly Review*, XXXIX, 345–59 (April, 1829), by John Barrow.

An Address Delivered before the Antiquarian and Historical Society of Illinois, at Its Second Annual Meeting, in December 1828, by James Hall, President of the Society. Vandalia: Printed by Robert Blackwell. 1829.
Copy in AmPS.

An Oration, Delivered at Vandalia, July 4, 1830; by James Hall. Vandalia: Printed by Blackwell and Hall, 1830.
Copy in AmPS.

Legends of the West. By James Hall, Author of Letters from the West, Etc. Philadelphia: Published by Harrison Hall, 133 Chestnut Street. 1832.
Other editions: Second Edition, Philadelphia: Key and Biddle, 1833; Author's Revised Edition, New York: G. P. Putnam & Co., 1853; Cincinnati: Applegate and Company, 1853; New York: T. L. Magagnos and Company, 1854; New York: J. C. Derby, 1855; Cincinnati: H. W. Derby & Co., 1855; Cincinnati: Applegate & Co., 1857; Cincinnati: D. Clarke, 1869; Cincinnati: R. Clarke & Co., 1874; Cincinnati: R. Clarke & Co., 1885. Parts reprinted: "The Emigrants," in A. B. Hulbert, *Historic Highways of America* (Cleveland, 1904), XI, 175–201; and in *Golden Tales of Our America*, ed. M. L. Becker (New York, 1929). "The Seventh Son," in *Representative American Short Stories*, ed. A. Jessup (Boston, 1923), pp. 89–101. Reviews: *American Monthly Review*, II, 162–66 (Aug., 1832); *New England Magazine*, III, 169–70 (Aug., 1832); (Cincinnati) *Mirror and Ladies' Parterre*, Sept. 15, 1832.

The Soldier's Bride and Other Tales. By James Hall, Author of "Legends of the West." Philadelphia: Key and Biddle, No. 6 Minor Street. A. Waldie, Printer. 1833.
Reviews: *Cincinnati Mirror and Ladies' Parterre*, April 13, 1833; *American Monthly Review*, III, 400–405 (May, 1833). Copy in HU.

The Harpe's Head; A Legend of Kentucky. By James Hall, Author of "The Soldier's Bride," "Legends of the West," &c. Philadelphia: Key & Biddle—23 Minor Street. 1833.
Foreign edition: *Kentucky. A Tale*. By James Hall. In Two Volumes. London: Printed for A. K. Newman and Co., 1834. Reprinted in *Legends of the West* (New York, 1853) and in subsequent editions. Reviews: *American Monthly Magazine*, II, 138 (Oct., 1833); *Knickerbocker*, II, 310 (Oct., 1833).

An Address Delivered before the Erodelphian Society of Miami University, on the Twenty-fourth of September, 1833, at Their Eighth Anniversary Celebration. By James Hall. Cincinnati: Published by Corey and Fairbank. 1833.

Review: *American Monthly Magazine,* II, 333–38 (Jan., 1834).

The Western Reader; A Series of Useful Lessons, Designed to Succeed Corey and Fairbank's Elementary Reader. Selected and Arranged by James Hall. Cincinnati: Corey and Fairbank, and Hubbard and Edmunds [*sic*]. 1833.

Another edition: Cincinnati: Corey and Faikbank [*sic*], 1834. Review: *Cincinnati Journal,* April 4, 1834. Copy of each edition in WRHS.

Sketches of History, Life, and Manners in the West; Containing Accurate Descriptions of the Country and Modes of Life, in the Western States and Territories of North America. By James Hall. Volume I. Cincinnati: Hubbard and Edmands. 1834.

Only the first volume was published by Hubbard and Edmands. Review: *Cincinnati Mirror & Western Gazette,* May 24, 1834.

Sketches of History, Life, and Manners in the West. By James Hall. In Two Volumes. Philadelphia: Harrison Hall, 62, Walnut Street. 1835.

Other editions: (having the title, *The Romance of Western History: or Sketches of History, Life, and Manners in the West,* with twenty-two of its twenty-six chapters rearranged and reprinted from the original) Cincinnati: Applegate & Co., 1857; Cincinnati: D. Clarke, 1869; Cincinnati: Robert Clarke & Co., 1871; 1885. Reviews: *New England Magazine,* VIII, 235–36 (March, 1835); *Buckeye and Cincinnati Mirror,* Oct. 31, 1835; *Knickerbocker,* VI, 483 (Nov., 1835); *American Monthly Magazine,* VI, 239–40 (Nov., 1835); *Western Messenger,* I, 675–87 (May, 1836) by Mann Butler; *North American Review,* XLIII, 1–4 (July, 1836), by James Freeman Clarke; *Southern Literary Messenger,* II, 67–68 (Dec., 1835).

Tales of the Border. By James Hall, Author of "Legends of the West," &c. &c. Philadelphia: Harrison Hall, No. 47, South Third Street. 1835.

Reviews: *Cincinnati Chronicle and Literary Gazette,* Jan. 31, 1835; *Cincinnati Democratic Intelligencer & Commercial Advertiser,* Jan. 30, 1835; *Knickerbocker,* V, 73–75 (Jan., 1835); *American Monthly Magazine,* V, 9–15 (Jan., 1835); *Cincinnati Mirror & Western Gazette,* Feb. 7, 1835.

The Catholic Question, to Which Are Annexed Critical Notices, of A Plea for the West; from the Western Monthly Magazine, of 1835. By James Hall, Esq. Cincinnati. [On verso of title page: Catholic Telegraph Office. 1838.]

The *Cincinnati Journal and Western Luminary* of Oct. 9, 1835, reports that two editions had then been published. I have not found a copy of any edition before 1838.

A Memoir of the Public Services of William Henry Harrison, of Ohio. By James Hall. Philadelphia: Edward C. Biddle, 23 Minor Street. 1836.

Another edition: Cincinnati: Corey and Webster, 1836.

Statistics of the West, at the Close of the Year 1836. By James Hall. Cincinnati: Published by J. A. James & Co. 1836.

Another edition: Cincinnati: J. A. James & Co., 1837. Revised editions printed as: *Notes on the Western States; Containing Descriptive Sketches of Their Soil, Climate, Resources and Scenery,* Philadelphia: Harrison

Hall, 1838; another printing, 1839; London: Wiley & Putnam [1839?];
The West: Its Soil, Surface, and Productions, Cincinnati: Derby, Bradley,
& Co., 1848 [actually 1847]. Reviews: *Western Messenger,* III, 497–99
(Feb., 1837), by James Freeman Clarke; *Knickerbocker,* XII, 76–77
(July, 1838); *American Monthly Magazine,* XI, 199–200 (Aug., 1838);
Southern Literary Messenger, IV, 659–63 (Oct., 1838); *North American
Review,* XLVII, 499–501 (Oct., 1838), by James Freeman Clarke;
(London) *Athenæum,* Feb. 9, 1839, 111–13; *Western Quarterly Review,*
I, 201–3 (Jan., 1849).

History of the Indian Tribes of North America, with Biographical Sketches
and Anecdotes of the Principal Chiefs. Embellished with One Hundred
and Twenty Portraits, from the Indian Gallery in the Department of
War, at Washington. By Thomas L. M'Kenney, Late of the Indian
Department, Washington, and James Hall, Esq. of Cincinnati. Volume I.
Philadelphia: Published by Edward C. Biddle, 23 Minor Street 1836.
Volume II. Philadelphia: Published by Frederick W. Greenough, 23
Minor Street. 1838. Volume III. Philadelphia: Published by Daniel
Rice and James G. Clark, 132 Arch Street. 1844.

Another edition the same except Volume II has on the title page:
Philadelphia: Published by Daniel Rice and James G. Clark, 132 Arch
Street. 1842. Other editions: Philadelphia: J. T. Bowen, 1848–1850;
Philadelphia: D. Rice & A. N. Hart, 1854; Philadelphia: Rice, Rutter
& Co., 1870; Edinburgh: John Grant, 1933–1934. Reviews: *Western
Monthly Magazine,* N.S. I, 73 (Feb., 1837); *North American Review,*
XLVII, 134–48 (July, 1838), by Jared Sparks and C. C. Felton;
(London) *Athenæum,* April 14, May 12, 1838, 265–67, 342–44.

Reply to Strictures on Sketches of the West, in the North American Review,
No. 92; Being the Preface to Notes on the Western States, Just Published.
Philadelphia, H. Hall, 1838.

Notes on the Western States
See under *Statistics of the West.*

[Western Armory Report]
Title taken from *Cincinnati Daily Gazette,* Nov. 10, 1841, which
attributes the authorship to Hall and states that the work was published
in pamphlet form. Reprinted in the *Cincinnati Daily Gazette,* Nov. 10,
11, 12, 1841, and in the *Cincinnati Weekly Gazette,* Nov. 17, 1841. I have
been unable to find a copy of the pamphlet.

Memorial of the Citizens of Cincinnati, to the Congress of the United States,
Relative to the Navigation of the Ohio and Mississippi Rivers. Cincinnati: L'Hommedieu & Co., Printers 1843.

The *Cincinnati Daily Gazette* of Jan. 13, 1843 states that the pamphlet
was "written by Judge Hall." This edition consists of 36 pages. Another
edition (53 pp.) : Printed at the Daily Atlas Office, 1844. Copies of both
editions in HPSO.

Address before the Young Men's Mercantile Library Association, of Cincinnati, in Celebration of Its Eleventh Anniversary, April 18, 1846. By
James Hall. Cincinnati: Published by the Association. 1846.

The Wilderness and the War Path. By James Hall, Author of Legends of
the West, Border Tales, Sketches of the West, Notes on the Western
States, Etc., Etc. New York: Wiley and Putnam, 161 Broadway. 1846.
Another edition: New York and London, J. Wiley, 1849.

Memoir of Thomas Posey, Major-General, and Governor of Indiana; by James Hall.
> In *The Library of American Biography,* ed. Jared Sparks, Second Series, Vol. IX, 359–403. Boston: Charles C. Little and James Brown, 1846.

The West: Its Soil, Surface, and Productions
> See under *Statistics of the West.*

The West: Its Commerce and Navigation. By James Hall. Cincinnati: H. W. Derby & Co., Publishers. 1848.

The Romance of Western History
> See under *Sketches of History, Life, and Manners in the West.*

D. WORKS EDITED BY HALL

The Illinois Gazette
> Published weekly at Shawneetown, Illinois. Hall's editorship: May 27, 1820–November 16, 1822.

The Western Souvenir, A Christmas and New Year's Gift for 1829. Cincinnati, N. & G. Guilford [1828].

The Illinois Intelligencer
> Published weekly at Vandalia, Illinois. Hall's editorship: January 17, 1829–March 3, 1832.

The Illinois Monthly Magazine
> Published at Vandalia, Illinois. Hall's editorship: October, 1830–September, 1832.

The Western Monthly Magazine
> Published at Cincinnati. Hall's editorship: January, 1833–June, 1836.

III.   SECONDARY SOURCES

A. BOOKS

AARON, DANIEL. "Cincinnati, 1818–1838: A Study of Attitudes in the Urban West." Doctoral dissertation, Harvard University, 1942.

ALLEN, GARDNER W. *Our Navy and the Barbary Corsairs.* Boston: Houghton Mifflin & Co., 1905.

AMERICAN PHILOSOPHICAL SOCIETY. *Early Proceedings of the American Philosophical Society for the Promotion of Useful Knowledge, . . . from 1744 to 1828.* Philadelphia: Press of McCalla and Stavely, 1884.

ANDERSON, W. P. *Anderson Family Records.* Cincinnati: Press of W. F. Schaefer & Co., 1836.

ANDREWS, J. CUTLER. *Pittsburgh's "Post-Gazette."* . . . Boston: Chapman & Grimes, 1936.

Annual Register of the Proceedings of the Western Literary Institute and College of Professional Teachers. [Cincinnati?], 1833.

ANTHONY, IRVIN. *Decatur.* New York and London: Charles Scribner's Sons, 1931.

AUDUBON, JOHN JAMES. *Audubon's America: The Narratives and Experiences of John James Audubon,* ed. DONALD CULROSS PEATTIE. Boston: Houghton Mifflin & Co., 1940.

BALDWIN, CHARLES SEARS (ed.). *American Short Stories Selected and Edited with an Introductory Essay on the Short Story by Charles Sears Baldwin.* New York: Longmans, Green & Co., 1906.

BARINGER, WILLIAM E. *Lincoln's Vandalia: A Pioneer Portrait.* New Brunswick, N.J.: Rutgers University Press, 1949.

BARNES, GILBERT HOBBS. *The Antislavery Impulse 1830–1844.* New York and London: D. Appleton-Century Co., 1933.

BATEMAN, NEWTON, AND SELBY, PAUL. *Biographical and Memorial Edition of the Historical Encyclopedia of Illinois.* 2 vols. Chicago: Munsell Publishing Co., 1915.

BEECHER, LYMAN. *Autobiography, Correspondence, Etc., of Lyman Beecher,* ed. CHARLES BEECHER. 2 vols. New York: Harper & Bros., 1864.

BEECHER, LYMAN. *A Plea for the West.* Cincinnati: Truman & Smith, 1835.

BELL, JAMES C. *Opening a Highway to the Pacific 1835–1846.* New York: Columbia University Press, 1921.

BERNHARD, DUKE OF SAXE-WEIMAR EISENACH. *Travels through North America, during the Years 1825 and 1826.* 2 vols. Philadelphia: Carey, Lea & Carey, 1828.

BILLINGTON, RAY ALLEN. *The Protestant Crusade 1800–1860: A Study of the Origins of American Nativism.* New York: Macmillan Co., 1938.

BIRKBECK, MORRIS. *Notes on a Journey in America, from the Coast of Virginia to the Territory of Illinois.* . . . London: Printed by Severn & Co. for J. Ridgeway, 1818.

BLACKBURN, E. HOWARD, and WELFLEY, WILLIAM H. *History of Bedford and Somerset Counties, Pennsylvania with Genealogical and Personal History.* Bedford County by E. Howard Blackburn; Somerset County by William H. Welfley. 3 vols. New York: Lewis Publishing Co., 1906.

BLACK HAWK. *Life of Ma–ka–tai–me–she–kia–kiak or Black Hawk . . . With an Account of the Cause and General History of the Late War . . . Dictated by Himself.* Cincinnati, 1833.

BLAINE, HAROLD A. "The Frontiersman in American Prose Fiction (1800–1860)." Doctoral dissertation, Western Reserve University, 1936.

BLAIR, WALTER. *Native American Humor 1800–1900.* New York: American Book Co., 1937.

BOYD, THOMAS. *Light Horse Harry Lee.* New York: Charles Scribner's Sons, 1931.

BRACKENRIDGE, HENRY MARIE. *Recollections of Persons and Places in the West.* 2d ed. Philadelphia: J. B. Lippincott & Co., 1868.

348

BRADSHER, EARL H. *Mathew Carey: Editor, Author, and Publisher.* New York: Columbia University Press, 1912.

BRAINERD, M. *Life of Rev. Thomas Brainerd, D.D., for Thirty Years Pastor of the Old Pine Street Church, Philadelphia.* Philadelphia: J. B. Lippincott & Co., 1870.

BUCK, SOLON JUSTUS. *Illinois in 1818.* Springfield: Illinois Centennial Commission, 1917.

BULEY, R. CARLYLE. *The Old Northwest Pioneer Period 1815–1840.* Indianapolis: Indiana Historical Society, 1950.

BUTLER, MANN. *An Appeal from the Misrepresentations of James Hall, Respecting the History of Kentucky and the West.* . . . Frankfort, Ky.: Printed by A. G. Hodges, 1837.

CARNEGIE LIBRARY OF PITTSBURGH (comp.), *Pittsburgh in 1816 Compiled by the Carnegie Library of Pittsburgh on the One Hundredth Anniversary of the Granting of the City Charter.* Pittsburgh: Carnegie Library, 1916.

CARNOCHAN, JANET. *Inscriptions and Graves in the Niagara Peninsula.* ("Publications of the Niagara Historical Society," No. 19.) 2d ed. Wellington, Ont.: The *Tribune,* 1910.

Catalogue of the Members of the Second Presbyterian Church, in Cincinnati. Cincinnati: Printed by F. S. Benton, 1835.

CHITTICK, VICTOR L. O. *"Ring-Tailed Roarers": Tall Tales of the American Frontier 1830–1860.* Caldwell, Idaho: Caxton Printers, 1941.

COGGESHALL, WILLIAM T. *The Poets and Poetry of the West: With Biographical and Critical Notices.* Columbus, O.: Follett, Foster & Co., 1860.

COWIE, ALEXANDER. *The Rise of the American Novel.* New York: American Book Co., 1948.

CRAMER, ZADOK. *The Navigator, Containing Directions for Navigating the Monongahela, Allegheny, Ohio and Mississippi Rivers . . . and a Concise Description of Their Towns, Villages, Harbors, Settlements, &c. . . .* 11th ed. Pittsburgh: Cramer & Spear, 1821.

CRUIKSHANK, E. A. (ed.). *The Documentary History of the Campaign upon the Niagara Frontier Collected and Edited for the Lundy's Lane Historical Society.* 9 vols. in 5. Welland, Ont.: Printed at the *Tribune,* 1896–1908.

CUBBERLEY, ELWOOD P. *Public Education in the United States: A Study and Interpretation of American Political History* . . . Rev. ed. Boston, Houghton Mifflin Co., 1934.

DAVIS, W. W. H. *The Fries Rebellion 1798–99: An Armed Rebellion to the House Tax Law, Passed by Congress, July 9, 1798, in Bucks and Northampton Counties, Pennsylvania.* Doyleston, Pa., 1899.

Debate at the Lane Seminary, Cincinnati. Speech of James A. Thome, of Kentucky, Delivered at the Annual Meeting of the American Anti-Slavery Society, May 6, 1834[.] *Letter of the Rev. Dr. Samuel H. Cox, against the American Colonization Society.* Boston: Garrison & Knapp, 1834.

DENNIE, JOSEPH. *The Lay Preacher. Collected and Arranged by John E. Hall, Esq.* [Philadelphia]: Harrison Hall, 1817.

DODDRIDGE, JOSEPH. *Notes, on the Settlement and Indian Wars, of the Western Parts of Virginia and Pennsylvania from the Year 1763 until the Year 1783 Inclusive* . . . Wellsburgh, Va.: Printed at the Office of the *Gazette* for the Author, 1824.

DRAKE, DANIEL; BAKEWELL, J. W.; and WILLIAMS, J. S. *Rail-Road from the Banks of the Ohio River to the Tide Waters of the Carolinas and Georgia.* Cincinnati: James & Gazlay, 1835.

DUMOND, DWIGHT L. *Antislavery Origins of the Civil War in the United States.* Ann Arbor, Mich.: University of Michigan Press, 1939.

EDWARDS, NINIAN. *The Edwards Papers; Being a Portion of the Collection of the Letters, Papers, and Manuscripts of Ninian Edwards,* ed. E. B. WASHBURNE. Chicago: Fergus Printing Co., 1884.

EDWARDS, NINIAN WIRT. *History of Illinois from 1778 to 1833; and Life and Times of Ninian Edwards.* Springfield, Ill.: Illinois State Journal Co., 1870.

EGLE, WILLIAM HENRY. *Pennsylvania Genealogies.* . . . Harrisburg, Pa.: L. S. Hart, Printer, 1886.

ELLIS, HAROLD MILTON. *Joseph Dennie and His Circle; A Study in American Literature from 1792 to 1812.* Austin, Tex.: University of Texas, 1915.

ERSKINE, JOHN. *Leading American Novelists.* New York: H. Holt & Co., 1910.

EVEREST, CHARLES W. (ed.). *The Poets of Connecticut.* Hartford, Conn.: Case, Tiffany & Burnham, 1844.

EWING, LUCY E. LEE. *Dr. John Ewing and Some of His Noted Connections.* Philadelphia: Press of Allen, Lane & Scott, 1924.

FAUST, BERTHA. *Hawthorne's Contemporaneous Reputation: A Study of Literary Opinion in America and England 1828–1864.* Philadelphia, 1939.

FEARON, HENRY BRADSHAW. *Sketches of America. A Narrative of a Journey of Five Thousand Miles through the Eastern and Western Parts of America.* . . . 3rd ed. London: Longman, Hurst, Rees, Orme, & Brown, 1818.

FLETCHER, ROBERT SAMUEL. *A History of Oberlin College from Its Foundation through the Civil War.* 2 vols. Oberlin, O.: Oberlin College, 1943.

FLINT, TIMOTHY. *Recollections of the Last Ten Years, Passed in Occasional Residences and Journeyings in the Valley of the Mississippi.* Boston: Cummings, Hilliard & Co., 1826.

FOOTE, JOHN P. *Memoirs of the Life of Samuel E. Foote, by His Brother.* . . . Cincinnati: Robert Clarke & Co., 1860.

FORD, THOMAS. *A History of Illinois from Its Commencement as a State in 1818 to 1847. Containing a Full Account of the Black Hawk War, the Rise, the Progress, and Fall of Mormonism, the Alton and Lovejoy Riots.* . . . Chicago: S. C. Griggs & Co., 1854.

FOSTER, MORISON. *My Brother Stephen.* Indianapolis: Privately Printed, 1932.

FOX, EARLY L. *The American Colonization Society 1817–1840.* Baltimore: Johns Hopkins Press, 1919.

FRENEAU, PHILIP. *The Poems of Philip Freneau,* ed. FRED LEWIS PATTEE. 3 vols. Princeton, N.J.: University Library, 1902–1907.

GOODMAN, NATHAN G. *Benjamin Rush Physician and Citizen 1746–1813.* Philadelphia: University of Pennsylvania Press, 1934.

350

GRAHAM, WALTER. *English Literary Periodicals.* New York: Thomas Nelson & Sons, 1930.

GRATZ, REBECCA. *Letters of Rebecca Gratz,* ed. RABBI DAVID PHILIPSON. Philadelphia: Jewish Publication Society of America, 1929.

GREENE, EVARTS B., and ALVORD, CLARENCE W. (eds.). *The Governors Letter Books 1818–1834.* ("Collections of the Illinois State Historical Society Library," Vol. IV.) Springfield, Ill.: Trustees of the Illinois State Historical Library, 1909.

GRISWOLD, RUFUS WILMOT. *The Prose Writers of America.* Philadelphia: Carey & Hart, 1849.

GROSSMAN, JAMES. *James Fenimore Cooper.* New York: William Sloane Associates, 1949.

HALL, HAROLD E. "James Kirke Paulding: A Pioneer in American Fiction." Doctoral dissertation, University of Pennsylvania, 1953.

HALL, JOHN ELIHU (ed.). *The Philadelphia Souvenir; a Collection of Fugitive Pieces from the Philadelphia Press. With Biographical and Explanatory Notes.* . . . Philadelphia: Harrison Hall, 1826.

HALL, JOHN POSEY. *The Case of John Posey Hall, Late a Master in the Navy of the United States.* Washington, D.C.: W. H. Moore, [1858].

HALL, SARAH EWING. *Selections from the Writings of Mrs. Sarah Hall, . . . with a Memoir of Her Life.* [Edited by Harrison Hall, Preface by James Hall.] Philadelphia: Harrison Hall, 1833.

HARPER, JOSEPHINE LOUISE. "John Reynolds, 'The Old Ranger' of Illinois." Doctoral dissertation, University of Illinois, 1949.

HEITMAN, FRANCIS B. *Historical Register and Dictionary of the United States Army, from Its Organization, September 29, 1789, to March 2, 1903.* 2 vols. Washington, D.C.: Government Printing Office, 1903.

HERRICK, FRANCIS H. *Audubon the Naturalist: A History of His Life and Time.* 2d ed. New York: D. Appleton-Century Co., 1938.

HILTZHEIMER, JACOB. *Extracts from the Diary of Jacob Hiltzheimer, of Philadelphia. 1765–1798,* ed. JACOB COX PARSONS. Philadelphia: Wm. F. Fell & Co., 1893.

History of Gallatin, Saline, Hamilton, Franklin and Williamson Counties, Illinois. From the Earliest Time to the Present. . . . Chicago: Goodspeed Publishing Co., 1887.

[HOFFMAN, CHARLES FENNO]. *A Winter in the West. By a New Yorker.* . . . 2 vols. New York: Harper & Brothers, 1835.

HOWARD, LEON. *Herman Melville: A Biography.* Berkeley, Calif.: University of California Press, 1951.

JAMES, MARQUIS. *The Life of Andrew Jackson.* Indianapolis: The Bobbs Merrill Co., 1938.

JARRELL, HAMPTON M. "William Gilmore Simms: Realistic Romancer." Doctoral dissertation, Duke University, 1932.

JOHNSTON, GEORGE. *History of Cecil County, Maryland.* . . . Elkton, Md.: The Author, 1881.

JOHNSTON, GEORGE (ed.). *The Poets and Poetry of Cecil County, Maryland.* Elkton, Md.: The Editor, 1887.

Journal of the House of Representatives [sic] *of the Second General Assembly of the State of Illinois at Their First Session, Begun and Held at the*

Town of Vandalia, on Monday the 4th Day of December A.D. 1820. Vandalia, Ill.: Brown & Berry, 1821.

Journal of the House of Representatives of the Fourth General Assembly of the State of Illinois, at Their First Session, Begun and Held at the Town of Vandalia, November 15, 1824. Vandalia, Ill.: Robert Blackwell & Co., 1824.

Journal of the House of Representatives of the Seventh General Assembly of the State of Illinois, at Their First Sesstion, Begun and Held at the Town of Vandalia, December [1830]. Vandalia, Ill.: Robert Blackwell, 1831.

Journal of the House of Representatives of the Tenth General Assembly of the State of Illinois, at Their First Session, Begun and Held in the Town of Vandalia, December 5, 1836. Vandalia, Ill.: William Walters, 1836.

Journal of the Proceedings of the South-Western Convention Began [sic] and Held at the City of Memphis, on the 12th November, 1845. Memphis, Tenn., 1845.

Journal of the Senate of the Fifth General Assembly of the State of Illinois, at Their First Session, Begun and Held at the Town of Vandalia, December 6, 1826. Vandalia, Ill.: Robert Blackwell, 1826.

Journal of the Senate of the Sixth General Assembly, of the State of Illinois, at Their First Session, Begun and Held at the Town of Vandalia, December 1, 1828. Kaskaskia, Ill.: Robert K. Fleming, 1829.

Journal of the Senate of the Seventh General Assembly of the State of Illinois, at Their First Session, Begun and Held at the Town of Vandalia, December 6, 1830. Vandalia, Ill.: Robert Blackwell, 1831.

KILLIKELLY, SARAH H. *The History of Pittsburgh Its Rise and Progress.* Pittsburgh: B. C. & Gordon Montgomery Co., 1906.

KNAPP, SAMUEL. *Female Biography; Containing Notices of Distinguished Women.* New York: J. Carpenter, 1934.

Lane Theological Seminary General Catalog. Cincinnati, 1899.

Laws, of a Private Nature, Passed at the Eighth Session of the General Assembly of the State of Illinois, Begun and Held at Vandalia, on Monday the Third Day of December, 1832. Kaskaskia, Ill.: R. K. Fleming, 1833.

LEVASSEUR, AUGUSTE. *Lafayette en Amérique, ou Journal d'un Voyage aux Etats-Unis en 1824 et 1825.* 2 vols. Paris: Baudouin, 1829.

LINDER, USHER F. *Reminiscences of the Early Bench and Bar of Illinois.* 2d ed. Chicago: Chicago Legal News Co., 1879.

LOSSING, BENSON J. *The Pictorial Field-Book of the War of 1812. . . .* New York: Harper & Bros., 1869.

MACKENZIE, GEORGE N. (ed.). *Colonial Families of the United States of America. . . .* 7 vols. New York: Grafton Press, 1907–1920.

MAHAN, ASA. *Autobiography Intellectual, Moral, and Spiritual.* London: T. Woolmer, 1882.

MANSFIELD, EDWARD D. *Memoir of the Life and Services of Daniel Drake M.D., Physician, Professor and Author; with Notices of the Early Settlement of Cincinnati. . . .* Cincinnati: Applegate & Co., 1855.

———. *Personal Memories Social, Political, and Literary with Sketches of Many Noted People 1803–1843. . . .* Cincinnati: Robert Clarke & Co., 1879.

352

MARTINEAU, HARRIET. *Retrospect of Western Travel.* 2 vols. Cincinnati: U. P. James, 1838.

———. *Society in America.* 3 vols. London: Saunders & Otley, 1837.

MITFORD, MARY RUSSELL. *The Life of Mary Russell Mitford . . . Related in a Selection from Her Letters to Her Friends,* ed. REV. A. G. L'ESTRANGE. 3 vols. London: Richard Bentley, 1870.

MONROE, JAMES. *Oberlin Thursday Lectures Addresses and Essays.* Oberlin, O.: Edward J. Goodrich, 1897.

MORRIS, GOUVERNEUR. *The Diary and Letters of Gouverneur Morris,* ed. ANNE CARY MORRIS. 2 vols. New York: C. Scribner's Sons, 1888.

MOTT, FRANK LUTHER. *A History of American Magazines 1741–1850.* New York: D. Appleton & Co., 1930.

MUSSER, PAUL H. *James Nelson Barker, 1784–1858, with a Reprint of His Comedy "Tears and Smiles."* Philadelphia: University of Pennsylvania Press, 1929.

Narrative of the Late Riotous Proceedings against the Liberty of the Press, in Cincinnati. With Remarks and Historical Notices, Relating to Emancipation. Addressed to the People of Ohio, by the Executive Committee of the Ohio Anti-Slavery Society. Cincinnati, 1836.

NORTON, MARGARET CROSS (ed.). *Illinois Census Returns 1820.* ("Collections of the Illinois State Historical Library," Vol. XXVI). Springfield, Ill.: Trustees of the Illinois State Historical Library, 1934.

———. *Illinois Census Returns 1810, 1818.* ("Collections of the Illinois State Historical Library," Vol. XXIV). Springfield, Ill.: Trustees of the Illinois State Historical Library, 1935.

NUTTALL, THOMAS. *A Journal of Travels into the Arkansa Territory, during the Year 1819. . . .* Philadelphia: Thos. H. Palmer, 1821.

OGDEN, H. A. and NELSON, HENRY LOOMIS. *The Army of the United States Illustrated by Forty-four Fac-simile Plates from Water Color Drawings. . . .* New York: G. H. Buck & Co., [1886].

OWEN, WILLIAM. *Diary of William Owen from November 10, 1824, to April 20, 1825,* ed. JOEL W. HIATT. Indianapolis: The Bobbs Merrill Co., 1906.

PAINE, ALBERT BIGELOW. *Mark Twain, a Biography: The Personal and Literary Life of Samuel Langhorne Clemens. . . .* 3 vols. New York: Harper & Bros., 1912.

PATTEE, FRED LEWIS. *The Development of the American Short Story: An Historical Survey.* New York and London: Harper & Bros., 1923.

[PAULDING, JAMES KIRKE]. *Letters from the South, Written during an Excursion in the Summer of 1816.* 2 vols. New York: James Eastburn & Co., 1817.

PEASE, THEODORE CALVIN. *The Frontier State 1818–1848.* Springfield, Ill.: Illinois Centennial Commission, 1918.

Pennsylvania Archives, Sixth Series, ed. THOMAS LYNCH MONTGOMERY. 15 vols. Harrisburg, 1906–1907.

Pennsylvania Archives, Ninth Series, ed. GERTRUDE MACKINNEY. 10 vols. N. p., 1931–1935.

POE, EDGAR ALLAN. *The Letters of Edgar Allan Poe,* ed. JOHN WARD OSTROM. 2 vols. Cambridge: Harvard University Press, 1948.

POWELL, WALTER A. *A History of Delaware*. Boston: Christopher Publishing House, 1928.

QUINN, ARTHUR HOBSON. *American Fiction: An Historical and Critical Survey*. New York: D. Appleton-Century Co., 1936.

RANDALL, EMILIUS OVIATT and RYAN, DANIEL J. *History of Ohio; the Rise and Progress of an American State*. 5 vols. New York: Century History Co., 1912.

RANKIN, JOHN. *A Review of the Statement of the Faculty of Lane Seminary, in Relation to the Recent Difficulties in That Institution*. Ripley, O.: Campbell & Palmer, Printers, 1835.

REYNOLDS, JOHN. *The Pioneer History of Illinois Containing the Discovery in 1673 and the History of the Country to the Year 1818. . . .* 2d ed. Chicago: Fergus Printing Co., 1887.

REYNOLDS, JOHN C. *History of the M. W. Grand Lodge of Illinois, Ancient, Free, and Accepted Masons, from the Organization of the First Lodge . . . to . . . 1850*. Springfield, Ill.: H. G. Reynolds, Jr., 1869.

ROBERTSON, DAVID (comp.). *Reports of the Trials of Aaron Burr . . . for Treason, and for a Misdemeanor . . . to Which Is Added, an Appendix, Containing the Arguments and Evidence . . . To Commit A. Burr, H. Blannerhasset [sic] and I. Smith To Be Sent for Trial to the State of Kentucky. . . . Taken in Short Hand*. 2 vols. Philadelphia: Hopkins and Earle, Fry and Kammerer, Printers, 1808.

ROSA, MATTHEW WHITING. *The Silver-fork School: Novels of Fashion Preceding "Vanity Fair."* New York: Columbia University Press, 1936.

ROTHERT, OTTO A. *The Outlaws of Cave-in-Rock: Historical Accounts of the Famous Highwaymen and River Pirates Who Operated in Pioneer Days upon the Ohio and Mississippi Rivers and over the Old Natchez Trace*. Cleveland: Arthur H. Clark Co., 1924.

ROURKE, CONSTANCE. *Audubon. . . .* New York: Harcourt Brace & Co., 1936.

RUSK, RALPH LESLIE. *The Literature of the Middle Western Frontier*. 2 vols. New York: Columbia University Press, 1925.

RUXTON, GEORGE F. *Ruxton of the Rockies*, ed. L. R. HAFEN. Norman, Okla.: University of Oklahoma Press, 1950.

SAFFORD, WILLIAM H. (ed.). *The Blennerhassett Papers, Embodying the Private Journal of Harman Blennerhassett, and the Hitherto Unpublished Correspondence of Burr, Alston, Comfort Tyler, Devereaux, Dayton, Adair, Miro, Emmett, Theodosia Burr Alston, Mrs. Blennerhassett and Others. . . .* Cincinnati: Moore, Wilstach & Baldwin, 1864.

————. *The Life of Harman Blennerhassett Comprising an Authentic Narrative of the Burr Expedition. . . .* Cincinnati: Moore, Wilstach, Keys & Co., 1859.

SCHARF, J. THOMAS and WESTCOTT, THOMPSON. *History of Philadelphia 1609–1884*. 3 vols. Philadelphia: L. H. Everts & Co., 1884.

SIMPSON, HENRY. *The Lives of Eminent Philadelphians, Now Deceased. . . .* Philadelphia: William Brotherhead, 1859.

SMITH, THEODORE CLARKE. *The Liberty and Free Soil Parties in the Northwest. . . .* New York: Longmans, Green & Co., 1897.

[SNELLING, WILLIAM JOSEPH]. *Tales of the Northwest; or, Sketches of Indian Life and Character. By a Resident beyond the Frontier*. Boston: Hilliard, Gray, Little & Wilkins, 1830.

354

A Statement of the Reasons Which Induced the Students of Lane Seminary, To Dissolve Their Connection with That Institution. Cincinnati, 1834.

STEWART, RANDALL. *Nathaniel Hawthorne: A Biography.* New Haven, Conn.: Yale University Press, 1948.

STOWE, CHARLES E. *Life of Harriet Beecher Stowe Compiled from Her Letters and Journals.* . . . Boston and New York: Houghton Mifflin & Co., 1889.

STUART, JAMES. *Three Years in North America.* 2d ed. 2 vols. Edinburgh: Printed for R. Cadell, 1833.

STURTEVANT, JULIAN M. *An Autobiography,* ed. J. M. STURTEVANT, JR. New York: Fleming H. Revell Co., 1896.

SUTTON, WALTER. *The Western Book Trade: Cincinnati as a Nineteenth-Century Publishing and Book-Trade Center, Containing a Directory of Cincinnati Publishers, Booksellers, and Members of the Allied Trades, 1796–1880, and a Bibliography.* Columbus, O.: Ohio State University Press, 1961.

SWIFT, LINDSAY. *William Lloyd Garrison.* Philadelphia: George W. Jacobs & Co., 1911.

THOMPSON, HAROLD W. *Body Boots & Britches.* Philadelphia: J. B. Lippincott Co., 1940.

THOMPSON, RALPH. *American Literary Annuals and Gift Books 1825–1865.* New York: H. W. Wilson Co., 1936.

TILLSON, CHRISTIANA HOLMES. *A Woman's Story of Pioneer Illinois* . . . Chicago: R. R. Donnelley & Sons Co., 1919.

TODD, CHARLES B. *Life and Letters of Joel Barlow. LL. D. Poet, Statesman, Philosopher.* . . . New York and London: G. P. Putnam's Sons, 1886.

VENABLE, W. H. *Beginnings of Literary Culture in the Ohio Valley: Historical and Biographical Sketches.* Cincinnati: Robert Clarke & Co., 1891.

WADE, JOHN D. *Augustus Baldwin Longstreet: A Study of the Development of Culture in the South.* New York: The Macmillan Co., 1924.

WALTERS, RAYMOND. *Stephen Foster: Youth's Golden Gleam a Sketch of His Life and Background in Cincinnati 1846–1850.* Princeton, N.J.: Princeton University Press, 1936.

WARDEN, ROBERT B. *An Account of the Public Life and Public Services of Salmon Portland Chase.* Cincinnati: Wilstach, Baldwin & Co., 1874.

WATSON, MELVIN R. "The Essay Tradition and the Magazine Serials (1731–1820)." Doctoral dissertation, Johns Hopkins University, 1944.

WELD, THEODORE; WELD, ANGELINA GRIMKÉ; and GRIMKÉ, SARAH. *Letters of Theodore Dwight Weld[,] Angelina Grimké Weld[,] and Sarah Grimké 1822–1844,* ed. GILBERT H. BARNES and DWIGHT L. DUMOND. 2 vols. New York: D. Appleton-Century Co., 1934.

WENDER, HERBERT. *Southern Commercial Conventions 1837–1859.* Baltimore: Johns Hopkins Press, 1930.

WEYGANT, CHARLES H. *The Sacketts of America: Their Ancestors and Descendants 1630–1907.* Newburgh, N.Y.: [Journal Print], 1907.

WILLER, WILLIAM H. "Native Themes in American Short Prose Fiction, 1770–1835." Doctoral dissertation, University of Minnesota, 1944.

WILLIAMS, STANLEY T. *The Life of Washington Irving.* 2 vols. New York: Oxford University Press, 1935.

WILSON, FORREST. *Crusader in Crinoline: The Life of Harriet Beecher Stowe.* Philadelphia: J. B. Lippincott Co., 1941.

WOODS, JOHN. *Two Years' Residence in the Settlement on the English Prairie, in the Illinois Country, United States.* . . . London: Longman, Hurst, Rees, Orme, & Brown, 1822.

YOUNG, JOHN RUSSELL (ed.). *Memorial History of the City of Philadelphia.* . . . New York: New York History Co., 1895–1898.

B.   ARTICLES

Space does not permit a complete list of either the periodicals or the periodical articles used or cited in this study. Newspaper articles particularly are too numerous to mention here, but may be found cited in the chapter notes. The following newspapers and magazines were especially helpful; they are listed in the order in which they are cited, and newspapers are distinguished from magazines by the inclusion, either in the title or in subsequent parentheses, of the name of the city in which they were published.

The Port Folio
Poulson's American Daily Advertiser (Philadelphia)
Western Sun & General Advertiser (Vincennes, Indiana)
Pittsburgh Gazette
Pittsburgh Commonwealth
Mercury (Pittsburgh)
Pittsburgh Statesman
Illinois Gazette (Shawneetown)
Illinois Intelligencer (Vandalia)
Vandalia Whig and Illinois Intelligencer
The Western Monthly Review
Athenæum (London)
The Illinois Monthly Magazine
Cincinnati Chronicle and Literary Gazette
Daily Cincinnati Gazette
The Western Monthly Magazine
Cincinnati Mirror and Ladies' Parterre
Cincinnati Mirror and Western Gazette
Cincinnati Mirror and Chronicle
Buckeye and Cincinnati Mirror
Cincinnati Journal
Cincinnati Journal and Western Luminary
Cross and Baptist Journal (Cincinnati)
Catholic Telegraph (Cincinnati)
Daily Cincinnati Republican and Commercial Register
Cincinnati Chronicle
Cincinnati Daily Chronicle
Daily Cincinnati Advertiser and Journal

Lowell Journal (Lowell, Massachusetts)
Daily Cincinnati Atlas
Cist's Daily Advertiser (Cincinnati)
Cincinnati Commercial
The Western Messenger
Transactions of the Western Art Union

ADKINS, NELSON F. "James Kirke Paulding's *Lion of the West,*" *American Literature,* III (November, 1931), 249–58.

AGNEW, DANIEL. "Address to the Allegheny County Bar Association, December 1, 1888," *Pennsylvania Magazine of History and Biography,* XIII, No. 1 (1889), 1–60.

BRIGHAM, CLARENCE SAUNDERS. "Bibliography of American Newspapers, 1690–1820," American Antiquarian Society, *Proceedings,* N.S. XXIII–XXXVII (October, 1913–April, 1927).

BRIGHTFIELD, M. F. "Lockhart's *Quarterly* Contributors," *Publications of the Modern Language Association,* LIX (June, 1944), 491–512.

BURNHAM, J. H. "U. S. Senator John McLean," Illinois State Historical Society, *Transactions for the Year 1903* (Springfield, 1904), pp. 190–201.

CHEVALIER, MICHAEL. "Letters from France," *Western Monthly Magazine,* IV (November, 1835), 317–23.

———. "Letters on America," *Western Monthly Magazine,* IV (December, 1835), 404–14.

CONKLIN, WILLET T. "Paulding's Prose Treatment of Types and Frontier Lore before Cooper," University of Texas, *Studies in English,* XIX (1939), 163–71.

COTTERILL, R. S. "Southern Railroads and Western Trade, 1840–1850," *Mississippi Valley Historical Review,* XII (March, 1917), 427–21.

DONALD, DAVID (ed.). "The Autobiography of James Hall, Western Literary Pioneer," *Ohio State Archaelogical and Historical Quarterly,* LVI (July, 1947), 295–304.

DONALD, DAVID and PALMER, FREDERICK A. "Toward a Western Literature, 1820–1860," *Mississippi Valley Historical Review,* XXXV (December, 1948), 413–28.

[DRAKE, BENJAMIN]. "Cincinnati at the Close of 1835," *Western Monthly Magazine,* V (January, 1836), 26–31.

[FLINT, TIMOTHY?]. "Cincinnati in 1826," *Western Monthly Review,* I (May 1827), 61–66.

[FLINT, TIMOTHY]. "Progress of the West," *Western Monthly Review,* I (May, 1827), 25–26.

GOCHENOUR, N. C. "One Hundredth Anniversary of the Presbyterian Church of Vandalia, Illinois," Illinois State Historical Society, *Journal,* XXI (January, 1929), 547–55.

HALFIELD, EDWIN F. "Jonathan Dickinson Sergeant," *Pennsylvania Magazine of History and Biography,* II, No. 4 (1878), 438–42.

HALL, JOHN E. "Narrative of John E. Hall," *Interesting Papers Illustrative of the Recent Riots at Baltimore* [Philadelphia?, 1812], pp. 52–60.

HALL, SARAH EWING. "Sketch of a Landscape in Cecil County, Maryland," *Port Folio,* VIII (July, 1819), 81–83.

357

HEINL, FRANK J. "Newspapers and Periodicals in the Lincoln-Douglas Country, 1831–1832," Illinois State Historical Society, *Journal* (October, 1930), 371–438.

"Hiram Powers," *Western Monthly Magazine,* III (April, 1835), 245.

HOFFMAN, DANIEL G. "Irving's Use of American Folklore in 'The Legend of Sleepy Hollow,'" *Publications of the Modern Language Association,* LXVIII (June, 1953), 425–35.

HORNBERGER, THEODORE. "Literary Regionalism: Three Self-Conscious Wests," *Southwest Review,* XXVI, No. 4 (1941), 428–48.

JOHNSTON, CHISTOPHER. "Hall Family of Calvert County," *Maryland Historical Magazine,* VIII (September and December, 1913), 291–301, 381–82.

JOHNSON, EMORY R. "River and Harbor Bills," *Annals of the American Academy of Political and Social Science,* II (May, 1892), 782–812.

KEAGY, WALTER R. "The Lane Seminary Rebellion," Historical and Philosophical Society of Ohio, *Bulletin,* IX (April, 1951), 141–60.

"Life of John Ewing, D.D. Late Provost of the University of Pennsylvania," *Port Folio,* I (March, 1813), 214–25.

"Literature," *Cincinnati Chronicle and Literary Gazette,* July 19, 1834.

MELINE, J. F. "Biography of the Late Judge Hall, of Cincinnati," *Cincinnati Commercial,* Oct. 16, 1868.

"Meridies Atticae," *Cincinnati Mirror and Chronicle,* June 27, August 1, 1835.

MERRITT, WILLIAM HAMILTON. "Personal Narrative," Niagara Historical Society, *Publications,* No. 9 (1902).

NEVILLE, MORGAN. "Reminiscences of Pittsburgh," *Illinois Monthly Magazine,* I (February, 1831), 233–38. Reprinted from the *Cincinnati Chronicle and Literary Gazette,* January 8, 1831.

ORIANS, G. HARRISON. "The Indian Hater in Early American Fiction," *Journal of American History,* XXVII, No. 1 (1933), 33–44.

PEARCE, ROY HARVEY. "Melville's Indian Hater: a Note on the Meaning of *The Confidence-Man,*" *Publications of the Modern Language Association,* LXVII (December, 1952), 942–48.

PERKINS, JAMES HANDASAYD. "Charity in the Counting House and out of It" *Cincinnati Daily Gazette,* March 17, 1849.

PURCELL, JOHN. "Bishop Purcell's Journal, 1833–1836," ed. SISTER MARY AGNES MCCANN, *Catholic Historical Review,* V (July–October, 1919), 239–56.

RANDALL, RANDOLPH C. "Authors of the *Port Folio* Revealed by the Hall Files," *American Literature,* XI (January, 1940), 379–416.

RUSSELL, S. G. "John Russell, of Bluffdale, Illinois," Illinois State Historical Society, *Transactions for the Year 1901* (Springfield, 1901), pp. 103–7.

SCHROEDER, JOHN W. "Sources and Symbols for Melville's Confidence-Man," *Publications of the Modern Language Association,* LXVI (June, 1951), 363–80.

WATKINS, FLOYD C. "James Kirke Paulding's Early Ring-Tailed Roarer," *Southern Folklore Quarterly,* XV (September, 1951), 183–87.

358

INDEX

Hall, James: works—*Continued*
   of North America, 256-62; "If I
   were Persia's king, my dear," 40;
   "The Indian Hater," 149, 151, 154,
   274; "Indian Hating," 210, 218–
   19; "The Indian Maid's Death
   Song," 136–37; "The Isle of the
   Yellow Sands," 178; "La Belle
   Riviere," 148; "A Legend of Carondelet," 187, 188, 192; *Legends
   of the West,* 171–72, 187, 190,
   276; *Letters from the West,* 101–2,
   138–45, 255, 299; "Major General
   Thomas Posey," 130; "The March
   of Intellect," 245–46; *Memoir of
   the Life of William H. Harrison,*
   252, 316; *Memoir of Thomas
   Posey,* 276; *Memorial* [on the
   Western Rivers], 266–68, 269, 276;
   "Michel De Coucy," 187; "The
   Missionaries," 189; "My Cousin
   Lucy and the Village Teacher,"
   180, 181, 187; "The New Moon,"
   216–17, 218; "New Year's Address," 105–6; "Notes on Illinois,"
   183–84, 210, 255; "Obediah Mifflin," 99; "On Miss Maria Mer-
   ritt," 31–32; "On Novel Writing,"
   231–32; "On the Intercourse of the
   American People with the Indi-
   ans," 184, 210, 218, 259; "Othello,"
   20–21, 66; "Pete Featherton," 149,
   151–53, 154, 192, 193, 274; "The
   Philadelphia Dun," 188, 189, 193;
   "The Pioneer," 216–17; "The
   Power of Madeira," 76; "The
   Public Domain," 229, 255, 267;
   "The Red Sky of the Morning,"
   274; "Reminiscence of the Last
   War," 184; *Reply to Strictures on
   Sketches of the West,* 214; "The
   Rose," 73; "The Serenade," 178–
   79; "The Seventh Son," 188; "The
   Shawanoe Warrior," 149; "The
   Silver Mine," 188, 216; "Sketch
   of the Life of General Harrison,"
   252; *Sketches of History, Life and
   Manners in the West,* 209–16, 309;
   "The Smile," 76; "The Soldier's
   Bride," 146–47; *The Soldier's
   Bride and Other Tales,* 187; "The
   Soldier's Invitation," 38; "Song,"
   76; "The Spy," 216; "Stanzas,"
   56; *Statistics of the West,* 214,
   225, 276, 317; *Tales of the Bor-
   der,* 172, 216–18; "There's Nothing
   True but Heaven," 146; "To a

Coquette," 136; "To a Young
   Lady Who Mended the Author's
   Stockings," 76; "To Fanny," 131;
   "To Mr. Cook," 106–7; "To My
   Glass," 146; "To the People of
   Illinois," 108; "Travels in Hot
   Weather," 229; *The Trial and
   Defence of First Lieutenant James
   Hall,* 78; "The Useful Man," 189;
   The Village Musician," 189; "The
   Wanderer, by Edward Ennui," 70,
   71, 291; "The War Belt," 274;
   "Wedded Love's First Home,"
   148; *The West: Its Commerce and
   Navigation,* 276; *The Western
   Reader,* 207–8; "Western Scen-
   ery," 229, 255; *The Wilderness
   and the War Path,* 274–76, 320

Hall, John, father of James Hall,
   3, 5–6, 9, 13–14, 16–17, 61, 62,
   94, 132

Hall, John Elihu, brother of James
   Hall, 5, 77, 94, 121, 122, 129–30,
   131–32, 138, 282; contributor to
   Analectic Magazine, 19; contributor to *Port Folio,* 12; death of,
   168, 282; editor of *Port Folio,* 75–
   76, Federalism of, 13, 14; jurist
   in Baltimore, 19–20; "The Narrative of John E. Hall," 20; *Practice and Jurisdiction of the Court
   of Admiralty,* 20, 38; quoted, 45,
   69–70, 71, 146

Hall, John Posey, son of James Hall,
   178, 196, 198

Hall, Julia Rush, great-aunt of James
   Hall, 5

Hall, Lucy Frances, daughter of
   James Hall, 178, 196, 198, 314

Hall, Mary Louisa Anderson Alexander, wife of James Hall, 261,
   262

Hall, Mary Posey, wife of James
   Hall, 118, 119, 120–22, 128, 135,
   178, 195–97, 208, 231, 296

Hall, Richard, 4–5

Hall, Sarah Ewing, mother of James
   Hall, 3–6, 9, 12–13, 63–64, 71, 127,
   177; *Port Folio,* 12, 14, 76; *Conversations on the Bible,* 129–30;
   education of, 7–8; friendship with
   Cooper, 105; quoted, 17; *Selections from the Writings of Mrs.
   Sarah Hall,* 168, 177; studies
   Hebrew, 17; teaches James Hall,
   10–12